Regulating the Global Information Society

Edited by
Christopher T. Marsden

London and New York

First published 2000
by Routledge
11 New Fetter Lane, London EC4P 4EE

Simultaneously published in the USA and Canada
by Routledge
29 West 35th Street, New York, NY 10001

Routledge is an imprint of the Taylor & Francis Group

© 2000 Selection and editorial matter Christopher T. Marsden; individual
chapters © the contributors

Typeset in Baskerville by Taylor & Francis Books Ltd
Printed and bound in Great Britain by TJ International Ltd, Padstow,
Cornwall

British Library Cataloguing in Publication Data
A catalogue record for this book is available from the British Library

Library of Congress Cataloging in Publication Data
Regulating the global information society / edited by
Christopher T. Marsden.
Includes bibliographical references and index.
1. Computer networks–Law and legislation. 2. Telecommunication–Law
and legislation. 3. Digital communications. 4. Information society.
I. Marsden, Christopher T.
K564.C6 R44 2000
343.09'944–dc21

00–042485

ISBN 0–415–24217–7 (hbk)
ISBN 0–415–24218–5 (pbk)

Contents

Notes on contributors   viii
Series editor's preface   xiii
Acknowledgements   xv
Acronyms   xvii

1 **Introduction: information and communications technologies, globalisation and regulation**   1
   CHRISTOPHER T. MARSDEN

   PART I
   Theoretical perspectives   41

2 **The role of the public sphere in the information society**   43
   NICHOLAS GARNHAM

3 **In search of the self: charting the course of self-regulation on the Internet in a global environment**   57
   MONROE E. PRICE AND STEFAAN G. VERHULST

4 **Will electronic commerce change the law? Towards a regulatory perspective based on competition, information and learning skills**   79
   PAUL NIHOUL

   PART II
   The limits of telecommunications regulation   91

5 **How far can deregulation of telecommunications go?**   93
   MARTIN CAVE

 6 **Realising social goals in connectivity and content:
    the challenge of convergence**   108
    RICHARD COLLINS

 7 **Commentary: when to regulate in the GIS? A public
    policy perspective**   116
    FOD BARNES

 8 **The rise and decline of the international
    telecommunications regime**   124
    WILLIAM J. DRAKE

 9 **After Seattle: trade negotiations and the New Economy**   178
    JONATHAN D. ARONSON

    Comment on Jonathon D. Aronson, 'After Seattle:
    trade negotiations and the New Economy'   188
    DIMITRI YPSILANTI

    **PART III
    International self-regulation and standard setting**   191

10 **Locating Internet governance: lessons from the standards
    process**   193
    MARK GOULD

11 **Semi-private international rulemaking:
    lessons learned from the WIPO domain name process**   211
    A. MICHAEL FROOMKIN

    **PART IV
    Standard setting and competition policy**   233

12 **Will the Internet remake antitrust law?**   235
    MARK LEMLEY

13 **The problems of the third way: a Java case study**   243
    DAVID MCGOWAN

PART V
The limits of government regulation   263

14 **China's impact on the Global Information Society**   265
PERRY KELLER

15 **Freedom versus access rights in a European context**   285
AD VAN LOON

16 **Pluralism, guidance and the new media**   304
THOMAS GIBBONS

17 **Five challenges for regulating the Global Information**
    Society   316
PAMELA SAMUELSON

Bibliography   331
Index   358

Contributors

Jonathan D. Aronson is Director and Professor of the School of International Relations at the University of Southern California, and is also a Professor in the Annenberg School for Communication. He is a specialist on international aspects of trade and communications policy, and has also written on finance, trade in services, and intellectual property. His books include *Managing the World Economy: The Consequences of International Corporate Alliances* (Council on Foreign Relations 1993) and *When Countries Talk: International Trade in Telecommunications Services* (Ballinger 1988). His most recent work has focused on the implications of new communications technologies for international financial and trade policies and developments. He is a Harvard graduate and received doctoral training in political science and applied economics at Stanford. He has been a visiting fellow at Harvard, the London School of Economics and US Trade Representative (USTR), and is a member of the Council on Foreign Relations, the Pacific Council on International Policy, and the Asia Society.

Fod Barnes specialises in the regulation of public utilities and the application of competition law and principles to regulated industries. His early career was in consumer affairs, both at the Consumers' Association (Senior Project Officer) and the National Consumer Council (Head of Public Affairs). In 1989 he became a consultant. From 1989 to 1998, he was Policy Adviser to the Director General of Telecommunications (OFTEL), where he advised on all aspects of the regulation of the UK telecommunications industry: in particular the measurement of BT's profitability, and the regulatory and market implications of convergence. In addition he has also advised a number of other private- and public-sector clients on competition and regulation. In 1999 he was adviser to the Chairman of the UK Banking Review (the Cruickshank Review). He has recently joined Oxford Economic Research Associates as an Associate Consultant.

Martin Cave is Professor of Economics and Vice Principal at Brunel University. For the past fifteen years he has specialised in regulatory economics, especially of the communications industry. In this field he has published a number of books and articles dealing with regulatory problems in both western economics and economies in transition. He has acted as an advisor to OFTEL and is a member of the Competition Commission.

Richard Collins is Deputy Director and Head of Education at the British Film Institute. In a former life he taught media studies at universities in the UK, Australia and the USA and latterly at the London School of Economics and Political Science. He's written several books and numerous articles including *Culture, Communication and National Identity. The Case of Canadian Television* (University of Toronto Press 1990 and 1994) and, with Cristina Murroni, *New Media New Policies* (Polity 1996). He established the Media and Communication Programme at the Institute for Public Policy Research (IPPR) and was research director of the programme from June 1993. From August 1996 he was advisor on broadcasting and convergence to Don Cruickshank, the Director General of Telecommunications at OFTEL.

William J. Drake is a Senior Associate and the Director of the Project on the Information Revolution and World Politics at the Carnegie Endowment for International Peace (http://www.ceip.org). Previously he was Associate Director of the Communication, Culture and Technology Program at Georgetown University, and Assistant Professor of Communication at the University of California, San Diego. Among his publications are *Toward Sustainable Competition in Global Telecommunications* (Aspen Institute 1999) and the edited volumes, *Telecommunications in the Information Age* (United States Information Agency 1998), and *The New Information Infrastructure: Strategies for US Policy* (Twentieth Century Fund Press 1995).

A. Michael Froomkin is a Professor at the University of Miami School of Law in Coral Gables, Florida, specialising in Internet Law and Administrative Law. He is a member of the Royal Institute of International Affairs in London, the Advisory Board of the BNA Electronic Information Policy and Law Reports and the Editorial Board of *Information, Communication and Society*. In 1999 he served on the 'Panel of Experts' of the World Intellectual Property Organisation's Internet Domain Name Process. He is also a director of Out2.com, an Internet startup, and disputes.org, an online dispute settlement provider. Professor Froomkin writes primarily about electronic commerce, electronic cash, privacy, Internet governance, the regulation of cryptography, and US constitutional law. His homepage can be found at http://www.law.tm and he can be reached at froomkin@law.tm.

Nicholas Garnham is Professor of Media Studies, University of Westminster. He is also Managing Editor, *Media, Culture and Society*. Major works include *Capitalism and Communication: Global Culture and the Economics of Information* (Sage 1990) and *Emancipation, the Media and Modernity* (Oxford University Press 2000).

Thomas Gibbons is Professor of Law at the University of Manchester. Author of *Regulating the Media* (Sweet and Maxwell 1998, 2nd edn), he recently completed a three-year interdisciplinary study of the regulation of media concentration in the UK, Germany and the European Community. He is currently working on a book about media power and the law. He is a member of the Editorial Board of the *Yearbook of Copyright and Media Law* and the Advisory Board of the *International Journal of Communications Law and Policy* (*IJCLP*).

Mark Gould is a Lecturer in Law at the University of Bristol, and a graduate of the University of Warwick and the European University Institute, Florence. He has been researching issues of Internet law since 1995, and Internet governance since 1996. He is currently writing *Foundations of Internet Governance*, which will be published by Hart Publishing in early 2001.

Perry Keller is a lecturer at King's College London where he teaches undergraduate and postgraduate media law. He qualified as a lawyer in Canada and later in the United Kingdom and has worked in the legal department of the Hong Kong government. He has also lived in other parts of China and has published articles on various developments in Chinese law. He is currently writing a book on the failing grasp of national media regulatory regimes and the prospects for effective regulatory co-ordination or co-operation at regional and international levels.

Mark Lemley is a Professor of Law at the Boalt Hall School of Law, University of California at Berkeley, and a Director of the Berkeley Center for Law and Technology. He teaches intellectual property, computer law, patent law, antitrust, electronic commerce and regulation of the Internet. He is of counsel to the law firm of Fish and Richardson, where he litigates and counsels clients in the areas of antitrust, intellectual property and computer law. He is the author of six books and thirty articles on these and related subjects, has taught intellectual property law to federal judges at numerous Federal Judicial Center programmes, and has testified before Congress and the Federal Trade Commission on patent and antitrust matters. Before joining the Boalt faculty in January 2000, he was the Marrs McLean Professor of Law at the University of Texas School of Law.

David McGowan is an Associate Professor of Law at the University of Minnesota Law School. He has written and co-authored several articles dealing with legal and economic issues relevant to technology and competition policy. Before joining the faculty at Minnesota, Professor McGowan practised law in San Francisco, California.

Christopher T. Marsden is 1999–2000 Research Fellow of the Information Infrastructure Project at the Kennedy School, Harvard, Lecturer at the University of Warwick Law School from 1997 to 2000, and an Associate of the ESRC Globalisation Centre. He has consulted for various government and corporate bodies on competition, institutional and content issues, including the Council of Europe MM-S-PL Committee in 1999. Publishing manager at Maxwell Business Communications (1989–91) and Euromoney Publications (1993–4), he was Legal Advisor to the LSE Information Society Observatory in 1996. He has published many articles in UK and US publications, including three recent pieces in *info*, the ITS official journal. He has been since 1997 founder co-editor of the *IJCLP* (www.ijclp.org), and editor of *Convergence in European Digital TV Regulation* (Blackstone 1999, with Stefaan Verhulst).

Paul Nihoul is a Jean Monnet Professor of Law on the European Information Society and Director of the Telecom Unit at the Royal University of Groningen (the Netherlands) and at the Université Catholique de Louvain (UCL, Belgium). He holds a Licence in Philosophy and Letters (UCL), a Licence in Law (UCL), a Master of Laws (Harvard) and a Doctorate in Law (UCL). Formerly, he was an Attorney (New York, USA), a Counsellor of the Minister of Finance (Belgium) and a Referendaire at the European Court of Justice (Luxembourg). Dr Nihoul sits on the board of *info* the official journal of the International Telecommunications Society (ITS).

Monroe E. Price is co-director of the Programme in Comparative Media Law and Policy at the University of Oxford and a professor of law at the Benjamin N. Cardozo School of Law in New York. He has been a Member of the Faculty of Social Sciences, Institute of Advanced Study, and a visiting lecturer at the Yale Law School. A graduate of Yale University and Yale Law School, Professor Price clerked for Justice Potter Stewart, was Deputy Director of the Sloan Commission on Cable Communications and Dean of Cardozo Law School. He was a Fellow of the Markle Foundation and of the Media Studies Center.

Pamela Samuelson is a Professor at the University of California at Berkeley, with a joint appointment in the School of Information Management and Systems as well as in the School of Law, where she is Co-Director of the Berkeley Center for Law and Technology. In June of 1997 she was named a Fellow of the John D. and Catherine T. MacArthur Foundation. She has also been a Public Policy Fellow of the Electronic Frontier Foundation and a Fellow of the Association of Computing Machinery. A 1976 graduate of Yale Law School, she practised law with the New York law firm Willkie Farr and Gallagher. From 1981 to 1996 she was a faculty member at the University of Pittsburgh Law School, visiting at Columbia, Cornell, and Emory Law Schools. She has written and spoken extensively about the challenges that new information technologies pose for traditional legal regimes, especially for intellectual property law.

Ad van Loon is a lawyer who is Senior Co-ordinator, Public and Regulatory Affairs at VECAI, the association of cable communication companies in the Netherlands, Co-ordinator of International Research at the Institute for

Information Law at the University of Amsterdam and Consultant to the drafting group of a Bill on the Economic Relations in the Russian Media Sector. Previously, he worked in the Media Section of the Council of Europe, where he was Secretary to the Standing Committee of the European Convention on Transfrontier Television and to the Group of Specialists for the Protection of Rightsholders in the Media Sector. Among his other previous roles: legal adviser of the European Audiovisual Observatory and Secretary to an expert panel advising the Netherlands media authority. He is writing his PhD thesis on comparative media ownership and control regulatory issues in Europe, the US and Australia.

Stefaan G. Verhulst has been the Director of the Programme in Comparative Media Law and Policy (University of Oxford) since its inception in 1996. Prior to that, he was a lecturer on communications law and policy issues in Belgium before becoming Founder and Co-director of the International Media and info-comms Policy and Law studies (IMPS) at the School of Law, University of Glasgow. He has served and serves as consultant and researcher for numerous organisations including the Council of Europe, European Commission and UNESCO. He is the co-editor of the *IJCLP* and the *Communications Law in Transition Newsletter*. Contact: pcmlp@csls.ox.ac.uk.

Dimitri Ypsilanti is Head of the Telecommunication and Information Policy Section at the Organisation for Economic Co-operation and Development (OECD). Mr Ypsilanti's work has included telecommunication economic and policy analysis in a range of areas, including trade in telecommunication services, international telecommunication tariff and accounting rates issues, analysis of regulatory issues and comparative analysis of telecommunication performance among the OECD member countries. Mr Ypsilanti is the author of a number of articles and books published by the OECD and papers presented to international conferences. He has studied economics at the University of Bristol (UK), and at Memorial University and Queen's University in Canada.

Series editor's preface

The Centre for the Study of Globalisation and Regionalisation (www.csgr.org), founded in October 1997, is funded by the Economic and Social Research Council of the UK. With an initial grant of over £2.5 million, the Centre is rapidly becoming an international site for the study of key issues in the theory and practice of globalisation and regionalisation. The Centre's agenda is avowedly inter-disciplinary. Research staff in CSGR are drawn from international relations, political science, economics, law and sociology. The Centre is committed to scholarly excellence but also strives to be problem solving in methodological orientation.

Three broad categories of activity inform and underwrite the research programme of the Centre: (1) What is globalisation? (2) Can, and if so how, do we measure its impacts? (3) What are its policy implications? Understandings of globalisation are seen to be multi-dimensional – political, economic, cultural, ideological – so CSGR sees globalisation in at least two broad ways: first as the emergence of a set of sequences and processes that are increasingly unhindered by territorial or jurisdictional barriers and that enhance the spread of transborder practices in economic, political, cultural and social domains; and second, as a discourse of political and economic knowledge offering one view of how to make the post-modern world manageable. For many, globalisation as 'knowledge' constitutes a new reality. Centre research will ask what kinds of constraints globalisation poses for independent policy initiative on the part of national policy-makers and under what conditions these constraints are enhanced or mitigated.

Within these broad contexts, empirical work at CSGR focuses on (1) particular regional projects in Europe, North America and the Asia-Pacific; (2) the enhancement of international institutions, rules and policy competence on questions of trade competition and international finance and investment; (3) normative questions about governance, sovereignty, democratisation and policy-making under constraints of globalisation. Indeed, Centre research is sensitive to the wider normative nature of many of these questions, especially in research into the counter-tendencies towards, or sites of resistance to, globalisation at regional and local levels that give rise to different understandings of the importance of space and territoriality. *Routledge/Warwick Studies in Globalisation* provides an avenue for the publication of scholarly research monographs, policy-oriented studies and collections of original themed essays in the area of the research agenda of CSGR.

Increasingly, CSGR has also become interested in the impact of the Information and Communication Revolutions on global processes. It is in this context that CSGR was keen to sponsor the conference on Regulating the Global Information Society out of which this splendid collection of essays edited by Chris Marsden has emerged. *Regulating the Global Information Society* investigates the institutional governance of the most international and ubiquitous technologies of what Daniel Bell many years ago describes as 'post-industrial society'. Rather than undertake an exercise in prediction, or a historical, philosophical or sociological critique of the meta-narrative of the knowledge or information society (two very different concepts) the contributors to this volume consider the most directly tangible elements of the emerging information industries and their social impact. Written by predominantly legal and political economy scholars, the papers share two important characteristics: they focus on the socio-economic impact of their case studies and, in a wider context, the global impact of those technologies and markets which they analyse.

The emphasis in the volume on the role of non-state actors in the international political economy is a characteristic it shares with previous volumes in the Series. The case studies focus on contemporary substantive issue areas, chosen for the light they shed on the processes of co-regulation or self-regulation which are a common feature of governance in this most dynamic of environments. The contributions blend positivist and normative themes, acknowledging explicitly the impact of techno-economic developments on the future role of the public sphere and freedom of expression. The substantive issue areas demonstrate the absorption of international political economic issues into domestic politics and policy processes. Global communications networks exhibit advanced opportunities for regulatory arbitrage between states and regions, notably the European Union and the United States.

A remarkable element of *Regulating the Global Information Society* is that 'global' is not used merely as a slogan bandied around by either the American hegemon or the 'information dispossessed'; rather, it is fully incorporated into the volume's case studies, whether this is an examination of Microsoft's *de facto* global standard for computer software or China's challenge to the information sovereignty (sic) of the Internet. We hope the volume will prove an indispensable guide to the future development of regulation in this increasingly important element of the global policy process.

Richard Higgott
Director
Centre for the Study of Globalisation and Regionalisation

Acknowledgements

This volume arose out of a transatlantic workshop held at Warwick University on 3–5 June 1999. I acknowledge with gratitude the sponsorship of the seminar of the Legal Research Institute at Warwick Law School, and its Directors Lee Bridges and Mike McConville, together with the ESRC Centre for the Study of Globalisation and Regionalisation, Warwick, its Director Richard Higgott and Co-Director John Whalley. The seminar was held in connection with the 'European Media Regulation Group' seminar award R45126474197 from the Economic and Social Research Council (ESRC).

The transatlantic nature of this collection and workshop is a legacy of Susan Strange's willingness to share her insights and network of contacts in the months before her death in October 1998. It is also a tribute to the motivational skills of Mark Lemley and Michael Froomkin, and the goodwill of all those brought across the Atlantic to a location 'near Stratford'. The regulatory contribution is a tribute to the co-organisation arranged by John Dryden and especially Dimitri Ypsilanti, as well as Robert Pepper and Jonathan Levy. The FCC Office of Plans and Policy has been an outstanding supporter of the seminar award. Pamela Samuelson supplied the blueprint on how to organise a conference in the outstanding *The Legal and Policy Framework for Global Electronic Commerce: A Progress Report*, at Berkeley in March 1999[1], and the workshop example was Jon Aronson's in May 1999 at the University of Southern California, which led to the *e-conomy* project. To all, my thanks.

Corporate support for the seminar was given by BBC Policy and Planning, Cable Communications Association, Energis plc, Telenor, Telia AB, VNU Business Publishing. As the ESRC award holder, I also gratefully acknowledge the help given by Martin Kender at the ESRC in expediting the award, and Warwick's Giles Carden, Simon Bailey, Annabel Eccles and Irene Blood in supervising the administration. Within the Law School, Barbara Gray and Aileen Stockham were invaluable.

I also warmly acknowledge the support given by corporate and regulator panelists in the seminars. I express here my gratitude to those presenters of papers at the conference whose contribution could not be included here but whose advice and counsel helped to inform the debate to which this collection contributes: Andrew Graham, Wolf Sauter, Debora Spar and Larry Lessig. I am particularly grateful to Colin Blackman, Andy Clark, Campbell Cowie and Bill Melody, whose chairing of vital sessions helped to ensure the relative seamlessness of the discussions which followed. Richard Higgott and John Whalley also chaired sessions with wit and efficiency. Regulatory contributors whose advice to participants ensured a real academic–government discourse were Lee Tuthill, Alain Servantie, Robert Pepper.

Dennis Gilhooly[2] and Peter Grindley[3] provided contributions which were so timely that they were published immediately online in the *International Journal of Communications Law and Policy*, of which I am co-editor, together with Beth Noveck, Andreas Grunwald, Campbell Cowie, Stefaan Verhulst and Gunnar Bender. My co-editors, and the distinguished editoral advisory board, helped to ensure the success of the conference. Christian Sommer provided the conference video, available freely online at http://www.digital-law.net/warwick. Professor Dr Bernd Holznagel helped to support this continuing effort. The seminar and award would never have been brought to any kind of fruition without the outstanding administrative, secretarial, organisational and not least morale [sic] support of Aileen Stockham. She was a calm in the centre of various institutional storms throughout. I also record thanks to Mike McConville and Lee Bridges for timely advice.

The contributions are dated 6 March 2000, except where otherwise stated. In Internet years, there were five years to revise contributions. Publication will take a further five years. (The Internet in its most ubiquitous form, the World Wide Web (WWW), is only a decade old in human terms. It is already a venerable seventy years old in Internet terms.) A decade will have passed in the sixteen months between the workshop and your reading this section. The debate will continue to mature: this is an early step into the debate surrounding the global information society.

Finally, I am aware that the ultimate success of the seminars and this volume is entirely owed to the contributors, whose expertise, enthusiasm and willingness to hone their contributions to deadline and within their over-stretched schedules is a tribute to their organisations and particularly to them. Any dedication must be to contributors' colleagues and families, whose patience, support and suffering is otherwise unchronicled in an edited collection.

Chris Marsden
Brockenhurst, Hampshire and Cambridge, Mass.
14 March 2000

Notes

1   See *Berkeley Technology Law Journal* 14(2) (Spring 1999).
2   Gilhooly, Denis (1999) 'Toward the global Internet infrastructure', *International Journal of Communications Law and Policy* 3(9) at http://www.ijclp.org/3_1999/ijclp_webdoc_9_3_1999.html.
3   Grindley, Peter, David J. Salant and Leonard Waverman (1999) 'Standards WARS: the use of standard setting as a means of facilitating cartels in third generation wireless telecommunications', *International Journal of Communications Law and Policy* 3(2) at http://www.ijclp.org/3_1999/ijclp_webdoc_2_3_1999.html.

Acronyms

ABA	Australian Broadcasting Authority
ABC	American Broadcasting Corporation
ADC	Access deficit contribution
AOL	American Online
APA	Administrative Procedure Act
API	Applications programme interface
ARPA	Advanced Research Projects Agency
BBC	British Broadcasting Corporation
BSC	Broadcasting Standards Commission
BSkyB	British Sky Broadcasting plc
BT	British Telecommunications plc
CADCAM	Computer-aided design and manufacture
CAP	Competitive access provider
CBS	Columbia Broadcasting System
CCITT	Consultative Committee on International Telegraph and Telephone
ccTLD	Country code top-level domain
CEC	Commission of the European Communities
CNN	Cable News Network
CPD	Central Propaganda Department (China)
CPE	Customer premise equipment
CoE	Council of Europe
DNS	Domain name system/server
EBU	European Broadcasting Union
EC	European Community
ECHR	European Convention for the Protection of Human Rights and Fundamental Freedoms
ECJ	European Court of Justice
ECLR	European Competition Law Review
ECMA	European Computer Manufacturers' Association
E-Commerce	Electronic commerce
ECOSOC	Economic and Social Committee
EEC	European Economic Community

EMU	Economic and Monetary Union
EPG	Electronic programme guide
ETSI	European Telecommunications Standards Institute
EU	European Union
EuroISPA	Pan-European Association of the Internet Services Providers Associations
FDI	Foreign direct investment
FPI	Foreign portfolio investment
GATS	General Agreement on Trade in Services
GATT	General Agreement on Tariffs and Trade
GBDe	Global Business Dialogue on E-commerce
GBT	Group on Basic Telecommunications
GDP	Gross domestic product
gTLD	Global top-level domain
gTLD-MoU	Global top-level domain Memorandum of Understanding
HTTP	Hypertext transport protocol
IAB	Internet Architecture (formerly Activities) Board
IAHC	International Ad Hoc Committee
IANA	Internet Assigned Numbers Authority
ICANN	Internet Corporation for Assigned Names and Numbers
ICC	International Chamber of Commerce
ICCPR	International Covenant on Civil and Political Rights
ICT	Information and communication technology
IESG	Internet Engineering Steering Group
IETF	Internet Engineering Task Force
INTA	International Trademark Association
INTUG	International Telecommunications Users' Group
IP	Internet protocol
IPE	International political economy
IPTO	Information Processing Techniques Office
IPR	Intellectual property rights
ISDN	Integrated Services Digital Network
ISO	International Standards Organisation
ISOC	Internet Society
ISP	Internet service provider
ISR	International simple resale
IT	Information technology
ITC	Independent Television Commission
ITU	International Telecommunications Union
JVM	Java Virtual Machine
LLU	Local loop unbundling
M&A	Merger and acquisition
MNC	Multinational corporation
NBC	National Broadcasting Corporation
NGO	Non-governmental organisation

NII	National Information Infrastructure
NSF	National Science Foundation
NSI	Network Solutions, Inc.
NTIA	National Telecommunications and Information Administration
NTSC	National Television Systems Committee
OECD	Organisation for Economic Cooperation and Development
OFT	Office of Fair Trading
OFTEL	Office of the Telecommunications Regulator
OSI	Open systems interconnection
PAS	Publicly available specification
POC	Policy Oversight Committee
PSTN	Public switched telephone network
PTO	Public telecommunications operator ('telco')
PTT	Ministry of Posts, Telegraphs and Telephones
RPOA	Recognised private operating entity
SIO	Scientific and industrial organisation
SKA	Sender keeps all
SRA	Self-regulatory agency
TLD	Top-level domain
TNC	Transnational corporation
TRAM	Trade-related anti-competitive issue
TRIPS	Trade-related aspects of intellectual property
TVWF/TWF	'Television Without Frontiers' Directive
UCITA	Uniform Computer Information Transactions Act
UETA	Uniform Electronic Transactions Act
UNCITRAL	United Nations Commission on International Trade Law
UNCTAD	United Nations Commission on Trade and Development
US TAG	United States Technical Advisory Group
USO	Universal service obligation
USTR	United States Trade Representative
VAN	Value-added network
W3C	World Wide Web Consortium
WATTC	World Administrative Telegraph and Telephone Conference
WG	Working groups
WIPO	World Intellectual Property Organisation
WTO	World Trade Organisation
WWW	World Wide Web

1 Introduction

Information and communications technologies, globalisation and regulation

Christopher T. Marsden

Regulating the Global Information Society (GIS) involves analysing three separate but interconnected concepts, each of which has become so much a part of a contested socio-political dynamic that each individually has become something of a cliché. The three are: regulation as a means of control; globalisation as a phenomenon; the information society as a reality. This collection aims to examine the means by which the GIS can be regulated.

My primary task in this introduction is therefore to demonstrate that there is an object of regulation, as a problem set in a defined location, and as an objective of the regulatory actors. I therefore proceed by explaining the dynamic development of information and communication technologies (ICTs), which have the potential to lower information, and hence transaction, costs. The key to the transformative effect of these productivity gains is that the model of ICT deployment is through networks, which increase the productivity effect with each new addition to the network, thus creating an exponential 'bandwagoning' growth in the adoption of ICTs. This is seen most clearly in the development of social and economic transactions on the Internet, where in September 1999 over 200 million individuals were able to send and receive email, and to explore the information network for leisure, education, shopping or research. The potential productivity increases thus realised have economic and social ramifications, in that each extends the distant communication and execution of transactions. The socio-economic impact has been more rapid than any previous technological advance in its permeation of markets and societies.

This collection is a contribution to the debate into the role of governments in the 'Information Society', 'Information Superhighway', or digital networked economy.[1] As Luc Soete defined it:

> The information society is the society currently being put into place, where low-cost information and data storage and transmission technologies are in general use. This generalisation of information and data use is being accompanied by organisational, commercial, social and legal innovations that will profoundly change life both in the world of work and in society generally.[2]

While definitions of the GIS are thus almost impossibly wide, the attempt in the second part of this collection is to focus largely on tangible, substantive issues. Regulation is the focus of the substantive chapters, focusing on the inter-action between states and non-state actors, primarily multinational corporations (MNCs). This focus on international corporate behaviour illustrates the regula-tory lag in the policy treatment of the GIS. Ayres and Braithwaite state:

> Practical people who are concerned with outcomes seek to understand the intricacies of interplays between state regulation and private orderings ... If we accept that sound policy analysis is about understanding private regu-lation ... then interesting possibilities open up to steer the mix of private and public regulation.[3]

As Richard Whish more bluntly puts it: competition between MNCs occurs in 'the Real World'.[4] Ultimately, it will be seen that it is the virtual world of the GIS which raises the most profound issues of public–private interaction.

Globalisation is often an implicit element in the collection, as the global impact of a decision in, for instance, the Californian courts, regarding the tech-nical specification for the Intel Pentium II microprocessor, is obvious to any computer user (see Mark Lemley at Chapter 12). A comprehensive broad defini-tion of globalisation is adopted by Held *et al.*:

> A process, or set of processes, which embodies a transformation in the spatial organisation of social relations and transactions – assessed in terms of their extensity, intensity, velocity and impact – generating transconti-nental or interregional flows and networks of activity, interaction and the exercise of power.[5]

The ubiquity, rapid penetration and commonplace necessity of international data flows over digital communications networks (consider Internet email), combined with the economic and social effects of such flows, makes the Internet the paradigm of globalisation: it was 'born global'. That is not to deny the disparities in Internet usage between and within nation-states, nor the control over information flows which nation-states can exercise. Indeed, a useful purpose of this book is to expose the fallacy of 'unregulability' of the Internet by nation-states. The decision whether, when, how, why and whom to regulate is political, however bounded by technological factors.[6]

The collection analyses the regulation of the GIS from a variety of view-points, from which readers will draw differing insights on the degree of globalisation which governments and non-state actors will create in the GIS. It is widely acknowledged that there are three basic approaches to globalisation, what Held *et al.* classify as hyperglobalisation, sceptical and transformative views. The first 'hyperglobalisation' approach, which views the emergence of a global society and economy as an all but inevitable development in late capitalism, predicting the end of the nation-state and the rise of global forms of political authority and resonating somewhat with anarcho-libertarian and neo-classical economic approaches, is broadly rejected in this collection. Both strands, economic globalism and a global governance approach based on liberal interdependence, are seen as overly optimistic, failing to take account of the continuing pervasive legitimacy and influence of state actors. The second 'sceptical' approach (which can be termed the 'regionalisation' thesis) draws on historical comparisons to suggest the limited economic and social integration of the present stage of globalisation compared to earlier historical epochs, and predicts the clash of regional blocs such as the EU, North America and East Asia. This approach is contentious, in that it is still too early to state with any certainty whether the GIS will rapidly outgrow the developed world and become a truly global phenomenon. One view of this regionalisation thesis is that it represents a triumph of American values and hegemonic influence, to which the other major blocs react defensively, and this narrative is found in many of the contributions.[7] Nevertheless, it is clear that the degree of economic and social integration already evident in the GIS is unprecedented in human history. The third 'transformative' approach, which draws on the realist school of international relations, is contingent, based on an interdependent view of nations and non-state actors which redefines sovereignty based on emerging global social and economic structures, more incrementalist and institutionally based. It is the view which predominates in this collection, both more conservative than a hyberglobalist thesis, and more cognisant than the sceptics of the transformative effects of the GIS and its technologies on human interaction. Nevertheless, the collection does not seek to prematurely assert a particular view, different papers adopt differing approaches, institutional and historical legacies are fully considered, and the contingency and uncertainty in analysing regulation of the GIS, which is still very much a work in progress, is admitted. There are no easy answers, and certainly no single answer.

This introduction is made up of four parts: first, an explanation of the Information Economy, focusing on the dynamic technological convergence of voice, data, video and audio transmissions by digital communications networks.[8] Second, I offer an explanation of the challenge which integrated global networks pose to previous notions of sovereignty, and to study of globalisation as a phenomenon. Third, the regulation of these global networks will be considered in the light of existing and emerging contributions to the literature on international regulation, particularly regulatory arbitrage. Fourth, I introduce the contributions and explain the structure of the book. The normative element in regulatory design will be explicitly examined.

Not all contributions are written by academics, very few general readers will be familiar with the disciplinary background upon which all authors draw, and there will therefore be a higher degree of unfamiliarity with the subject matter than will be the case in contributions to a more established field. The contributors, cognisant of this fact, have written in as straightforward and non-technical a language as possible. Specialists in their particular fields will refer to their more technical work, while gaining from the insights such an interdisciplinary examination can offer. I begin by briefly narrating the development of the Internet, before considering the broader effects of information and communications technologies (ICTs).

Information Economy

The commercialisation of the public Internet

When Democratic Party presidential candidate Al Gore claimed in January 2000 that he 'created' the Internet in a Cable News Network (CNN) interview, he was ridiculed by even former Vice President J. Danforth Quayle, who immediately announced that he had invented Spellcheck.[9] That the Vice President's exaggeration could be considered so outlandish demonstrates a strange disjuncture of myth and reality. The Internet was largely a US government creation, though developed by university science departments, as later in European universities. Developed as ARPANET by the US government's Advanced Research Projects Agency, with architecture originally intended to survive thermo-nuclear strike, it became a cultural artifact in its public goods stage of development, and is now a key driver of economic integration across national boundaries. Much of the WWW is self-regulated, for instance, by W3C (World Wide Web Consortium), a US–EU consortium of private and public organisations, and the similarly constituted IETF (Internet Engineering Task Force) and ICANN (Internet Corporation for Assigned Names and Numbers), with minimal direct government interference. The British inventor of the WWW, Tim Berners-Lee, did so at CERN (European Centre for Nuclear Research), the particle accelerator laboratory which was an intergovernmental-funded research initiative in Switzerland. The original open standards on the WWW, for intellectual property and navigation standards, and even the property of WWW domain name addresses, were developed by engineers and university researchers in collaboration: the W3C is such an organisation, as is the IETF. Such organisations are international in character and were begun as non-commercial self-regulatory organisations.[10] Berners-Lee has explained that the open standard of the WWW describes:

> a vision encompassing the decentralized, organic growth of ideas, technology, and society. The vision I have for the Web is about anything being potentially connected with anything. It is a vision that provides us with new freedom, and allows us to grow faster than we ever could when we were fettered by the hierarchical classification systems into which we bound ourselves.[11]

Larry Lessig explains what that architectural principle of any-to-any[12] means in practice:

> This end-to-end design frees innovation from the past. It's an architecture that makes it hard for a legacy business to control how the market will evolve. You could call it distributed creativity, but that would make it sound

as if the network was producing the creativity. It's the other way around. End-to-end makes it possible to tap into the creativity that is already distributed everywhere.[13]

It is only with the phenomenal success of the WWW that companies such as Netscape, and later AOL and Microsoft, began to create economic value from the Internet, from the mid-1990s. The Internet has of course gone through many maturing phases since its anarcho-libertarian and vehemently anti-trust (big business) origins up until the early 1990s. A new type of radical free market libertarianism grew up from then, consistent in its espousal of free speech but more concerned with avoiding government economic and access, as opposed to social, regulation. The US governmental adoption of this free market libertarian approach was encapsulated in the Magaziner Report of 1997.[14] Michael Froomkin has described this Report as a paradoxical mix of heavy government intervention to secure property rights for corporations, combined with a libertarian language designed to minimise regulation in areas other than property rights. As for its claim to be providing a 'global framework', he claims that it 'fails to grasp the consequences of the means proposed to achieve its short-term ends for long-term global governance'.[15] European observers present at the two-year review of Magaziner's 'framework', or strategy at best as Froomkin described it, could rightly be mystified by the word 'global' in its title, as it referred so little to co-operation with the European Union (EU). In fact, references to the EU were to the morality of its 'anti-business' privacy policy.[16] By contrast, the European attitude was more cautious, a 'middle way' between the social market approach and this US libertarianism. The Bangemann Report of 1994[17] shared many free market characteristics with the US 'Information Superhighway' which Al Gore had claimed prior to the 1992 presidential campaign in which Bill Clinton was elected president, but it was critically differentiated by the deliberate adoption of the term 'Information Society'.

The growth of the GIS – despite its phenomenal US national growth – was therefore hampered by rival visions of the role of the state.[18] For several years during the development of the WWW, competing visions co-existed. Their separate development was possible within the technologically limited capability of the Internet, and a negotiating interval between the conclusion of the Final Act of the Uruguay Round in 1993 and the commencement of pre-negotiation for the Millennial Round in 1999. The application of e-commerce is dependent on security of encryption, itself controlled by governments (especially Pentagon export licensing controls), the global reach of US online content has led to large-scale redistribution of telecommunications revenues from developing nation telcos to US carriers (see Drake Chapter 8), and the enduring dominance of that content is driving the cultural hegemony of export-oriented US media products and consequently social values.[19] Interim policy discussions held under the auspices of variously the OECD, ITU and the United Nations Conference on Trade and Development (UNCTAD) have succeeded in reaching some consensus regarding infrastructure technical standards and telecom network liberalisation and privatisation. The two approaches, which as suggested above shared far more issues than differences, were somewhat reconciled in the Brussels G7 conference of 1995, at which point the term 'Global Information Society' first became a common usage. Note that 'global' was in this instance the European Union, North America and Japan, Kenichi Ohmae's famous 'triad'.[20]

What the brief narrative illustrates is that self-regulation is a highly developed – even dominant – regulatory form in the Internet, that national, regional and multilateral/plurilateral issues are interconnected, that economic, social and cultural issues are converging, and that 'joined up' analysis needs to consider the variable geometry of policy fora and issue areas. However, the Internet is only the latest, consumerist stage in the development of globally integrated communications networks, which began with the telegraph in the last century.

Information and communication technologies

Two structural forces are creating a dynamic information revolution in time and space: technology and globalisation. It is the outflanking of traditional notions of national law by these forces which creates the challenge to existing notions of the nation-state, of regulation, and, ultimately, of spatial and temporal parameters: a new dynamic digital environment is taking over many of the characteristic nation-state static parameters around which analysts formerly built static frameworks. Michalski predicts that:

> A decade from now, information technology will in all probability have penetrated every aspect of human activity ... In order to realise the promises of twenty-first century technologies – in particular information technology – individuals, business and governments need to embrace a culture of creativity, experimentation and openness to change.[21]

The growth of ICTs, which has fostered all the structural transformations above, will change the global political economy because the structure of ICTs (the 'Nintendo economy' as Quah (1996) has termed it) will increasingly take over that of other industries (the 'heavy metal' economy, in Quah's memorable description). The digitalisation of the economy will be as profound as Fordism, and will be based on digital networks. These networks will not take data everywhere, or at least not at the same speed, nor will the networks be available to everyone, as much of the network architecture will be privately owned and managed. Nor will the information passed lead to knowledge, without human manipulation. However, it is confidently predicted that economies in the developed world will by 2005 increasingly demonstrate the characteristics of the digital economy.

The digital economy is based on bits.[22] Information products, such as financial flows, are a combination of these bits. Software is another combination of bits, which includes music, video, data, all of which are computer code. Production no longer requires analogue communication: consider the extraordinary advances made using CADCAM (computer-aided design and manufacture) from the 1980s.[23] More obviously, the value chain in commercial transactions is no longer necessarily analogue: suppliers, designers, manufacturers, final assemblers, wholesalers, distributors, retailers, can all be seamlessly connected by digital ICTs. Parts of that value chain are already redundant, and Quah has compared knowledge-challenged workers as 'roadkill on the Information Superhighway' (though acknowledging the hyperbole in the description). Where products can be made using bits (such as music or academic journals or airline reservations and tickets), it is possible to substitute the 'real' product with a 'virtual' digital version. Short-range predictions focus on digital software, which is already creating a process of creative destruction (the phrase of Josef Schumpeter), and the hardware networks which transport that software.

Consider three levels of creative destruction: micro-, macro- and meta-level. First, micro describes the effect of ICTs on the individual, from consumer to entrepreneur to business: ICTs here have the effect of exponentially increasing productivity. Second is the effect of the network at macro-level: industries become 'super-competitive', upstream and downstream supplier and distributor must adapt to new efficiencies, restructuring takes place, and customers drive rapid tipping of markets away from inefficient businesses. There is thus a step change in the economy. Competition policy must react to the new actors, allowing entrants into markets and preventing the emergence of long-run dominance. Meta-level changes focus on the effect of ICTs on political and social organisation, especially the resultant regionalisation or globalisation of power structures, and the state-firm diplomacy which is creating these networks far removed from traditional nation-state boundaries.

While studies of economic globalisation, for instance financial markets and industrial organisation, have previously focused on foreign exchange or automobile manufacturing as sectoral case studies of international economic integration, it is apparent that the relative neglect of digital communications networks as agents of economic, social and political structural transformation is in immediate need of remedy. There is broad agreement that knowledge-driven industries are the primary engine of structural change in the international economy and society, particularly in developed nations, accounting on OECD measures for over 50 per cent of GDP within its member economies (see note 37). The diffusion of information is essential to the generation of knowledge, and this in turn is dependent on ICTs, of which the most dynamic is, in turn, the Internet. Computer and telecommunications hardware and software account for 7 per cent of GDP in OECD countries. The price of personal computers (PCs) and portable computers demonstrates the extraordinary dynamic innovation and competition in the industry, with prices falling in the six years to end-1998 by 85–90 per cent. Computers cost one-tenth of their price level six years ago. While 'Internet' will be used as shorthand for the digital communications networks delivering information over telephony systems, it should be understood that many other types of information exchange are possible over this same infrastructure (for example, intranets, Virtual Private Networks and others).

Nevertheless, the structural transformation of the global economy caused by digital communications networks, which promises to transform societal and political structures in its wake, will be referred to, using the shorthand which is prevalent in the current policy discussion, as 'Internet'.

Trans-Pacific fibre-optic cables are being laid which have capacities in excess of 4 petabits: 4,000,000,000,000,000,000 bits of information. These travel at the speed of light from San Francisco to, for instance, Singapore, where the bit stream is instantly converted back into voice, data or video. The computer which powers both the bit stream and the terminal on which the data is received will in all likelihood contain products from Europe, the US and East Asia, and be powered by software developed or supported in India or China. It is the transformative effect of digital communications networks, both creating and paid for by the transnational capital flows with which it has a symbiotic relationship – how else did Reuters become a global financial information and telecommunications systems provider? – which has created the dispersed control of manufacturing and services value chains, which has itself led to further hardware and software development. Even this simplified explanation of the value chain lends itself to puncturing the myth that globalisation is somehow a simple or even reversible process. Carnoy *et al.* assert that:

> The world economy is becoming more competitive, more global and increasingly dominated by information and communications technology … (but) we are convinced that multinational enterprises are a product of their national origins and still depend on their home bases for economic strength.[24]

The growth of the e-conomy in the year to March 2000 has proved to most sceptics that the economic model in developed societies is no longer predominantly manufacture, but information services dominated. The valuation of 'new economy' firms in the United States has increased to the point that the services firms, Microsoft and Cisco Systems, are far higher valued than manufacturers Intel and IBM, even though the latter manufacture for the new economy. Further, AOL–TimeWarner, a content supplier, is now more valuable than either. 'Dot.com' frenzy in the New York NASDAQ index spread in late 1999 to European and East Asian bourses, e-commerce grew exponentially (both business-to-business, B2B, and business-to-consumer, B2C), and the real economy was increasingly being restructured by Internet – or 'new economy' – companies, whose valuations had enabled a spate of historic acquisitions of both 'new' and 'old economy' rivals. On 7 March 2000, the NASDAQ index of technology shares rose to an intraday high above 5000, with the Dow Jones All Industrial index at 9796.[25] At the start of 1999, the Dow Jones had been almost five times higher than the NASDAQ. In London, the largest ever change in capitalisation of the top hundred companies took place on 8 March 2000. Both markets saw technology company capitalisations increase while 'old economy' valuations slid, by a third in the six months to March 2000 in the case of large UK companies.[26]

The predicted crash may have occurred by the time you read these words, but it is unlikely that this transformation will have reversed altogether. Sceptical comparisons with Wall Street 1929, when radio station and aircraft stocks led the bubble, do not remove the underlying trend for Internet companies to replace 'old economy' companies (even if that means the 'old economy' companies re-investing themselves and their business processes with 'new economy' models).

Measuring the effect of ICTs on economic growth and international trade and investment flows is problematic. A narrow definition would examine the ICT sector of the economy in isolation, in which ICTs account for 5 per cent of GDP and 10–12 per cent of capital stock for the US economy. A broader defini-tion of the share of ICT in increasing productivity in the US economy 1994–8, conducted by the Department of Commerce in June 1999, estimates 35 per cent of total growth attributable to the use of ICT. Narrower estimates for future e-commerce expenditure are even less definitive: European Commission estimates for 2002 at $654 billion contrasts with Forrester Research estimates for $1.5 tril-lion in the US alone, or 13 per cent of GDP. However, e-commerce figures are misleading in that predictions are based on total revenue rather than value-added. In an international context, the US comparisons are at best indicative of potential, as e-commerce and ICT increasingly play as ubiquitous a part in the other OECD economies as in the US. The figure which appears most reliable is that of the Department of Commerce, as it measures productivity, the feature most commonly associated with international competitiveness. The attribution of 35 per cent of increases over a 5-year period to ICT gives some indication of the importance of ICT in the next 5 years of growth in Europe. There is no direct causation: the US is the world leader in hardware and software produc-tion.

The European economy is therefore operating in a framework in which US ICT dictates the progress of other economies, to an increasing extent. B2B – not B2C – is the real growth area in e-commerce. Predicted e-commerce revenues grew from $350 billion in the US in 1998 to an estimated $1500 billion in 2000. Europe lags behind, in that 60 per cent of 'Club Nord' businesses – Britain, Ireland, Scandinavia, Finland, Germany, Austria – use the Internet, but only just over a third of 'Club Med' – France and Italy. Nevertheless, B2B is growing rapidly. Europe's economy is not yet converging with the US model. Rather than reheat the 1980s 'regionalisation' Rhineland stakeholder capitalism with Anglo-Saxon shareholder value debate, I focus here on the transformation of markets. The combinations of Vodafone–Mannesman with variously Vivendi and BSkyB have created a web of content and infrastructure companies which rival AOL–TimeWarner.[27] Where PC penetration into businesses and homes has exceeded US rates only in Nordic countries, the European penetration of mobile telephony, and soon Internet mobile telephony, has greatly exceeded that in the US, led by Nokia and Ericsson manufacturers and Psion software development. The ubiquity of digital mobile telephones, PCs and Internet access for European businesses and households is a feature of the year from March 1999.

Content is critical to the AOL–TimeWarner merger. TimeWarner is a movie-television-magazine-cable TV conglomerate. In Europe, government ownership or control of television, which may have hampered the national film industries' economies of scale despite subsidy designed to overcome this handicap compared with the strength of Hollywood, has been replaced with private digital channels, delivered by cable systems newly divested from privatised national telcos (such as in Germany and Holland) and by digital satellite networks (even in Sweden and the UK by digital terrestrial TV). As a result, many European households – and even more US cable and satellite households – receive digital TV, which also permits Internet access at higher speed than conventional analogue telephone wires. This combination of mobile, PC and TV Internet access promises pervasive access to the services of the GIS within a few years. Given that Internet years are dog years (seven to each calendar year), by the publication date of this book more than half of all European Union and US households will probably access Internet services at home.

The legal and regulatory environment of states is a key determinant of investment in ICTs. Where services are 'location bound',[28] rather than tradable, foreign direct investment (FDI) is a pre-requisite, as in utilities, including digital communications networks. Entry and establishment is therefore critical, both in terms of laws specifically aimed at foreign investors, and domestic regulation, especially the market for corporate control, which is determined by private ownership and government acquiescence in foreign ownership. Both of these factors have resulted from reforms dating to the 1990s, based on liberalisation in the mid-1980s driven by US, UK and European Commission initiatives. It has become a commonplace to describe the huge growth in merger and acquisition (M&A) more generally, and particularly in the case of telecoms networks. UNCTAD established that in the period 1980–96, FDI doubled in the global economy as a percentage of GDP, both in combined inflows and outflows (from about 1 per cent to 2 per cent) and total inward plus outward stock (from 10 per cent to over 20 per cent), while world trade (imports plus exports) fluctuated at about 35–45 per cent.[29] Regional distribution confirms the 'triad' analysis of East Asia, Western Europe and North America. See Table 1.1.

Table 1.1   Outward FDI stock 1980–97 as per cent of global total[30]

Region / country	1985	Stock 1990	Stock 1997
W. Europe	44.4	50.8	50.4
USA	36.4	25.5	25.6
Japan	6.4	11.8	8.0
Other	4.3	4.4	9.7

This continuing domination of outward FDI is itself dominated by M&A: acquisitions by FDI reached $236 billion in 1997, almost 60 per cent of total FDI inflows, above historic trend rates of 50 per cent of all inflows. UNCTAD explains that liberalisation and deregulation – especially in telecoms and financial services – have contributed to the M&A trend.[31] The OECD goes further in its analysis of 1997, a record year for the members in which outflows reached $382 billion and inflows $257 billion.[32] It explains three causes for continued growth in FDI in the 1990s:

- deregulation – especially in telecoms;
- privatisation – where foreign ownership has been permitted;
- reform of trade and foreign investment regimes.

The UK three-year (1995–7) average for inflows was 12.2 per cent of the OECD total, and outflows 14 per cent of the OECD total,[33] both second only to the USA but far larger as a share of GDP.[34] The OECD, based on KPMG figures, explains that M&A is the dominant method of entry into host OECD economies, with 90 per cent of US inflows from M&A in 1996.[35] These mergers are individually becoming far larger in size, but numerically less common. Cross-border M&A is even more concentrated in OECD countries than FDI overall.[36]

On almost any measurement, the internationalisation of ICTs is far more advanced than any other industry, with computing and telecom hardware the most internationally integrated product.[37] The increase in mergers and strategic alliances, which have driven international investment to new records, is concentrated in these industries. Data to the end of 1998 (a record year for total international mergers at $550 billion) fails to account for the recent telecoms mergers, which have grown from the $50–60 billion valuations of late 1998 to the $70–80 billion of early 1999, and on to the $120–140 billion of late 1999. The enormous paper wealth generated by stock market gains has led to a restructuring of the economy. The acquisitions of TimeWarner by America Online (AOL), of Mannesman by Vodafone, of MediaOne by AT&T, of Telecom Italia by Olivetti, and – most spectacular of all – of Hong Kong Telecom by Pacific Century Cyber Works, a 'shell' owned by the Li family, were the largest mergers in history, larger than any bank, automobile, utility or energy merger. Curwen has shown that over 20 per cent of the world's largest companies (the FT500) at end-1998 were telecoms companies, this prior to the recent 'dot.com' frenzy, and asks rhetorically, 'Have telcos taken over the world?'[38] It is without doubt that the largest merger wave in history has resulted, further strengthening the structural dominance of telecom, software and content companies in the developed economies.

Globalisation and sovereignty

The chapters in this collection offer some projections into the medium-term impact of ICTs on globalisation and regulation, focusing on both the growing role of international co-operation in regulation, and the challenge which this further pooling of sovereignties poses to the national public interest and policy process. Its impact on national economies is uncertain, but we can observe that the growth of cross-border information exchange has resulted in both bilateral negotiation, and regional regulation, of communications. Digital pay-TV, broadcast by satellite, shares these characteristics, with satellite transmission from one country (normally Luxembourg, in the EU context)[39] to another in its region, and national regulation of the local cable operator which distributes content to the customer. Satellite television has been the political scientist's regional communications case study *par excellence*. The Internet is a global phenomenon: unsurprisingly, regulation of both Internet content and e-commerce is pursued in multilateral as well as bilateral and regional fora. The UK E-Commerce Green Paper of 1999 states:

> E-commerce is essentially a global, rather than a national, issue ... recent years have witnessed a remarkable growth in the nature and range of bodies engaged in discussion of this issue. The Government believes that it is important to monitor these developments carefully to ensure consistency with our own policies.[40]

It further states that initiatives have been taken by the OECD in a cryptography conference of October 1998,[41] by the United Nations Commission on International Trade Law (UNCITRAL) in a Model Law on Electronic Commerce,[42] and in other EU initiatives.[43] Consider further the issue of e-commerce in the World Trade Organisation (WTO). Despite the global reach of e-commerce, for the US government, Aaron has explained:

> there are other countries that would insert the WTO into e-commerce issues as authentication, commercial contracts, privacy, consumer protection and content. These matters are already *under consideration in more appropriate fora* – such as the Global Business Dialogue on E-Commerce [GBDe], OECD, UNCITRAL, WIPO [World Intellectual Property Organisation], and others.[my emphases][44]

US Trade Representative Charlene Barshefsky explained:

> we are seeking extension of the WTO's current moratorium on application of tariffs to electronic transmissions. We will also embark upon a program to ensure that our trading partners avoid measures that unduly restrict development of electronic commerce; ensure WTO rules do not discriminate against new technologies and methods of trade; accord proper treatment of digital products under WTO rules; and ensure full protection of intellectual property rights (IPRs) on the Net.[45]

Many social scientists continue to believe that an irrational optimism is evident in too many liberal economic predictions of an increasingly borderless world. Globalisation raises the question whether the global political economy driven by ICTs is better explained by dynamic or by static models. It has become increasingly evident that the dynamic model is the better, though this evidently increases contingency. Henderson explains:

> Forecasters from many disciplines: economics, technology assessment, game theory, ecology, or chaos and complex adaptive system models, now agree that equilibrium models drawn from Cartesian–Newtonian worldviews of a deterministic, 'clockwork' universe no longer fit.[46]

The broader effect of ICTs on globalisation and the meta-narrative of structural transformation of the world economy and civil society is therefore somewhat neglected in traditional analysis: it does not 'fit' within a static state-centric or neo-classical worldview.

In this introduction I hope to have performed two services: first, to persuade the sceptic to at least suspend disbelief and accept that the 'new economy' exists and is by its nature global, due to the dispersal of digital communications networks. The costs and access to the GIS for the disadvantaged are perhaps the primary political challenge of the early twenty-first century, but the GIS is by its nature global. In the US, the Internet and the 'new economy' are the new facts of social, economic and even political life. The late adoption of Internet services by Europeans, dating to the free ISP service, provided first by Freeserve in the UK in November 1998,[47] means that mass business and consumer adoption of the Internet is taking place while this book is in production in the middle half of 2000. It may be that these two assertions are accepted by the time this is read.

Second, I aim to persuade the US reader and the English speaker – including the US Trade Representative – that the Internet is global in its societal and political impact, and thus its governance, rather than being an American invention which must adopt American values, will equally become global. The Internet can be regulated, and will be regulated. The section following will describe why and how this can be achieved. In spring 2000, the following joke applies. A Chinese woman logs on to the Internet for the first time, and is guided through the use of email, chatrooms, discussion lists, news sites, special interest sites and so on, by her grandson. She observes government-approved Chinese sites, illegal but constantly flouted sites from overseas Chinese, sites in Japanese, in German, in all the languages of the world, dealing with religion, politics, sex, health, travel. She speaks to people from countries she has never even heard of before. Finally, she comes to the AOL site. Her son explains that this is a very special site, behind whose walls its 23 million customers spend 75 per cent of their time. 'Don't disturb them,' he tells her. 'They think they're the only ones here.'

The regulation of the Internet is largely US in its value system and its economic governance. This surely cannot last for ever, just as Britannia could not always rule the waves, and Greenwich Mean Time at the end of the last millennium was observed by those in Fiji and Samoa who may not know why the world's time is named for the standard set by the Royal Observatory above the Royal Navy's former staff college in East London. The globalisation of the Internet, and the potential for governance, is explained in the second part of this section.

There is a twist, which is built into the architecture of the Internet. The Internet is global, even if early adoption is local – and particularly US. Lessig's drawing of the constitution reflects the fact that cyberspace was made in the US.[48] Even the latest figures reveal that twelve North Americans are online for every five Europeans, and three Asians, 112 million to 47 million and 33 million respectively in September 1999. The next stage in 'constitutionalising cyberspace' is to consider the international dimension in which the GIS – and cyberspace more narrowly – sits, and which Lessig touches upon in his largely American treatment. Having considered commerce and code in the US, much research is needed into the effects of *le defi americain* in GIS architecture and governance in an international setting. Regulation must be global to be effective. To take the sensational example which is all too prevalent, should child pornography be discovered, who is responsible in law for its dissemination over the Internet? The questions are compounded by the any-to-any architecture of the Internet: all too often, the sender of information resides in a different physical jurisdiction to the (willing or unwitting) recipient.

The increasing role of private law, added to the phenomenon of self-regulation, may suggest a creeping 'deconstitutionalisation' of communications regulation, or even a privatization of the public sphere. In truth, it appears to be more a matter of 'variable geometry', of sovereignty being pooled where appropriate, and employed uninationally where advantageous to the nation-state. This growing role for governments in setting policy to encourage inward investment by footloose MNCs challenges traditional notions of sovereignty in the nation-state. The speed of action of individual governments[49] is the main advantage of regulating in this manner. However, though such rapid reaction may allow regulatory advantage for domestic firms and eliminate regulatory lag in reacting to market developments, it also creates the possibility of regulatory arbitrage, where MNCs can choose from a menu of successively more liberal trading environments, designed for their competitive advantage. Regulatory arbitrage is more commonly known as 'the race to the bottom'. There are unparalleled opportunities for trading in the convergent environment, as well as regulatory avoidance strategies. The largest economies, nevertheless, can set the rules of the game, as seen in the example of the infamous Compuserve obscenity trial in Bavaria.[50] The UK is one such nation, Germany another, but the US decisively the most important. The major trading powers, and it is the EU and US which dominate, can set regulatory standards which include or exclude market actors from other regions of the world.[51] The theoretical framework for the competition and co-operation among the leading states (phrased 'co-opetition' by the UK e-commerce minister)[52] is considered in detail in the following section.

Given the brief description of the Internet's transformative effect, it is perhaps also questionable whether academics have maintained an irrational cynicism and pessimism regarding the extent to which the international economy is now integrated. The Australian government has reported on Douglass North's assessment that 45 per cent of total costs in the economy are transaction-related, which creates opportunities for productivity increases through 'net effects', productivity gains through Internet-related transactions.[53] To claim, as many have, that the world economy was more integrated prior to the Great War in 1914, based on a higher proportion of trade relative to gross domestic product (GDP), is to fail to factor in the further flows, beyond trade, which have transformed the world economy, and latterly global society. These are flows of capital, foreign direct investment and digitised information flows. All three are at levels which would be completely beyond the imagination of pre-Great War businessmen or politicians, or even economists, lawyers and political scientists of a decade ago. Further, the extent of strategic alliances and joint ventures between ICT actors is evidence of even more profound international linkages, which Portnoy describes as political and economic linkages.[54] Further evidence to support globalisation must disentangle the trend towards international economic integration with the associated trend towards the globalisation of the formerly national (or even more parochial) societies and individuals, whose activities staff the MNCs, and support the political systems in which they are based. The empirical evidence for economic globalisation, itself more or less based on liberal economics, does not remove the normative case for government intervention or a broader sociological critique of globalisation. Accepting the evidence of globalisation which is now all around us does not end politics or history: *homo economicus* still battles against *homo sociologicus*. However, the presence of the Internet in the corner of the room, with instant access to all other users globally, and thus the opportunity for all users to engage in what were considered the privileges of a transnational class, does transform our view of the national polity or society. In essence, globalisation has arrived.[55] The hard choices are now to re-introduce politics and sociology into the globalised environment paradigmatically represented by the Internet.

Regulation

Regulatory intervention is both necessary and highly demanding, in that the complexity, dynamism and globalisation of the markets often render traditional top-down regulation obsolete, and make intervention on the market a strategic choice for competition authorities. There are bottlenecks almost everywhere. Many may be unblocked by the sheer dynamism of competitors, and the trick for regulators is to analyse which are more permanent in character, and of greater strategic importance in the economy. In the US, the MS-DOS operating system is an example, in the UK the British Interactive Broadcasting 'Open ...' interactive TV services platform. The European competition authorities have also concentrated on physical telecoms and cable television networks, controlled by former monopolists.[56] Open standards ensure maximum compatibility between software, as long as technical integrity is maintained. It is a 'free lunch' if there are enough competent and willing volunteers, and open code development continues with the Linux operating system, for instance. However, the increasing complexity and the enormous profits available to private standards have encouraged attempts to create *de facto* standards, either by industry consortia more or less in the interest of the network, or by single companies who give away product freely in order to build dominance, before charging monopoly rents having achieved that dominance. In operating systems, MS-DOS is one example, with Java an attempt by Sun Microsystems to displace the Microsoft product in favour of its own. In Chapter 13, David McGowan considers the Sun strategy of attempting to licence the specifications for its Java source code through the International Standards Organisation (ISO), and its ultimate failure to secure a favourable outcome. In Chapter 12, Mark Lemley considers the developing standards debate in US litigation in the microprocessor market, a hardware market critical to the operation of PCs.

The problem of collective action which the Internet and globalisation presents is intensified by the capabilities and potential of the technology, and the characteristics of information markets. In contrast to broadcast public goods which are non-excludable and non-rivalrous, the privatisation of information flows offers possibilities for private monopoly and sub-optimal exclusion of social groups and individuals. This is a justification for the strong European tradition of public service broadcasting, and the US provision of free-to-air terrestrial broadcasting. The high fixed and low marginal costs of information goods have been exacerbated by the Internet, and the potential benefits of positive externalities from the wider flow of information are threatened by the closure of this formerly open network. Where initial European consumer reaction to the Internet resembles the moral panic associated with environmental pollution, and negative externalities are highlighted for public concern (literally where pornography is considered a polluting 'moral hazard')[57] it is the potential removal of the positive externalities which is focused upon in the chapters by David McGowan, by Richard Collins, and by Monroe Price and Stefaan Verhulst. The excludability of information from users by strong cryptography, secure payment systems and the like is essential in order to advance e-commerce, but changes the nature of the medium from a public to an increasingly private sphere. Nevertheless, the advantages of freedom of choice offered remain compelling, and Nicholas Garnham's contribution in Chapter 2 seeks to establish the autonomy of the individual over the mass conformity of the late twentieth-century mass media. The regulation of this new global space is essential to maintain global public goods, free information, privacy, interconnectedness and development.

Information market failure: network effects

In ICT markets, which increasingly influence investment and economic growth trends more generally, interconnection and access issues are critical. Without access to ICT bottlenecks, firms, states, regions and consumers are excluded from the 'Information Society'. Governments no longer attempt to control access through widespread provision of public goods, as in a static policy model, as it is recognised that this may stifle innovation. However, Internet and telephony access, control of content and educational capacities of ICTs are central to societal development, and controlled by private (often foreign) corporations. The Freeserve, Hotmail or Amazon model for e-commerce success is to attract and retain customers – often by incurring enormous losses in providing free services until critical mass is accomplished – thus creating a 'bottleneck' where other service providers needing to access those customers can be excluded, or exploited. This strategy of brand building and audience retention is very similar to broadcasting channels, the difference being that it is market forces which determine success, rather than government allocation of spectrum. These bottlenecks can be secured by fair means or foul, by marketing or by technology, and the sums of money involved in a successful model are so vast as to create incentives for anti-competitive conduct.

Competition policy analysts, whether lawyers or economists, have long experience of regulating international economic actors, more so since the inception of European Commission DGIV regulation of almost all significant international mergers from 1990.[58] Thus, the profound changes in the international political economy (IPE) ushered in by international telecoms joint ventures such as Concert, Atlas, and AT&T–Unisource[59] are well known to competition analysts despite their recent approval by the Commission. This competition policy approach to mergers, considering future developments, has two especially pertinent features. First, it is forward looking, though historical trends influence the predictive analysis. It can therefore prove more inaccurate than historical accounts, but – for our purposes – has the great advantage that the economist's tools permit policy-making which takes full account of dynamic technological change. This dynamism is complemented by a second factor: the globalisation of industry structures inherent in such widespread merger activity is fully factored into predictive analysis. The often sterile 'reality check' academic analysis of globalisation which dominated debate in the mid-1990s is less important to the competition analyst than the emerging reality of truly global communications markets. Thus, while arguably most academic discourses surrounding globalisation somewhat 'missed the trick' with the growth of the Internet, competition policy analysis was centrally concerned with the mergers which were making this new reality.

The substantive benefit of considering the leading edge of economic analysis is often obscured by a set of analytical constructs which assume a neo-classical reality where none such exists. However, this is very clearly not the case in the European policy analysis which is so much criticised by the Chicago School element of US competition economists. Europeans, they accuse, see market failure everywhere – perhaps mitigated by the obvious legal requirement to break up, not extend, national oligopolistic markets in aiding the creation of a single European market since 1992. Further emphasis on market failure is supplied by the school of micro-economics which considers networks as economic constructs.[60] Even more so, the normative failures of neo-classical economics are challenged in law-and-economics by the Second Wave of 'New Chicago School' analysts, who factor normative, technological and even socio-psychological constructs into a 'bounded rationality' which is more human than the neo-classical *homo economicus*. This new model permits far more perceptive understanding of information markets, which are prevalent in the GIS, and adds greatly to our previous understanding of information economics.

Competition policy regulates software markets, which afford two particular challenges: first, software is the basis of the intellectual property which is the commercial basis of the Internet; second, the ability of computers to 'speak' to each other, and for programmes to communicate within computers, depends crucially on standard setting. First, consider software. It is clear that the granting of a state monopoly for a limited period to an IPR holder is a suspension of competition in itself.[61] This raises competition issues, in that the IPR granted may be the basis for the entire global computer system. This is only a slight exaggeration: consider Java or MS-DOS software. Where real or intellectual property forms a 'bottleneck' facility, and this appears as true of Windows operating systems as railway terminals, it may be that the consumer interest is best served by requiring the owner to permit access on reasonable and non-discriminatory terms. Other examples of such are telecoms networks, pay-TV platforms and interactive services offered via closed digital platforms.[62] In each case, competition authorities must be convinced that a position of dominance on a permanent basis has been created, and that the facility is economically unfeasible to duplicate.

Second, consider standards.[63] Network markets – and here I refer to the economics of networks, not the politics – tend to 'tip' in favour of a single dominant standard due to positive externalities. An addition to the network increases its utility for all existing users. This addition may be a physical effect – your friend purchases an Internet connection and can thus receive and send email – or a virtual effect – you subscribe to a pay-TV network and spread the service's reputation by bragging about it to friends. The email example also shows that the interactivity of 'two-way' telephony-type network effects has increased effectiveness – all else being equal – over 'one-way' TV-type network effects. The Internet has physical two-way (email) and virtual one-way (video and content reception): this combined attraction explains its extraordinary impact, though the 90 per cent decline in terminal equipment costs undoubtedly helps. Information markets are network markets in which 'winner takes all' strategies often succeed, in which market failure is endemic, and in which predatory pricing, bundling of dominant products with others (tied sales), and refusal to deal in the IPR which forms a bottleneck, are common strategies.

Microsoft

The *US* v. *Microsoft* case is relatively well known, if imperfectly understood by non-specialists, and raises interesting issues, very few of which will be resolved by the case itself. The possible anti-competitive effects of the Microsoft monopoly have been considered in the US and EU since 1994. In 1995, Microsoft consented to certain conditions relating to the 'tying' – bundling – of its Windows 95 software with other Microsoft products. The Department of Justice considered that Microsoft broke these conditions (the EU kept a watching brief on events, though it also theoretically held jurisdiction). That case has proved as litigious as the great anti-trust cases of the early 1980s, AT&T and IBM, which helped free the computer hardware and telco industries for the recent innovatory competitors – such as Microsoft – to enter.

In late 1999, Richard Posner was appointed mediator between the parties, following a finding of fact in the case which was damaging to Microsoft. The previous expert appointed to the court, Lawrence Lessig,[64] had been released. While the case may still be appealed to the Supreme Court, its importance can be summarised by reference to the writing of these two experts, Posner and Lessig. The former is a legal analyst of 'Chicago School' neo-classical economics.[65] The latter, who studied under Posner, is a 'post-Chicago School' analyst, whose observations on market failure in the software market have been developed by reference to institutional analysis. Lessig views software as the 'code of cyberspace', not in a narrow engineering sense but, more widely, in the civil law sense as the constitution of cyberspace. Lessig sets out the 'New Chicago School' agenda:[66] in essence – and my summary here is unbelievably crude – it is law *and* economics *and* normative values *and* architecture. The last such is the code.

Should governments cede that space, and therefore sovereignty, to corporations such as Microsoft, as the dominant operating systems provider or, even more damagingly in his view, strengthen the already dominant position by extending IPRs into cyberspace and then internationally through TRIPS, they would be failing to assert the public interest in free expression in cyberspace. The US government appears to be following exactly that path, allowing corporations every non-pornographic wish in the pursuit of an economically rational online environment. This is a not merely a national matter, in that privacy, security, taxation and other issues spill over national boundaries, especially where the hegemon, the US, is in cyberspace even more that figure, and the rest of the world, the EU notwithstanding, is placed in the position of dependent rule-taker. It is perhaps indicative that academic dissenters from the US government's position are actively explaining why public interest intervention is necessary. Examples are Reidenberg (privacy), Froomkin (domain names), Lemley and Samuelson (intellectual property),[67] McGowan and Lessig (competition and constitutional law).

Regulatory arbitrage[68]

National and regional policies for attracting the investment of MNCs, are claimed to create a dynamic of regulatory arbitrage,[69] also known as competition between rules – the 'race to the bottom' as it is characterized by many critics. Whether acceded to or resisted by national and regional policy-makers, the impetus which the mobility of MNCs creates for 'forum-shopping' necessarily influences policy. This influence is strongest in strategically and politically important sectors of the economy, and the regulations of the nation-state which plays host to the most important market – which has the hegemony – set precedents which enable policy-makers in that market to entrench their advantage. In the video, computing hardware and software and telecoms industries that leading market is undoubtedly the US; European regulators operate in a framework which is coloured if not dominated by US experiences of regulation, and the overwhelming success of US communications products. This regulatory arbitrage is increasingly important in an interdependent international economy, especially where sub-sectors of an industry are asymmetrically regulated. This is of profound importance for economic integration and globalisation of economies, because national regulatory arbitrage[70] may demote competition to a second-order concern, favouring competitiveness.[71] ICTs increasingly are characterised by market failure on a global scale, which is enforced – if at all – by either the hegemon, the US, or by the EU, as largest regional trading bloc with most advanced supranational enforcement powers. Lessig states that for the first time we are confronted with the fact that 'anyone could be a multinational … routinely living in multiple non co-ordinating jurisdictions'.[72]

Federal jurisdictional competition has been extensively analysed in law and economics literature, concentrating on federal-state disputes in the US. Briefly summarised, public choice analysis[73] of central government in the US: 'diagnosed regulatory capture and unchecked central government growth as principal ailments … [critics] looked in part to the devolution of regulatory authority to junior levels of government for a cure'.[74] Part of this analysis examines the 'free rider' problem, that interest groups can actively promote a narrow agenda in order to divert resources from wider utility in favour of their sectional interests. However, public choice theory assumes:

- the footloose investor (no costs in relocation);
- perfect information;
- optimal sized communities;
- no externalities.

Critics of public choice indicate that public actors are not necessarily efficiency maximisers in a narrow monetary sense.[75] Government is not discrete – consider the European Union; externalities are rife – especially in information markets – and investors are not footloose, especially in network industries where sunk costs are critical to network formation. As will be seen, the information asymmetries between government and market actors lead to regulatory distortions in favour of the market actors. Therefore, the assumptions in the Tiebout model cannot be maintained in these empirical case studies.

Public choice has a weakness beyond the over-simplistic reliance on economic resources: it reveals taxpayer preferences where mobility is assumed (and hence competition between geographically fixed regulatory jurisdictions) rather than the total electorate, and therefore the interests of business rather than those of the disadvantaged:

Competition causes the content of regulation and the level of public goods and taxation to be dictated by the private preferences of a narrow, arbitrarily identified class of itinerant at-the-margin consumers or investors ... competition can force the pursuit of policies ... removed from the public interest.[76]

North explains that:

It is hard – maybe impossible – to model [efficient institutions] with wealth-maximising actors unconstrained by other considerations. It is no accident that economic models of the polity developed in the public choice literature make the state into something like the mafia ... the traditional public choice literature is clearly not the whole story.[77]

He then explains why the parameters of investigation must be broadened from the narrowly neo-classical economic to encompass prior institutional structures and practices: 'Informal constraints matter. We need to know much more about culturally derived norms of behavior and how they interact with formal rules to get better answers to such issues.'[78]

This leads to reliance on the state-firm diplomacy as a framework. Lindblom[79] noted that: 'Businessmen do not appear simply as the representatives of a special interest, as representatives of interest groups do. They appear as functionaries performing functions that government officials regard as indispensable.'[80] Thus: 'Public affairs in market-oriented systems are in the hands of two groups of leaders, government and business, who must collaborate.'[81] This public role for businessmen, who are responsible for the generation of national competitiveness, and hence taxation revenues, creates a position of interdependence: 'Market and private enterprises thus introduce an extreme degree of mutual adjustment and political pluralism.'[82] This statement of public policy shares much with public choice in its assumptions, and provides empirically provable and robust assertions which are demonstrated in these case studies. Lindblom considers it critical that businessmen have access to a far greater range of resources than interest groups, and even government actors, and thus are able to influence the policy debate in their favour. He demonstrates this by analysing presidential election funding.[83] Further, he demonstrates the 'circularity of polyarchy' by demonstrating the commercial control on US mass media, in an analysis developed radically by Chomsky and Herman.[84]

Sovereignty, law and international relations

Jayasuriya claims that: 'Globalization is reshaping the fixed and firm boundary between domestic and international spheres and changing our conceptions of the proper domain of domestic and international politics and law'.[85] In support of his view, he quotes MacCormick, who suggests that, for scholars, '[E]scape from the idea that all law must originate in a single power source, like a sovereign, is thus to discover the possibility of taking a broader, more diffuse, view of law'.[86] Conceptualising a variable geometry of regulatory arrangements,[87] inclusive of international self-standardisation as well as traditional Westphalian notions, leads to a notion of 'complex sovereignty': 'The transformation and reconstitution of the notion of State and sovereignty in the face of the globalization of economic relations.'[88] Jayasuriya explains that as regulatory complexity increases in response to the global economy:

> The reconstitution of sovereignty represents the nationalization of international law. What this signifies is that the operation of the global economy requires extensive regulatory changes at the national level ... the focus is more decidedly on the way the form of sovereignty changes in relation to a fundamental transformation in the structure of social and economic relations. This represents not an erosion (as a formalist perspective might imply) or a dissolution (within a constructionist perspective) but a fundamental transformation of the form of sovereignty.[89]

One must distinguish the approach between 'market and social structures paradigms'.[90] He notes the work of both Strange and Rosenberg,[91] without qualifying which approach is the more satisfactory: Strange's view of structuralism which is bound in a non-ideological critique or Rosenberg's historical Marxism. He notes that:

> The important point to observe is the way in which structural changes in the global political economy lead to changes in the form of State sovereignty; these changes serve to radically reconstitute our understanding of the traditional boundaries between the international and the domestic spheres because agencies such as independent central banks are simultaneously part of the domestic order and a range of global governance mechanisms.

and observes that 'perhaps the best exemplar of this polycentric legal order and its disruption of the internal sovereignty of the State is the EU'.[92] One should always observe that, while more complex and therefore innately appealing than overblown paradigmatic claims, this 'transformation' is 'indeterminate, tentative and contingent', to employ the description of McCahery *et al.*[93]

Such is the (theoretical) geographical mobility and distributional efficiency which the new technologies offer, that one can view communications regulation as a microcosm of the globalisation debate: 'Globalisation is not a leap into an economic cyberspace that renders obsolete existing frameworks for understanding the influence of markets on regulation, and regulation on markets.'[94] Note the deployment of the term 'cyberspace' to designate a globalised libertarian utopia. The truth or otherwise of McCahery's tentative and contingent 1996 conclusions will be examined in the substantive case studies in this collection.

In her final unfinished article,[95] Strange explains that mainstream international relations scholars, based on the example set by international lawyers, delineated artificial disciplinary walls, failing to explain domestic–international interaction in regulatory regimes:

> The basic assumption is that world politics – international relations – are conceptually different from national/domestic politics, and must therefore be studied separately … the conceptual wall that was built to define the study of international relations has become a prison wall putting key questions … off-limits in the study of international politics.

She identifies sanction and enforcement of power relations, and therefore international law, in the same constricting conceptual straitjacket, though the case is somewhat overstated given the increasing recent attention paid to dynamic convergence of national approaches to regulation, both in European law[96] and in broader international comparisons, not least in broadcasting regulation.[97] Strange explains that, despite the static nature of much realist international relations and legal theory: 'This sharp distinction between international law and domestic law, and correspondingly between international politics … and domestic politics is being widely questioned. The evidence of overlap and of reciprocal influence is abundant.'[98]

International negotiations can therefore be conducted entirely on a local domestic basis, in that the state is fully aware that both home and host-state firms have the option to invest in other, more investor-friendly jurisdictions.[99] Domestic regulatory decisions thus have international political economic consequences, of which the shrewd regulator is cognisant, and which influence the policy choices taken by government. Hence, it is valid to employ dynamic institutional analysis theory[100] in order to explore the changing institutional political economy of the MNC and the state. This search for a more holistic explanation is approached from law by Weiler, in his study of the European Union constitution[101] 'with particular regard to its living political matrix: the interaction between norms and norm-making, constitution and institutions, principles and practice'. In analysing GIS regulation, we need make no apology for explicitly examining the efficiency claims of various institutional arrangements. The examination of the legal and political in such a case was made three decades ago by Hirschman, and remains valid: 'I hope to demonstrate to political scientists the usefulness of economic concepts and to economists the usefulness of political concepts. This reciprocity has been lacking in recent interdisciplinary work.'[102]

Weiler goes on to explain that 'The same can be said about the interplay between legal and political analysis'.[103] I therefore employ what I hope will be seen as a careful eclecticism, of particular value in such a value-loaded study as that of 'convergence': the effect of ICTs on the global economy. As Muchlinski has stated:

> A complex series of hitherto distinct regulatory fields – foreign investment, privatisation and competition … [are] used as a means of protecting and

furthering the competitiveness of business enterprises. Furthermore, the discretion enjoyed by the authorities in the application of these laws has created opportunities for active lobbying on the part of interested parties.[104]

McCahery *et al.* explain that:

Struggles to open up markets entail extended processes of economic diplomacy focusing on regulatory requirements and enforcement ... Business firms themselves, co-operatively and through groupings and associations, can act to ensure international coordination and enforcement of regulation in their interest, with the support of professional brokers of norms, the lawyers and accountants.[105]

McCahery *et al.* discuss the public and social choice models, which begin from market or institutional perspectives. They note that: 'Commonalities emerge despite paradigmatic differences – market models adapt to institutional frameworks and institutional explanations encompass competitive behaviour and outcomes.'[106] I see this commonality as emerging most relevantly in the work of North, which is followed by Levy and Spiller.[107] It is instructive to compare the views of McCahery *et al.*, who set out a three-point 'primary and interrelated concerns' in study of regulation with a globalisation agenda:

1   institutional response to dynamic economic change;
2   the 'functional policy concern' regarding the utility and geometry of regulation;
3   the democratic deficit, resulting from the institutional (i.e. constitutional) underdevelopment of the regimes formed to regulate international economic actors.[108]

As McCahery *et al.* put it: 'competition influences results traditionally thought to lie in the discretion of sovereign regulators'.[109] These questions of how, where and with what tools to regulate in an increasingly complex and interdependent environment are important to this collection. How do regulatory institutions respond to dynamic change in economic conditions? How are these governance reforms influenced by political (social, cultural and ideological) and economic factors? To what extent do national and regional regulators diverge in their response to global technological factors? These questions form the research hypothesis addressed in the school of institutional analysis termed the New Institutional Economics. It is the first question which predominates: how has the state reacted to the dynamism of technology and market development in the communications industries?

Structure of the collection: regulating the GIS

Melody suggests that the changes in the IPE described loosely as the 'information revolution', which really implies digital convergence at the micro level considered, may prove the catalyst for analysis of market failure in the IPE: 'The most relevant market model for examining the consequences of competition in the information age is one of indeterminate, unstable oligopoly.'[110] The role of government in promoting its national champions is critical:

> The international success of home-based TNCs ... becomes a primary objective of government policy ... the real change is a much closer identification of the national and public interests with the corporate interest of the dominant home-based TNCs ... competition in the domestic market can be seen as potentially damaging to the ability of home-based TNCs to compete successfully in global markets.[111]

If one accepts market failure as the result of the economies of scale and scope that ICT provides for corporations, then: 'There are unlimited opportunities for institutional analysis and theoretical developments to make complementary contributions.'[112] Paul Nihoul considers some of these theoretical implications in Chapter 4, in asking 'Will electronic commerce change the law?' He expressly considers whether industrial regulation has led to a systematic hierarchical confrontation between public and private spheres, a distinction which may be unhelpful as the intermediation of state between individuals, communities and economic actors becomes less clear.

Contributors largely focus our attentions on regional rivalry in this public–private bipolar economic sovereignty contest, in substantive issues surrounding 'standards wars'. There are three types of fora chosen:

1   the national legacy regulation of telecommunications (Chapters 5–7);
2   self-regulatory solutions adopted at national levels based on media and content regulation (Chapters 14–16); and
3   bilateral (perhaps bi-regional) negotiations between EU and US states and firms, whether unilaterally considered by national courts (Chapter 12) or continued within
    • plurilateral fora such as OECD, ICANN, International Standards Organisation (Chapters 10–13); and
    • multilateral negotiation within the World Trade Organisation and United Nations Agencies (Chapters 8 and 9).

The chapters in this collection describe the interplay of economic and normative values in the regulation of cyberspace. The contributors also acknowledge a plurality of actors as well as venues: the step forward in the past decade from a state-centric Cold War dominated, neo-imperialist hegemon-dependency view of globalisation within international relations literature, towards a more multipolar view of states, firms and societies is explicitly favoured in the structure. A matrix may help aid comprehension of this increasingly complex interplay of public, private and social forces: see Table 1.2.

Table 1.2   State and non-state actors in national, regional and international fora

	National	*Regional*	*Plurilateral / multilateral*
States	Westphalian realism: US as hegemon, developing nations as dependent; security structure provides national public goods	Trading blocs (e.g. NAFTA, ASEAN, Mercosur) and supra-national blocs (EU); security structures e.g. NATO, Warsaw Pact	UN; 'Washington consensus' of IMF-World Bank; developed 'clubs' (G7, G15, BIS); developing bloc (G77, NAM)
Firms (based on UNCTAD definitions)	'Uninational' industrial concerns ('champions') export trade, often promoted by government to balance trade flows	MNCs; intra-firm transfers; EU economic interest groupings (EIGs) – e.g. Airbus Industries	Transnational corporations (TNCs); multipolar operations, devolved strategy and research – theoretical construct
Social movements (environment examples)[113]	Political parties and community groups	Regional entities – e.g. ECOSOC members in EU, Greenpeace, European Parliament Green Party	Global social movements (GSMs); World Wide Fund for Nature (WWFN), less formal 'eco-warrior' alliances

The focus is on co-ordination issues, particularly competition and the private standards setting coalitions which have rapidly developed to manage global networks,[114] in 'open' and 'closed' structures which increasingly characterise regulatory approaches, and which both reflect state–firm partnerships and/or diplomacy.[115]

These issues have a fascination for comparative lawyers and political scientists because all too often the national legal machinery, and thus power of the sovereign, is found wanting in these international transactions, which address issues which have traditionally been dealt with at national level. Whereas crime, business transactions, financial regulation and competition law increasingly operate across frontiers (and here I refer to boundaries beyond the single European market, though this is the obvious federalism–subsidiarity case in the UK, comparable with the US federal–state literature), the same is not true for human rights and other core constitutional values, such as freedom of expression. The international bodies which consider these issues, such as the Council of Europe (CoE) and UNESCO, are notoriously unsupported by national jurisdictions, and beset by political infighting and institutional redundancy. In the earlier technological test cases, including short-wave radio and satellite television, the ability of international constitutional organisations to agree a code of practice to deal with human rights issues was found wanting, whereas the functionalist organisations such as the ITU and WIPO, as well as regional economic groupings, were more successful. Now, globalisation and technological innovation have outflanked even the latter, and state control of the economic and normative appears to have become an interdependence between state and non-state actors, particularly MNCs.

Content differences remain intractable: whether domain names, self-censorship of adult content, or digital copyright is at issue, transatlantic governance differences continue.[116] In the absence of effective multilateral/plurilateral regulation, self-regulation has been instituted, by not-for-profit organisations affiliated with corporate interests. As this self-regulation regularly produced leverage for dominant industry interests and their *laissez-faire* policy proposals, it also proved a classic opportunity for governments to pursue unilateral regulatory arbitrage, or the 'race to the bottom' in an attempt to capture footloose investment.[117] (Locational choice is a critical and unique property of Internet content providers, if not telecoms network providers.) There are therefore competing visions of Internet, or Information Society, governance. Cultural as well as economically rational motivations differentiate state and market actors. This is illustrated by self-standardisation processes.[118]

International organisations present further complexity, built on this intersectoral rivalry. For instance, at a regional level competing Information Society visions are offered by the EU and CoE, the former built on economic rationalisations under the Treaty of Rome as amended, the latter on the European Convention on Human Rights (especially Art.8 – privacy, and Art.10 – freedom of expression). At a multilateral level, three competing visions can be identified: those of the United Nations agencies, UNESCO, UNCTAD and the ITU, reflecting the organisations' commitments to, respectively, cultural protection, autonomy and development, economic efficiency and fairness, and technological development and co-operation. Grand multilateral solutions may therefore be theoretical solutions to intractable real-world problems.

To take a concrete example, the jurisdiction necessary to control the ubiquity of Microsoft software standards is graduating from national[119] to regional, and prospectively global. Jackson has indicated[120] that the major unfinished business from the Uruguay Round multilateral trade negotiations relates to the establishment of a global anti-trust authority.[121] The revisiting of the issue of standardisation and competition becomes all the more important in a global economy in which MNCs have outgrown territorial jurisdiction, and now are colonising the GIS. The OECD attempts to grasp e-commerce as a set of issues which it will analyse, co-ordinating between government and business in ensuring effective self-regulation, leads to fears that US hegemony will be replaced by MNC hegemony in e-commerce governance. The interaction between the GBDe (Global Business Dialogue on e-commerce) and OECD, as also that within ICANN (a WIPO initiative) demonstrates the lack of e-democracy on a global level.

The privatised and public–private rule-making which such state–firm diplomacy reveals is a fascinating and richly rewarding substantive case study.[122] In Chapter 3, Monroe Price and Stefaan Verhulst consider further the variety of shades of 'self-regulation', and shed light on the role of public and private actors. It is evident here, and throughout the collection, that the US government plays a reduced but interdependent role with private actors, and maintains ultimate sovereignty. The EU is also an important actor, as Mark Gould and Ad van

Loon reveal in Chapters 10 and 15. The role of more marginalised states is more precarious, as one might expect. Perry Keller's examination of China policy towards information in Chapter 14 demonstrates the degree of freedom of movement of information, and the degree of state intervention considered possible by the most powerful of the non-OECD economies. His surprising conclusion regarding the pragmatic limits on government discretion are of wider interest for smaller and less powerful developing economies and societies.[123]

Economic efficiency and rights-based regulation

There are two arenas of regulation which we can immediately identify: the 'superhighway' carriage type of sectoral regulation which has grown out of telecommunications, media and computing regulation; and broader societal issues surrounding the usage of, and access to, the content which comprises the GIS. The differences between the two are somewhat more blurred than this distinction suggests, as social and economic regulation co-exist in most of the content and carriage arenas described in this book. Those looking for easy answers to hard regulatory questions, or clear principles where none exist, are advised to consult more libertarian or technical texts. Nevertheless, the artificiality of this distinction is maintained in the book's structure, because issues explored in telecoms – including the critical question of access to networks – are not yet converged with those arising in media regulation, which begins from a rights-based approach. Further, the apparently unregulated arena of computing is actually a blend of media and telecoms regulation, though this truth is often obscured by the relative paucity of regulation to this point, and the tendency towards self-regulation, whether *de facto* or through industry-wide agreement.

First, telecoms regulation. Access to the Internet requires access to a telephone, which is still an urban and developed country phenomenon. Even where telephone access is assured, the capacity of that telephone line varies enormously, the call charges vary hugely, and terminal equipment is needed. Users of the Internet will know that access to the GIS requires a sophisticated PC, whether that looks like a desk-top screen, a television or a mobile telephone, which is always online when the user is near, and which can access the Internet at above the current copper wire 56Kps. The GIS is currently the 'World Wide Wait', and Internet access devices are vastly more expensive than telephones. The investment required for the developed world to achieve high-speed ('broadband' is the term used for this high capacity link) access to an always-on Internet is enormous. The further investment for all consumers to so do, not simply the rich and technologically literate, is an even greater challenge.[124] For developing countries, particularly those with limited physical infrastructure and great geographical size, such as Sudan, the challenge is far greater even than this. With the benefits of the Industrial Revolution so clustered within regions of the world, and regions within those regions, the Information Revolution risks further separating the affluent few from the desperate many. In describing a GIS, we begin with the challenge of a global information infrastructure.

The most apparent and real transformation of the GIS has occurred in telecoms, where a mixture of asymmetrical regulation of the former national monopolist through price control, introduction of competition in mobile, long-distance and international services, and social pricing of access to ensure provision of service to the economically disadvantaged, has generally succeeded in transforming the pricing of telecoms services. This has been most dramatically the case for business in economies which liberalised earliest, such as the Nordic countries, Netherlands, Japan, as well as Britain and the US. However, the liberalisation of all Western European telecoms in 1998 has profoundly affected pricing in latecomers to liberalisation, such as Germany and France. Arguably, this has been a triumph for price caps, duopoly regimes and social regulation of access, rather than the result of free market competition, which has only emerged in the most profitable sectors of multinational and urban business, international and long-distance calling. As Martin Cave reveals in Chapter 5, the extent to which competition has been permitted in telecoms markets is very much a secondary consideration to these more intrusive regulatory factors. Fod Barnes, ten years at OFTEL, the UK regulator, reveals in Chapter 7 that free market competition was always a longer-term goal. Though arguments familiar to telecoms economists, these regulatory improvements with relatively little competition demonstrate the limited competition possible in markets. Both Barnes and Richard Collins argue that the basic policy choices are political, not economic, and Barnes and Cave agree that competition policy is not yet a dominant theme in telecoms.

The real retail competition which will drive down local telephone costs will have to emerge in the local loop. The cost of constructing a rival local network to the incumbent former national telephone company is staggering. For students of globalisation, it is a little-noted fact that the largest 'greenfield' foreign direct investment ever undertaken is that of US telephone companies in the UK, which are now reduced to NTL and Telewest plc, at approximately \$15–20 billion over the period since 1991. This enormous investment was necessary to build a fibre-optic hybrid network which passes almost two-thirds of all UK households, and is able to supply cable TV, and broadband cable with upgrading. However, real competition has not yet emerged at the retail level, with British Telecom likely (as this is written) to have its price cap retained after 2001. Other European governments recently privatised their state-owned or controlled cable TV networks (or are in the process of so doing), which can be upgraded to provide a rival local loop. In consequence, European local loop competition is not yet a reality. In the US, AT&T has embarked on the enormous investment needed to purchase and upgrade local loop through cable TV networks, buying in 1999 both TCI and MediaOne, while AOL is buying the third of the big networks, TimeWarner. Thus, local loop competition – and that between two companies – is not yet in place in any major market. This long-standing 'phoney war' over consumer access to cheap Internet has permitted the entry of alternative networks, though their bandwidth is still inferior to fixed line. The most common, indeed ubiquitous in the 'triad' countries, is mobile telephony. By the publication date of this book, Internet-able telephony will be possible. Further forwards, broadband Internet access will be possible by about 2003 through 'third generation' (3G) mobiles. In the meantime, the standards which will form the basis for 3G mobiles have been set.

Richard Collins in Chapter 6 looks forward beyond the public–private Mark I/Mark II regulation of broadcast and telecoms, towards a more balanced Mark III, where open/closed, public/private extremes are replaced by a more inclusive approach. In similar vein, David McGowan in Chapter 13 looks beyond both government and private market failure in his assessment of network effects in software markets, terming the approach adopted by Sun Microsystems in their attempted international adoption of Java programming code a 'third way' of examining the open–closed debate. Mark Lemley in Chapter 12 adds further analysis of the complexity of assessing IPRs, and the intensely fought battles between private property and publicly available standards. All three reveal the complexities in considering a balanced regulatory approach to the social, economic and competition issues raised in this most rewarding of economic case studies, where the potential for both negative and positive externalities is so great.

International institutional standard setting

One element of reform often posited as the extreme state response to the extreme globalisation thesis – that MNCs are rapidly developing into stateless TNCs, able to evade jurisdictional regulation – is that a form of world government be adopted, based on the United Nations or possibly the international economic bodies, including the recently formed WTO (from 1995). It will be seen that – the fiasco in Seattle aside – the choices of regulatory venue adopted have been chosen in public–private partnership between the economic superpowers, the US and EU, and their high-technology private partners. The choices made have been largely private, from the ICANN domain names procedures to the self-regulatory standards setting procedures which have overtaken the traditional United Nations agency, the ITU. Formal legitimacy is offered by ITU, or WIPO in the case of ICANN, but there is no doubt that private actors such as Motorola, IBM, Bertelsmann, NEC, Nokia, Ericsson, Lucent and others, play a critical role as non-state actors. Bill Drake in Chapter 8 describes the formation of the ITU as a classic government-sponsored functionalist problem-solving activity, and its latter history as shaped largely by the US government and its clients, whether carriers or manufacturers. His lengthy treatment leaves no doubt of the fact that non-state actors are intimately involved in the formerly state-controlled process of rule and standard-setting for the Internet and telephony. Both he and Jonathan Aronson in Chapter 9 consider the incarnation of telecom liberalisation in the 1997 Agreement on Basic Telecoms (ABT) by almost a hundred signatories under the auspices of the World Trade Organisation, as a critical diplomatic confirmation of the liberal economic agenda pursued by the US and its allies in the previous two decades.

The need for re-engineering, or at least redefining, e-commerce was an essential set of US issues at the WTO meeting in Microsoft and Boeing's home of Seattle, in order to launch (or abort) the Millennial 'Clinton Round' in November 1999. This represented the US version of open standards for global e-commerce, market-driven by self-regulation and not subject to extra taxation or tariffs. The future of international organisational regulation as revealed in the poor choice of Seattle as venue for the aborted 'Clinton Round' reveals the crashing lack of sensitivity to government – especially in developing countries – which does not whole-heartedly embrace the US lead in Internet regulation. Aronson sees the failure to achieve any consensus at Seattle as indication of the need for a new realism from the US, which cannot unilaterally drive its agenda in such a multinational forum.[125] He asks how future ICT applications for international trade will be classified. As services? Trade? Intellectual property? Often, products traded electronically are all three: software is a good which can be distributed over the Internet, servicing that product is also electronic, and clearly the value in the product is an IPR. Therefore, the three WTO regimes, GATT, GATS and TRIPS, all apply. Ypsilanti of the OECD indicates that the US can simply side-step developing country opposition by using the auspices of the OECD, which is at the leading edge of Internet and e-commerce policy. It is a moot point as to whether OECD initiatives might go the way of the previous attempt to short-circuit the WTO, the doomed Multilateral Agreement on Investment. Given the lesser dependence on investor-unfriendly unionists and environmentalist activists in rich countries, and on relatively poor faith regimes which commodity extractors deal with in very underdeveloped economies, the ICT companies might meet less organised opposition to their exclusive dialogue.

Constitutionalism, legitimacy and self-regulation

The formal legitimacy offered by these functionalist UN-affiliated bodies does not disguise the lack of formal democratic process involved, which was the ostensible cause of the Seattle November 1999 and Davos February 2000 disturbances by an alliance of anarchists, trade unionists and environmentalists. The choice of protest on the Internet has more traditionally been by hacking into government or corporate sites, or spreading viruses which incapacitate recipients' PCs via email. Formal democratic decision-making for the global issues which Internet governance raises are extremely immature, as Michael Froomkin in Chapter 11 demonstrates in his assessment of ICANN processes, of which he was a member, and to which he subjects the high standard of US administrative law transparency and due process. Unsurprisingly, ICANN falls far short of the inclusive participatory standard required. Mark Gould in Chapter 10 demonstrates that the consensual model of standard setting which sufficed in the development of the Internet, a legacy model which is still effective in the more technical policy arena, is increasingly placed under strain by the advanced consumer – and therefore democratic – adoption of the Internet. Larry Lessig has characterised this as the 'newbie' issue of pervasive adoption of the Internet, creating a cultural problem where there is less common knowledge of 'netiquette'. These consumers' demand for protection and security creates a classic global public goods issue, which governments are now addressing.

Environmental, labour and financial market analysts will find these reflections unsurprising examples of both the limitations of global governance and the rapid maturing and thus increasing complexity of a global social movement (GSM). Where anti-pollution, exploitation and capitalist demonstrations and consumer boycotts have identified clearly defined and emotive targets in real space – for instance, the Brent Spar oil platform, the Ogoni people's exploitation as revealed in the execution of Ken Saro-Wiwa, or the economic dislocation caused in Indonesia by the Asian financial crisis of 1997–8 – the group identity of cyberspace is more diffuse, and the identification of 'rallying points' for protest less obvious.

Adult pornography has proved one such place. Students of media history are well aware of the moral panic which new media induce, and adult pornography is a regular target, from printed press and colour photography to cinema to video recording to satellite television. The difference with the Internet is that knee-jerk government regulation has only taken place in special circumstances (the Australian federal government has introduced such legislation as a *quid pro quo* in order to secure a partial privatisation of its state telco Telstra), with regulated self-regulation – or co-regulation as it is increasingly known – the norm. Monroe Price and Stefaan Verhulst assert in Chapter 3 the limits of both government and private action in this sphere, and assert the interdependence of both – there is little purity in self-regulation without at least a lurking government threat to intervene where market actors prove unable to agree. They draw on regulatory theory and empirical studies of advertising and newspaper regulation, demonstrating that in areas of speech, the Internet included, government preference in liberal democracies is for self-regulation.[126]

All the contributions concern standards and networks, as well as sharing a common concern with non-state actors. Standards have been described, and are critical. It has been seen that there are normative as well as technical standards which are critical to the future governance of cyberspace, though the latter have predominated in the technological evolution of the medium. Only now, with the growing ubiquity of the Internet for businesses and particularly consumers, are normative values – beyond a crude cyber-libertarianism – being taken more seriously. If technical standard setting in the Internet environment draws on the law and economics of information, the normative standard setting which is increasingly superimposed on that earlier model reflects an extension of law and economics into the moral and social universe.

Networks are also important for both technical and regulatory purposes. First, digital networks serve a technical and economic purpose which provides a further rich seam in the law and economics of information. However, it is the social interaction which contributes to 'virtual' network effects – as seen in broadcast networks, for instance, where 'word-of-mouth' recommendation leads to increasing consumer take-up of the services – which demonstrates the intersection of technical and social networks in practice. The dynamism of the social networking, combined with rapid technological advances, has led to the extraordinary speed of development of the Information Society and e-conomy. It is not just the much-vaunted anonymity and dispersed architecture of the Internet which creates regulatory challenges. The innovatory benefits of a self-regulatory and flexible approach to such an incredibly rapidly developing network, driven by entrepreneurial sellers and purchasers and the exponential growth of consumer adoption of the Internet, are obvious to government. It is the social, and technological, phenomenon which makes Internet regulation through traditional long-winded legislative and regulatory processes an unattractive legacy for governments.[127] There is an urgent need to secure democratic participation, checks and balances, in a more reflexive, flexible form.

Consider a second set of 'network effects', the elite socio-political networks of regulators and corporate actors, and the stakeholder (consumer, labour, local government etc.) networks with which national, regional and even international regulators interact.[128] These social networks are critical contributors to the participatory, hierarchical or elite regulatory processes which are described in the collection. These social networks can no more be described without reference to digital networks than can digital networks be described without reference to networks of users. The power of the Internet to provide a global interactive discourse between regulators and other stakeholders has transformed regulatory models.[129] Michael Froomkin's description of the ICANN process demonstrates both the limitations on, and possibilities of, such an approach. Mark Gould's overview of ICANN and other Internet regulatory processes demonstrates the blending of technical and social regulation, from regulatory network theory based on Rhodes' analysis. However, they both beg the question which is often termed the 'Digital Divide': access to online processes is possible for the well-resourced, in time and technology. Who represents the interests of the dispossessed, other than a token law professor or two?

Perry Keller in Chapter 14 addresses the uncomfortable division between economic and democratic processes in China, where the rapid penetration of the Internet is embraced by the state for economic and technological purposes, but a highly discrete and often apparently random enforcement of the state's absolute control over internal dissemination of information is applied. It is apparent that the First Amendment standard of free speech which Froomkin sees as exported with the Internet is not acceptable to the Communist Party in the largest single nation. A global First Amendment standard is unlikely. There is, of course, a more state-directed policy of ensuring access to information, which shares its legacy in freedom of expression, but which is based on the European public service broadcast tradition and broadcasting notions of both internal and external pluralism in corporate supply of information.[130] Far from the 'marketplace of ideas' which press freedom permits, this tradition holds that state regulation of the consumer's access to information can be benevolently justified by reference to the need for impartiality, political and social balance in the material consumed by individuals who are required to make informed voting decisions in a plural democracy. Tom Gibbons in Chapter 16 establishes the democratic case for extending this model from a world of scarcity of technical resource to one constrained by the information choices of the consumer, drawing on political theory and the pluralism theory and policy which the Council of Europe has commissioned in the period 1996–9. Ad van Loon in Chapter 15 explains the highly controversial progress of proposed European law in the EU, a process which has had minimal results, and the more consensual but less legally effective processes of the CoE, culminating in Recommendation 99(1) of the Council of Ministers (the CoE comprises forty-one members, including Russia and Israel, and is therefore a broader church than the predominantly Western European EU with fifteen members).

The first and last contributions to the collection confront the reality of the sloganised title of this collection. Both Nicholas Garnham in Chapter 2 and Pamela Samuelson in Chapter 17 question the propaganda value of the term 'society' to describe the emerging socio-economic form. They believe that economic imperatives occupy the policy domain, and that society has been left to follow. While Garnham challenges the basis of a 'golden era that never was' in his Kantian response to Habermas' public sphere theory, Samuelson holds policy-makers to their rhetoric, exploring the social policy goals of regulation from five legislative principles.

Will the Internet change everything? Writing in March 2000, this appears probable, based on financial data, economic restructuring, consumer and social usage of the Internet, and government espousal of the 'e-conomy'. Indeed, while predictions of the Information Age were made in the 1970s, their arrival appears to have been delayed but not cancelled, and 1999 was as likely as any other year to herald the 'new economy' as a ubiquitous mass phenomenon. It seems increasingly inevitable that the Internet, and information and communications technology more generally, will transform the economies of developed, and increasingly developing, economies, societies and polities. For social scientists, it is no longer possible to avoid the question. In this collection of chapters, essays and commentaries by an international, interdisciplinary group of expert commentators on the emerging Global Information Society, an interim, contingent answer is attempted.

Notes

1   See Gilhooly, D. (1998) *The Twilight of Telecommunications: Towards the Global Information Infrastructure*, paper presented to Global Information Infrastructure Commission Annual Forum 1998, 12 October, at: http://www.gii.org/events/ann4GDandTL .htm.
2   Soete, L. (1997) *Building the European Information Society for us all*, final policy report of the High Level Group. Brussels: DGV – Social Policy Directorate General.
3   Ayres, Ian and Braithwaite, John (1992) *Responsive Regulation: Transcending the Deregulation Debate*, Oxford: OUP, p. 3.
4   Whish, R. and Wood, Diane (1993) *Merger Cases in the Real World*, Paris: OECD.
5   Held, D., McGrew, A., Goldblatt, D. and Perraton, J. (1999) *Global Transformations: Politics, Economics and Culture*, Cambridge: Polity Press, Cambridge, Introduction, p. 16.

6 Florini, A.M. (2000) 'Who does what? Collective action and the changing nature of authority', Chapter 1, pp. 15–31 in Higgott, R., Underhill, G. and Bieler, A. (eds) *Non-State Actors and Authority in the Global System*, London: Routledge, especially pp. 20–27.

7 Higgott *et al.* (2000) 'Introduction: globalisation and non-state actors', pp. 3–6 in Higgott R., Underhill, G. and Bieler, A. (eds) *Non-State Actors and Authority in the Global System*, London: Routledge.

8 Blackman, C., and Nihoul, P. (eds) (1998) *Telecommunications Policy* 22(3): Special Issue *Convergence Between Telecommunications and Other Media: How Should Regulation Adapt?*; Marsden, C. (2000c) 'The European digital convergence paradigm: from structural regulation to behavioral competition law?', Chapter 20 in Erik Bohlin *et al.* (eds) *Convergence in Communications and Beyond*, Amsterdam: Elsevier Science.

9 Turque, W. (2000) *Inventing Al Gore*, New York: Houghton Mifflin, and extract in 'Thank you, Dad', *Sunday Times*, 'News Review', 6 March 2000.

10 See Lemley, M. (1999a) 'Standardizing government standard setting policy for electronic commerce', *Berkeley Technology Law Journal* 14(2): 745–58; and Lessig, L. (1999c) 'The limits in open code: regulatory standards and the future of the net', *Berkeley Technology Law Journal* 14(2): 759–70.

11 Berners-Lee, Tim, with Fischetti, Mark (1999) *Weaving the Web: The Original Design and Ultimate Destiny of the World Wide Web by Its Inventor*, HarperCollins, at http://www.harpercollins.com/catalog/redir.aspl?0062515861.

12 Saltzer, Jerome W., Reed, David P. and Clark, David D. (1984) 'End-to-end arguments in system design', *ACM Transactions in Computer Systems* 2(4): 277–88.

13 Lessig, L. (14 November 1999) *Architecting Innovation* at http://www.thestandard.com/article/display/0,1151,7430,00.html.

14 Clinton, William J. and Gore, Albert, Jr (1997) *A Framework for Global Electronic Commerce* at www.ecommerce.gov/framewrk.htm (henceforth the Magaziner Report after the head of the President's taskforce and Senior Adviser to the President for Policy Development).

15 Froomkin, M. (1999c) 'Of governments and governance', *Berkeley Technology Law Journal* 14(2): 617–33, quote p. 620.

16 Comments of Peter Harter, Global Public Counsel, Netscape Communications, but see Reidenberg, J. (1999) 'Restoring Americans' privacy in electronic commerce', *Berkeley Technology Law Journal* 14(2): 771–92.

17 Bangemann, M. *et al.* (1994) *Europe and the Global Information Society, The Report of the High Level Group* http://www.ispo.cec.be/infosoc/backg/bangeman.html; see further Bangemann, Martin (1997a) '*A new world order for global telecommunications – the need for an international charter*', Telecom Inter@ctive 97, International Telecommunications Union, Geneva, 8 September 1997 (http://www.ispo.cec/be/infosoc /promo/speech/geneva.html); Bangemann, Martin (1997b) *Europe and the Information Society: The Policy Response to Globalisation and Convergence*, speech presented in Venice, 18 September, available at http://www.ispo.cec.be/infosoc/promo/speech/venice.html; Bangemann, M. (1999) 'Which rules for the online world? The European Union contribution', *info* 1(1): 11–15.

18 Reidenberg, J. (1996) 'Governing networks and rule-making in cyberspace', *Emory Law Review* 45, adapted for B. Kahin and C. Nesson (eds) (1997) *Borders in Cyberspace: Information Policy and the Global Information Infrastructure*, Cambridge: MIT Press.

19 Schiller, D. (1999) 'Deep impact: the Web and the changing media economy', *info* (1): 35–52.

20 See Ohmae, Kenichi (1990) *The Borderless World: Power and Strategy in the Interlinked Economy*, London: Collins.

21 Michalski, Wolfgang (1999) *21st century technologies: a future of promise*, OECD Observer No. 217/218, Summer 1999, at http://www.oecdobserver.org/news/fullstory.php3?aid=48.

22 Pratt, Andy C. (1999) *Making digital spaces: a constructivist critique of the network society*, mimeo.

23 Hodges, M. and Turner, L. (1992) *Global Shakeout*, London: Century Business, describing the increasing dynamism and competition in manufacturing and financial industries.

24 Carnoy, Martin, Castells, Manuel, Cohen, Stephen S. and Cardoso, Fernando Henrique (1993) *The New Global Economy in the Information Age; Reflections on Our Changing World*, London: Macmillan, pp. 1–2.

25 Mathieson, C. (2000) 'FTSE review pushes trackers into tech stocks', *Times 2*, 8 March, cover story, p. 29.

26 Ibid. There was therefore not the conventional bull market for all stocks, but movement out of profitable 'old economy' stocks into loss-making Internet and technology stocks, which was somewhat reversed in the following week.

27 See Marsden, C. (2000a) 'Not so special? Media pluralism merges with competition and industrial policy', *info* 2(1).

28 Dunning, J. (1993) Chapter 6, 'The internationalisation of the production of services: some general and specific explanations', in Aharoni (ed.) *Coalitions and Competition: The Globalization of Professional Business Services*, London: Routledge, quote p. 91.

29 UNCTAD (1998) *World Investment Report 1998: Trends and Determinants*, Figure 1.1, p. 7.

30 Ibid., Table 1.3, p. 5.

31 Ibid., Figure 1.1, p. 19.

32 OECD (1999c) *Recent Trends in Foreign Direct Investment*, p. 1.

33 Ibid., from Table 1, p. 2.

34 This ranking is unsurprising, given that USA and UK account for approximately 50 per cent of OECD inflows and outflows, and the UK 40 per cent of US outflows. However, over the period 1990–6, the UK total inflows and outflows were only 10 per cent higher than the French total (UK $326.5 billion to France $308.4 billion), signalling increasing competition for both inward and outward FDI.

35 OECD (1999c) *Recent Trends in Foreign Direct Investment*, p. 6.

36 Figures from Table 5, p. 7. UK firms accounted for a total $87.8 billion in cross-border M&A in 1997, 92.1 per cent of total in- and outflows at $95.3 billion. By contrast, French M&A total of $35.0 billion was under 60 per cent of the $58.75 billion total flows, and a lower figure for inflows. In 1997, a record year and therefore possibly distorted compared with the general trend, it appears that the UK was the most attractive inward investment location in Europe and that almost all of that inward investment was conducted through M&A, a market-seeking and acquisitive strategy.

37 OECD (1999b) *OECD Science, Technology and Industry Scoreboard 1999*, Paris: OECD.

38 Curwen, P. (1999) 'Telcos take over the world?' *info* 1(3): 239–51, quote p. 243.

39 See Nobre-Correia, J.-M. (1995) 'Luxembourg: local, regional, national or transnational?', Chapter 9 in Spa, M. de M. and Garitaonandia, C. (eds) *Decentralization in the Global Era: Television in the Regions, Nationalities and Small Countries of the European Union*, London: John Libbey.

40 Department of Trade and Industry (5 March 1999) 'Building Confidence in Electronic Commerce: A Consultation Document', *International Context*, 6.

41 See Ypsilanti, D. (1999) 'A borderless world: The OECD Ottawa Ministerial Conference and initiatives in electronic commerce', *info* 1(1): 23–34. For a critical perspective see Love, J. (1999) 'Democracy, privatization and the governance of cyberspace: An alternative view of the OECD meeting on electronic commerce', *info* 1(1): 15–22.

42 See United Nations General Assembly Resolution 51/162 of 16 December 1996 at http://www.un.or.at/uncitral/en-index.htm.

43 Additionally, work in this field is conducted through various self-regulatory bodies. See Bangemann, M. (1999) .

44 Aaron, Ambassador David L. (1999) Seattle, Washington, 12 November, at http://www.usia.gov/topical/econ/wto99/ec1112.htm.

45 Barshefsky, Ambassador Charlene (1999) *Services in the New Round*, Senate Banking Committee, Washington, DC, 2 November 1999, at http://www.usia.gov /topical/econ/wto99/se1102.htm.

46 Henderson, Hazel (1998) 'Viewing "the New Economy" from diverse forecasting perspectives', *Futures* 30(4): 267–75.

47 Marsden, C. (2000b) MM-S-PL 1999–12 Final: *Pluralism in the Multi-Channel Market: Suggestions for Regulatory Scrutiny*, section 5, at http://www.ijclp.org/4_2000 /ijclp_webdoc_5_4_2000.html.

48 Lessig L. (1999b) *Code and other Laws of Cyberspace.*

49 Especially the UK whose combination of effectively unicameral legislature, unwritten constitution, unitary state and majoritarian electoral system allows 'policy-making on a heroic scale'. Prosser, T. (1997) presentation to SPTL Media Law Section, Warwick, 16 September, mimeo.

50 Bender, Gunnar (1998) *Bavaria v. Felix Somm: The Pornography Conviction of the Former CompuServe Manager* http://www.digital-law.net/IJCLP/1_1998/ijclp_webdoc_14_1_ 1998.html.

51 As the Warsaw Pact nations excluded commercial communication from the West in the Cold War period.

52 Hewitt, P. (2000), Harvard Information Infrastructure Project 1999–2000, 15 March, Cambridge, Mass.

53 Commonwealth of Australia (1998) *A Strategic Framework for the Information Economy: Identifying Priorities for Action*, December: 4.

54 Portnoy, B. (2000) 'Alliance capitalism as industrial order: exploring new forms of interfirm competition in the globalising economy', Chapter 9, pp. 157–73 in Higgott *et al.*.

55 See Florini, A.M. (2000), pp. 19–27.

56 Cave, M. (1997) 'Regulating digital television in a convergent world', *Telecommunications Policy* 21(7), Special Issue: 'The Economics Regulation of Pay Broadcasting': 575–96; Nolan, D. (1997) 'Bottlenecks in pay television. Impact on market development in Europe', *Telecommunications Policy* 21(7): 597–610.

57 See Whitehead, Phillip (1997) *Draft Report on the Commission Green Paper on the Protection of Minors and Human Dignity in Audiovisual and Information Services* (COM[96]0483–C4–0621- /96) PE 221.804 of 24 April 1997.

58 Cook, C.J. and Kerse, C.S. (1996) *E.C. Merger Control*, 2nd edn, London: Sweet and Maxwell.

59 Media ventures including two vetoed attempts to merge interactive businesses by Kirch, Deutsche Telekom and Bertelsmann's broadcast subsidiary. See specifically Harcourt, A. (1998) 'Regulation of European media markets: approaches of the European Court of Justice and the Commission's Merger Task Force', *Utilities Law Review* 9(6): 276–91.

60 Shapiro, C. and Varian, H.R. (1999) *Information Rules: A Strategic Guide to the Network Economy*, Cambridge MA: Harvard Business School Press.

61 Barton, John H. (1997) 'The balance between intellectual property rights and competition: paradigms in the information sector', *European Competition Law Review* 7: 440–45.

62 Cave, M. and Cowie, C. (1996) 'Regulating conditional access in European pay broadcasting', *Communications and Strategies* 23(3): 119, Montpellier: IDATE. Cave, M. and Cowie, C. (1998) 'Not only conditional access: towards a better regulatory approach to digital TV', *Communications and Strategies* 30(2): 77–101. Cowie, C and Marsden, C. (1999) 'Convergence: navigating through digital pay-TV bottlenecks', *info* 1(1): 53–66.

63 David, P. and Shurmer, M. (1996) 'Formal standards setting for global communications and information services: towards an institutional regime transformation?' *Telecommunications Policy* 20(10): 789–816.
64 Posner, R.A. (1998) 'Social norms, social meaning and economic analysis of law: a comment', *Journal of Legal Studies* XXVII (Part II): 553–65; Lessig, L. (1998) 'The New Chicago School', *Journal of Legal Studies* XXVII (Part II): 661–91. For examples of Lessig's recent work, see e.g. http://cyber.law.harvard.edu/works/lessig/tv.pdf.
65 See his survey of regulatory literature: Posner, R.A. (1984) 'Theories of economic regulation', *Bell Journal of Economics and Management Science* 5: 335.
66 Lessig (1999b) *Code*, Chapter 7, 'What things regulate'.
67 See Lemley, M. *et al.* (forthcoming 2000) *Software and Internet Law*, Washington DC: Aspen Law and Business.
68 An excellent property-rights based treatment of regulatory arbitrage in Internet governance is Burk, Dan L. (1999) 'Virtual exit in the global information economy', *Chicago Kent Law Review* 73(4): 943–95.
69 A. Michael Froomkin (1997) 'The Internet as a source of regulatory arbitrage', in Kahin and Nesson (eds) *Borders in Cyberspace: Information Policy and the Global Information Infrastructure*, Cambridge MA: MIT Press.
70 Woolcock, S. (1996) 'Competition amongst forms of corporate governance in the European Community: the case of Britain', Chapter 7 in Dore, R. and Berger, S. (eds) *National Diversity and Global Capitalism*, Ithaca and London: Cornell University Press, p. 180. McCahery, J., Bratton, W.W., Picciotto, S., and Scott, C. (eds) (1996) *International Regulatory Competition and Co-ordination*, Oxford: OUP, n. 31.
71 Sauter, W. (1997), *Competition Law and Industrial Policy in the EU*, Oxford: Clarendon.
72 Lessig (1999b) *Code*, pp. 193–4.
73 Moe, Terry M. (1997) 'The positive theory of public bureaucracy', in Dennis C. Mueller (ed.) *Perspectives on Public Choice: A Handbook*, Cambridge: Cambridge University Press.
74 McCahery, J., Bratton, W.W., Picciotto, S., and Scott, C. (eds) (1996) *International Regulatory Competition and Co-ordination*, Oxford: OUP, p. 12.
75 Bear in mind that academic economists who design these theories have chosen policy entrepreneurship and intellectual satisfaction above budget maximisation – McCahery *et al.* (1996), p. 7.
76 Ibid., p. 15.
77 North (1990), p. 140.
78 Ibid.
79 Lindblom, C. (1977) *Politics and Markets: The World's Political-Economic Systems*, New York: Basic Books.
80 Ibid., p. 165.
81 Ibid., p. 165.
82 Ibid., p. 179.
83 Ibid., p. 194.
84 Ibid., pp. 212–3.
85 Jayasuriya, K. (1999) 'Globalization, law and the transformation of sovereignty: the emergence of global regulatory governance', *Global Legal Studies Journal* 6: 425–55, quote p. 425.
86 MacCormick, Neil (1993) 'Beyond the sovereign state', *Modern Law Review* 56(1): 8, from Jayasuriya *op. cit.*, p. 426.
87 He takes as his case study the Bank of International Settlements and the domestic implementation of capital adequacy rules, a case study also examined by Underhill, Picciotto and Strange.
88 MacCormick *op cit.*, p. 426.
89 Jayasuriya *op. cit.*, p. 447.
90 Jayasuriya *op. cit.*

91 Jayasuriya *op. cit.*, pp. 432, 434.

92 Ibid., p. 441.

93 McCahery *et al.*, p. 7.

94 Ibid., p. 3.

95 Strange, S. (1998) *What Theory? The Theory in Mad Money* (November) http://www.warwick.ac.uk/fac/soc/CSGR/wpapers/wp1898.PDF visited 10 June 1999, pp. 2, 8.

96 For a theoretical discussion of policy convergence, accompanied by communications case studies, see Levy, D.A.L. (1997a) 'Regulating digital broadcasting in Europe: the limits of policy convergence', *West European Politics* 20(4): 24–42. Holznagel, Bernd (1998) 'European audiovisual conference – results from Working Group III', *International Journal of Communications Law and Policy* 1(1) at http://www.digital-law.net/IJCLP/final/current/ijclp_webdoc_9_1_1998.html;. The more general role of the ECJ is examined by Weiler, J. (1991) 'The transformation of Europe', *Yale Law Journal* 100: 2405; (1993) 'Journey to an unknown destination: a retrospective and prospective of the European Court of Justice in the arena of political integration', *Journal of Common Market Studies* 31: 417; and (1994) 'A quiet revolution: the ECJ and its interlocutors', *Comparative Political Studies* 17: 510.

97 Beltrame, F. (1996) 'Harmonising media ownership rules: problems and prospects', *Utilities Law Review* 7: 172; Hitchens, L.P. (1994) 'Media ownership and control: a European approach', *Modern Law Review* 57(4): 585–601.

98 Strange (November 1998), p. 3.

99 See Spar, D.L. (1996) 'Ruling commerce in the networld', *Journal of Computer-Mediated Communication* 2: 1.

100 See Mueller, Milton (2000) 'Technology and institutional innovation: Internet domain names', unpublished manuscript available from author.

101 Weiler, J.H.H. (1999) *The Constitution of Europe*, Cambridge: Cambridge University Press, p. 15. His Chapter 2, from which this methodological note is taken, is updated from his classic 1991 essay 'The transformation of Europe', *Yale Law Journal* 100: 2403.

102 A. Hirschman (1970) *Exit, Voice and Loyalty – Responses to Decline in Firms, Organisations and States*, Cambridge MA: Harvard University Press, quoted in Weiler, *op. cit.*, p. 17.

103 Weiler (1999) ibid.

104 Muchlinski, P. (1996) 'A case of Czech beer: competition and competitiveness in the transitional economies', *Modern Law Review* 59(5): 658–74, quote p. 659.

105 McCahery *et al.* (1996), p. 2.

106 Ibid., p. 3.

107 North, Douglass C. (1990) *Institutions, Institutional Change and Economic Performance*, Cambridge: Cambridge University Press; Levy, Brian and Spiller, Pablo (1994) 'The institutional foundations of regulatory commitment: a comparative analysis of telecommunications regulation', *Journal of Law, Economics and Organisation* 10(2): 201–46.

108 McCahery *et al.* (1996), p. 2.

109 Ibid., p. 3.

110 Melody, W.H. (1994) 'The Information Society: implications for economic institutions and market theory', Chapter 2, pp. 21–36 in Murphy, C.N. (ed.) *The Global Political Economy of Communication*, Basingstoke: Macmillan, p. 29. He applies this generally, with the case study of Northern Telecom, a Canadian-based MNC engaged in telecommunications equipment manufacture.

111 Ibid., pp. 26–7.

112 Ibid., p. 34.

113 Established potential negative externality of pollution – environmentalism shares externality and public goods factors with information goods (e.g. consider pornography).

114 See Mansell, Robin E. (1993) *The new telecommunications: a political economy of network evolution*, London: Sage.

115 A closed society to ICTs may not realise productivity gains or lowered costs, and therefore not realise ICT effects at all; by contrast an open society will increasingly resemble Silicon Valley today, with ubiquitous communications, intensive socially destructive and unstable work patterns, and an excluded information underclass.

116 Mayer-Schonberger and Foster (1997), p. 246.

117 Froomkin (1997), p. 142.

118 Cowie and Marsden (1999), *info* 1(1).

119 See *The Economist*, 20 December 1997, p. 18: 'Persecuting Bill'.

120 Jackson (1995) and (1993).

121 *Financial Times*, 20 July 1997, 'WTO urged to act on competition rules', p. 6, detailing the espousal this policy by Sir Leon Brittan, EUer responsible for external relations.

122 Levy, D.A.L. (1997b) 'The regulation of digital conditional access systems. A case study in European policy making', *Telecommunications Policy* 21(7): 661–76; Cawley, R. (1997) 'European aspects of the regulation of pay television', *Telecommunications Policy* 21(7): 677–91; Watson Brown, Adam (1999) *Industry Consortia and the Changing Roles of Standards Bodies and Regulators*, 325 IPTS Report, Institute of Prospective Technology Studies, Seville, Spain, also through DGXIII, at http://www.jrc.es/pages/f-report.en.html.

123 See by comparison Walter, A. (2000) 'Globalisation and policy convergence: the case of direct investment rules', Chapter 3, pp. 51–73 in Higgott *et al.*, 2000.

124 See Shelanski, H. (1999) 'The speed gap: broadband infrastructure and electronic commerce', *Berkeley Technology Law Journal* 14(2): 721–44.

125 Schneider, V. (1997) 'Different roads to the Information Society: comparing the US and the European approaches from a comparative public policy perspective', in Kubicek *et al.* (eds) *The Social Shaping of Information Superhighways*, Cambridge, MA: MIT Press.

126 Though one must acknowledge the strength of the democratic principle enunciated: see Mayer-Schonberger and Foster (1997) 'A regulatory web: free speech and the global information infrastructure', in Kahin and Nesson (eds) *Borders in Cyberspace*; Volkmer, I. (1997) 'Universalism and particularism: the problem of cultural sovereignty and global information flow', in Kahin and Nesson (eds) *Borders in Cyberspace*; Price, M. (1995b) *Television, the Public Sphere and National Identity*, Oxford: OUP.

127 See Freedman, J.O. (1978) *Crisis and Legitimacy in the Administrative Process: A Historical Perspective*, Cambridge: Cambridge University Press; also Baldwin, R., Scott, C., Hood, C. (1998) *A Reader on Regulation*, Oxford: OUP.

128 Reidenberg, J. (1996) 'Governing networks and rule-making in cyberspace', *Emory Law Review* 45, adapted for Kahin and Nesson (eds) (1997) *Borders in Cyberspace*.

129 Braun, Phillip and Schaal, A. (1998) *Federalism, the Nation State and the Global Network: The Case of German Communications Policy* http://ksgwww.harvard.edu/iip/iicompol/Papers/Braun-Schaal.html.

130 Doyle G (1998) 'Media consolidation in Europe: the impact on pluralism', study prepared on behalf on the Committee of Experts on Media Concentrations and Pluralism, MM-CM (97) 12, Directorate of Human Rights, Council of Europe; Graham, A. (1995) 'Exchange rates and gatekeepers' in T. Congdon *et al.*, *The Cross Media Revolution: Ownership and Control*, Luton: John Libbey, pp. 38–49.

Part I

Theoretical perspectives

2 The role of the public sphere in the information society

Nicholas Garnham

In recent years, a major strand of thinking about the media and its role within the theory and practice of democratic politics has been based upon the concept of the public sphere, particularly as developed in the writings of Habermas, and in the various critiques of Habermas' position by, among others, feminists, communitarians and post-modernists.

I should stress at the outset that I use the term 'media' advisedly, to refer to the channels of social communication between human beings, because I am forced to reject the term 'information society' as devoid of any objective co-relative, and thus void of any analytical, as opposed to ideological, usefulness. Even the most cursory examination of the claims made for the existence or coming into being of an information society reveals this inadequacy. This is not to deny that a combination of technical and socio-economic developments have re-articulated the structure and somewhat modified the conditions of access to and usage of those channels of social communication. But the fundamental questions raised by the relation between those media and democracy, and the role of regulation within that relationship, to which the term 'public sphere' points, have not fundamentally changed.

In order to address the question of the role of the public sphere we need to be clear as to what we mean by the public sphere. And I wish to suggest that although the public sphere is now a fashionable concept and has undoubtedly served a useful purpose in critical thinking about the relationship between economic developments in the information sector and the maintenance or development of democratic politics, as it is now used it often disguises rather than clarifies the issues at stake. In particular I want to argue that the usage of the term 'public sphere' mobilises a range of conflictual views about the nature of the division between the public and the private and about the relative normative evaluations of those two spheres; that contemporary societies and polities are increasingly riven by a shifting range of border disputes between the private and the public and by deep normative confusion about them; that it is around this division and our different normative attitudes to it that many of the regulatory policy disputes revolve. In order to clarify what I think those disputes are really about, what in short is at stake, it will be necessary, I am afraid, to visit areas of political and social theory with which many readers may, as economists, be unfamiliar.

It is easy, I think, to understand the attraction of the public sphere approach. It provided, against the background of the turn away from Marxism associated with the collapse of 'actual existing socialism', an alternative to theories of dominant ideology or hegemony as an explanation for the coincidence, within what used to be called 'bourgeois democracies', of growing social inequality and political apathy on the one hand with the relative stability and increasingly consensual, non-ideological nature of representative party politics on the other. Its emphasis on discursive practices and on communicative action as central to democratic practice and legitimation fitted well with the wider 'linguistic turn' in the human and social sciences and the associated growth of what Nancy Fraser (1997) has called the politics of recognition. At the same time its use of the spatial metaphor of sphere, and its stress on the necessary institutional foundations for the realisation of those citizen rights to free expression and debate central to democratic theory, addressed the problems arising both from the perceived empirical reality in the mature democracies of an increasingly media-saturated plebiscitory politics dominated by public relations, image manipulation and political marketing (and the associated growth of both political cynicism and apathy) and the problem of constructing the institutions and practices of democracy at the level of both state and civil society in newly democratised countries with little or no historical traditions of democracy to call upon.

Drawing upon a Kantian heritage that links freedom to a personal autonomy grounded in the exercise of public reason, Habermas and his followers have stressed the role of the public sphere as a site within which the formation of public opinion, and the political will stemming from and legitimised by such opinion, is subject to the disciplines of a discourse, or communicative ethics, by which all views are subjected to the critical reasoning of others. At the same time a democratically legitimate public sphere requires that access to it is open both to all citizens and to all views equally, provided only that all participants are governed by the search for general agreement. This general model is then applied as a normative test against which the performance of contemporary media, in terms of political effects and democratic potential, can be judged on the basis of either the rationality of their discourse or the range of views or speakers accorded access.

This view of the public sphere has then been criticised on three main grounds.

- First, that its procedural rules are too rationalist – that the persuasive use of rhetoric can never, and indeed should never, be excluded from political communication – and that to impose such discursive norms in practice excludes from the public sphere as illegitimate not just a range of culturally specific discursive forms but also those who do not posses the cultural capital required to mobilise those discursive forms. Here we find the criticism that the model of procedural rationality being deployed is in fact a model of a certain intellectual practice and thus excludes, in a movement of symbolic violence, those who are not members of the social group who are the carriers of that practice, whether conceived as intellectuals or as the white male bourgeoisie, and that it leads to a privileging of certain genres of media, especially to an assumption that news and overt political coverage are 'serious' and thus to an evaluation of its absence as a sign of 'dumbing down' or 're-feudalisation', at the expense of entertainment and its role in the formation of publics and as a site for the development of an under-standing of issues of public importance or, *à la* Bakhtin, the carnivalesque subversion of imposed norms and hierarchies of significance.

- Second, the public sphere model of procedural rationality is criticised for drawing the distinction between public and private in such a way as to exclude both key groups of citizens, e.g. women, or key matters of potential public political concern, e.g. the regulation of domestic, intra-familial or sexual relations.
- Third, it is criticised on the grounds that it has valued general agreement around a set of universal values or norms (however rationally discursively arrived at) which, its critics argue, derive in turn from a liberal model of proceduralism, abstract individual rights and ethical neutrality which priori-tises the just over the good and thus denies difference and thus the inevitability of perpetual normative conflict within modern societies. This in its turn, so critics argue, leads to an over-centralised model of *the* public sphere incompatible with the politics of identity in multicultural societies, whereas what is needed is a decentralised model of multiple public spheres expressive of each distinct collective identity, culture or form of life.

In this paper I wish to examine these issues through the optic of the distinction between public and private. It is clear that the use of the concept of the public sphere mobilises this distinction, and critics of Habermas' position and his followers rightly pointed to the ways in which this distinction operates norma-tively as well as descriptively; to how the conceptualisation of the boundary between public and private has shifted historically and to the ways in which the boundary has been mobilised to exclude both topics for debate and action and social actors from legitimate participation in the public realm. The key argument here is that we can only clarify what is at stake in these arguments – what it is that the protagonists are actually talking about – if we go behind this apparently simple distinction and begin to unpick the range of meanings, both descriptive and normative, that these terms mobilise and the differing intellectual traditions, or strands of thought and associated problems, from which those different mean-ings are drawn.

In particular in current debates about the media, the concepts of public, and private as its opposite, are mobilised in three ways. First, around the concept of the public sphere within a general institutional debate about the practice of democratic politics in general. Second, in a debate about the content and prac-tice of the mass media which focuses on issues of privacy. Third, in debates about media regulation which, in the face of technological convergence and the growth of the Internet, turn on the distinction between the rights and obligations attaching to public and private communication respectively. In each case two issues are at stake:

- where to draw the boundary between the public and private both generally and within specific spheres of social action, which in its turn depends upon the ways in which we choose to distinguish the public from the private;
- what relative normative valuation to attach to each sphere – that is to say, do we regard, for instance, the private as a sphere to be protected against the encroachment and domination of the public or, on the contrary, do we regard the public as a sphere of superior shared social values to be fostered at the expense of selfish, corrupting private interests?

Because both the boundaries and the relative evaluations are in fact mobilised, both for intellectual analysis and political debate, in shifting, confused and often mutually contradictory ways, it is necessary, I think, to unpack the roots of these distinctions and evaluations in order to clarify their entailments.

The debate on the validity and usefulness of the concept of the public sphere uses the distinction between public and private in two ways related to two distinct defining attributes of the public sphere – one epistemological and the other institutional. The public sphere is defined, for instance classically in the writings of Habermas, as being public in two senses: because the opinions, 'truths' or agreements arrived at within it have to be validated by publicly presented and challengeable arguments, and because the sphere is equally open to the access of all citizens. The reason that this distinction is important is because advocates of differing positions within the debate around the public sphere may place their emphases on one or the other and the two sets of values may be in conflict. Thus those who stress the discourse or communicative ethics side will stress the importance of public standards of argument – of a certain procedurally based form of rational rhetoric – but by so doing will, either implicitly or explicitly, exclude those who are not prepared or are incapable of obeying those rhetorical rules. It is on this basis, for instance, that one form of feminist critique of the public sphere approach has been mounted on the grounds that the form of discourse defended as appropriate for public dispute and opinion formation is inherently masculine. Similarly, debates over the evaluation of the political implications of talk shows, or of the so-called 'dumbing down' or tabloidisation of news and political reporting in both newspapers and broadcasting, has in part turned on a difference between those who stress the populist and emotive nature of the discourse as dangerously anti-rational and thus anti-democratic on the one hand, and those on the other who stress the democratically positive nature of the increased access of 'ordinary' people to arenas of public debate previously dominated by political and intellectual elites. It is easy to see how defenders of a discourse ethics approach can at a minimum be blind to the ways in which socially created cultural incapacities – such as those extensively analysed by Bourdieu – create barriers to full and effective access to the public sphere and maximally can lead to the elitist defence of rule by experts. On the other hand, a stress on access can easily lead to the defence of demagogic populism and the view that the lowering of material or cultural barriers to access is *ipso facto* democratic – the kind of argument that is only too easily mobilised by the Murdochs of this world in defence of the *Sun* or Sky TV against the toffs, the chattering classes, the educated middle-class professionals running broadsheet newspapers or the BBC.

The debate over privacy in particular, and media ethics more generally, is now pervasive. It is in essence a debate about what subjects, in both senses of the word – persons and subjects of discussion – should be the legitimate object of media coverage and thus of public exposure or display. This issue has recently been raised by the moral panic surrounding the role of the paparazzi in the death of Princess Diana and by so-called 'Zippergate' in the USA, which has raised centrally the issues of what areas of behaviour it is or is not appropriate to subject to the glare of 'publicity', and of the relationship between then-President Clinton's 'private' sexual behaviour and the performance of his 'public' political duties. Similar issues are currently raised in the UK over the 'outing', that is to say the publication of the legal sexual preferences and behaviours, of gay politicians which they, for whatever reason, would prefer to keep 'private'. We can see played out here a more central drama of our times, namely the increasing stress on the personal and individual and on interpersonal relations as the supreme source of value on the one hand and the obsession with celebrity on the other – on both of which the media feed and the latter of which they are crucial in creating and sustaining. This was one of the paradoxes of the media discourse in the wake of Princess Diana's death. On the one hand there was the condemnation of the hounding paparazzi and the ecstatic praise for the personal, 'touchy-feely', 'feminine' values that Diana supposedly represented and expressed, in opposition to what were represented as the repressive, formal values of traditional public life and duty. On the other there was condemnation of the royal family for its failure to mourn in public for popular delectation, coupled with a more general claim to the socially therapeutic role of the public expression of private feelings.

Thus in the debate over privacy and media reporting we find, first, those defending privacy against media intrusion – including celebrities and 'public' figures such as politicians objecting to intrusions in their 'private' as opposed to their 'public' lives. Second, we find the media defending their behaviour as in the 'public' interest because it makes publicly available information necessary for the making of informed political judgements as to the suitability for public office of the individuals concerned. What is at issue here are two different distinctions between public and private. On the one hand there is the issue of whether in the case of a given individual private and public behaviour can or should be distinguished, and, on the other, whether there is a range of subject matter (or behaviour) which is appropriate or inappropriate for discussion and/or display in public. And in both cases whether morality is a public or private matter.

The public/private distinction is also, of course, central to the regulatory debate set in motion by so-called convergence and the development of the Internet mode of communication. To date, two models of communication have underpinned regulation. On the one hand, the traditional mass media of the press and broadcasting have been seen as media of public communication and thus as institutions straddling the private economic sphere and the public political sphere, in a way that legitimised public policy intervention to ensure that these media fulfilled their public functions, functions ultimately underpinned by a liberal freedom of expression theory. To what extent this involved an intervention by the state in the private economic activities of corporations, and if so what forms of intervention, has been and remains a matter of continuous political debate. On the other hand, telecommunication networks developed as carriers of private communication between individual private persons. While regulation of the network was considered legitimate any regulation of the messages passing over the network was and is regarded as an illegitimate infringement of individual freedom, autonomy and privacy, as indeed an infringement of the right to free speech. Within the Internet environment these two traditions of thought now come into conflict because it is possible, for instance, to regard a website as either, because of the individual addressibility and transactional nature of each communicative relation with the site, a site for a series of private individual transaction on the model of the market or, because of its general accessibility, a site for public communication within the public sphere with associated rights and responsibilities for those who control and use it. Which view we take will make a difference to the normative evaluations of the activity and any resulting regulatory policy we might wish to advocate or impose.

The roots of public sphere theory

> We do admittedly say that, whereas a higher authority may deprive us of freedom of *speech* or of *writing*, it cannot deprive us of freedom of *thought*. But how much and how accurately would we *think* if we did not think, so to speak, in community with others to whom we *communicate* our thoughts and who communicate their thoughts to us? We may therefore conclude that the same external constraints which deprives people of the freedom to *communicate* their thoughts in public also removes their freedom of *thought*, the one treasure which remains to us amidst all the burdens of civil life, and which alone offers us a means of overcoming all the evils of this condition.[1]

The concept of the public sphere, and the related conceptual and normative distinctions between public and private, has been mobilised as a normative concept with which to pass judgement on the performance of the media from the perspective of the creation and maintenance of democracy. In making a judgement on its efficacy from this perspective, and on the criticisms made of it, we need to be clear about the problem to which it is addressed.

The problem of the relationship between communication and politics can be traced back to the Enlightenment and the basic paradox that modernity posed; the paradox of what Kant called the 'unsocial sociability' of human beings. We might think of this as the inherent tension between liberty and fraternity. If we take as granted the key characteristics of modernity as the development of ever more complex forms of social specialisation, associated with a separation between human identity formation and life chances on the one hand and ascribed roles on the other, and with the death of tradition as a guide to social behaviour, then we are unavoidably faced by the task of constructing forms of social co-ordination, social bonds, whether seen as polities, communities or societies, which are compatible with free individual subjects, in the sense of rational reflexive and autonomous beings whose identities and moralities must unavoidably be post-conventional. We do not need to concern ourselves, interesting as that is, with the historical roots of this shift out of traditional societies, nor indeed with its desirability or morality. It is simply the fate with which we are now faced and with which we have to deal.

In essence, modern democracy is about how we handle the relationship between individual freedom and moral agency on the one hand and the necessary and unavoidable social norms and structures within which alone such freedom can be exercised on the other. As Rousseau put it in *The Social Contract*:

> the problem is to find a form of association ... in which each, while uniting himself with all, may still obey himself alone, and remain as free as before. This is the fundamental problem of which the social contract provides the solution.
>
> (Rousseau 1968)

Kant's answer was epistemological and placed what has become known as a discourse ethic centre stage. Thus the key foundation of a democratic polity was the ability and duty to exercise Public Reason. Free citizens could not depend upon the mere ungrounded opinion of others. They had to think for themselves and subject their opinions to the discipline of public criticism. This argument then linked up with a tradition of political thought stemming from the community of saints, and the need to discover the truth of God through the free public exchange of views derived from private faith and conscience, to found the liberal social contract theory of democratic legitimacy within which free expression, and thus tolerance, are the supreme political virtues, and to the supremacy of the right over the good. The crucial point is that upon this epistemological foundation is built a theory of the relation between communication and politics which builds a limited sphere for public action upon the prior existence of private, autonomous individual subjects whose individual rights it is the purpose of the public realm equally to protect, but whose autonomy, and therefore potential for freedom, is itself built on public discourse.

The alternative response to the paradox of modernity can also be derived from Rousseau. It stems from the stress that he laid on the centrality for the formation of human identity and the maintenance of social bonds of the human desire for recognition or the love or esteem of others. As Charles Taylor has argued, our modern politics of identity, whether individual or collective, and the problems and disputes surrounding it, stems from the attempt, following Rousseau, to make honour egalitarian. Drawing upon a tradition of civic republicanism the political realm was seen as the realm where the common values of the collective were expressed and where agonistically individual citizens competed for honour and respect – or, in modern terminology, recognition. This is why for Rousseau in the utopian republic all citizens would be permanently and perpetually on mutual show. If feudalism had been a theatre in which the ruler performed for a spectating public then in an egalitarian republic all citizens were at the same time actors and spectators for each other in a permanent social theatre (Taylor 1994).

This view was then developed by Hegel, in his critique of Kant, in two key directions; first, by developing a theory of human subjectivity as essentially socially constructed in a process of reciprocal interaction and mutual recognition; second, by stressing the problem of what he called *Sittlichkeit*, namely the shared values upon which membership of any social collective not held together by mere force must be based and as that which motivated free individuals to belong to a given collectivity – to feel at home in it – such that they owed loyalty to it and then, in the ultimate test of citizenship, were prepared to subordinate their private interests to the public interest by being prepared to die for their country. From the perspective of public sphere theory this tradition prioritises fraternity or solidarity.

It is out of this tradition that the communitarian critique is mounted against what they see as the abstract, rationalist, rights-based characteristics of discourse ethics and the public sphere. For these critics the problem of public discourse is one of constructing discourses which recognises cultural and individual diversity and which is capable of motivating and providing a sense of belonging, or *heimat*, to human agents rather than of fostering critical self-development.

The political problem to which the public sphere tradition of analysis addresses itself is then two sided, and many of the problems with current uses of the term 'public sphere', and criticisms of it, derive from a confusion about which of the two sides of the dilemma are being addressed.

The public sphere involves both questions of discourse and their relationship to the formation of human identities, and to the motivation of action on the one hand and questions of the institutional structures, forms of social relationship and appropriate spheres of social effectivity of spheres of discourse and action we can call public, on the other. In particular, differences between positions turn on the relative weight given, within more general views of society, identity formation and politics, to discourse or action. In particular, is the purpose of the public sphere, and of politics more generally, to reach agreement and substitute persuasion for force as the dominant mode of social co-ordination? Or, on the contrary, is the public realm, in Arendt's words, 'where freedom can appear' because 'men act in concert'?

Let us start from the side of discourse. Central to Habermas's public sphere theory is a concept of communicative or discourse ethics, and a specific test of rationality applied to communicative interchange appropriate to the public sphere and legitimate as the foundation for public opinion and will formation. And a central criticism of this tradition from communitarians and post-modernists has been that it is based upon the no longer tenable rational subject of the Enlightenment, and also therefore upon the liberal rights model of politics with its supposed denial of differentiated life worlds, and the inevitable irreducibility of the relativity of values that stem from those life worlds.

It is clear that this strand in Habermas' thinking derives from Kant's concept of the relationship between the formation of autonomous individual subjects and the use of what Kant called Public Reason. It is crucial to stress that Kant's position was explicitly anti-foundationalist. It has in my view been unfortunate that Habermas has combined a Kantian approach to public reason with a search for a foundationalism in the basic structure of communicative action, which is both unnecessary and probably unsustainable. The reason for this move by Habermas is clear. It was an attempt to find a substitute for a need- and interest-based, and thus ultimately instrumental, foundationalism that underpinned Marxist-inspired versions of ideology and ideology critique. We will need to return to this question of interests and the problem of the source of the motivations for political action shortly.

But to return to the problem of discourse ethics. It is important to register that for Kant the autonomy of the individual subject and thus her or his freedom, upon which any theory of democracy must rest and from which much of the liberal tradition of political thought derives, rested upon the ability to think for oneself. In a situation of all-enveloping doubt this involved freeing oneself both from dogmas – the pre-packaged thoughts of others or of society at large, what has become known as ideology – *and* from the subjectivity of individual desires and the individual point of view. On this view the rationality which was the founding condition for autonomy and thus for freedom depended upon the exercise of public as opposed to private reason. It is important to stress that the distinction does not turn upon the number of people to whom a discourse is addressed or who have access to the discourse, but upon the discursive conditions. For Kant, public reason must be offered in such a way that it is potentially acceptable by any other human being, and this in its turn involves the effort of putting oneself in the position of the other. This involved the exercise of reflective judgement or a *sensus communis*, what Hannah Arendt has termed 'enlarged thinking'. This Kant defines as:

> the idea of a public sense, i.e. a critical faculty which in its reflective act takes account (*a priori*) of the mode of representation of everyone else, in order, as it were, to weigh its judgement with the collective reason of mankind, and thereby avoid the illusion arising from subjective and personal conditions which could readily be taken for objective ... This is accomplished by weighing the judgement, not so much with actual, as rather with

the merely possible judgements of others, and by putting ourselves in the position of everyone else.[2]

Arendt glosses this passage as follows:

> The power of judgement rests on a potential agreement with others, and the thinking process which is active in judging something is not, like the thought process of pure reasoning, a dialogue between me and myself, but finds itself always and primarily, even if I am quite alone in making up my mind, in an anticipated communication with others with whom I know I must finally come to some agreement … From this potential agreement judgement derives its specific validity. This means on the one hand that such judgement must liberate itself from the 'subjective private conditions', that is from the idiosyncracies which naturally determine the outlook of each individual in his privacy and which are legitimate as long as they are only privately held opinions but are not fit to enter the market place, and lack all validity in the public realm. And this enlarged thinking, which as judgement knows how to transcend its individual limitations, cannot function in strict isolation or solitude; it needs the presence of the other 'in whose place' it must think, whose perspective it must take into consideration, and without whom it never has the opportunity to operate at all.[3]

Thus, for Kant, public reason is closely tied to the categorical imperative and the particular form of universalisability that, in Kant's view, must be the founding condition for any social grouping that did not infringe the autonomy of its members. For Kant this could ultimately be extended to all human beings (indeed the possibility of other reasoning species being included was not excluded). Thus, and this is crucial in the current climate of thought which places such emphasis on identity, for Kant and for that strand of the public sphere tradition which stems from it, identity, except in the sense of the most basic and minimal perception of self-consciousness without which, Kant argued, we would not be moral beings at all but merely instinct-driven animals, does not pre-exist social interaction. The autonomous moral agent who is the necessary subject of democratic politics can only be formed within the exercise of public reason as Kant defined it. The essence of such public reason is that it is always offered for possible critique by others. Public reason is distinguished from private reason – here Kant gives the example of a sermon – on the grounds that acceptance of the sermon depends upon the prior unquestioned and unquestionable acceptance of a range of given religious dogma. For public reason, no issues are off limits. This is why within this tradition intellectual tolerance and free communication are the supreme values.

Thus the publicness of discourse as a condition for a society of agents who are free and autonomous, not in the sense that they are not subject to social and material constraints, but that they think for themselves, is based on the nature of the discourse and its potential accessibility rather than upon the number of people who actually have access to it.

Here we are brought back to the Hegelian concern for *Sittlichkeit* and to critiques of Habermas' public sphere approach from a communitarian and neo-Aristotelian perspective. Here the debate over the public sphere has to be seen as part of the wider debate between advocates and defenders of the theory and practice of rights-based liberalism and the various proponents of communitarianism and identity politics (Benhabib 1992; Gray 1995; Guttman 1994). What is the problem here?

The communitarian critique is a response to the political dilemma of modernity that stems from Hegel's critique of Kant and from an alternative response to the dilemma raised by Rousseau. Rousseau posed the dilemma in terms of the relationship between freedom and social conditioning. Having argued that humans were by nature good and altruistic but had been corrupted by society, he was then faced by the problem of how to create a free society out of agents who had been conditioned to be undemocratic and enslaved. This dilemma is, of course, an old one, stemming from Greek thought which saw the moral life as essentially social and thus socially conditioned. How then could one create a just commonwealth out of an unjust one? The Platonic solution, as is well known, was the philosopher king. Where then to find these philosopher kings remained a problem. But the crucial point is that this leads to the opposite solution to that of social contract theory and the liberalism based upon it. Now political values are social before they are individual. Politics is embedded in, and ideally expresses, a set of pre-existing social values, or a way of life, and the role and legitimacy of the state, or the public realm, is then to foster and uphold those communal values and defend that way of life. The citizens find their identity in, and give their loyalty to, not a set of abstract rights but a way of life, an ethos, that embodies a set of moral values. From this perspective, liberalism, and the particular forms of democracy that it supports, is but one way of life among many possible alternatives (Gray 1995). From this perspective the role of the media is then to foster and defend this shared way of life, sometimes described, in the nationalist model of communitarianism, as national identity or culture.

The communitarian position on the public/private divide, and the approaches to both politics and the media that stem from it, is in a sense contradictory. The core of identity politics – or what Nancy Fraser (1997) has called the politics of recognition – is the call for the recognition in the public realm of values hitherto deemed private, both in the sense of being excluded from the public gaze and from public debate, but also in the sense of stemming from private group interests and identities rather than from a generally shared interest and identity, and thus for the acquisition of rights that recognition of these values as public entails, while at the same time drawing for its evaluative arguments upon a range of sources which must exclude the very concept of the public, and its liberal valuation of rights and the recognition and equal treatment of the diversity of private interests, that they are demanding.

What Benhabib (1992: 68–88) has called the integrationist strand within communitarianism seeks *Sittlichkeit* in an attempted return to the moral certainties and social unities of pre-traditional societies. Here everything is in a sense public; the values that motivate people and give them their social anchorage are derived from and shape a whole shared way of life. In a theocracy there is no room for the individual or the private. Indeed, this strand in communitarianism criticises the liberal tradition precisely for creating, and philosophically justifying as the highest good, social arrangements that separate political or public spheres of action and value on the one hand from private spheres of action and value on the other to the impoverishment, in their view, of both (MacIntyre 1981, 1988).

On the other hand the participationist strand wishes to build its way out of the alienation and formalism of liberalism by both accepting the conditions of modernity which are liberalism's starting point – namely post traditional societies and reflexive individuals – while at the same time arguing for a refounding of political communities on the universalisation of the discourse ethic and its practices, whereby in a sense the systems world can sink back into the life world. The more post-modern end of communitarianism, which links to so-called new social movements and the politics of identity or recognition, makes this attempt by, in effect, advocating the fragmentation of societies into small-scale or specialised communities of interest or identity, each with their own public sphere. They tend to see more universalistic and unified definitions of the public sphere as repressive of difference and thus anti-democratic. What is at issue here is both whether within a polity we should be looking at one or multiple public spheres and how we think the relation between public and private. It is clear, I think, that an integrationist communitarianism, and the politics of recognition that stems from it, demands a unified public sphere and places continuous pressure on the existence of a meaningful private sphere. Its aim is a one-to-one fit between a unitary set of values, a single public sphere (if this term any longer has meaning here) and single polity. If diverse communities exist within a single territory or polity the aim is fragmentation, not co-existence and the toleration of diversity. It is clearly incompatible with the exercise of public reason in the Kantian sense and with media practices and institutional forms in harmony with such an ideal.

The case of participatory communitarianism and the identity politics that stems from it is more complex. Here the problem arises from the ambivalence of the liberal value of tolerance *vis-à-vis* the public/private divide. On the one hand, toleration can be taken to mean the acceptance by public authorities of a range of practices and beliefs by defining them as private and outside the realm of public regulation, for instance religious observance. Such toleration, of course, rests, as the communitarian critics quite rightly point out, on a prior judgement that the practice or belief in question is not in any sense a threat to the public weal or interest. This form of toleration can be rejected by certain advocates of the politics of recognition because, it is argued, it implicitly downgrades, and thus in some sense fails to fully recognise, the importance or centrality of the practice or belief in question. On the other hand, we can also understand toleration as giving public recognition to and bringing into the public realm people, practices or belief. By so doing, we signal that we give them equal value to those already so recognised and with which we are prepared to live and argue within a shared culture and polity. Thus we need to distinguish those demands for recognition and for multiple public spheres that seek, in effect, to extend the private, so that their group identities remain unthreatened by the risk of corrosion brought by participation in the critical discourse of the public sphere and the need for compromise that the agreement on common courses of action inevitably carries, from those that are demands for a widening of the definition of what is public to let them into what remains a common arena for critical public debate and decision-making, with the acceptance of the duties and risks that such entry carries with it. In the former case what is being demanded in the name of difference is the dissolution of any shared culture, polity and set of rights and associated obligations. Here the question is how much such private fragmentation any society or polity can sustain while remaining viable, and whether in fact we will only regard such demands as democratically legitimate where the group identity claimed is itself subject to the disciplines of the discourse ethic. In the second case, the liberal polity is being asked, rightly, to live up to its ideals and is prepared to accept that those values it considers central to its way of life must always be held provisionally and be subject to the review of critical discourse. Here we need to distinguish between a truly private realm, the irreducible site of individual autonomy (a realm which from a true social constructivist view does not, of course, exist) from the multiple public spheres within which we necessarily live and have our being, defined by Benhabib as any occasion or situation where people share views on matters of common interest, multiple public spheres that all contribute to the formation of our identities and which may be more or less democratic in the sense of meeting the requirements of the discourse ethic. The media are integral to these multiple public spheres and should be judged in each case on the basis of the identities and practices they foster. But these multiple public spheres then need to be distinguished from the political public sphere where discussion is necessarily aimed at the common agreement necessary for concerted action within a unified polity. Of course, one of the matters legitimately discussable must always be the extent of the reach of such debate and action, in the sense of the proper boundary at any time of the public and the private, and the continuing legitimacy of the particular polity.

Privacy

If the Kantian approach to the distinction between public and private, and the view of politics that stems from it, can be seen as the search for individual autonomy via public discourse, the Hegelian tradition from which the communitarian critique of public sphere thinking is mounted can be seen as a search for an identity that only the recognition and esteem of others can create. If the autonomous identity upon which democracy must be founded is created within the Kantian model by mutual criticism, the bonds of sociality in the Hegelian model are based upon our recognition of ourselves in the gaze of others. As Rousseau then argued, an egalitarian social order must be founded on the equality of public exposure that his metaphor of all citizens being at once performers and spectators in the theatre of life expresses.

This approach leads to a notion that runs continuously through the debates over privacy and the media – namely the role played in the construction of a viable modern social order of the behaviour-controlling effects of public exposure. To illustrate how complex the division between public and private can be I want here to turn to Adam Smith who, within the regulatory debate, is constantly summoned in support of a position which equates competitive markets with individual rights and liberties against concepts of the public and the public interest. In fact, Adam Smith's primary founding argument was in favour of the market as a public institution and sphere of public behaviour, and it was made on moral grounds. He argued that we could never know how our fellow humans really thought and felt, but that what mattered was how they behaved towards one another. He then argued, on lines similar to Rousseau, that a driving human motivation was the desire to be liked and respected by others, and thus that the best way to ensure that people behaved well towards one another was to expose their behaviour to public view. It was this that the market achieved.

But one finds a general extension of this view in the wider assessment of urban life and the development of the division of labour as widening the range of both actual, and perhaps more important, potential human interactions outside a person's immediate personal and private sphere, in particular outside kin relations, as a force for civilisation, as the root of the word indicates; in the view that urbanity, again with the same root, is a desirable human character trait. One finds perhaps the ultimate development of this view in Elias' *The Civilizing Process* (1978) where he argues, drawing ultimately on Durkheim, that it was the increasing density of social contact between strangers, the increased and necessary publicness of modern life, that led to the internalisation of a set of socially collaborative norms and greater levels of self-control, which made a harmonious and relatively non-violent modern social order possible. Ironically here we find an internalisation of social control, its personalisation, individuation and in a sense privatisation caused by the increased publicness of social interactions. It is precisely these self-disciplining effects of public display that Foucault and his followers attack, using the metaphor of the Benthamite Panopticon as epitomising modernity, in the name of a difference whose source and place of refuge they then seek in the privacy of a body which lies outside both discourse and politics.

Notes

1   Kant (1970), 'What is orientation in thinking' in *Kant's Political Writings*, p. 247.
2   Kant, *Critique of Judgement*, p. 151, quoted in Benhabib (1992: 133).
3   Benhabib ibid.

3 In search of the self

Charting the course of self-regulation on the Internet in a global environment

Monroe E. Price and Stefaan G. Verhulst[1]

Each day, societal demand grows for some form of control or supervision over something that appears inherently beyond governance: the Internet. The gulf between community aspiration and the perceived limits on government capacity forces each entity, industry and regulators, to conduct a thorough and painstaking search for an appropriate solution. The resolution to this dilemma requires the innovation of regulatory design for the Internet. Without flexibility and responsiveness, traditional law and regulation cannot adequately address the transnational, intangible, and ever-changing Internet space. The Internet challenges 'classic patterns of regulation' in terms of the identity of the rule makers and the instruments used to establish rules (Reidenberg 1996). With some notable and largely unsuccessful exceptions,[2] the initial attempts at Internet regulation have tended to move away from direct legal control and towards more flexible variations of 'self-regulation'.

Internet self-regulation involves many regulatory subjects such as e-commerce,[3] technical protocols and domain names management (ICANN).[4] However, most of the public concern and debate has focused on illegal and harmful content.[5] This concern has prompted substantial and public industrial response. But despite the growth and importance of these self-regulatory approaches and institutions, there are fundamental questions about the nature of these that remain unanswered. These problems are not addressed, in part, because the Internet community takes certain aspects of self-regulation for granted. However, a failure to understand completely the mechanisms of self-regulation may hinder the development and implementation of policy.

This essay examines the tremendous growth of institutions and self-regulatory systems on the Internet. It also looks at how self-regulatory entities and systems handling on-line content relate to other quasi-legal and state institutions, what powers self-regulatory institutions undertake or apprehend, and how the use of self-regulation can contribute to the effective and efficient realisation of both economic and societal goals. In the first part of this chapter, we discuss the conceptual components of self-regulation, review various definitions, examine the relationship between self-regulation and other regulatory models, and look at the role of self-regulation as a regulatory tool. In the second part, we apply this analysis and structure to current efforts at self-regulation and content control on the Internet. We conclude with some thoughts and recommendations on how to achieve systematic self-regulation as a foundation.

Self-regulation: general concept and characteristics

Defining self-regulation

The initial problem of every approach to self-regulation pertains to definition and semantics. There is no single definition of self-regulation that is entirely satisfactory, nor should there be. Not only does self-regulation differ from industry to industry and from time to time, it also evolves as the nature of the Internet alters. Different profiles of self-regulation emerge and adjust to the varying aspects of the Internet that are regulated. Self-regulation has and will continue to have different meaning depending on the sector and state. Moreover, whatever its implication or suggestion, self-regulation is almost always a misnomer. Self-regulation rarely exists without some relationship between the industry and the state, which is a relationship that varies greatly. The actual meaning of self-regulation changes depending upon the extent of government action, the history of the relationship between industry and government, and the nature of the public's perceptions of the relationship between the private sector and the state.

Governments, industries and other groups employ the term 'self-regulation' almost indiscriminately, without considering that such indiscriminate use may have consequences. Ways to examine the various definitions of self-regulation may include: considering the variables underpinning self-regulation, looking at the processes behind self-regulation with an essentialist approach, or comparing the concept of self-regulation geographically[6] and with other models of regulation.

The breadth of possible meanings for self-regulation is impossible to capture in a single thought. When government maintains the power to regulate, it can consider avenues of self-regulation for industry. However, it is the sector that is subject to the regulation that establishes the process and formula for regulation. Because self-regulation is thought to exist when private entities have been commanded to act or become the delegates of state power, the intertwining of state and private industry is implicitly recognised, although the governmental nature of self-regulation may differ again across sectors (Baldwin and Cave 1999: 125).

At the heart of misunderstandings and misapplications of the term is the complex question of what constitutes the process behind self-regulation. An essentialist approach to self-regulation would require that all elements of regulation – formation of norms, adjudication, enforcement and others – be self-generated. Even 'subcontracting' of rules might violate the purest ideal of self-regulation if the contractor is the government.

Huyse and Parmentier distinguish among several processes that may be labelled self-regulation. They use the term 'subcontracting' to describe the situation where the state limits itself to setting the formal conditions for rule making while leaving it entirely up to the parties to shape the content. 'Concerted action' describes the circumstance where the state sets not only the formal but also the substantive conditions for rule making by one or more parties. Finally, 'incorporation' is established where existing but non-official norms become part of the legislative order when lawmakers insert them into statutes or when they declare the outcome of private negotiations generally binding for a whole sector (Huyse and Parmentier 1990: 260).

All of these forms of self-regulation are present in the debate over content control on the Internet. Elements of the Internet industry often seek forms of self-regulation where none of these forms of state participation is overtly present, where structure and norms seem to emerge from the industry itself. For those who foster self-regulation, the important quality is the vector: maximising private or self-regulation as a supplement, substitute, or delegate of the state.

Self-regulation and other regulatory models

Another closely linked way of defining self-regulation is by determining its particular place and role among other regulatory models.[7] It is now a commonplace to classify means of governing or controlling the behaviour of industry players through three forms of economic and social organisation: government organisation, industry self-organisation, and market organisation. These principal types, again, are said to constitute a continuum along which regulation is more or less formalized. Government or public regulation is the most formal (the so-called command and control type of regulation), where non-compliance may lead to public or private law sanctions. Market organisation (the laissez-faire approach) is the least formal, where compliance is usually based upon voluntary action (Sinclair 1997: 529). In practice, however, the three forms overlap and create inter-dependencies as a result of market or policy failures, or even wider public concerns – such as the protection of minors – that cannot be addressed purely by one form. The early experience with the Internet and with media-related content regulation supports this view. Experimentation with command and control regimes has given way to a plethora of national efforts that combine regulation and self-regulatory initiatives. Constitutionally, a preference exists for self-regulation in the area of speech. But in terms of management and efficiency, many authors have concluded that self-regulation and formal legal systems work best when they are combined (Doyle 1997: 35–42). Two-tiered regulation is especially relevant in industries and areas that are complex and transnational in character, for example in content regulation. It is convenient and logical to consider these co-regulatory mechanisms as a form of self-regulation. Hoffmann-Riem calls this 'regulated self-regulation' (Hoffman-Riem 1996).

Self-regulation versus deregulation and non-regulation

Self-regulation ought to be perceived as a paradigm different from deregulation or non-regulation. Deregulation directly aims at removing any regulation

perceived to be excessive and hindering market forces. Self-regulation, as a regulatory doctrine or approach to management, does not aim primarily to dismantle
or dispense with a framework for private activity (Ukrow 1999: 15). Self-
regulation is not an alternative or substitute for some types of direct regulation,
such as antitrust (Breyer 1982: 157). Considering self-regulation as the antithesis
of legal regulation is thus far too simple a characterisation of the limits to law
(Prosser 1998: 271). It is important, however, to be clear about the differences
between regulation by government and self-regulation by those largely operating
apart from government. Regulation by government always implies the use of
government power to ensure certain actions by parties. Self-regulation, on the
other hand, consists of a series of representations, negotiations, contractual
arrangements and collaborative efforts with government. Self-regulation on the
Internet is a subtle and changing combination of all of these forms of activity.
Further, self-regulation can be seen as that range of activity by private actors
undertaken to prevent more intrusive and more costly action by government
itself. In that sense, self-regulation can be explained as a collective economic decision, an intersection of maximisation of profit and expressions of public interest.

Self-regulation and negotiation

Too few discussions of self-regulation pay attention to disparate meanings of the
self-regulatory process in various national settings. Approaching the topic
without a comparative perspective has particular perils in the Internet context.
To start with, self-regulation everywhere is a function, in large part, of historic
relationships between business and government. Self-regulation involves a
dialogue between government and an association or grouping of businesses. The
state is not, however, the only party that might develop co-regulatory arrangements with the industry. It is possible to argue that self-regulation is rarely
effective or legitimate without outsider involvement and negotiation. Outside
participants may be considered in four categories: public members (also called
'independents'), consumer representatives, experts and professionals. In practice,
most self-regulatory systems use some mixture of these four types (Boddewyn
1988: 52). Self-regulators may thus be subject to negotiation and non-member
controls in a host of ways (Baldwin and Cave 1999), for example through:

- statutory prescriptions and objectives;
- rules drafted by or approved by other bodies or ministries;
- ministerial guidelines or criteria for consideration by the self-regulator;
- parliamentary oversight of the delegated legislation that guides the self-
  regulator;
- departmental purse strings;
- regulatory agency oversight;
- informal influences from government exerted in the shadow of threatened
  state regulation;
- judicial review;

- complaint and grievance-handling mechanism (e.g. ombudsmen); and
- reporting and publication requirements set down by government or parliament.

Regulation and regulatory tools

Justification of regulation and self-regulatory agencies

The starting point of every regulatory intervention, including self-regulation, must be the policy objective, not the means of achievement. Justifications for intervention often arise from an alleged inability of the marketplace to deal with particular structural problems. Here a distinction must be made between economic self-regulation and social self-regulation. While the former is concerned with the adjustment of markets or other facets of economic life, the latter 'aims to protect people or the environment from the damaging consequences of industrialization' (Hawkins and Hutter 1993: 199). Social self-regulation is thus usually taken to include mechanisms whereby firms or their associations, in their undertaking of business activities, seek to assure that their actions avoid unacceptable consequences to the environment, the workforce, or consumers and clients. The establishment of such social norms of behaviour is one of the most complex aspects, theoretically and practically, of self-regulation (Rees and Gunningham 1997: 376–80).

In its 'collective form', self-regulation is sometimes a deliberate delegation of the state's law-making powers to an agency, the membership of which wholly or mainly comprises representatives of the industries or individuals whose activities are being regulated. Self-regulatory agencies can also be seen as involving a delegation of individual and user interests to a private body because of its specific expertise and knowledge. The 'self' here can be institutionalised into (separate) self-regulatory agencies (SRA) (or in some cases cartels) that combine the governmental function of regulation, and in some cases enforcement, with the institutional and often legal structure and interests of a private body (Black 1996).

Self-regulatory agencies have the delicate task of helping to define norms, bringing them to public notice, and creating a sense of 'industrial morality'. One of the key tasks of an SRA might be to ensure accountability of its members through monitoring or enforcement of standards. One of the principal mechanisms to reach accountability is transparency. The first step towards transparency is often the public announcement of the principles and practices that the industry accepts as guides to its behaviour and as standards for evaluating and criticising performance. The next critical step is the development of an information system for collecting data on the progress of member companies in implementing the industry codes or practices. Building transparency into the social structure of the industry by those categories sets the stage for a 'theatre of external judgement', and as transparency increases so does the likelihood among members of being called to account for industrial conduct (Rees and Gunningham 1997: 383–5).

Self-regulatory tools

A wide array of self-regulatory tools have proven track records as substitutes for government regulation. Codes of practice or good conduct are the most common instance, but they are often merely declarations of principles. At times, however, they embody mutual obligations by competing actors, for example, in the form of agreements, that each of them will take certain action to restrict content that would give any one of them a temporary competitive advantage. Codes provide an indication of the nature of the self-regulatory authority, including whether or not it will impose sanctions for breaches of the code, and upon whom. Codes are often the instrument for the generation or refinement of norms. In the Internet setting, they are usually the codification of norms negotiated between the industry and government authority. There are a number of industry initiatives underway directed at developing codes of conduct and a number of national governments specifically endorse codes as a front-line mechanism for addressing content issues.

Regulatory process

Self-regulation, both generally and in terms of the Internet, can also be analysed against the standard components of the regulatory process. These include: (1) policy-making, i.e. enunciating principles that should govern enterprises; (2) legislation, i.e. defining appropriate rules; (3) enforcement, i.e. initiating actions against violators; and (4) adjudication, i.e. deciding whether a violation has taken place and imposing an appropriate sanction. The transnational process of building self-regulatory institutions for the Internet must involve each of these components, but to different degrees. More important, in each state, as the self-regulatory agencies are built, the division between industry initiatives and government initiatives for each component can be quite different. Merely to understand the nature of self-regulation in a given setting, it is necessary to determine, in each particular version of the exercise of regulation, how the roles are divided between the state and industry (Campbell 1999). For example, an industry may be responsible for the definition of standards for content (through developing a code of practice) but leave enforcement to the government. Similarly, responsibility for enforcement may be divided, with the state prosecuting for certain speech and the self-regulating entity self-policing and removing other kinds of speech.

   In the context of Internet content regulation, at the policy level, both industry and government are engaged, though the extent to which policy is the product of meaningful consultation among sectors varies substantially from state to state. Government legislation may take the form in some contexts (e.g. Australia) of administrative approval of industry established codes. Moreover, enforcement and adjudication pose problems for the Internet that are similar to and yet different from those of other self-regulatory contexts.

Cost–benefit analysis

A fashionable way of looking at the characteristics and merits of self-regulation is to examine how it addresses the limitations of government regulation. The increasing significance of self-regulatory mechanisms suggests, not surprisingly, that they offer a number of benefits that cannot be achieved through government regulation. But self-regulation imposes costs as well. A key question in the debate on self-regulation, therefore, is whether and in what ways self-regulatory systems can effectively monitor and control the behaviour of market players without generating the bureaucratic and legal costs of traditional regulatory regimes.

Costs

Implementing and complying with regulation entails significant costs, and efficiency losses associated with regulation can be high (Ministry of Consumer Affairs, NZ, 1997). In contrast with command and control type of regulation, the 'voluntary' nature of self-regulation implies, sometimes misleadingly, that the costs associated with compliance are lower and fall on those markets at which regulation is targeted. It is, however, naive to suggest that self-regulation does not itself involve significant costs. For any system, regulatory or self-regulatory, costs are determined by a combination of the policy goals they envisage and the structures and dynamics of the economic and social activities they regulate.

Enforcement and 'free riders'

The nature of a voluntary system creates a potential 'free-rider problem' (OECD 1998), where some actors expend significant resources on the development, monitoring and implementation of codes and standards while others ignore their existence. Self-regulation can quickly become moribund without strong and committed support for its development, implementation and enforcement among those professing participation in the regime. This situation may not be entirely disadvantageous to more resourceful actors, as they can set benchmarks that can convey benefits in terms of consumer confidence and recognition in market formation and social responsibility. Commercial and social prominence is critical for the success of the major actors on the Internet as it is in any industry (AOL is an example of the process[8]). And once a critical mass of participants has been reached a 'voluntary' system of codes and controls can become very hard to evade because of increased peer-pressure and public expectations.

Free speech and globalisation

Self-regulation has the seeming benefit of avoiding state intervention in areas that are sensitive in terms of basic rights, such as freedom of speech and information, while offering standards for social responsibility, accountability and user protection from offensive material. But private censorship can be more coercive and sweeping than its public form. And the dangers of constitutional violation are particularly striking where the self-regulatory entity is acting in response to government or as a means of pre-empting its intervention. Here is an important area where the efficiency aspects of self-regulation, the very aspects that may be deemed a benefit by some, can be deemed a cost or deficiency of self-regulation for others.

Moreover, self-regulation may better accommodate the transnational conflicts inherent in the global architecture of the Internet. An emphasis on self-regulation may be a more effective alternative wherever one state is highly dependent on consensus with other states. Finally, government regulation can be inflexible and not as adaptable to the rapid changes taking place in the Internet as other policy alternatives. Robert Pitofsky, Chairman of the US Federal Trade Commission, explained recently that '[l]egitimate and fair self-regulation will become more important as the economy grows faster than government regulation' (Pitofsky 1998). He also referred to the fact that self-regulation sometimes is more 'prompt, flexible, and effective than government regulation', and that 'the judgement and experience of an industry also is of great benefit, especially in cases where the government has difficulty defining "bright-line rules". On-line content is clearly such a case.'[9]

Democratic deficit and accountability

The 'democratic deficit' or 'corporatist character' (Schmitter 1985) of self-regulation in comparison with state regulatory activities can be seen as an important cost. As John Braithwaite has put it: 'Self-regulation is frequently an attempt to deceive the public into believing in the responsibility of an irresponsible industry. Sometimes it is a strategy to give the government an excuse for not doing its job' (Braithwaite 1993: 91). It is clear that legitimacy plays an important role within the debate about government versus self-regulation. Effective self-regulation requires active consumer and citizen participation at all stages of development and implementation. Without user involvement, a self-regulatory mechanism will not accurately reflect user needs and will not be effective in delivering the standards it promotes. Moreover, self-regulatory institutions may not impose meaningful sanctions on industry players. Self-regulatory standards are, according to critics, usually weak, enforcement is ineffective and punishment is often secret and mild.

Taxonomy of self-regulation

Individual versus collective self-regulation

Within this wide range of dimensions of the 'self', it is important to distinguish between individual firm self-regulation (where an entity regulates itself, independent of others) and self-regulation by a group. Self-regulation may speak to the specific actions of each actor, but it often refers to a collective constraint, which binds the individual actors. In the Internet setting, one could consider as a matter of individual self-regulation the decisions by each entity that operates as a service provider, a bulletin board, or a program supplier regarding what each will post or what rules each will consider itself governed by, including rules to rate or label content. Several major service and content providers (such as AOL, MSN (Microsoft Network), and others)[10] have developed explicit guidelines and user protection guarantees (especially for minors), often labelled 'netiquette', in order to establish and maintain confidence among their users. One might even speak of self-regulation by the vast community of individual users that subscribe to a set of principles established by their Internet service provider or by other sources or, as self- generated.

Agreed upon and codified self-regulation is not the province solely of large multinational enterprises, even though its executives may feel the most pressure to protect investments and to respond to societal influences. Multinational enterprises may prefer self-regulation to preserve their market position and investment from the risk of more restrictive state regulation. In terms of content regulation on the Internet, self-regulation has come to mean some degree of collective or community constraint, with some form of rules imposed upon members or actors by an entity created by some or all of the actors, who are often under pressure from government. This collective action or, in some cases, the initiative of a private regulatory entity engenders outcomes that would not be reached by individual behaviour alone. As such, self-regulation is a process of 'collective self-governance'.

Enforced versus voluntary self-regulation

There is a difference in scope if self-regulation is a consequence of government threat (enforced self-regulation) or a consequence of a civic culture in which the government co-operates with industry (voluntary self-regulation). Self-regulation cannot totally replace government regulation entirely in the media and communications related sectors (Federal Government Commissioner 1999). The state retains ultimate responsibility for protecting the public interest.

In general, one can identify four types of relationships between industry and the state. The distinctions among these relationships may be subtle, but they are significant. They include: mandated self-regulation, in which the industry is virtually required by the government to formulate and enforce norms within a framework defined by the government; sanctioned self-regulation, in which the collective group itself formulates the regulations, which are then subjected to government approval; coerced (or enforced) self-regulation, in which 'the collective group itself' formulates and imposes regulation in response to governments' threats of statutorily imposed regulations (such as the creation of the Press Complaints Commission in the United Kingdom, for example); and voluntary self-regulation, where there is no active state involvement.

To determine how to structure the symbiosis between the self-regulating entity and the state, a number of questions can be asked:

- Will the regulating entity be generated from within the industry or as a consequence of government action?
- Are the broad standards to be administered by the regulating entity developed by the government or by the entity itself?
- Who will appoint the members of any administering board?
- Will the administering board or the regulating entity or the industry require state intervention to protect them from liability?
- Will users have a right of review within the self-regulatory process?
- Will users have a right of review in the state's judicial system or other processes elsewhere for review?
- Should there be a public body that periodically reviews the work of the self-regulating entity?
- Will the industry act through a self-regulating board, or does self-regulation mean that each firm has some responsibility that they are privileged or required to exercise as a result of industrial consensus?
- Will there be a duty or privilege of the entity to co-operate with the state's law enforcement agencies (for example, to monitor and then provide information of potential violation of a law)?
- Should the responsibility for process of norm-refinement (e.g. what constitutes violence for improper material) rest wholly within the self-regulatory sector, and if not, how should that responsibility be shared?

These questions, while often overlooked by regulatory planners, are part of a taxonomy of self-regulation. It is rare, as we have emphasised, that a self-regulatory body has, in terms of these questions, no relationship to the state. It is often the case – and this is certainly true in the Internet context – that the generation of self-regulation has its foundation in the possibility or fear of government regulation (Gibbons 1998: 275–85). In some states, the process of generating self-regulation is a co-operative effort, which suggests that some states view self-regulation as a more effective approach towards achieving improved standards than the expansion of the definition of illegal conduct. Thus, self-regulation becomes a body of action in which the industry itself can prevent the imposition of more extensive, costly, and intrusive regulation by government.

Self-regulation that results from a more positive relationship between state and industry may turn out to be more flexible and may also lead to better co-operation, while maintaining a sense of common experience. In the arena of content control, one of the perceived virtues (though not unalloyed) of self-regulation is the capacity of users to establish their own standards rather than be subject to a singularly imposed government standard.

Furthermore, self-regulation has proven to work best where there is a degree of coincidence between the self-interest of the industry and the wider public interest (Gunningham *et al.* 1998: 53), and where both parts of the equation share an understanding of this commonality. In the advertising industry, for instance, self-regulation has voluntarily emerged as suppliers have realised the benefits of acquiring public credibility for their products and from creating an image of professional responsibility (Boddewyn 1991: 27).

However, where a substantial lag exists between the public interest and the moral intuition of some industry players, it would be naive to rely upon an industry association to take the initiative. Government or other external pressure, usually in a carrot and stick approach, is one response to fill that gap. Government policy may not always, however, lead to the formation of a common interest platform. External pressure may come from a variety of sources, but the most important ones are the threat of direct government intervention (enforced self-regulation), broader concerns to maintain credibility and legitimacy (and as a result commercial gain), and the market itself.

Lessons from other industries

While structures of self-regulation vary across industries, the evolution of self-regulation on the Internet will share important common structural elements with other histories and industries. Our analysis echoes the work of J.J. Boddewyn, whose classic study of self-regulation in the advertising industry found substantial support for a set of clearly relevant hypotheses concerning the effectiveness of such self-regulatory bodies (Boddewyn 1988: 30–33). For example, he concluded that the existence of an industry-wide decision-making system (such as a capstone trade association) increases the probability of effective industry self-regulation (Boddewyn 1988: 30–33). Industry self-regulation is more effective when it involves all interrelated levels. Just as a scheme that included only advertisers was strengthened if it included distribution systems (such as television networks), a self-regulatory system for the Internet would also grow strong if it included a range of content providers as well as service providers. Boddewyn also found that the development and effectiveness of an industry-wide self-regulatory system are enhanced by government threat and oversight (Boddewyn 1988: 30–33). The corollary for an Internet context involves, for example, monitoring and pressure from such bodies as the European Commission or national legislatures on the private sector to take productive action.

It was Boddewyn's view that the strength and effectiveness of an industry self-regulatory system is a function of its essentiality and non-substitutability (Boddewyn 1988: 330–51). In other words, self-regulation is most effective when (for reasons of practicality, technology and ideology) there is a coherent preference for self-regulation over government action. In addition, the existence and effectiveness of industry self-regulation is not measured by formal rules alone, but also by cultural factors. The transnational character of self-regulation, the experience of each state, and the relationship between government and business are examples of such potential influences. Other 'Boddewyn hypotheses' include the idea that industry self-regulation is more likely in those situations where self-policing can increase the overall demand for the industry's product and many of the participants. States that encourage self-regulation must convince the industry that effective implementation of self-regulatory measures is beneficial, in that it may well enhance industry credibility among consumers and reduce the threat of costly government regulation. Industry self-regulation is more likely in those situations where the externally imposed cost from not undertaking self-regulation would be greater than the cost of undertaking self-regulation.[12] The decisions made in the process of devising a structure of self-regulation will, therefore, reflect the careful calibration that is part of all business decisions.

Finally, the threat of government regulation precipitates the creation and improvement of an industry-wide self-regulatory system. For all of the criticism of 'jawboning' or other modes of implying government intervention, the dialogue between government and industry is central to key structures of self-regulation. Also, encouragement and support of industry self-regulation as an instrument of public policy is more likely to result when the limits of government intervention have become apparent. This may be true from the outset in the area of content regulation where free speech and similar concerns underscore the limited role for the state.

The Internet

We turn now to the Internet itself and its relationship to self-regulation. It is frequently said that the Internet is unregulable, or that regulation is beyond the control of the state. We differ with this assumption, not because we think regulation is necessary, but rather because the evidence and the cogency of the argument that states will find ways of asserting regulation and its bringing the force of the state to bear. Self-regulation will, in some circumstances, become the handmaiden of government regulation and facilitate its efficacy. It would be ostrich-like to deny that regulation (or regulation facilitated by self-regulation) of Internet content can and will occur. It may be preferable to acknowledge that the likelihood of regulation is increased by the willing or forced co-operation of the industry, and subsequently try to assess the conditions and consequences of such co-operation (Goldsmith 1998: 1209–10).

The 'self' of Internet self-regulation

The Internet is a consummate demonstration of the complexity of determining what ought to be included in the 'self' of self-regulation. It includes a cornucopia of institutions that partake of self-regulatory characteristics. Voluntary institutions, generated by the Internet and not by government, are the very backbone of efforts to deal with harmful content.[11] In many discussions, governments have failed to recognise that the Internet industry is not monolithic and that there is no single 'industry' that speaks for the whole of the Internet.[12] Moreover, the fact that the Internet is relatively young and still in a rapid growth stage also means that in many cases effective co-operative action (e.g. creation of industry associations) is also in its early stages. An interesting example of such co-operation is the EuroISPA, the pan-European association of the Internet services providers' associations of some EU member states.[13]

The 'self' cannot be divided in terms of sectors of the industry that form cohesive communities. Indeed, it has been suggested that self-regulation operates more effectively when it involves interrelated levels of the industry, which often do not form one coherent body. For example, Boddewyn's study of the advertising industry found that self-regulatory systems were strengthened when they included distribution systems (such as television networks) (Boddewyn 1988). Many of the Internet self-regulatory bodies contain representatives from different sectors of the industry. For example, Internet Access Australia (IIA) in Australia has a membership that includes telecom carriers, content creators and hardware developers.[14] In contrast, the self-regulatory organisations in the United Kingdom tend to have a narrower membership, with the Internet Service Providers' Association (ISPA)[15] and the London Internet Exchange (LINX)[16] the two leaders whose memberships are restricted to providers.

There is also an increasing social demand for breadth in the definition of 'self' for self-regulation on the Internet. If the function of self-regulation is to minimise harmful and illegal conduct on the Internet (particularly as it affects young people), then it must become more, rather than less, extensive. Albert Gidari, Executive Director of Internet Law and Policy Forum has stated that, often, the 'self' in self-regulation too narrowly focuses on the business sector alone (Gidari 1998). A narrow conception of self-regulation places too much of the burden on industry to solve the legal and policy issues, and it fails to recognise individual users of Internet services and other participants as 'independent Internet stakeholders and possible administrators' in a larger self-regulatory regime (http://www/ilpf.org 3 March 2000).

Internet and competitive self-regulation

The multi-sectoral nature of many Internet services means that we should expect a wide variety of self-regulating communities or mediating institutions to come into existence. Moreover, competing self-regulatory regimes may emerge within any given sector. As Ogus has described:

> [C]ompetition of this kind is inherent in systems of private ordering: suppliers compete to attract consumers by the quality (as well as the price) of their products and services. Quality is, to some extent at least, a consequence of standards and other forms of control imposed internally by the management of a firm. The standards may reflect general regulatory requirements but more often they are voluntary, representing the firm's response to assumed consumer demand and, in some cases, incorporating industry-wide practices. To signal to consumers the relationship between standards and quality, some form of voluntary accreditation or certification can be used. Suppliers who aim at

different quality standards, and have difficulty in communicating that fact to consumers, will have an incentive to establish a rival certification system.

(Ogus 1992)

In addition, resulting patterns and institutions of self-regulation will differ geographically. Each state has different social demands, each state has a different constitutional structure, and each state has different traditions of industry–government co-operation in the fields of media and speech. One study of self-regulation and self-generation of standards that compared the experiences in Canada and the United States demonstrated marked differences in the scope of co-operation with the government, shared standards, and the notion of self-regulation as a social and collaborative act (McDowell and Maitland 1998).

When it comes to the Internet, differences in self-regulation, state to state, will also turn on the speech traditions in each society and the way that each conceptualises the Internet. Where the Internet is perceived as derived or related to telephony, self-regulatory practices and standards that have emerged in telecommunications may predominate. In the United States, partly because of the First Amendment tradition, self-regulation is distinctively a form of avoidance of, confrontation with and studied separation from government. However, a comparative overview of self-regulatory systems in the media in all EU member states identified clear differences in meaning and structure of the self-regulatory systems (Brohmer and Ukrow 1999).

Justification for Internet regulation: illegal and harmful content

Politicians have expressed concerns about the proliferation of pornographic and illegal material on the Internet.[17] In many instances this has led to pressure being placed directly on the Internet industry to regulate itself. This pressure has often been in the form of a threat that if the industry does not regulate itself the imposition of more extensive, more costly and more intrusive regulation by government will follow. Certainly this has been the background to self-regulation, albeit in different ways, in the United Kingdom and Australia. In the United Kingdom, concern over Internet content has not led to specific legislation or licensing controls. However, it has led to the establishment in September 1996 of the Internet Watch Foundation (IWF).[18]

In Australia the self-regulatory framework is even more clearly the product of direct pressure from the government. The Internet Industry Code of Practise created in 1999 by the Internet Industry Association, a trade body covering different sectors of the Internet industry, was the direct product of the enactment of the Broadcasting Services Amendment (Online Services) Act 1999. The industry became considerably more proactive in self-regulating when the Online Services Bill was going through the legislature in an attempt to ameliorate the likely impact of legislation which many in the industry considered 'heavy-handed' (Fair 1999: 13).

This does not mean that Internet self-regulation should be understood as being simply foisted, unwelcomed, on an unwilling industry. For various reasons, members of the Internet industry itself have often independently supported self-regulation. Self-regulation can have the effect of enhancing the credibility of the industry in the eyes of the consumer, making the industry, or part of it, appear responsible and trustworthy. For this reason many individual actors in the Internet industry have chosen to institute their own 'regulatory' schemes similar to those of the self-regulatory associations, at times working in co-operation with them.[19]

Two complex issues should be taken into consideration in identifying the most appropriate legislative approach for controlling Internet content. The first issue is to define the types of content that is unacceptable and/or illegal, and the second is to evaluate the different methods or platforms of exchanging information on the Internet.

A discussion of illegal, harmful or offensive content is always a complex matter (OECD 1997b) that is not unique to the Internet, especially, in terms of definition. Several EU documents have outlined that it is necessary to differentiate between these categories of content (Commission of the European Communities 1996d), but a fully satisfactory definition has yet to emerge. The Green Paper on the Protection of Minors and Human Dignity in Audio-Visual and Information Services (Commission of the European Communities 1997f) produced broad agreement on objectives and the action to be taken within Europe. Generally, the concept of 'illegal' seems a relatively simple reference to content that is contrary to law. However, legality becomes a particularly difficult issue in the international context, where what is illegal in some countries is not necessarily illegal in others. It was only recently that Japan's lower house of Parliament banned the production and sale of child pornography. Furthermore this question can be exacerbated in a discussion of civil and criminal law, where 'illegal' may only refer to that which is a criminal offence, and 'harmful' might indicate that content which raises civil law issues because of questions of 'harm' to another party. What one considers to be harmful or appropriate depends on cultural differences and can be distinct according to different age groups. All this has to be taken into account in defining appropriate approaches to protect children against undesired material whilst ensuring freedom of expression.

Self-regulatory mechanism

Modes of self-regulation on the Internet are functions of the industry's platforms for exchanging information. The World Wide Web is only one of the means by which content is exchanged on the Internet. Other methods of information exchange include e-mail, ftp (file transfer protocol), news groups and real-time chats. As the KPMG review of the Internet Watch Foundation highlighted, each route has different characteristics and is used for different purposes and may require different regulatory and protective approaches. For instance, many considered chat and news group platforms as the most widely used communications platform on the Internet by paedophiles because of the difficulty in 'traceability'. Moreover, filtering and blocking of such dynamic content has proven to be problematic and in some cases impossible. All this confirms that a multiple approach of regulatory tools will be necessary to control Internet content satisfactorily.

Several ISP associations have now developed or are in the process of developing different codes concerning, among other things, the protection of minors.[20] Codes of practice on the Internet gain practical efficacy when tied to seals of approval or other accrediting signals. The specific software of the Internet and its increasingly sophisticated capacity to provide filtering devices heightens the importance of such signals. Under some filtering systems, whether voluntarily or by regulation, only websites that have the appropriate seal or accrediting signal are allowed through a filter and then, depending on the nature of the legal and technological architecture of the filtering system, into a home or into a state or region. There are many discussions of the workings of such filtering software, the efforts under way to improve them, and the implications and dangers from a free speech perspective. Aside from codes of conduct and filtering systems, there are agreements specifically to label pages or other elements of content. The institution of hotlines and complaint handling procedures by industry actors is also an important element of content self-regulation on the Internet. Hotlines can provide a mechanism for users to report illegal or harmful content that they see on the Internet. Based upon a public–private partnership, such direct reporting options can have a crucial evaluation and monitoring function.

In addition, an underestimated aspect of self-regulation is consumer education. Education, in this context, can constitute more than a media campaign. It can be an adjustment in the navigational system of the software, so that a choice of filtering mechanism is the default position. It can mean investment in a system like GetNetWise, which contains information about content management, and assurance that the GetNetWise or similar option is more clearly before the consumer.

Legal controls are not unimportant, but there is a set of options available as part of self-regulation that enables a shift from 'hard law to software' (Wacks 1997: 93–112). Because this shift can empower the user, consumer and citizen, it seems to have a high value. Hence the major response to the call for self-regulation involves processes that promote filtering and rating systems.

Current examples and Internet practices

It is too early to assess the current status of self-regulatory practices in a comparative way. Often self-regulatory efforts are neither public nor reported, and they take different forms in different areas of the world. There are flaws in survey techniques since categories for description may vary between the surveying entity and the businesses or the governments being surveyed. As the Internet changes, and as social needs are defined, self-regulatory practices also change, and do so rapidly.

Europe

The majority of efforts to self-regulate and consequently to draft codes of conduct for the Internet in Europe came in 1997, when there was an explosion of self-regulatory activity. To protect their interests *vis-à-vis* the intentions of the government, working parties or industry associations were established in Belgium (ISPA), France (AFPI), Ireland (ISPA), Italy (@IIP), and in Germany (ICTF/FSM). All have since drafted codes of conduct, including references to rating and filtering mechanisms and rules to protect minors. Some of these codes also created a complaints mechanism, or hotline: e.g. Newswatch (Germany), Meldpunt (Netherlands), IWF (UK), AFA (France). These efforts were preceded by the earlier organisation of self-regulation on the Internet in both the Netherlands (NLIP, 1995) and in the United Kingdom (ISPA, 1995, and Internet Watch Foundation, 1996). Recent efforts in Spain (Anprotel), Denmark (FIL), Austria (ISPA) and Finland (ISPA) have followed these forerunners. Further, Internet service providers in Greece were, in early 2000, in the process of setting up an official association, and Sweden's leading Internet service providers were also in the process of holding discussions to create a framework for self-regulation in their country. Some of these efforts have been combined across Europe through the creation of EuroISPA, the pan-European association of the Internet services providers associations of the countries of the European Union. Other pan-European efforts include INCORE (Internet Content Rating for Europe), funded by the European Commission, to create a forum to examine questions of content rating and subsequent filtering, and INHOPE (Internet Hotline Providers in Europe).

Recently there has been an international effort to develop, implement, and manage an internationally acceptable voluntary self-rating system. Among the founding members of this effort are the Internet Content Rating Association (ICRA), British Telecommunications PLC (BT), Demon Internet, IBM, Internet Watch Foundation, the Electronic Network Consortium (Japan), EuroISPA Microsoft, T-Online and the Bertelsmann Foundation.[21]

North America

There has been a great deal of activity in connection with self-regulation in the United States and Canada. In November 1995, the Task Force on Internet Use of the Information Technology Association of America (ITAA) issued a report on *Internet, Free Speech and Industry Self-Regulation*. It concluded by stating that ITAA

> believes a reasonable and rational middle ground exists that allows the Internet to continue to flourish, while at the same time giving parents and families the tools necessary to negotiate safely on the information super-highway. This approach recognises the need for industry self-regulation rather than legislative intervention. ITAA intends to continue pursuing a balanced approach, what it views as the better alternative.
>
> (http://www.itaa.org)

This approach has been followed by several high-level summits, like the Bertelsmann Internet Content Summit, on Internet content and child protection. In addition, several ISP associations have been created at the state level. For example, in Texas the non-profit Texas Internet Service Providers Association (TISPA) was founded in 1996. According to TISPA's bylaws, initiatives will be developed 'to disseminate legislative, educational and other useful information and to inspire Members to further inform themselves in the practical and ethical issues of the Internet industry'.[22] State law requires all Texas Internet service providers to link to blocking and filtering software sites. In 1997, during its 75th Regular Session, the Texas legislature passed House Bill 1300 (HB 1300). The bill requires Internet service providers to make a link available on their first World Wide Web page (home page) which leads to Internet 'censorware' software, also known as 'automatic' blocking and screening software. The Florida Internet Service Providers Association (FISPA) was founded in May 1996 'to facilitate discussion and educate the public about the importance of the Internet industry'.[23] A code of conduct was drafted that reflects general principles of good conduct. In Canada, the Canadian Association of Internet Providers (CAIP), created in 1996, has issued a voluntary code of conduct with an accompanying commentary.[24]

Australia

On 21 April 1999, the Minister for Communications, Information Technology and the Arts introduced Internet legislation, known as the Broadcasting Services Amendment (Online Services) Bill 1999. Among the listed provisions, the Australian Broadcasting Authority (ABA) will be given powers to issue notices to service providers aimed at preventing access to prohibited material which may be the target of complaints if it originates in Australia. If the material is sourced overseas, the ABA is authorised to take reasonable steps (i.e. technically feasible and commercially viable) to prevent access. Such 'reasonable steps' are to be detailed in an industry code of practice to be developed in consultation with the ABA. There are several associations at the state level such as the South Australian Internet Association, the ACT Internet Association, the Tasmanian Internet Association and the Western Australian Internet Association. At a national level there is the Internet Industry Association, which incorporates the Australian Internet Alliance, and the Internet Industry Association of Australia.

Asia

In Japan the Electronic Network Consortium developed General Ethical Guideline for Running Online Services in 1996.[25] Similar guidelines called 'Codes of Practice for Internet Service Providers' were approved by the Telecom Services Association on 30 January 1998.[26] A Practice Statement that recommends guidelines for members of the Hong Kong Internet Service Providers Association (HKISPA) was developed to protect young people and public morals.[27] In particular, the guidelines were designed to enhance the regulation of obscene and indecent material transmitted on the Internet. Finally, in Singapore, in exercise of the powers conferred by Section 18 of the Singapore Broadcasting Authority Act, the Singapore Broadcasting Authority issued the Internet Code of Practice, effective as of 1 November 1997.[28]

Conclusions and recommendations: systematic self-regulation as a foundation

Given the competing societal interests in controlling content on the Internet, meaningful and effective self-regulation is more effective than the exclusive exercise of government authority. Self-regulation has a greater capacity to adapt rapidly to quickening technical progress and to the transnational development of the new communications medium. In addition to flexibility, self-regulation presents the benefits of greater efficiency, increased incentives for compliance, and reduced cost. A carefully structured programme of self-regulation, often developed in co-operation with government, is in harmony with the new technology, mirroring the Internet itself as a global, essentially private and decentralised network of communication.

Effective self-regulation requires active consumer and citizen consultation based upon shared responsibility at all stages of development and implementation. Moreover, the effectiveness of self-regulation and its enforcement will depend largely on the full collaboration and commitment among all industry players. Self-regulation can then yield a responsive, acceptable and systematic solution to current concerns.

The development of an effective self-regulatory regime for the Internet includes the formation of multiple, carefully considered, comprehensive and complementary mechanisms to achieve public interest objectives. The establishment of self-regulatory mechanisms that gain social acceptance will, in general, be the product of public input and co-operation among Internet service and content providers, self-regulatory national, international and state bodies.

Self-regulatory agencies (SRAs) should be established to create, promulgate and enforce self-generated codes. Furthermore, SRAs should strive to gain public confidence by ensuring accountability, monitoring members and enforcing standards.

Codes of conduct should be adopted to ensure that Internet content and service providers act in accord with principles of social responsibility. These codes should meet community concerns and industry needs and operate as an accountability system that guarantees a high level of credibility and quality. To be effective, these codes of conduct should be the product of and enforced by the self-regulatory entities themselves, though they may at times work in collaboration with the government. Because of the transnational nature of Internet communications, co-ordinated activity among these agencies is an essential element of self-regulation.

There should be comprehensive use of rating and filtering technology and a mobilisation of content producers worldwide to empower users of the Internet to make more effective choices about program content. Such technology is especially necessary for content directed at children or content that might, in the absence of mechanisms, enter homes without the capacity of guardians to exercise judgement. Such a comprehensive system requires citizen content response and complaint systems, such as hotlines, that may add accountability and credibility to self-regulation mechanisms. In addition, public education is essential to increase awareness of the means to filter and block content, to present complaints for effective redress and to obtain the level of compliance that is promised by the industry. Finally, industry members must develop techniques to measure the effectiveness of self-regulatory measures and to determine what national and transnational measures, if any, are necessary to compensate for their deficiencies.

Notes

1   The authors would like to thank Nancy Edlin, Lillian Choi and Suwha Hong for their editorial support.
2   USA Communications Decency Act and the Supreme Court; Germany and CompuServe, subsequent retreat.
3   The Global Business Dialogue on e-commerce (GBDe) and the OECD are examples of institutions that focus on self-regulation in the e-commerce context. GBDe is a company-led effort to strengthen and co-ordinate international co-operation. It works to establish and empower a number of working groups that will span the breadth of significant e-commerce issues, facilitate outreach within the business community and assess the actions and responses of business, government and non-governmental organisations. The GBDe works to identify and offer solutions and guidance on regulation or business self-regulatory codes of conduct in conjunction with governments/administrations and international governmental organisations (http://www.gbd.org). Another organisation that focuses on e-commerce issues is the Organisation for Economic Co-operation and Development (OECD). The OECD examines the implications of, and possible policy responses to, electronic commerce in policy areas such as taxation, consumer fraud and protection, privacy and security. It is also examining the broader economic and social impact of this new activity on jobs, education and health. The OECD groups twenty-nine member countries in an organisation that, most importantly, provides governments a setting in which to discuss, develop and perfect economic and social policy. They compare experiences, seek answers to common problems and work to co-ordinate domestic and international policies that increasingly in today's globalised world must form a web of even practice across nations (http://www.oecd.org/subject/e_commerce).
4   The Internet Corporation for Assigned Names and Numbers (ICANN) is an organisation that addresses issues of domain name management. ICANN is a non-profit corporation that was formed to assume responsibility for the IP address space allocation, protocol parameter assignment, domain name system management, and root server system management functions now performed under US government contract by IANA and other entities (http://www.icann.com).
5   A three-country survey conducted in Australia, Germany and the United States by the German-based Bertelsmann Foundation in conjunction with the Australian Broadcasting Authority during June 1999 found that the majority of those surveyed in each country were concerned about the presence of pornographic material and racist messages on the Internet. In Australia, 53 per cent of those surveyed said they would

block pornographic content in all circumstances, while a further 33 per cent said they would block this content in certain circumstances. The equivalent figures for racist messages are 60 per cent and 21 per cent respectively (http://www.aba.gov.au, http://www. stiftung.bertelsmann.de/internetcontent/english/frameset_home.htm).

6 Despite the global nature of the Internet, almost each country and region has highly differentiated approaches to the process of content regulation on the Internet, regarding its scope, structure and design.

7 Joseph Rees somewhat idiosyncratically likens the general regulatory system, in his landmark book *Reforming the Workplace*, to the proverbial iceberg, the tip being government regulation, while the massive body represents society's great array of private regulatory systems (Rees 1988: 6).

8 AOL's recent advertising campaign assures customers of their ability to determine access to content, using AOL's age-referenced system (http://www.aol.com). AOL has also enacted a 'Safe-Surfin' ' campaign, outlining basic parental options in relation to children and Internet use (http://www.safesurfin.com).

9 The US courts recently invalidated the Communications Decency Act and granted a preliminary injunction against enforcement of the Child Online Protection Act (*Reno* v. *ACLU*, 117 S. Ct. 2329 (1997); *Reno* v. *ACLU*, 31 F. Supp. 2d 472 (1999)).

10 Industry corporations are also working with public interest groups such as the Internet Education Foundation (http://www.neted.org) and America Links Up (http://www.americalinksup.org) to further consumer choice in content selection alternatives.

11 However, the history of a voluntary association such as the Internet Corporation for Assigned Names and Numbers (ICANN) indicates how seeming autonomy begins with government encouragement. The Internet Corporation for Assigned Names and Numbers (http://www.icann.org) (17 February 2000).

12 Albert Gidari, 'Observations on the state of self-regulation of the Internet', prepared for the Ministerial Conference of the OECD (7–9 October 1998).

13 EuroISPA (http://www.euroispa.org/index.html) (19 February 2000).

14 Internet Access Australia (http://www.iia.net.au) (19 February 2000).

15 ISPA UK (http://www.isps.org.uk) (20 February 2000).

16 London Internet Exchange Ltd (http://www.linx.net) (19 February 2000).

17 As early as 1986, US government officials expressed concern about the use of computer networks for the communication and distribution of child pornography; Attorney General's Commission on Pornography: Final Report. (1986) (the Meese Commission). See also, e.g. 'Senator Harradine launching Child Protection Week,' *Canberra Times* (13 September 1998).

18 Nevertheless it would be misleading to characterise this as arising solely from the perceived need of the private sector to regulate itself. The impetus for the establishment of the IWF clearly came from the government. The decision to set up the IWF was, at least in part, the result of pressure from the Home Office. The industry's proposals were developed in discussions with the Home Office and the police in the shadow of the threat of more intrusive legislation and of criminal prosecution. See the Internet Watch Foundation (http://www.internetwatch.org.uk) (20 February 2000).

19 For example, AOL has a hotline and 'notice and take down procedure' and works in co-operation with IWF in England. It has done so, to some extent, as a marketing tool.

20 Organisation for Economic Co-operation and Development (OECD) (http://www.oecd.org/dsti/sti/it/index.htm) (20 February 2000).

21 ICRA's mission is to develop, implement and manage an internationally acceptable voluntary self-rating system which provides Internet users worldwide with the choice to limit access to content they consider harmful, especially to children. ICRA has

received the RSAC assets including the RSAC system that provides consumers with information about the level of nudity, sex, language and violence in websites.

22 Texas Internet Service Provider's Association (TISPA) (http://www.tispa.org/bylaws. htm) (20 February 2000).

23 The Florida Internet Service Provider's Association (FISPA) (http://www.fispa.org/ fispa_code.html) (20 February 2000).

24 The Canadian Association of Internet Providers (CAIP) (http://www.caip.ca/caip-code.htm) (20 February 2000).

25 The Electronic Network Consortium, *General Ethical Guidelines for Running Online Services* (http://www.nmda.or.jp/enc/guideline.html) (20 February 2000).

26 Telecom Services Association (TELESA) (http://www.telesa.or.jp/e_guide /e_guido1.html) (3 March 2000).

27 The Hong Kong Internet Service Providers Association (HKISPA) (http://www. hkispa.org.hk) (20 February 2000).

28 Singapore Broadcasting Authority (SBA), *The Internet Code of Practice* (http://www. sba.gov.sg/netreg/code.htmn) (20 February 2000).

4 Will electronic commerce change the law?

Towards a regulatory perspective based on competition, information and learning skills

*Paul Nihoul**

The purpose of this chapter is not to analyse proposals currently under discussion regarding the regulation of e-commerce, in Europe or the United States.[1] My intention is rather to examine such proposals, in line with our conception of regulation. The question, in that regard, may be phrased as follows: what do these proposals tell us about the vision that we have about regulation, i.e. the rules which are adopted by authorities in order to ensure compatibility of economic activities with social values? The perspective is meant to help us understand how, and to what extent, regulation is being affected by the Information Society.

A confrontation among actors

The basic idea is that human attitudes change with the Information Age. Our perspective has been influenced during a long period by an 'industrial' vision. Industrialisation is generally associated with labour and production organisation. However, industrialism also affected the law – the mechanisms which are used to ensure compliance with social values. The industrial vision of the law appears to be based on a 'macro-legal' attitude, where regulation is seen as:

1 a set of normative principles;
2 imposed by an authority;
3 expressing a project to be implemented by the members of society under a threat of a penalty.

That vision has led to a systematic confrontation among economic and social actors. One example may be taken from discussions surrounding e-commerce regulation.[2] In this debate, two positions are generally opposed.[3]

First, the position adopted by businesses. As we know, businesses endeavour to minimise costs and maximise benefits. Such attitude is said to be necessary, as customers are to be attracted to collect the resources which will be necessary for the survival and the future development of the undertakings. In that context, regulations are regarded as burdens. As a result of the law, undertakings are to commit resources to behaviour they would not otherwise have contemplated (e.g. the protection of personal information on customers). The rules also prevent them from engaging in activities that might have proven profitable (e.g. the installation of electronic devices in software in order to monitor customer behaviour and gather marketing information).

Second, the position adopted by customers. Cost minimising and profit maximising are not limited to businesses. Such behaviour may also be found with customers. The pattern is, however, generally different, as an action bringing a benefit to an undertaking often implies a cost for customers (and vice versa).[4] By customers, rules are generally regarded as remedies – not burdens. They are supposed to provide a protection against risks.[5]

As we can see, different solutions may be adopted in various situations. These solutions are decided upon by authorities.[6] The latter are supposed to occupy a central and intermediary position in society. Most of them are elected, or are at least submitted to some form of (sometimes indirect) electoral control. For that reason (and probably others as well), they may be sensitive, in general, to some of the concerns expressed by the consumers.

It has long been recognised, however, that electoral results do not only depend on the behaviour of the citizens. Money is essential on that market too. The marketing activity which is related to elections depends to a substantial extent upon the sum collected by the candidates. In many instances, the electoral money is handed over by corporations. It is thus essential for authorities and their members to be sensitive as well to the ideas – and suggestions – put forward by the undertakings.[7]

The political process

On the basis of these remarks, a general presentation may be proposed of the regulatory process as it is analysed by many observers.

In *economic* terms, rules may be said to provide a tool for the allocation of costs and benefits among social and economic forces. Take the discussions on the allocation of damages caused by illicit information posted on the web. Various solutions are contemplated by law makers. The damages can be imposed on the victim, by deciding that no reparation will be granted. A payment may also be requested from the service provider, or from other intermediaries (firm providing storing facilities, etc.). The choice in favour of one option will determine who will pay the costs associated with the activity.

The regulatory process may be described in *political* terms as a struggle to obtain legal protection. Interest groups are aware of the prevalence that may be given by the law to their position. That prevalence means that their position will be accepted, and defended with the authority of the state, as long as other groups are not in a position to articulate a coherent counter-proposal and mobilise social forces to have that proposal adopted by the legitimate representatives.

The struggle clearly appears in many economic areas. One may cite, as an example, the discussions which oppose undertakings for the adoption of technical standards, particularly within the European Union.[8] From a logical point of view, these discussions may be divided into two components, in view of their object. In a first instance, social and economic actors fight in order to have their position adopted by the authority, with respect to the question of knowing whether or not a standard should be fixed by an authority (and not, for instance, progressively elaborated by the markets). Actors may in that regard have diverging interests, depending on their situations. When a decision has been made with respect to the principle (determination of the technology by an authority and not by the market), undertakings have to fight again. This time, the objective is, for each of those concerned, to impose their own standards on the markets via the authority.

The attitude adopted by these undertakings may easily be understood: the 'winner' – i.e. the undertaking whose innovation will be regarded as the standard – will receive payments from intellectual property rights licences;[9] it will be placed in an excellent position to undertake research and development for related innovations; and it will command the knowledge now necessary to manufacture the goods and services related to that standard.[10]

A locked society?

These patterns are inherent to an industrial vision, where the positions to be occupied by the actors are centrally defined. They have led many observers to consider that our society is somehow locked. Parties are trying to obtain legal or economic advantages to the detriment of others, with the result that satisfactory compromises are rarely attained.

A good example of that situation may be found in the discussions that have taken place in Europe with respect to the universal service in the telecommunications industry.[11] As we know, that sector was reserved for decades to national monopolies. With the advent of competition, authorities wondered about the implementation of the political objectives which were pursued under the former regime, in particular the broad dissemination of telecom goods and services throughout the population and the territory.[12] They decided that a political action should be undertaken apart from competition.

The question was, however, to determine who would pay the costs associated with the universal service. The new entrants were rather opposed to a substantial public intervention. They feared that the costs would be imposed on undertakings including themselves. Their concern was that they would then be hampered in their ability to compete/enter markets dominated by former operators and to innovate and develop new services/technologies.

By contrast, the former telecom operators supported a large version of the universal service. Due to their command on the public network, they were the only ones able to perform the relevant services. For that reason, they were sure to be entrusted with the exclusive responsibility for the programme. They would thus be protected from competition in these markets and would receive a remuneration which would compensate their relative inefficiency in other fields as well.

The position advocated by the former telecom operators was supported to some extent by certain consumer groups. The latter have traditionally been wary of changes coupled with competition. They hope that prices will decrease as a result of a change in the market organisation. At the same time, they are concerned that undertakings might be forced to cheat in a competitive environment – i.e. to grab resources from customers while providing little to them.

The debate led the Member States to discuss an amendment to the EC Treaty during the Amsterdam intergovernmental conference. The partisans of both attitudes submitted proposals supporting their stance. A compromise was reached for a new provision to be inserted in the Treaty. That provision, however, is hardly comprehensible. It contains a summary of the positions expressed by the parties, without clear indication as to the option which was finally chosen. All parties were thus in a position to claim victory. The confrontation was not resolved, and is likely to occur whenever the question is raised again.[13]

Rules with various origins

Rules created by authorities

As was said at the outset of this article, the regulation that we experience nowadays in many sectors of the economy is inspired by an industrial vision. In many respects, industrialisation is accompanied by some sort of centralisation. With industrialisation, workers gathered from villages to urban centres. Their work was organised as the implementation by many of tasks determined by a few. Such economic and social concentration found an echo in political organisations, with large territories being administered from a single place.[14] In that organisation, the law was no exception. As observed above, the legal system was regarded as a body of binding sentences expressing a project designed by a central authority. That project was supposed to become reality, i.e. to be implemented by the members of society under the threat of sanction.

Compared with that organisation, a change is under way with the development of the Information Society. The latter does not imply, nor rest upon, any centralisation. It may rather be associated with a dispersion or dissemination of the decision-making power. The evolution may be illustrated with the changes which are occurring in the labour markets, as a result of the development of our information- and knowledge-based culture. In that sector, we are witnessing the possibility of workers increasingly performing duties away from traditional premises. Workers are increasingly independent. They do not remain seated in the main office of their undertaking, but are dispatched to the client's premises, where they sometimes stay for months. Contacts are kept within the firm through electronic and telecommunications devices such as telephone, electronic mail or video conferencing.

Can we draw any conclusions from that evolution with regard to regulation? In our era of increasing individual independence, is it appropriate to maintain the industrial view of regulation? Should we still consider that the law is created principally, if not exclusively, by public authorities?[15] Are we not in a position to consider alternative sources of regulation, which may gain momentum with the Information Society? That perspective is essential for the development of future regulatory tools to be used in the Information Society. It is also important for the democracy, as the latter implies (and presupposes) the possibility for citizens to participate in the 'the norm-making process'.

To me, a positive answer must be given to the question. Rules are not – and should not be – created in an exclusive manner by authorities. Research is only starting in that direction, but it is essential to demonstrate that new areas are progressively discovered in that field. In this article, three sorts of project will be shortly introduced with an emphasis on the last one.

Rules created by communities

Rules are created by communities, apart from those which are adopted by authorities. Seminal reflections may be found in that regard in the work of Robert C. Ellickson.[16] These works are based on a study related to a small farming community in the United States. The objective of Ellickson was to identify how the members of that community resolve their conflicts, i.e. to determine what regulation was used in order to manage their sometimes conflicting interests. Surprisingly, the study showed that most of the time parties did not resolve conflicts using the laws enacted by the local and/or the federal government. Rather, they referred to norms which had progressively developed in their community and which remained unaffected by the official legal production.

The work initiated by Professor Ellickson was continued in other projects. It was certainly essential to determine whether the pattern observed in a farming community could be found in other, probably more sophisticated, circles, such as those formed by businesses in the modern economic world.

A project of that kind is currently being undertaken with respect to the Internet in the Berkman Center for Law and Society at Harvard Law School. In that project, Larry Lessig regards electronic software as a sort of legal code. That code is to be used by Internet users to reach the goal they are pursuing – realise a given operation, attract customers, etc.[17]

Another legal scholar, Yochai Benkler, looks at the impact of technical choices on behaviour.[17] For him, the Internet is to be regarded as a medium which allows virtually everyone to post creations on the web. By contrast, when it comes to television, creation is severely restricted to some entities or people – basically those who can collect the funds necessary to finance televisual content. For Benkler, the choice in favour of one or the other medium has an impact on democracy, as it determines the ability to participate in the creation and dissemination of ideas.[19]

Rules created by individuals

Another research direction is related to the rules which are created by individuals, or by entities. In the industrial vision, society is regarded as homogenous. On one side are the public authorities, which enact rules supposed to govern society. On the other side are the members of society, who are expected to abide by instructions given by public authorities. Non-compliance implies a penalty, as the objective is to ensure a homogenous behaviour – that which is deemed appropriate by authorities.

That representation corresponds with the perspective adopted by the authorities. In that context, regulation is seen as a project designed by authorities for society. People – who are affected by regulation – have no existence on their own. They constitute mere tools for the realisation of the public project. In that respect, the industrial vision conforms in many regards with a centralised version of the regulatory phenomenon.[20]

Yet, as we have seen, the Information Society is characterised by a movement to the contrary. Rather than concentrating, it expands organisations in space and volume. With the Information Society, the economy, labour and the political process appear to move away from concentration towards decentralisation. For the study of regulation, that evolution necessitates a perspective not restricted to the authorities but, rather, based on the views adopted by the people.

In that regard, it is essential to set aside the classical tradition in legal analysis, where rules are analysed from the authorities' perspective. A research project is currently taking place in that direction at the Telecom Unit. Our focus is placed on the process whereby individuals and entities forge their own rules on the basis of a variety of external influences, including: social pressure, threat of sanction, etc. The scheme is based on an ordinary question: 'Who really makes the law?' It is conceded that public authorities adopt propositions which pretend to govern behaviour. However, the real lawmaker appears to be located elsewhere. Nobody can really be forced to obey the law. If you do not want to comply, you will always find a mechanism which will allow you to bypass the law – legally or not.

Rules created by economic interactions

More concrete examples are available in the third direction, which also forms the focus of research undertaken at the Telecom Unit. That third category is related to interactions among society members – business interactions, in this case. The analysis is based on an example concerning competition regulation. European states now have competition laws similar or analogous to those embodied in the European Treaty (prohibition of cartels and dominant-position abuses). Prior to that stage, most of them already had rules related to competition ('rules on fair competition'). Both bodies of regulation contained in effect the same kind of prohibitions, with differences as to modalities.

The example focuses on one practice which is considered illegal under both sets of rules: the refusal to supply a good/service if the customer does not accept the acquisition of another – related or not – market (tying). Under the rules of unfair competition, that practice was prohibited in all circumstances. The approach is different with the rules of competition as they now exist, where the prohibition is only directed against dominant firms adopting that behaviour. The reason underlying that latter approach may be described as follows.

- In normal circumstances, a customer may change supplier if dissatisfied – for instance if confronted with tying-in practices. An economic pressure is then placed on the supplier to change its behaviour, or face the departure of dissatisfied customers. No specific rule appears to be necessary to bring about a change in behaviour on the part of the supplier.
- The mechanism will only be effective if the customer has the possibility of changing supplier, should he be dissatisfied. That possibility is seriously hampered in cases where the supplier holds market power. The concept describes a situation where the undertaking has the possibility to behave independently on the markets. It does not have to take into account the possible reactions of dissatisfied customers, nor those of competitors, who are in effect unable to attract customers.[21]

Under both sets of regulation, a negative consequence is attached to a specific behaviour. It is hoped that this consequence will force the undertaking to change behaviour. The only difference is related to the nature of the sanction. In one case (absence of market power under competition rules), an economic sanction is applied by business actors (change of supplier). In the other ones (fair competition and presence of market power under competition rules), the sanction is applied by an authority and takes the form of a civil and/or criminal penalty.

	Former rules of competition	*Present rules of competition*
Attitude *vis-à-vis* tying-in	Tying-in is prohibited in all situations	Tying-in is prohibited where the firm holds market power, and only discouraged in other circumstances[22]
Sanction	A criminal and civil penalty is imposed	A criminal and civil penalty is imposed where the firm holds market power; the firm suffers a decrease in market share in other circumstances[23]
Reason for which a sanction is imposed	The hope is that tying-in will be dropped by the firm as a result of the imposition of the sanction It is even hoped that the practice will be dropped before the sanction is imposed (anticipation of the sanction on the part of the firm)	The hope is that tying-in will be dropped by the firm as a result of the imposition of the sanction It is even hoped that the practice will be dropped before the sanction is imposed (anticipation of the sanction on the part of the firm)

Changes related to the Information Age

The regulatory mechanism

Let us identify the mechanism underlining the approach in both sets of regulation. Three ingredients may be isolated.

- *Information*   In both sets, the purpose is to avoid a behaviour deemed incompatible with social values. To ensure that goal is achieved, information is provided to the potential trespasser: 'Tying-in is not deemed desirable and the company resorting to that practice will face a sanction.'[24] In the absence of such information, the behaviour is likely to be adopted as businesspeople may have the impression that their benefits will increase if the customers are forced to buy goods or services they would otherwise have left aside.
- *Learning capacity*   Information is not sufficient *per se*. A change will only occur if the undertaking is able to assess the situation, to understand the necessity of a change and to modify effectively behaviour on the basis of that assessment.
- *Incentive*   Another ingredient must be added to information and learning skills, to ensure a change will occur in behaviour. No change will take place if the agent is not encouraged, or pushed, to do so. The incentive may take several forms. In this case, we have examined the incentive which may be derived from the application of a sanction should the criticised behaviour be adopted. [25]

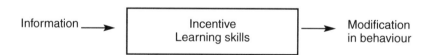

Impact of the Information Age on regulatory mechanism

Here is the final word of the analysis. The ingredients examined above may be associated to a substantial extent with the Information Society.

- *Information*   With the Information Society, we witness the development of electronic means of storage, analysis and transmission which all affect the volume and quality of available information. These media offer unprecedented manners to influence business behaviour – which is the purpose of regulation.
- *Learning skills*   A similar explosion may be witnessed in the capacity of actors – businesses or customers – to use learning capabilities. That development weights on the design of regulatory tools for the future – especially for those which are related to the Information Society. The proposal put

forward by the US administration, which has been shortly alluded to above, appears to be based on such process. In that proposal, customers may obtain information as to how data concerning their behaviour might be used by companies they are in contact with. On that basis, they may decide to alter their behaviour – e.g. break their relation with a company that would not respect privacy.

- *Incentive*   An incentive may be found in competition, which dominates the Information Society. Competition is greatly enhanced by new possibilities for customers to compare offers (monetary union, bargain hunter software, etc.). It is also reinforced by the pace of technology innovation, through which undertakings are forced to offer wider choice to the customers. Yet competition acts as a powerful incentive in the business community: it brings increasing wealth to those who can find their way in the business labyrinths (positive incentive), and sanction to others (negative incentive).

Conclusion

With the Information Age, we are entering a new stage in society. That development has an impact on regulatory tools available to ensure compatibility of economic activities with social values. Regulation implies the use of information and incentive to obtain changes in behaviour. It also requires learning skills, to ensure effective change in undesired business behaviour. These ingredients are now undergoing major changes: information can be produced, collected and transmitted more easily; with competition, businesses must provide better answers to customers; learning skills ensure that economic objectives and targets are effectively attained. As a result of these changes, we are in a better position to overcome the opposition – traditional in the Industrial Age – between customers and businesses. That development may offer a model for the solution of other conflicts of interest as well.

Notes

*   The Telecom Unit is a research institute which focuses on issues related to the Information Society. The emphasis is placed on regulatory issues, examined in an interdisciplinary perspective (law, management and engineering). On electronic commerce in the UK and in Europe, see Chissick and Kelman 1999.

1   For a global overview of telecom regulation in Europe, including aspects of Internet regulation, see Nihoul 1999. For a similar study on US law, see Benkler 1996.

2   For an excellent presentation of the discussion related to that subject matter, see the first issue of February 1999 of the review *info – The Journal of Policy, Regulation and Strategy for Telecommunications, Information and Media*, published by the Camford Group and endorsed by the International Telecommunications Society as its membership journal. One may also consider Spar 1999, who discusses the attitude generally adopted by businesses with respect to the Internet (as free a space as possible), and yet the necessity to elaborate rules in order to govern activities in cyberspace.

3   This description is simplified for the sake of presentation. Groups are not as homogenous as one may think. For instance, the rules of privacy protection may be considered as a burden by consumers who might prefer a simpler – hence cheaper –

treatment, contrary to what is generally suggested. Some businesses might also consider these rules as a source of profit. That is the case for the undertakings whose business is rating the policy adopted by e-commerce companies with regard to privacy. Furthermore, and assuming that groups are rather homogenous, the status of the rule among businesses and consumers often depends on its content. For instance, many e-commerce businesses will consider the rules on privacy as constraints, but they will have a different view with respect to the rules protecting their intellectual property. Such rules will then be considered as absolutely necessary, even though they may place a constraint on the behaviour to be adopted by other economic agents – in this case the customers. Similarly, rules may be considered positive by customers with respect to the protection of privacy, while some customers will complain about the intellectual property rules which, they say, prohibit the free circulation of ideas and art.

4 A decrease in price will often be regarded as positive by the customers, but rarely by undertakings as it will imply a profit lower than would otherwise have been attained. By contrast, higher prices for a good or a service will require a larger share of the customer purchasing power to be allocated to the operation, whereas it will mean a bigger profit for the undertaking.

5 Suppose you want to underwrite securities via the Internet. The amount may be intercepted, or it may be allocated by the addressee to a destination which was not intended by the customer. That risk may be transferred to another party. For instance, the legislator may decide that the risks will be taken over by the financial institutions.

6 The authority has been identified with the term 'legislator', but may receive a different name in other legal systems.

7 Businesses also have an influence on politicians via the information they are able to collect and the intelligence they are in a position to produce and disseminate.

8 E.g. the standard for the third generation of mobile phones. More generally, one would benefit from a careful analysis of the positions adopted by, among others, Blackman (1999, on the messy future which is expected for standards) and Grindley *et al.* (1999, on the 'Standards Wars'). These authors claim that standard setting is nothing other than a procedure which allows cartels to exist and be maintained thanks to the intervention of the government.

9 The good or service may only be used and/or produced if the other undertakings resort to the intellectual property rights which are associated with the innovation.

10 For other examples, see Higgott *et al.* 2000.

11 See Nihoul 1998.

12 About the European rules on universal service, see Haag and Goldsing 1997; Nihoul 1999: 273; Rapp 1996.

13 On this, see, among others, Dehousse and Van den Hende 1997.

14 That was the case in France, Germany and the United Kingdom.

15 The question is thus not related to the determination of the entities (businesses, authorities, etc.) which should set the rules, as is often the case in discussions concerning e-commerce regulation. It is rather to identify sources of normativity, by trying to determine who in effect sets the rules by which the actors abide.

16 Ellickson 1991.

17 A description of the work of the programme, and of papers in progress, is available at cyber@law.harvard.edu. In the published literature, see, among others, Lessig 1997 and 1998.

18 See Benkler 1998.

19 The choice is realised by authorities, which may encourage the development of one or other technique. It also depends upon the community as a whole – the innovations which are made by its members and the kind of technology which is supported by the latter.

20 In that context it comes as no surprise that the legal profession has been articulated around activities carried out by authorities. Some legally educated people work for

institutions. In that capacity, they contribute to a definition of the project by public authorities. Others work in the private sphere. Their job is then aimed at trying to anticipate the decisions of authorities in order to counsel clients on how to implement their strategies without impairing the implementation of that project.

21 That situation may be for several reasons. Suppose that one firm commands the sole telecom (fixed and mobile) infrastructure available in a given territory. Customers have to deal with this firm if they want to use telecom services, whatever the conditions imposed by the firm. So it is for competitors attempting to enter the market, who would be forced to use the infrastructure during a temporary period.

22 In the present competitive world, undertakings are aware of the importance of retaining customers' confidence. Most of them understand that restrictive practices may undermine that confidence. Resorting to tying-in, for example, may cause customers to turn to other suppliers.

23 Customers dissatisfied as a result of the restrictive practice turn to other suppliers.

24 As we have seen, the sanction may take the form of a penalty imposed by an authority. In that case, information is provided via the publication of civil or criminal laws. The sanction may also be administered by the customer, who may choose another supplier. The information is then communicated through another channel – e.g. business books explaining to would-be managers the importance of customer satisfaction.

25 In that regard, two possibilities have been examined: the imposition of a sanction by an authority or by a customer. In both cases, the incentive takes the form of an economic loss should the behaviour be adopted.

Part II

The limits of telecommunications regulation

5   How far can deregulation of telecommunications go?

Martin Cave

Introduction

This chapter is concerned with the general issue of 'normalising' public policy towards the telecommunications and related industries. By normalisation, I mean the application of conventional competition policy approaches, rather than the use of industry-specific and interventionist regulation. If the latter approach is essentially prescriptive – the regulator, for example, fixes prices and quality standards directly, the competition approach is proscriptive, in the sense that certain courses of conduct are prohibited, but a firm avoiding such practices can do what it likes.

Governments all over the world are increasingly addressing these issues, but one country – New Zealand – resolved it as long ago as 1987, when it decided, with unimportant exceptions, to regulate its telecommunications industry solely on the basis of its general competition law, the Commerce Act 1986. The New Zealand experience has attracted considerable interest. In most countries, however, an evolutionary approach is envisaged in which the regulator progressively withdraws from detailed intervention and becomes more like a competition authority. If this approach is adopted, the time elapsed in the course of the process assumes considerable significance.

I outline the evolutionary approach in relation to the UK, where three stages of deregulation can be distinguished, two completed, the third in progress. The first was the duopoly policy (1984 to 1991), in which the UK government committed itself to licensing a single entrant, Mercury, to compete with the incumbent operator, BT. This was followed by a transitional period, characterised by increasingly complex regulation. First steps towards the third phase of 'normalisation' were taken in 1997, when a range of new approaches to most of the aspects of regulation considered below came into effect. Further progress is taking place in 2000/01.

The second section, 'Stages of regulation', deals with UK experience in regulating entry into telecommunications, the overall level of retail prices, the maintenance of universal service obligations, and the pricing of individual retail services. The third section deals at greater length with interconnection or wholesale prices. The fourth section evaluates the experience to date, while the final section asks how far deregulation can go.

Stages of regulation

Licensing and entry

The UK's 1984 duopoly policy is easily described. The government (which – rather than the regulator – licensed telecommunications operators) undertook to give the single licensed entrant, Mercury, a clear run at BT, undisturbed by further entry, for a period of seven years. In return, Mercury undertook certain obligations concerning the roll-out of its network. The results were meagre. Mercury followed BT's prices rigidly, with a discount in market segments which it was attacking. BT was relatively content to concede market share at a comparatively slow rate (estimated at about 4 per cent by 1991, although concentrated in the most profitable international business segment).

In 1991, the government conducted a review of the duopoly policy and decided to license entrants in local and long-distance markets, on minimal conditions. As a result of this liberalisation, several hundred licences have now been issued, notably to operators falling in the following categories:

- Cable television operators, now licensed to pass approximately two-thirds of UK homes and now passing approximately half of them, were permitted to offer telecommunications services.
- A number of competitive access providers (CAPs) have established networks for voice and data in major cities.
- Other utility companies have also gained licences and built networks, including Energis, which has established a long-distance network built on the high-voltage electricity transmission grid.
- The government also has licensed operators to provide international services, including facilities-based services.

Recent market share data are considered below.

Regulating overall retail prices

The progressive tightening of the overall cap on BT's retail prices to RPI$-7\frac{1}{2}$ for 1993–7 is shown in Table 5.1. Also of interest is the coverage of the controls, as measured by the proportion of BT's total turnover subject to a cap. Significant increases in this proportion took place when the cap was renewed in 1989. International calls were incorporated in it in 1991. Regulation thus became more, rather than less, pervasive.

OFTEL's decisions on BT's price cap from 1997 represented a significant diminution in coverage, in response to the development of competition. The new price control regime was confined to services provided to a subset of customers on BT's residential tariff, excluding the two deciles with the highest bills. The coverage of the basket was thus reduced by about two-thirds, to about 22 per cent of BT's total revenues. To reflect the fact that the scope for cost

Table 5.1   Retail price control

	Control	*Coverage*
1984–9	RPI−3	49%
1989–91	RPI−4½	55%
1991–3	RPI−6¼	67%
1993–7	RPI−7½	64%
1997–2001	RPI−4½	22%

reduction in serving such customers is less, the price cap in the period of 1997–2001 is RPI−4½. This represented a major step towards the elimination of overall control over retail prices.

However, whereas in 1997 there were hopes that retail price controls might be abandoned after 2001, a consultation paper issued by OFTEL in March 2000 (OFTEL 2000b) identifies a range of options for extending them. The probable continuation of the controls reflects the observation that BT's profitability on calls remains high and that unrestricted rebalancing would have an adverse effect on a significant number of customers.

Universal service obligations

During the duopoly policy in the UK, the burden of universal service obligations or USOs – the obligation to provide specified services at nationally averaged tariffs – was imposed on BT alone, although Mercury was under certain licence obligations to roll out its network. The scale of the costs associated with this obligation was given little thought, but as additional licences were issued in the period from 1991, the imposition of the obligation on a single, even if a dominant, competitor became more questionable.

As far as measurement of the costs of USOs is concerned, it was generally accepted in the UK that the appropriate method of computation is to identify those subscribers whose avoidable costs exceeded their avoided revenue (including revenue of incoming calls), and to sum the losses thus estimated. Empirical work suggested that these costs were a small proportion, perhaps 0.5 per cent, of telecoms revenue, before deduction of benefits which the USO operator derives. OFTEL determined that this amount was too small to justify the setting up of a Universal Service fund – a decision confirmed provisionally in 1999.

Anti-competitive pricing

As noted above, one of the hallmarks of normalising regulation in the telecommunications industry is the replacement of specific price controls by general prohibitions on anti-competitive pricing. These involve floors and ceilings on the price charged for any service, and limitations on discrimination in prices charged to different customers for the same service.

During the duopoly policy, OFTEL interpreted the prohibition in BT's licence of 'undue discrimination' strictly, and rejected proposals for optional tariffs and quantity discounts. After 1991, BT was allowed to offer quantity discounts, but a floor of fully allocated costs was established for call prices as a proxy for the unknown incremental cost, and additional restrictions applied. Initially, such quantity discounts contributed to satisfaction of the price cap, but after 1993 they ceased to count, thus discouraging BT from focusing price reductions on its larger customers. The reduction in coverage of the retail price cap from 1997 has focused attention on what limitations should be imposed upon the price of retail services no longer included within the cap. There has also been debate about appropriate floors and ceilings for services still within the proposed wholesale or retail caps.

A natural approach here would be to rely upon ordinary competition law to police anti-competitive conduct of this kind. The difficulty, however, was that the relevant UK legislation then current was widely criticised for the lack of penalties for engaging in anti-competitive practices. To deal with this problem, OFTEL introduced a new fair trading condition in the licences of UK telecommunications operators which gave it the power to enjoin an operator from behaving anti-competitively (but not to impose fines). OFTEL intended that its decisions under this fair trading condition (FTC) should be consistent with European competition law. The condition lapsed in March 2000, when the provisions of the Competition Act 1998 came into force.

The existence of the fair trading condition has in many cases given OFTEL a choice of routes for dealing with complaints – either to use the new condition and examine the conduct in terms of European Competition Law, or to utilise a more specific licence condition, such as the condition which prohibits BT from exhibiting undue discrimination or undue preference in its pricing behaviour. Because such licence conditions do not conform to the language of competition law, and because OFTEL is under no obligation to interpret them in accordance with the principles of European jurisprudence, they offer greater flexibility. This may be one of the factors explaining the relatively limited use to date of the fair trading condition.

Traditional interconnection

The early days

During the duopoly period, the structure of interconnection charges was very simple. Under the regulatory regime set out in BT's licence, the parties sought to form an interconnection agreement on a commercial basis. If that failed, then OFTEL would determine interconnection prices (and, if necessary, other aspects of the arrangements) on the basis of fully allocated historic costs. OFTEL made such a determination between BT and Mercury in 1985, setting charges for three services for three separate times of day, corresponding to the retail tariff gradient. The arrangement was indexed the following year at the value of X in the then current price control. It was widely believed that, if initially interconnection prices were set in a way advantageous to Mercury, by the time of the next determination in 1991 the laxity of the indexation formula had made the prices relatively generous.

Following a request from BT and Mercury, OFTEL determined a new set of interconnection charges in 1991, on the basis of the same principles. By this stage, the duopoly policy had been abandoned in favour of liberalised entry into domestic telecommunications markets. BT's licence had also been amended to allow supplementation of interconnection charges by an access deficit contribution (ADC), intended to take account of losses on access which BT might suffer as a result of regulatory restrictions on its ability to raise its quarterly rental charge. As these ADCs were proportional to the profitability (to BT) of the retail service the competitor was providing, the system gave BT considerable power to influence its rivals' costs. The similarity of the regime to the Baumol–Willig efficient component pricing rule is evident. The practical effect of the system was diminished, however, by OFTEL's discretion to grant ADC waivers in specified circumstances.

In 1992 OFTEL also inaugurated discussion on a staged programme of reform of the interconnection regime. The first major stage was completed by 1996, but left intact the accounting basis for setting interconnection charges – the use of fully allocated historic costs.

This first stage involved a number of key elements – relating not only to the level of interconnection charges and the range of services available, but also to the accounting requirements imposed upon BT. Since 1994/5 the company has been obliged to prepare and publish separate accounts for its access, network, and retail businesses. The accounts are presented both in historic cost terms, and in current costs where capital goods are valued, and depreciation computed, on a modern equivalent asset basis. In establishing transfer prices between its network and retail businesses, the company must apply the principle of non-discrimination: BT Network must sell services to BT Retail at the same prices as it would charge other operators purchasing the same services on an interconnection basis. The introduction of separate accounting thus translated the problem of interconnection prices between competing operators into a more general problem of setting network or wholesale charges for the dominant firm.

In addition, in place of individual determinations between pairs of companies, a standard price list was introduced for about 60 unbundled wholesale services. OFTEL also refined its approach to determining which of BT's costs should be included in network, and hence interconnection, charges. In 1995, it issued a new determination of standard charges which excluded a range of costs. A system was also introduced whereby interconnection payments were initially based upon an estimate of fully allocated costs, with adjustments being made as actual costs were revealed. As a result of these changes, and of the tightening of BT's incentives to cut costs through the retail price cap, network charges fell by a third between 1993/4 and 1995/6. A consultancy study carried out for BT in 1997 concluded that BT's interconnection charges in the UK were the lowest of eleven companies examined.

Switching to an incremental cost base

None of the changes described above involved departure from the fully allocated historic cost basis of setting interconnection charges, enshrined in BT's 1984 licence. However, it was increasingly recognised that this basis was unsatisfactory on two counts: first, because calculating fully allocated costs involved a distribution of common or joint costs on a purely conventional basis, and second, because the use in price setting of the depreciated historic costs of assets gave confusing signals to competitors. Thus the replacement cost of BT's trenches and ducts exceeds historic cost, whereas the replacement cost of switches falls short of historic cost. Prices based on historic costs might discourage entry by more efficient suppliers of access services, and encourage less efficient entrants into conveyance.

To overcome these difficulties, a project was inaugurated to calculate network costs on an incremental cost basis. Two alternative cost methodologies were adopted. The first, known as 'bottom-up' cost modelling, involves the construction of an engineering model of parts of a telecommunications network. The resulting network design is then costed, and the average incremental cost of providing a particular (in this case, fairly broadly defined) service computed. The alternative approach, known as 'top-down', involves utilisation of BT's management accounts. Starting from a summation of all network costs, including overheads, an attempt is made to identify costs associated with progressively more narrowly defined services. The similarity of the results from the two models will depend upon the closeness of their assumptions.

The bottom-up model attempts to cost a network of the same basic topology as BT's existing network. The definition of relevant increments is also the same in both cases. Not surprisingly, however, the estimated incremental costs of the same interconnection service derived using the two models were not identical for a number of reasons, including:

- *Capital equipment costs* – arising from differences in utilisation, pricing or asset mix;
- *Operating costs* – the bottom-up model uses an operating cost to capital cost ratio reflecting the experience of a range of operators, rather than BT's experience alone.
- *Cost causation* – there are differences in the implicit or explicit cost volume relationships in the two models.
- *Economic and accounting depreciation* – associated with alternative depreciation profiles.

When these factors were taken into account, a reconciliation between the two estimates was achieved for most services.

The network price cap and deregulation

The previous system of UK interconnection pricing involved the determination, on a cost plus basis, of charges for individual services. This had a number of disadvantages. First, incentives to reduce costs are limited, although this tendency is tempered by the existence of a cap on BT's retail prices: lax control of network costs would injure the margin in BT's retail business, as well as raising costs for its competitors. Second, there is no tendency towards efficient pricing of interconnect services; instead, an equal mark-up is enforced for each service. Moving to a network price cap could remedy both of these deficiencies.

Before examining the details of this development, it is useful to review a number of more general issues relating to the network price cap. First, there is the question of usage-dependent pricing – whether the same interconnection service can be charged at different rates depending on the nature of the final service produced. Usage-dependent network prices can promote efficient Ramsey retail prices. It is also possible that prohibiting usage-dependent pricing may prevent the emergence of new services. Thus, use of the standard call termination charge to price video on demand may render the service wholly uncompetitive. However, usage-dependent pricing may also offer the incumbent opportunities for controlling, in an anti-competitive way, the development of new services. It might, for example, keep a wholesale price exceptionally high and then lower it only when its associated retail arm was in a position to offer the new service. For this or other reasons, OFTEL has determined generally to exclude usage-dependent pricing, although exceptions to this rule may be allowed in special cases.

Second, there is the key issue of who is entitled to buy network services at wholesale prices. In the UK regime, such rights were initially restricted to firms with their own infrastructure, although the definition was stretched to include international simple resale (ISR) operators, and the difficulties in establishing qualification are recognised. The justification of this approach was the policy decision taken by the government in 1991 to promote infrastructure competition as well as, or even at the expense of, service competition. This restriction was, however, loosened in 1997 in response to European legislative changes. Further extension of rights to cost-based interconnection (including reselling of BT's line) is under consideration (OFTEL 2000b).

Third, there is the issue of how comprehensive the price cap should be. In principle, any network service subject to effective competition should be excluded from the cap, to diminish regulation and to prevent a situation arising in which the incumbent can finance price cuts in competitive services by raising the price of monopolistic services. OFTEL concluded in 1997 that less than half of BT's network services require continued price control.

Fourth, this question abuts on the issue of how to co-ordinate a network and a retail cap. The principal options here are to establish separate caps, with an implicit assumption about the network costs in a retail cap, so that the latter effectively controls only the retail margin, and to adopt a combined or global cap in which a higher wholesale price would have to be compensated for by a lower retail price.

This last approach can be shown to elicit efficient pricing, provided that appropriate remedies against a price squeeze are available. These desirable properties depend, however, upon having comprehensive caps at both wholesale and retail levels, thus discouraging price deregulation. In the event, OFTEL adopted the first approach described above of setting separate but linked caps. It was thus decided to choose progressive price deregulation service by service or customer group by customer group, and to reject a unified all-embracing price control.

Finally, there is the key issue of the mark-up of long-run incremental cost which BT should be allowed to recover under the network price caps. This issue has been widely, if not conclusively, debated at both theoretical and practical levels. In the event, OFTEL decided to adopt an equal mark-up approach, allowing a uniform (11 per cent) mark-up of incremental cost in BT's access and network businesses.

After an analysis of the competitive position of a number of network services, OFTEL concluded that some, such as Directory Enquiries, were already competitive and hence required no price control. Others – long distance and international conveyance – become competitive before 2001, and require only a 'safeguard cap' preventing any increase in real prices. This left a third category, amounting to about 40 per cent of revenues, which were neither actually nor potentially competitive and required price controls. Separate baskets were created, each subject to a separate price control. The first includes call termination services, the second call origination, conveyance from local to long distance exchanges and single transit (use of a single switch but no transmission over BT's network). Three separate baskets were established to prevent BT recovering an excessive proportion of its costs from call termination, the primary area of bottleneck control. All are subject to a cap of RPI−8.

Within each price cap, the prices of individual services are subject to a floor of actual incremental cost and a ceiling of the stand-alone cost of an efficient operator. Because the increment in the estimate of the floor is broadly defined, many costs are included. As a result, the difference between floor and ceiling for individual services is estimated to lie between 40 and 82 per cent.

Evaluation of UK experience to date

Market shares in fixed link telecommunications in the UK at the end of 1998 are shown in Table 5.2. The table reveals the loss by BT of market share in varying degrees: in international, its competitors will by now have more than half the market, whereas their share in exchange lines is only about 15 per cent. At the same time, about half of UK households now have access to the alternative local loop provided by cable operators, suggesting that, even in this market, BT is subject to significant constraints since it still has an obligation to average its tariffs geographically.

Table 5.2 Fixed market shares in the UK (%) – first quarter, 1999

Call revenues	BT	C&W	Cable	Others
All calls	70.4	12.1	6.5	11.1
Local	79.8	7.2	9.3	3.5
National	71	10.2	5.2	13.9
International	53.2	12.3	6.4	27.8
Calls to mobile	71.4	13.5	6.3	8.4
Exchange line rentals	88.4	4.8	5.7	1.1
Exchange lines 31 December 1998	85.4	4.6	8.8	1.2

Source: OFTEL

The price control regime has also generated substantial reductions to consumers in real terms. The distribution of these returns has, however, been open to question. When the retail price control covered all residential and all business customers, there was a natural tendency for BT to focus its price cuts on customers in more competitive markets – business customers and higher spending residential customers. This process was particularly marked between 1991 and 1993, when the company was first permitted to offer quantity discounts – those discounts qualifying for satisfaction of the price cap. In those two years, residential customers derived almost no benefit from the annual bill reduction in prices of 6.25 per cent. As a consequence, OFTEL introduced a requirement in 1993 that any additional quantity discounts offered by BT would not 'score' for satisfaction of the price cap. Then in 1997, the retail price cap was limited in scope to a basket based on purchases by the eight deciles of residential customers with the lowest bills. Because the line rental represented about half of this basket, a 1 per cent increase in line rentals would require an additional 1 per cent cut in call charges. This had the effect of limiting the scale of re-balancing, and hence increasing the benefits derived by those purchasing price control services.

This phenomenon is demonstrated in Table 5.3, which shows distribution of benefits of the retail price changes between 1990/91 and 1998/9. Despite a decline in the value of X in the RP1-X price formula from 6.25 per cent to 4.5 per cent, the first 80 per cent of residential customers derived an additional 1.7 per cent reduction in the real price of their services in the two years after 1997, compared with the seven previous years. High-spending residential and business customers fared worse than in the previous period. This experience illustrates the importance of ensuring that no price cap contains competitive and non-

Table 5.3 Distribution of benefits of retail pricing changes: average decline in real prices

	1990/1–1996/7	*1996/7–1998/9*
Official price controls (RPI−*X* formula)	6.7%	4.5%
First 80% of residential customers	2.9%	4.6%
Top 20% high-spending residential customers	5.8%	4.8%
All business customers	8.0%	6.9%

Source: OFTEL

competitive services. If it does, there is a serious risk that relative price structures will be distorted and that – in the limit – the regulated firm will have an incentive to engage in 'subsidised predation'.

How far can deregulation go?

The growing importance of access

As discussed above, traditional interconnection problems involve inter-operator transactions deriving from the need to complete calls and achieve any-to-any connectivity. Recent developments have, however, focused much more upon the more general question of access by one operator to another's facilities, particularly in circumstances where the access seeker achieves a direct commercial relationship with the access provider's customers. Examples of this form of access, drawn from recent UK regulatory discussions, include the following:

- local loop unbundling (LLU);
- access to set-top boxes;
- access for content providers and internet service providers to cable TV networks;
- access to mobile network infrastructures, for example on the part of virtual network operators.

These issues have been made more complex by the convergence of information and communication technologies. Whereas there is little difficulty in making a convincing argument in favour of a telecommunications entrant's access to the historic operator's call termination facilities, the problem becomes much more complicated where there is (for example) a variety of possible delivery mechanisms for entertainment services, including cable, satellite and terrestrial transmission (both analogue and digital), as well as a copper wire network combined with ADSL (Asymmetric Digital Subscriber Line) and (prospectively) third generation mobile radio. There is likely to be a fundamental and enduring conflict between opening a market to competition immediately, through mandated access, and the long-term development of infrastructure competition. I first examine this conflict before considering in broader terms the appropriate relationship between *ex ante* and *ex post* regulation, and between telecommunications and competition law.

The unbundling of the local loop provides an interesting example of how these tensions play out. OFTEL was initially sceptical about such unbundling, because it believed that it could jeopardise the development of existing network competition. In December 1998, it issued a consultation document on mandating local loop unbundling (LLU) for BT, inviting comment on the effect of such requirement on investment in alternative local networks. Then in July 1999 OFTEL published a further consultation document signalling that it accepted that there was a case for regulatory action. In particular, the Office had concluded that there were barriers to competition in the supply of higher band-width services at both wholesale and retail level, and that small and medium sized enterprises in particular were being denied service. BT's copper loops were likely to be the primary route for the delivery of high band width services to the mass market, as demand from such consumers would not generally be met by other means. This conclusion rested upon the observation that BT had a very strong market position in supplying 85 per cent of access lines, whereas cable networks at present passed only around 50 per cent of UK homes, of whom approximately one third took service.

The document also considers two principal variants for delivering LLU. The first involved a requirement on BT to make its local copper loop available as a leased circuit to other operators, which would then be able to upgrade the loop to provide higher bandwidth capacity by installing equipment at BT's local exchange and at the customer's premises. This would require a considerable investment on the part of the other operators. The principal alternative involved BT in upgrading its network to enable its copper loop to be used instead of higher bandwidth services. Connection between the service provider and the customer would not be through a discrete physical connection, but via a virtual circuit, in which data from many customers would be multiplexed together and the service provider benefit from a logical connection between each customer and the data packets flowing on the circuit.

As far as pricing is concerned, OFTEL recognised that in the presence of an unbalanced tariff, pricing the loop on the basis of BT's current retail charge, minus retail cost (retail minus), would provide competitors with a substantial commercial advantage over BT, since they would both buy loops at below cost and have access to the excess profits embodied in the prices charged for other services.

OFTEL agreed with BT the date of July 2001 for introducing LLU, but – with anxieties growing that the UK was being disadvantaged in its development of Internet access and e-commerce as a result of the delay – there was pressure to bring the date forward.

A second example of access problems is provided by the regime under which other broadcasters seek access to proprietary technologies for conditional access services for digital television. The need to introduce such a regime flowed from the European Union's Advanced Television Service Directives of 1995, which was transposed into UK legislation in 1997. These developments took place against a background of concern on the part of regulatory and competition authorities in the UK about the dominant role of BSkyB in the UK pay television market. The legislation required charges for digital conditional access services to be 'fair, reasonable and non-discriminatory'.

The interpretation of this phrase presented considerable difficulties for the following reasons:

- the cost structure of a conditional access system is complicated, consisting of fixed start-up costs, as well as costs driven by the number of channels serviced and by the number of subscribers served;
- digital conditional access services were developed on the back of equivalent analogue services, to some extent relying upon skills acquired in the development of analogue services which might reasonably be recompensed through digital charges;
- the development of digital television was promoted through extensive subsidisation of set-top boxes, raising the issue of the extent to which it was appropriate that competing digital broadcasters should contribute to those subsidy costs;
- the set-top boxes were used both for broadcasting services and for interactive services, such as home shopping – leaving open the question of how costs should be divided between the two classes of service;
- a requirement not to discriminate would clearly prevent broadcasters of the same kind (for example, premium pay TV channels or public service broadcasters) paying different charges, but this leaves open the question of whether the requirement of identical or similar charges should also apply to different types of broadcaster.

The purpose of these two illustrations is to demonstrate the complexities which arise in pricing access to facilities. OFTEL's most recent position, set out in its January 2000 strategy document, is that the regulatory requirements and pricing regime should depend upon the degree of market power exercised by the owner of the access facility (OFTEL 2000a). This can vary from dominance, through significant market power, to no market power, with the access obligation and pricing rule depending on where a particular case falls.

Telecommunications law versus competition law

One of the interesting things about this approach is that it borrows extensively from competition law. In effect OFTEL is proposing (and the European Commission's 1999 Communications Review (Commission of the EC 1999a) does the same) the application by regulatory authority on an *ex ante* basis of decisions which might emerge *ex post* from the application of competition law.

For example, in relation to local loop unbundling, the OFTEL principles would first involve market definition, in order to establish whether dominance or significant market power existed. The OFTEL consultation document quoted above implicitly identifies exchange lines as a relevant market at the national level, and answers the question relating to BT's dominance in the affirmative. Having satisfied itself of this fact, ideally through a more thorough discussion of both product and geographical dimensions of market definition, OFTEL could then proceed to apply the relevant pricing principle.

The approach a competition authority would take to the matter would be rather different. Essentially, it would have to address the question of whether the local loop satisfied the requirements for application of the European version of the essential facilities doctrine, which would involve an examination of what facilities were both technologically and commercially feasible as substitutes for the access facilities in question. Once that determination had been made it would broadly be up to the parties to negotiate an appropriate price. This might well be based on the same regulatory pricing principles as those enunciated by OFTEL, but it would depend on circumstances.

This suggests that the two approaches might lead broadly to the same result, but with a significant procedural difference. In the UK, regulation can be applied relatively speedily (subject to consultation requirements, etc.), and come into effect *ex ante*. Competition law, by contrast, has to be applied after an infraction. This does not mean, however, that competition law is only capable of modifying behaviour *ex post*, since the anticipation of legal action should act as a satisfactory *ex ante* disincentive. However, this assumes a degree of anticipation on the part of the regulated firm, which in the absence of clear legal precedents may be hard to achieve. It also requires the competition legislation to contain penalties of sufficient severity to deter illegal courses of conduct.

This last condition has until recently been lacking in the UK. But the passage of the Competition Act 1998, which came into force in March 2000, has changed that. Under the Act, OFTEL exercises concurrent powers with the general competition authority, the Office of Fair Trading. In practice, OFTEL will take the lead in matters relating to telecommunications, and the Director General will have the power, in the case of infractions, to levy fines (subject to appeal to a Competition Tribunal) of up to 10 per cent of a firm's UK turnover, or up to 30 per cent if the offence has continued for three years or more.

This new legislation is likely significantly to alter the balance of advantage between reliance upon the Competition Act and reliance upon the licensing conditions established under telecommunications legislation. Indeed, in its strategy document, OFTEL acknowledges that:

> Regulation of anti-competitive behaviour should increasingly be carried out under the Competition Act, which provides appropriate incentives through fines, on both dominant undertakings and on undertakings that are party to restrictive agreements, to encourage operators to put their own house in order and not to rely on OFTEL's licence compliance procedures. It is a key step in ensuring that as competition develops telecoms becomes more like other sectors of the economy wherever feasible.

Use licence conditions only where there is a need to promote competition. Rely solely on the Competition Act to police anti-competitive behaviour where there is effective competition.
(OFTEL 2000a, italics in original)

How far can deregulation go?

This discussion provides a suitable introduction to an attempt to answer the question in the title: what is the feasibly irreducible level of sector-specific legislation in telecommunications, once opportunities for the development of effective competition have – to all intents and purposes – been exhausted? Particular answers to this question might lead on to a further question, not addressed here, which relates to the identity of the organisation undertaking such regulation – the issue of whether it should be a sector-specific regulator, such as OFTEL, or the general competition authority.

It is useful to try to answer this question in terms of the five aspects of regulation identified at the beginning of this chapter. As far as licensing is concerned, there is no obvious basis for adopting an approach significantly different from the 'free for all' employed in other industries. This does not mean, of course, that environmental considerations such as the impact of rights of way should be neglected. These should, however, be enforced in a competitively neutral fashion. It is useful to note in this connection that the European Commission's 1999 Communications Review proposes the replacement of much licensing activity by the issuing of authorisations, as well as emphasising the desirability of 'one-stop shopping' within the European Union (Commission of the EC 1999a).

Provided the network pricing problem has been adequately resolved, there is no reason why retail price control should continue to be required. Service providers should be able to enter and exit the market fairly costlessly, in response to any opportunities to arbitrage between network and retail prices. This conclusion is contingent to some extent on the degree of geographical averaging imposed under the universal service obligation, because the latter permits competition in one area to be borrowed to the benefit of consumers in another area.

This deregulation of retail pricing is quite consistent with the persistence of regulatory measures to protect consumers, relating to such matters as contract duration and the transparency of prices.

The third facet of regulation concerned universal service obligations. The issue here more generally relates to the attainment of social or (more generally) non-economic objectives through the pricing of communications services. On the basis of experience to date, there seems to be no necessary contradiction between the attainment of universal service objectives and the development of competition. This is likely to remain true provided that obligations do not acquire such a magnitude that they risk overwhelming the ordinary process of market allocation, thus endangering competition. Similar observations apply to the achievement of other social objectives such as the protection of customer privacy.

The fourth element considered related to the control of anti-competitive pricing. This probably presents the least difficulty, because the natural means of policing anti-competitive pricing in any sector is via an appropriately specified competition law with sufficient deterrent capabilities.

Finally, we face the most persistent cause of continuing regulation of interconnection and access. Both the European Commission's Review and OFTEL's long-term strategies envisage that call termination is likely to remain a bottleneck which requires continuing price regulation. This argument is based upon the propositions that the only means of access to the called party is via its fixed-link operator, and that the called party is unlikely to choose its operator on the basis of whatever termination charges are rolled up into the retail price paid by the calling party. In fact, neither of these propositions is necessarily true. The increasing penetration of mobile phones offers an alternative means of access to a growing proportion of the population, and, to the extent that telecommunications take place within a closed user group (for example, a family or a firm), a subscriber's choice of operator may be influenced by the level of termination charges. Just the same, it is not unreasonable to assume that there will be a continuing necessity to control the prices of call termination set by dominant operators. Whether the same is required for other operators depends to a considerable extent upon the regulatory regime – particularly the extent to which retail prices of a call can be varied to take account of differing termination charges. There thus seems to be the medium- or long-term prospect of regulation, probably on an LRAIC basis, of call termination charges.

The speed with which technological developments take place is an argument against regulation which might be inhibiting or inadequate. Indeed, the experience of the Advanced Television Services Directive provides a useful illustration. The requirement for fair, reasonable and non-discriminatory pricing applied only to conditional access services. Yet it immediately became apparent that a variety of other technical services, not explicitly covered by the Directive, were potential barriers to entry.

In an ideal world, the matter would be resolved by the application of clear principles governing interoperability and access to proprietary information and standards, derived from competition law. In the absence of such information, there is an arguable if not overwhelming case for relying upon *ex ante* regulation, to maintain competition and protect consumers.

In summary, there is considerable scope for further deregulation of the telecommunications and related industries, and this is consistent with the attainment of non-economic objectives such as universal service and subsidised access to the resources necessary for a citizen to participate in the Information Society. The key problems requiring special treatment relate to interconnection and access, but it has been argued that even here there is considerable scope for narrowing considerably the area for *ex ante* regulation, and increasing reliance upon competition law. Perhaps what is required above all is an adequate set of legal precedents, which will introduce the necessary level of legal certainty. Unfortunately, it seems that the only way to achieve this objective is to take the risk of deregulation.

6 Realising social goals in connectivity and content
The challenge of convergence

Richard Collins

In both telecommunications and broadcasting, new market structures have emerged which change the context of and rationale for regulation. In both domains governments have lost control over market entry and, consequently, the old method of achieving regulatory goals (including social goals) by attaching conditions to licences no longer works reliably. So what? Some claim that this no longer matters and that competition will spontaneously achieve the goals which once could only be realised through regulation. But this view seems excessively optimistic for the following reasons:

- The future is constrained by the past – competition will not develop spontaneously because part of the legacy of the past is a number of dominant firms – often created by an earlier regulatory regime which controlled entry.
- Relevant markets fail in interesting ways. Regulation/intervention is likely to be required, not only to mimic the outcomes of a well-functioning market (dealing with dominant firms is one aspect of that) but because the economic characteristics of media and communications differ sufficiently from those assumed in economic theory for there to be perverse outcomes if markets work (or are made to work) in conventional ways.
- People don't enter markets equally endowed; allowing markets to work spontaneously may result in unacceptable levels of inequality and social exclusion.
- Economic efficiency may produce socially unacceptable outcomes (e.g. the monopolisation or oligopolisation of supply of information through concentration of ownership and/or control).

These objections do not mean that competition should be rejected either as a regulatory goal or as a conceptual template for the regulatory or public policy. On the contrary (to restate what is already on the public record as my view): 'Competition and markets have a valuable role in securing the public interest in media and communications' (Collins and Murroni 1996: 183). But whilst competition is necessary, both as a conceptual paradigm and as a policy goal, it is not sufficient.

Technological change has meant that markets which hitherto seemed naturally to be dominated by monopolies are now more open to entry than before. Monopoly provision (or at least highly limited entry) formerly seemed appropriate to both telecommunications and broadcasting: telecommunications because of both the levels of capital investment required to establish a comprehensive network and the economies of scale and scope which characterised wired networks; broadcasting because of scarcity in the radio frequency spectrum.

Convergence, the synonym for the intense process of technological change now taking place in communications, is customarily described as a process of integration. Integrated broadband intelligent digital networks enable users to communicate cheaply over long distances and for long periods exchanging sound, text, data, images and video over the same infrastructure. Text, images and data are reduced to a single bitstream, delivered over an integrated 'any-to-any' network, combining wired and wireless elements, and carrying messages spanning all communicative relationships: from the strictly private one-to-one communication characteristic of telephony to the one-to-every communication characteristic of broadcasting. But convergence is also substitutability between hitherto separate media and infrastructures. A voice message may be delivered over a wired or wireless network. Broadcast signals may be delivered through terrestrial free-to-air broadcasting or via satellite or cable. Kevin Werbach, of the FCC Office of Plans and Policies, defined the issue pithily by stating that one new medium, the Internet, is 'substitutable for all existing media' (Werbach 1997).

Both integration and substitutability mean that a single regulatory doctrine is required. Competition is usually seen as the name of this game. So pervasive is this notion that it comes as a surprise to be reminded of how recently this notion achieved its currency in the UK: in respect of telecommunications, with the Littlechild Report of 1983 (foreshadowed by the Beesley Report of 1981) and in respect of broadcasting, with the Peacock Report of 1986. The names by which these reports are customarily known, those of the distinguished economists who either authored the report (Stephen Littlechild) or chaired the authoring committee (Alan Peacock), signal the hegemony of economics and of economists in this field of policy wonkery.

Paradigm crash

But economics is one among several social sciences – it is not a theory of everything. That its foundational assumptions (e.g. that people do not behave altruistically, that the collective good is best realised through individuals seeking their own good) are neither incontestable nor comprehensive enough to embrace all human motivations and behaviour is undoubtedly important (and well known). But perhaps more relevant is the growing acknowledgement that key axioms in economists' cognitive arsenal are inadequate to address the strictly *economic* issues arising in media and communications.

De Long and Froomkin (1998), for example, argue that what they call the 'three pillars' of the market system – excludability, rivalry and transparency – are, at best, shakily present in the 'new economy'. Garnham (1994) and Graham (1999) have also argued that media markets have an intrinsic tendency to fail and offer further arguments to those succinctly made by de Long and Froomkin. Others (see Collins 1998) have contended that social benefits accrue from some forms of market failure in communications.

Garnham (1994) refers to the hit or flop phenomenon. Most new releases, whether TV programmes, films or CDs, are flops. The few hits make up for this extensive (and expensive) failure. Since industry professionals cannot predict success, they need to balance risk across as wide a slate of products as possible, i.e. larger companies are favoured. Second, Garnham refers to the importance of marketing – the media sector spends disproportionately on marketing, a classic barrier to entry, partly because viewers cannot try goods without consuming them (de Long and Froomkin's transparency point), and partly because new products are highly sensitive to fashion.

Graham (1999) points to the importance of externalities (not strictly an argument about intrinsic failure of media markets but rather an affirmation of the importance of non-economic criteria) and to the tendencies of individual consumers both to underfund provision of merit goods and not to know their own preferences. The potential for establishing and abusing a dominant position is inherent in network technologies (i.e. network externalities can operate negatively as well as positively).

Accordingly, the combination of barriers to entry, economies of scale and incentives to integrated distribution networks suggests that broadcasting[1] markets will continue to fail (see also Graham and Davies 1997). The old economics and its paradigms have crashed on the information highway.

Fairness

All do not enter markets equally endowed, all do not benefit equally – and some not sufficiently – from the allocations performed even by a technically perfectly functioning market. Implicit in the term 'sufficiently' is a proposition that even if efficient (producing Pareto optimal maximisation of outputs for a given set of inputs), a well-functioning market may produce outcomes which are so unequal as to be socially unacceptable. Unacceptable, that is, for reasons of pragmatism and principle. Even those who benefit from unfair allocation of resources may acknowledge pragmatic reasons for a more equitable distribution (the disadvantaged, in the absence of redistributive measures, might use violence to secure a bigger share). But as well as pragmatic arguments for fairness (which open up alternatives of increased expenditure on police, security and defence to protect unfair distribution as an alternative to re-distribution) there are principled arguments. Among the most persuasive are Rawls'.

It would be a life's work to rehearse different arguments from principle on and in which reasoned critiques of the social effects of market mechanisms might be grounded. But, of contemporary thinkers, Rawls' theory of justice (1971) is particularly germane, notably because of his notion of 'social primary goods'. For Rawls, these are goods which people need if they are to achieve a good life (and which are distributed through social institutions). Rawls argues that a just, or fair, level of access to social primary goods would be ensured if they were to be allocated as if everyone had chosen the principle for allocation as if 'behind a veil of ignorance' (Rawls 1971: 12). That is, by choosing a principle for the allocation of finite resources as we would if none of us knew:

> his [sic] place in society, his class position or social status, nor does any one know his fortune in the distribution of natural assets and abilities, his intelligence, strength and the like ... The principles of justice are chosen behind a veil of ignorance ... Since all are similarly situated and no one is able to design principles to favour his particular condition, the principles of justice are the result of a fair agreement or bargain.
>
> (Rawls 1971: 12)

Rawls' model recognises that we do not enter markets equally endowed, and that because some of us cannot signal our preferences through money as the medium of communication as strongly as can others, then we must have recourse to other signalling systems and allocative methods, notably politics, which better provide for justice. How then has politics defined the socially desirable outcomes that markets and competition may fail to deliver?

Social goals: connectivity and content

The social goals sought through regulation of the media and communications sectors can be described as 'connectivity' and 'content'. Connectivity, to ensure that all have access at affordable prices to the communication systems necessary for full social participation. Content, to similarly ensure both that all have access at affordable prices to the information they require for full social participation *and* to ensure that they do *not* have access to information, to content, that society deems to be damaging.

Connectivity has usually been considered under the rubric of the Universal Service Obligation (USO) which is vested in/imposed on network operators and, characteristically, has three elements:

*   geography – ensuring that services are available even in locations which are unprofitable to serve;
*   poverty – ensuring that services are available at affordable prices, even to the poor;
*   disability – ensuring that the disabled are not excluded from access to and use of services.

Content considerations have led to regulation designed to *restrict* access to content that is deemed to be damaging either to the individuals using it or to others (because of the undesirable actions that may follow use of the information in question). This can be stated as regulation designed to minimise the negative externalities attached to particular content. Varying levels of access to restricted content – that is negative content regulation – may be arranged according to the age, sex or professional status of users:

- taste and decency;
- violence;
- information likely to lead to crime or public disorder.

Content considerations have led to regulation designed to *promote* access to content that is deemed to be beneficial, to maximise the positive externalities attached to the information in question, i.e. positive content regulation:

- national content;
- quality;
- diversity;
- pluralism;
- information for political decision-making and participation;
- merit goods.

The extensive interrelated technological, commercial and policy changes to regulated media and communications sectors have led to review of both the substance and the means of regulation for content and connectivity. In both telecommunications and broadcasting there has been a shift of paradigms. Consider the differences between what we might call a 'Mark I' and a 'Mark II' model of regulation in each of the telecommunications and broadcasting sectors.

Telecommunications

The telecom model Mark I ensured universal (geographical) service at equalised (affordable) prices via cross subsidy undertaken by a monopoly (usually publicly owned). It was replaced by the telecom model Mark II where competition has shrunk the universal service obligation in voice telephony (at least when a mature built-out network exists) and where universal service at affordable prices is available under stand-alone costing.

Nonetheless, in spite of the very striking successes of the Mark II model in reducing the need for intervention to secure goals often imagined to be unachievable short of regulatory whip-cracking (e.g. in provision of public call boxes, extension of service to the previously untelephoned), some regulation continues to be required beyond that necessary for a well-functioning competitive market to operate: for example, to maintain the network externality and fulfil social – USO – obligations to the poor ('lifeline' service), the disabled (textphone), access to emergency services, etc.

However, changing patterns of connectivity demand reconsideration of the content and character of the USO. Should it be confined to voice telephony or, for example, should it be defined as a broadband digital line to every home at affordable prices? Because those with access to the basic infrastructure of a computer and a telephone line (and who have the skills to navigate the system) enjoy unprecedented possibilities of interrogating new information, participating in virtual communities, and in authoring new works, we may anticipate redefinition of the USO so that affordable access to broadband intelligent interactive networks is a prerogative of all.

Broadcasting

The European broadcasting model Mark I provided universal (geographical and content for all tastes and interests) service free at the point of use through a publicly owned monopoly. The broadcasting model Mark II permitted limited entry of licensed commercial broadcasters who, as conditions of licence, provided geographical universality of service and fulfilled positive and negative programming requirements (i.e. less sex and violence, more children's programming and news and current affairs than profit-maximising commercial services would offer).

In broadcasting, as in telecommunications, liberalisation and the growth of competition have realised striking benefits. But they have also put in question the established instruments through which social goals have been achieved. Satellite and cable television channels and establishment of a plethora of new commercial radio services have benefited consumers by extending choice and stimulating incumbents to tailor their programmes more closely to viewer and listener preferences. But regulation is still required to ensure that the plurality of information sources required by a healthy polity is available to all at affordable cost. Regulation must inhibit concentration of ownership; ensure that both 'positive programming requirements' and 'negative programming requirements' (the ITC's terms) are delivered; and ensure that services are available to all at affordable cost.

Positive programming requirements ensure that 'merit goods' – such as comprehensive, reliable and well-researched news, information and education programmes, innovatory drama, arts and music, programmes for economically powerless groups, and so on, which would not be provided in sufficient quantities by profit maximising commercial broadcasters – are supplied free at the point of use. Negative programming requirements are to inhibit the circulation of offensive material, misleading information, reckless claims in advertising and product promotion and so on. Positive programming has been achieved by public sector provision and by conditions in the licenses of commercial terrestrial broadcasters.

But new technologies (satellites and, soon, video via the Internet)[2] mean that the conditions under which social obligations were discharged, under both broadcasting Mark I and Mark II regimes, no longer obtain. Governments can no longer control entry to broadcasting markets and thus neither regulatory model remains viable. Just as in telecommunications, a Mark III regime is required. For each, hitherto separate, domain of telecommunications and broadcasting, the new regulatory paradigm, the Mark III paradigm, is an integrated 'converged' paradigm which unifies content and connectivity considerations.

Internet regulation – broadcasting and telecommunications Mark III

Internet regulation focuses the issues sharply. If, as Werbach suggests, the Internet is 'substitutable for all existing media' (Werbach 1997) then any regulatory provisions made, either for broadcasting or telecommunications, can be 'end run' by service providers using the Internet. Hyperbolic though this proposition may be, it conveniently identifies the scale of the challenge facing policy-makers, a challenge which the UK House of Commons Select Committee on Culture, Media and Sport acknowledged when stating that 'the Internet will become increasingly a platform for audio-visual content barely distinguishable from broadcast content' (House of Commons 1998: 520–I, para. 114).

Access to the Internet, and thus to the cornucopia of content considered by the Select Committee, is clearly a matter both of the availability of appropriate infrastructure (a suitable terminal, network and Internet service provider access) at affordable prices. But networks and infrastructure at affordable prices will not ensure effective participation. Citizens will need keyboarding skills and a level of computer literacy, as well as access to telecommunication services – however defined – if participation is to be real. Accordingly, the universal service obligation of the future, a Mark III model of regulation, is likely to include both affordable access to infrastructure and competence in the skills required for its use.

However, Internet content regulation, and thus the realisation of content social goals, poses distinctive challenges. These[3] resolve into the following list of difficult issues – difficult because of the problems of extraterritoriality and exercise of jurisdiction:

- 'negative' content regulation – how to stop unlawful and/or offensive material;
- 'positive' content regulation – how to ensure provision of beneficial material;
- allocation and regulation of Internet domain names and addresses – a problem similar to those associated with telephone numbering (portability, control of numbering, giving competitive advantage, etc.);
- the substitution of Internet content 'caches' and 'mirror sites' for transmission capacity means that distinctions between content and carriage provider are difficult to make;
- balancing consumer and producer interests in intellectual property accessed over the Internet;
- protecting consumers from fraud and other forms of misrepresentation, ensuring consumers are able to achieve adequate redress in the case of dissatisfaction.

This is not the place for an exhaustive discussion of possible strategies to address these problems, only to signal both that competition has not, and will not, fulfil all social goals in communications, and that an integrated approach drawing on telecommunications and broadcasting precedents is likely to be required.[4]

Conclusion

The composition and extent of social obligations which societies seek to deliver through communications regulation, i.e. the USO, will differ from time to time and from place to place. What one society identifies as essential another may see as trivial, but the following normative definition may provide a helpful general formulation:

> The universal service obligation for media and communications should be defined as universal access at affordable cost to the information and services necessary to participate fully in economic, social and political life.

However, globalisation, and the increasing sharing of sovereignty which accompanies it, means that inter-societal value differences of this kind will become less and less sustainable. Further, technological change, as shown above, makes achievement of whatever social goals a society, or societies, may define more and more difficult, if sought through established policy and regulatory instruments. The USO in content and connectivity is likely to remain a live regulatory issue even though both the contents of a USO basket and the means to deliver it have changed.

Notes

1 Broadly defined including cable, webcasting and other hybridised forms of electronic content delivery.
2 BBC Television's *Nine O'Clock News* is available via the Internet throughout the world (Birt 1999: 124).
3 See Australian Broadcasting Authority 1997 for a comparative study of Australia, Malaysia, Singapore and UK Internet content regulation.
4 See OFTEL 1997a for a well-worked-out model and ITC 2000 for evidence suggesting public tolerance for a self-regulatory Internet negative content regime (one of the key OFTEL propositions).

7 Commentary

When to regulate in the GIS? A public policy perspective

Fod Barnes

What fundamental rules are needed for the information economy?

There are contrasting views on what is required, from governments, producers and even consumers, for the new information economy (or the e-economy) to 'take off', and to deliver the 'best' outcome. The range of views is sufficiently different (see other chapters in this book, for example) to indicate that there is no general agreement as to what the problem is, rather than just being alternative approaches to the same problem. This chapter, based on the experience of being at the centre of regulating the UK telecommunications industry for nine years, is an attempt to better define the fundamental problem(s) that exist now (and are likely to persist), before going on to suggest where the solutions may lie.

Other chapters deal with the detail of what regulation is, or is not, needed – see for example the chapter by Richard Collins. My purpose is not to deal with the detail but, if possible, with the big (economic) picture. At best, the big picture may (with some more work) create the framework for resolving some of the apparent contradictions and disagreements in the detail. At a minimum it should create a framework that is capable of being shot down, and therefore improved.

There are three main issues I wish to deal with in this chapter:

- What are the really important characteristics of convergence?
- How do they change the underlying economic problems of (tele)communications?
- What does that mean for the proper 'regulation' of communications?

Not understanding the wood for the trees

But first it is necessary to dispose of a small problem of language: 'regulation', and hence 'deregulation', 'liberalisation' and 're-regulation' are politically charged terms, and mean very different things to different people. 'Regulation' is also often contrasted to 'competition' as if they were more or less mutually exclusive – which ignores probably the most important developments in telecommunications, *regulation for competition*. To try to avoid purely semantic disagreements

I am going to use the term 'rules', by which I mean the rules that producers need to conform to if they wish to operate commercially in the markets being discussed.

Where to start

To keep the analysis manageable this chapter takes the old world of telecommunications and broadcasting, including their respective rules, as a given, and concentrates on the implications of the changes (or lack of them) that convergence brings. This, however, should not be taken to imply that in the past we had the right set of rules.

What is changing?

The Internet changes everything – or does it?

It is often said (including elsewhere in this book) that the Internet changes everything. It certainly changes many things, and enables *services* that could not be economically provided in the past. But I am not so sure that, in terms of *economic regulation and competition* issues, the change is that profound. Indeed, the technical changes and developments that have enabled the creation of the Internet infrastructure (and hence the services run over it) may have made matters worse (or at least more complicated).

Traditionally telecommunication networks (of the 'voice telephony' kind) provided two services to customers – a transmission path (of limited bandwidth but unlimited capacity) and a *control* function, which (save for the odd wrong number) allowed the person making the call to direct that transmission path to a specific destination. This formed a single pair of points between which communication could place. Add a (relatively simple) telephone at each end, with the *network* specifying the technical characteristics of the telephone, and a telephone conversation could take place. (Note: these networks did not, strictly speaking, provide the service of voice telephony – that was provided by the caller and callee.) The bundle of transmission and control defined the service, and was provided by the same organisation.

Traditional broadcasting networks, in contrast, provided a transmission path (of much higher bandwidth, but severely limited capacity) and content, but no real control. The network again defines the technical specification of the customers' equipment. The bundle of transmission and content defined the service, and was provided by the same organisation. Indeed, although broadcasters like to see themselves as being defined by their content, historically it has actually been access to the transmission capacity that has been the crucial definition of any particular broadcaster.

To complete the convergence picture, the IT industry has traditionally provided content, but not (at least public) transmission capacity (and, therefore, control has not been an issue). There has been no guarantee of interoperability (or, indeed, operability).

What convergence is doing is breaking down these neat bundles – or, to be precise, what technical innovation is doing is changing these relationships, *the result of which is convergence*. The 'fully converged' network would provide high (apparent) bandwidth, would not be capacity constrained, delivers content, and would have good control. The Internet is moving in that direction, but so is digital satellite broadcasting (especially when bridged with a limited return path) and digital cable (in the case of cable and satellite, not because they are digital, but because they have good control – conditional access – systems).

There is no doubt that these changes are significant, but perhaps not quite in the way those who believe that the 'Internet changes everything' have in mind.

In my view the most significant implication of these developments is the breaking of the link between the telecommunications infrastructure and the service delivered over that infrastructure. This significance arises from two different impacts:

• Most existing rule sets are based on an implicit assumption that there is a one-to-one correspondence between the service and the network.
• Significant economies of scope across different economic markets arise, adding a further potential difficulty to making these markets work properly.

What are the economic implications of this change?

To understand the implications of the convergence, and the other technological developments, it is necessary to understand the characteristics of the existing systems and infrastructure. And in particular its economics. Unfortunately, a lot of the economics is hidden by the special rules that have been applied to this sector and, quite frankly, a lack of the normal information you would expect producers to collect. In addition, familiarity has made it more difficult to see the wood for the trees.

But generally speaking, looking backwards, (tele)communications networks have had the following characteristics set out in Table 7.1 (telephony) and Table 7.2 (broadcasting).

A considerable part of the resulting regulation of these two types of (tele)communication networks and services is 'justified' by the problems caused by a number of these economic characteristics:

• *Economies of density* mean that multiple provision at any one location is likely to be expensive and unstable. Where such economies are exhausted there may be limited multiple suppliers, but the threat of ongoing new entry is low.
• *Network effects* better than linear mean that a big network is 'worth' more than two little ones or, more realistically, a big network has market power in relation to a small network greater than the difference in size.

Table 7.1 Characteristics of fixed, switched telecommunications networks

Network part or operation	Economic implications
Local distribution networks (to the first point of switching)	Economies of density
Inter-switch distribution	Economies of route density and (limited) economies of scale
Network effects	Better than linear
Edge-to-centre interoperability	Relatively simple, fairly standardised across the world
Edge-to-edge interoperability	Simple (voice telephony) made interoperable by network translation. Fairly simple (fax), international standardisation
Bandwidth	Low
Capacity	Unlimited
Fixed costs (network)	High
Variable costs (network)	Low
Services	Voice telephony, then fax
Underlying service	Symmetric, controlled (addressable), unlimited connectivity, low bandwidth, transmission path

- *Edge-to-edge interoperability* means that a system is 'better' just because it has more users, not because it delivers better service.
- *Low variable costs/high fixed costs* mean that price discrimination is potentially welfare enhancing and the ability to price discriminate may determine producer success. (It may also be anti-competitive and 'unfair'.)

Looking forward, these problems can be mapped on to 'converged' networks:

- Convergence does nothing about the economies of *density*. If problems exist now, they will continue.
- *Network effects* increase. Compared to two-way point to point services (i.e. telephone network), two-way point to multi-point services (or multi-point to multi-point) have an even greater increase in the number of different transmission path patterns that are possible as the number of connected users increase, thus making big even better than small.
- The increasing complexity (i.e. telephone compared to PC, TV compared to TV plus set top box) of the services requiring *edge-to-edge interoperability* makes interoperability more difficult to achieve. This combines with the network effect of connection, making big classes of interoperating entities 'better' than small ones.

Table 7.2   Characteristics of unswitched telecommunications networks (broadcasting networks)

Network part or operation	Economic implications
Distribution networks	Economies of density
Network effects	Linear
Edge-to-centre interoperability	Complex, standardised by system and service (TV – country, radio – world-wide)
Edge-to-edge interoperability	None
Bandwidth	High
Capacity	Low
Fixed costs (network)	High
Variable costs (network)	Very low
Fixed costs (content)	High
Variable costs of continued production	High
Variable costs of consumption	Zero
Services	One way, broadcast 'entertainment'
Underlying service	Asymmetric (one-way), uncontrolled, restricted connectivity, high bandwidth transmission path

- If anything, convergence makes the problem of *high fixed costs/low variable costs* worse. As more services can be delivered electronically more services will use infrastructure with this cost characteristic. In addition, the *potential* for price discrimination is increasing, because of improvements in the control technology. This increases the competitive advantage of those suppliers who can, effectively, price discriminate. This advantage may be both legitimate (welfare enhancing) and non-legitimate (anti-competitive).

There is also a very important, second-order effect of the increasing scope of the services that can be delivered over the same infrastructure. Existing *regulation* tends to be based on an assumption that there is a one-to-one correspondence between the network (or system) and service. Thus broadcasting regulation identifies a 'broadcaster' with a system and, ultimately, uses the sanction that it will take away access to the system if the broadcaster misbehaves. Controls on telephone services assumed that the operator of the network 'knew' what end service was being delivered. The more the same system delivers different services, the less this is the case. The result is that existing regulation fails to work as expected, or at all. Depending on one's view of the need for rules, this is either a good thing or a bad thing. My view is that this regulatory failure will be exploited extremely efficiently by the powerful commercial forces now interested in convergence. Given the potential market failures I have identified, their interests may not coincide with those of society at large.

At this point in the analysis it is legitimate to ask the question: 'If convergence makes things worse, how come the actual impact of the Internet has been to make things better?'

I think there are two parts to the answer. The first part is that, with my definition of rules, the Internet is not, at present, 'unregulated'. Indeed, the Internet has been the beneficiary of a lot of 'special' rules that have given it a competitive advantage over other forms of activity, including 'old-fashioned' voice telephony. The differential application of access charges in the USA to two ways of achieving the same service – in this case a transmission path between a pair of terminals across a reasonable distance – gives the Internet a price advantage, without there necessarily being a cost advantage. It has also been subject to 'special rules' in the way the US government provided the backbone network and other crucial inputs like domain names. Therefore, the Internet has not been, and is still not, an 'unregulated' activity.

The second reason why, so far, the Internet has made things better, and not worse, is because it used to be considered a commercial irrelevance by the existing powerful players. Those people dealing with the interoperability problems, standards setting, interconnection pricing, etc., were not primarily, if at all, motivated by maximising the profitability of their bit of the action. This is no longer true. The past development of the Internet is, I believe, a very bad indicator of what will happen in the future. And looking at other manifestations of convergence which are, or were, really 'unregulated', the message is the same – these systems create significant market power, and producers will attempt to exploit it at the expense of consumers.

What needs to be done?

The answer is not to turn the clock back. The future is different. But it is possible to learn from the past. Many of the *underlying* problems of (tele)communication networks and services have not gone away, so there will be a number of points in the production chain where there are only a few suppliers: local access networks and conditional access systems, to name but two.

Given few suppliers and multiple services supplied through these bottlenecks, we need to develop a set of rules for access that maximises consumer benefit (in both a narrow and wider sense). This is probably some combination of a 'no anti-competitive price discrimination' rule and rules on access to the technical interfaces.

The price discrimination rule is particularly difficult. The high fixed costs/low variable costs means that uniform prices are likely to be significantly economically inefficient. But finding a methodology that allows welfare-enhancing price discrimination while catching anti-competitive price discrimination is, to say the least, difficult.

In addition, if suppliers are vertically integrated across both a bottleneck and other, non-bottleneck layers in the production chain – say, both conditional access and programme production – a non-discrimination rule applied to access to the problematic layer (i.e. the one with very few suppliers, or one supplier) always has to have a no cross-subsidy rule to go with it. This type of rule is also difficult to put into practice. (Indeed, under some circumstances, vertical separation might be the only practical answer.)

The technical interfaces are themselves far from easy to define, and do not stay put – as Microsoft likes to claim. There is also no doubt that requiring certain forms of technical interface will, at least in theory, reduce the range of possible services/products that can be produced. It may also constrain service quality and ease of use.

There is also a problem of current IPR law. Opening an interface to non-discriminatory access will (usually) require access to IPR as currently defined, and although the trumping of intellectual property rights by competition law (or regulation) does take place under some circumstances, this is rare and would need to be made more certain if it is to be widely used in this way.

So the costs of applying even simple rules that would tend to maximise competition within the various parts of the system as it develops could be high – but so are the potential benefits. The successful 'ring fencing' of the problematic layers in the vertical chain should allow competition to operate normally in the non-problematic layers. If this works, no special rules should apply in these layers.

Simple analysis, difficult solution

But even just applying a 'non-discrimination' rule to bottlenecks and requiring access to technical interfaces into and out of the bottleneck raises quite fundamental issues about what competition law and IPR are for. And here there may be an intellectual problem as well. To the extent that there is a substantive difference between competition law and regulation, it is in the type of market failure that they are designed to address. Competition law addresses market power that is 'unnatural', and looks for solutions that return the market to a competitive position. Economic regulation typically deals with natural monopolies, where customers did not get a choice. The problematic market structures that are emerging in the vertical layers within convergence are not 'monopolies' in the traditional sense, but nor is the creation of market power 'unnatural'. How to deal with these areas of activity in ways that maximise the long-term interests of consumers is, as far as I know, not worked out. Whether the rules that do emerge flow from developments in competition law or developments in regulation is a second-order issue. What the content of these rules should be is by far the most important issue to resolve.

And to do this requires someone to define what the objective is. Complex trade-offs are needed. For example, there will almost certainly be a trade-off between maximising the (static) economic efficiency of allowing vertical integration between a 'problematic' and 'non-problematic' layer – because this allows efficient price discrimination – and non-discriminatory access to the problematic layer – which is likely to maximise dynamic efficiency through increased competition in the non-problematic layer. There is also clearly a trade-off between allowing maximum exploitation of novel inventions – which increases the incentives to 'invent' – and the resultant economic inefficiency because prices are considerably higher than costs. And there may also be a countervailing increase in the scope for innovation in non-problem layers if access to the problem layers is open. For example, locking in the Internet browser to the operating system of a PC may increase the returns to the owner of the operating system's IPR, but reduce the scope for innovation in browsers (as, in effect, only one company can produce them, and it faces no effective competition).

Even if it was accepted that the balance between incentive to invent and free exploitation of ideas had, in the past, been set optimally by IPR law, and even if it is accepted that competition law was 'optimal' for the 'old' economy, it is not obvious that this balance would be right for the 'new' Internet/converged economy. Indeed, for the reasons outlined above – increased network effects, increased economies of scope, more services with very low marginal costs, etc., the *a priori* answer would be that they are not.

More importantly, the debate about what the rules should be trying to achieve, at this fundamental level, does not seem to be taking place. More often the debate concerns which of the 'old' structures should be applied, when actually something rather fundamentally new is needed. Those with an interest in ensuring the maximisation of long-term consumer welfare – which is, after all, the objective of a properly competitive market – do not seem to be engaged in the debate of what these new rules should look like. The running is being made by those whose interests (quite properly) are much more narrowly focused – namely the maximisation of profit both within and (less legitimately) outside the *existing* rules of the market.

Conclusion

The Internet (convergence) does change things, but not in a way that brings the characteristics of these activities into the mainstream economy. The old, special rules, applied to both broadcasting and telecommunications, are not sufficient for the new world – but it is unlikely that normal competition law or, indeed, existing information law, is adequate either. A much more fundamental review – a political review – of what should happen, given the characteristics of the new world, is needed if society is to gain maximum benefit from the technical potential of the Internet and related, convergent, technologies.

8 The rise and decline of the international telecommunications regime*

William J. Drake

International telecommunications is an issue-area in which multilateral cooperation is very deeply institutionalized. Long before governments recognized a need
to establish international mechanisms to manage global problems like trade,
human rights or the environment, they saw that nation-states could only benefit
from the possibilities of international telecommunications if there were shared
rules of the game governing how national networks would interconnect and
messages would be passed from one to the next. In consequence, the international telecommunications regime is the oldest multilateral regime in the world,
and the International Telecommunication Union (ITU) – which has historically
been the central forum for its negotiation – is the oldest intergovernmental organization in the world.

The telecommunications regime comprises the principles, norms, rules and
decision-making procedures that governments have agreed to govern the organization of international networks and services.[1] This chapter explores its
historical development, transformation, and contemporary decay. For 135 years,
governments have cooperated in the ITU and its predecessor, the International
Telegraph Union, to maintain a regime based on the overarching principles of
national sovereignty, network interconnection and joint service provisioning. This
framework allowed national carriers to slowly evolve a global network of
national networks while protecting themselves from competitive market forces.

In the post-World War II era, the progressive internationalization of pressures
unleashed by the United States' information control revolution fundamentally
redefined the policy environment. In particular, new technological opportunities
created by the merging of telecommunications, computing and microelectronics
provided large corporations – especially users of systems and services – with new
incentives to put pressure on governments for market liberalization at both the
national and multilateral levels. In parallel, the slow but steady spread of new
ideas about the role of telecommunications in an information-based economy
and its optimal governance encouraged governments, first in the industrialized
world and later in the developing world, to rethink the case for liberalization in a
more accommodating light.

From the mid-1970s to the mid-1980s, the asymmetric international spread of
these corporate pressures and new ideas generated substantial conflict between

pro-liberalization and pro-monopoly governments, especially within the industrialized world. But from 1988 to 1997, the once steadfast opposition to liberalization and commercialization collapsed, and governments renegotiated the regime's major instruments to facilitate a far-reaching shift towards a market-based and more privately controlled global order. Moreover, even where the regime's instruments were not formally altered, they were inter-subjectively understood in a very different way from what prevailed in the past. The cumulative result of these formal and informal shifts was a fundamental transformation in the social purposes, instruments, and meaning of the international telecommunications regime.[2]

But even with this relaxation of old regulatory approaches and accommodation of market demands, the regime has come under further pressure since 1998. The growing influence of the new trade in services regime negotiated in the World Trade Organization (WTO), the rise of the Internet, the spread of so-called "new modes of operation" that de-couple market behavior from multilateral disciplines, and the declining compliance of key member states – especially the United States – have thrown the world's oldest regime into a state of creeping decay. Indeed, in a privatized and liberalized global telecommunications market, the telecommunications regime is increasingly irrelevant and ignored by the major players. To the extent that multilateral telecommunications rules will be needed in the new global information economy, they will be provided by the WTO and other trade institutions and a diverse range of private sector-led standards bodies, and not in the ITU.

Development of the *ancien régime*

The organizational landscape

Evolution of the ITU

In the decade following the telegraph's invention in 1837, a number of early adopting countries entered into bilateral commercial treaties that included rudimentary provisions on the organization of their international telegraphic correspondence. Some of these provisions influenced the design of the Treaty of Dresden of 1850, which joined together Austria, Prussia, Bavaria and Saxony in the Austro-German Telegraph Union. In 1855, Belgium, France, Sardinia, Spain and Switzerland formed the West European Telegraph Union along essentially the same lines. After several years of coordination between the two groups, that included three formal inter-organizational agreements, these governments recognized that a single multilateral framework with a broader membership could reduce the transaction costs involved in establishing connections and promoting the orderly expansion of international communications.

Hence, in 1865, Napoleon III invited twenty European governments to Paris to create what would become the world's first formal international organization – the International Telegraph Union. The Treaty of Paris comprised a

Convention that laid out the political principles governing telegraph relations between members, and an annexed set of Regulations that established more detailed guidelines for the technical and economic organization of international networks and services. The Convention was intended to be revised by Diplomatic or Plenipotentiary Conferences only occasionally as circumstances warranted, while in 1875 it was decided that the Regulations could be revised by separate Administrative Conferences more frequently in light of technological progress and the growth of international correspondence. Governments designated their national telecommunications administrations to serve as their representatives in these conferences, which became the ITU's key decision-making forums. This dual-track treaty system, involving separately negotiated Conventions and Regulations, is still with us today.

Three other organizational features of the ITU are relevant here: first, in 1868, a permanent Bureau was established at Berne, Switzerland, to serve as an information conduit between members. Second, in 1906, twenty-nine governments met in Berlin to sign a Convention creating a separate International Radiotelegraph Union (IRU) to facilitate the management of the international frequency spectrum. For reasons of economy, the Berne Bureau was tasked with serving as the IRU's organizational center. In addition, the principles, norms, rules and decision-making procedures established by this convention constituted the creation of an international radio regime, which has existed separately from but loosely linked with the international telecommunications regime ever since.[3]

Third, in light of the increasing complexity of the developing technology, ITU members came to see a need for technical standards and operational procedures that were more detailed than would be necessary to include in the treaty instruments, and that would need to be revised more frequently than was possible by the periodic Diplomatic and Administrative Conferences. Accordingly, in 1924, 1926, and 1927 respectively, these governments created the International Consultative Committee on Telephone (CCIF), the International Consultative Committee on Telegraph (CCIT), and the International Consultative Committee on Radio (CCIR).[4] The committees were coordinated with but legally separate from the ITU, and adopted technical standards in the form of voluntary Recommendations. While they were not treaty instruments, in later years the Regulations routinely specified that ITU members should follow the Recommendations whenever possible, which created some ambiguity about their precise legal status. In any event, it is widely believed that most administrations generally did comply with the Recommendations most of the time.

With the accession of many new members from outside Europe and the increasing interrelation of telegraph, telephone, and radio issues, governments began to debate the merits of managing all international electrical communications issues within a single, broad-based multilateral organization. After several failed attempts in the early 1920s, at Madrid in 1932 they finally succeeded in merging the telegraph and radio unions to form the International *Telecommunication* Union. In parallel, the Berne Bureau was transformed into a more substantial permanent secretariat headed by an elected Secretary General.

And with the growing importance of telephony and the distinctive issues it raised, henceforth separate Regulations would be devised for telephone and telegraph networks and services.

At Atlantic City in 1947, the ITU was brought into the new United Nations system and restructured, with new organs added to deal with radio matters. The Berne Bureau was replaced by a permanent secretariat in Geneva, the three consultative committees were formally brought into the new organization, and an Administrative Council was created to meet annually to oversee organizational management and, at times, consider substantive policy issues.[5] Henceforth, the Administrative Conferences were to be called World Administrative Telegraph and Telephone Conferences (WATTCs). Organizational coherence was increased in 1956, when the CCIF and CCIT were merged to create the Consultative Committee on International Telegraph and Telephone (CCITT).

(While this section of the chapter is concerned with the *ancien régime* that lasted until 1988, on the subject of organizational matters it is worth noting additional changes made in the 1990s. The 1992 Plenipotentiary Conference revamped the ITU into a tripartite organization comprising a Telecommunication Standardization Sector, a Radiocommunication Sector, and a Development Sector. The first of these, which is commonly referred to as ITU–T, encompasses the CCITT's study groups and its Plenary Assemblies (now called World Telecommunication Standardization Assemblies) as well as a business Advisory Council. Moreover, the WATTCs are now World Conferences on International Telecommunications (WCIT), although one has yet to be held. And after decades of debate, the Convention was finally split into two, so that there is now a Constitution pertaining to the fundamentals of the ITU organizational operation and a Convention dealing with broad policy matters.)

In sum, the above narrative lays out in highly compressed form the main steps in the evolution of the ITU. The relationship between the relevant ITU organs and the telecommunications regime instruments they devise is depicted in Table 8.1. Against this backdrop, we can now consider the ways in which power was exercised in the ITU to shape the *ancien régime*.

Power dynamics

The international telecommunications regime has lasted for a century and a half, which makes it the world's most long-running multilateral institution. To what should we attribute this durability? The official story told by the ITU is that this is a testament to the functional necessity of international communications and the technocratically rational, engineering approach to problem-solving practiced in ITU bodies. Indeed, the ITU has traditionally characterized itself as a "technical" rather than "political" organization. There is something to the first of these claims, although it by no means tells the whole story, but the second claim is dubious. As with any other international institution, the ITU's activities always have been shaped by the power and interests of nation-states and have involved "political" calculations and negotiations. It is simply that despite any

Table 8.1

ITU bodies involved in telecommunications regime matters	Telecommunications regime instruments
Diplomatic or plenipotentiary conferences	Convention; from 1992, Constitution and Convention (binding treaties containing overarching principles and norms governing relations between members and the operations of the ITU organization)
Administrative Conferences (1865–1947), WATTCs (1947–92), World Conferences on International Telecommunications (1992–present)	Telegraph and Telephone Regulations; from 1988, renamed the International Telecommunication Regulations (binding treaties containing more elaborate principles and norms governing the organization of networks and services in light of the Convention's mandate)
CCIF/CCIT (1920s–56), CCITT (1956–92), ITU–T (1992–present)	Telegraph and Telephone Recommendations; from 1992, International Telecommunication Recommendations (non-binding guidelines containing detailed rules – technical standards and regulatory injunctions – operationalizing the higher order principles and norms)

disagreements they have had on specific issues, most states for most of the time had broadly symmetrical preferences on the fundamental architecture of international governance (a condition that, as we will see later, is evaporating today). To understand why this was so, we need to begin with the domestic sources of international objectives.

The European countries that created the regime generally had government Ministries of Posts, Telegraphs, and Telephones (PTTs) serving as monopoly or near-monopoly providers of their domestic and international telecommunications. The PTTs developed corporatist relationships with various social constituencies that supported them, including equipment manufacturers, labor unions, political parties, and residential consumers – a nexus Eli Noam has aptly labeled the "postal industrial complex."[6] The most important exception to this pattern concerned intercontinental connections, on which private cable companies (especially from the United Kingdom) predominated until the post-World War II period. In many cases states took control of the technology at the outset, while in a few others they attained their monopolies post hoc through the nationalization of private carriers. While some contemporary scholars have ascribed this state control to mere rent-seeking by greedy governments, the reasons were more complex and included a mix of national security, economic, social, and conceptual justifications that policy-makers and others considered to be perfectly valid at the time.[7] The European approach was also pursued by other industrialized countries like Japan and Australia, although Canada opted for a unique mixture of provincial government monopolies and regulated private firms.

In parallel, the telecommunications administrations of European colonies in

Asia, Africa, and the Middle East generally were branches or affiliates of the European PTTs. Notable exceptions to this pattern included the Caribbean islands and Hong Kong, where the British firm Cable & Wireless served as a private monopolist. After attaining their independence, these developing countries usually nationalized their telecommunication systems and established PTTs that operated along the same lines (albeit with far fewer resources) as their European counterparts. In contrast, Latin-American countries, which gained their freedom from colonialism early in the nineteenth century, often gave private monopoly concessions for their international connections to foreign firms like International Telegraph and Telephone (IT&T). But in the twentieth century, they too went the PTT route through nationalization.

The developing country majority had little independent influence on the *ancien régime*. The colonial administrations were given voting rights in ITU bodies until the United States successfully insisted on ending the practice at the 1947 Atlantic City conferences. In the plenipotentiaries, WATTCs, and their antecedents, the colonial and later post-colonial PTTs essentially followed the European agenda on regime issues, since the principles and norms contained in the Convention and Regulations generally served their monopoly interests as well. And the developing countries had even less influence on the regime-related agenda in the consultative committees, in which they lacked the technical expertise, resources, and direct stakes of the industrialized countries. Indeed, to the extent that developing countries even sent representatives to the meetings, these were often staff from their Geneva consulates who just showed up to pick up the documents and send them back to their national capitals.

While some countries and colonial territories had private national carriers at various times (especially during the nineteenth century), generally this was before they joined the ITU. No accident here; the European PTTs used other states' functional incentives to join to socialize newcomers into the ways of their club. For example, in the telegraph union of 1865–1932, "Nationalization or complete control over telegraph was always an unwritten prerequisite for membership."[8] In consequence, even the United Kingdom was not admitted until after it nationalized its telegraph system. Moreover, in countries that retained private national carriers longer and joined the new ITU after 1932, typically these firms had monopolies or near-monopolies which brought their preferences broadly into line with those of the PTTs. In short, while a global generalization inevitably does not capture all the local variations over time, it is reasonable to say that for much of the *ancien régime*'s reign, the overwhelming majority of ITU members had monopolies, especially government monopolies, and that this created a strong and nearly universal symmetry of interests regarding the type of international order they preferred.

The United States represented by far the most significant divergence from the growth of state control. This was in keeping with the wider pattern of American exceptionalism – little soccer and socialism, no PTT. The United States opted for private carriers and went through cycles of competition and industry concentration until after World War I, when the American Telegraph and Telephone

Company (AT&T) consolidated its power as a near-monopolist in most markets, a process which the federal government encouraged. The partnership between AT&T and the government deepened after the Communications Act of 1934 created the Federal Communications Commission (FCC) and the first semi-coherent national policy framework for telecommunications. AT&T reigned supreme on international voice routes alongside a handful of international record carriers that had entered the market earlier to provide telegraph and, later, telex services.

What is especially noteworthy here is that the United States (along with Canada and some Latin-American countries) never joined the telegraph union because it did not want to nationalize or impose treaty obligations on its private carriers. Indeed, the government claimed it had no constitutional authority with which to so do, and sometimes displayed a certain hostility towards the telegraph union. Nevertheless, with the burgeoning growth of international traffic and a strong desire to secure frequency spectrum allocations under the international radio regime, the United States did see its way to join in launching the new telecommunication union in 1932. Given the ITU members' desire to bring the American market into the multilateral framework, the United States was able to exact a number of concessions to its interests in exchange for joining.

In general, the US government was not a key player until late in the *ancien régime*. After all, the United States did not join the ITU for the first sixty-seven years of its existence, when the fundamentals of the regime were put in place. After joining in 1932, the US government spent much of its time in meetings arguing – often alone and unsuccessfully – against key elements of the PTT's agenda, which caused persistent consternation among its counterparts. The government exercised influence largely by saying no and trying to limit the application to US carriers of what it saw as excessively regulatory obligations. For example, the United States did not sign the International Telegraph Regulations and the International Telephone Regulations until 1949 and 1973, respectively, and even then took a number of important reservations. As one observer has concluded,

> These kinds of involvement appear to characterize what might be called the general, long-term approach of the US toward international telecommunication arrangements. It is a policy of minimizing the specificity of arrangements, diminishing the role of international organization, and effecting bilateral alternatives.[9]

This approach was in sharp contrast to the management of radio regime and organizational matters, on which the US government was much more active and influential.

What all this meant was that the European PTTs were the dominant governmental players on regime issues. Their control in the telegraph union era was absolute, and was only partially attenuated after the telecommunication union was launched and many new members joined. After all, since the vast majority of countries also had PTTs by this point, they shared in the Europeans' basic vision of a non-competitive global market that was split into a series of mutually exclusive monopoly jurisdictions. And the Europeans had the technical expertise and historical connections to provide leadership in setting the tone for the nearly worldwide PTT agenda. Hence, the ways in which issues could be defined had to map with their underlying material interests, technocratic organizational culture, and normative conceptions of how national correspondents should work together.

What about the influence of the private sector? In the nineteenth century, the vast majority of intercontinental submarine cables were controlled by a small cartel of private firms based largely in the United Kingdom.[10] Nevertheless, the PTTs were able to use their collective legal authority to bring these and subsequent corporate entrants into a uniform and predictable framework on their terms. The Rome conference of 1871 decided that henceforth private carriers would be admitted to participate without voting rights in all the administrative conferences (although they could "accede" to the treaties), and in consequence such meetings were sometimes animated by heated discussions of tariff and routing questions. But in the end, the cable companies had to go along with the PTTs if they wanted the landing rights and operating agreements needed to connect national markets, and they found financial benefits in having a stable and harmonized framework for handing off the expanding traffic and splitting the revenues with administrations.

At the birth of the telecommunication union in 1932, the United States insisted as part of its price for joining that the decision-making procedures be amended to ease the participation of countries with private carriers. Hence, the ITU developed the designation, "Recognized Private Operating Entity" (RPOA). To receive "recognition," a firm was bound to provide services to all customers on a non-discriminatory basis and be subject to the regime's instruments. This conferred upon RPOAs a measure of PTT-like "publicness," and in exchange for playing by the cartel rules they were granted the right to participate in the consultative committees and on government-led delegations to the treaty conferences.[11] On the other hand, they no longer could independently accede to the relevant treaties as had the cable companies of old.

As more and more countries nationalized their telecommunications systems in the first half of the twentieth century, the influence of RPOAs did not increase notably until the onset of liberalization in the 1980s. There were, however, exceptions, notably AT&T (which effectively determined US policy preferences) as well as Cable & Wireless and IT&T.[12] Even before the United States joined the organization in 1932, AT&T began to coordinate with its counterparts in the consultative committees, and its influence on technical standardization and operating procedures in particular grew steadily over the decades to follow. AT&T's centrality to trans-Atlantic communications, its technical prowess, and its status as a near-monopoly in the United States gave the European PTTs incentives to bend some of their preferences a bit to facilitate its active integration into the international system. Even so, where there was significant trans-Atlantic disagreement, notably on economic issues like tariffs, the European approach typically prevailed.

Other elements of the private sector had even less independent influence. Telecommunications equipment manufacturers could participate in the consultative committees' technical work in an advisory capacity as "Scientific and Industrial Organizations" (SIOs) and were important players on technical standardization matters, but they operated within the parameters set by the PTTs, who were their monopsony patrons. Organizations representing corporate users of telecommunications – e.g. the International Chamber of Commerce (ICC), the International Press Telecommunications Council (IPTC), and after 1974, the International Telecommunications Users' Group (INTUG) – also had advisory status in the consultative committees, but their persistent demands on matters like tariffs and the treatment of leased circuits were only partially and grudgingly accommodated by the PTTs until the 1980s.

In sum, then, power over the *ancien régime* was in the hands of a worldwide coalition of PTTs led by the Europeans. Not surprisingly, the substantive content of the regime reflected their largely symmetrical interests.

Regime attributes

The Treaty of Dresden that created the Austro-German Telegraph Union included, among other, the following principles:

Article 2   "… the provisions of the Union Treaty shall govern only international correspondence, namely, that telegraphic correspondence in which the originating and the terminal station belong to different Union administrations …"

Article 3   "Each government is at liberty to choose any system of transmission and equipment for its telegraph lines; accordingly, a message passing from one line to the other will normally be transferred at the point where the telegraph lines of two Union Governments meet …"

Article 6   "The use of the telegraphs of the Union Governments shall be open to all, without any exception. …"

Article 19   "The telegraph offices … are required to refuse to accept or transmit those private messages whose content offends against the laws or which are deemed to be unsuitable for communication on grounds of public good or morality."

Article 36   "The established transmission charge for each message shall, pending further agreement, be shared among those Union Governments."[13]

These key provisions also influenced the design of the West European Telegraph Union and were subsequently incorporated, with revisions and elaborations, into the 1865 Treaty of Paris that created the ITU. They have remained in place and defined the underlying foundations of the international telecommunications order ever since, even as the technological, economic, political, and conceptual fundamentals of global communications evolved and were ultimately transformed over the years. But as we will see later, what has changed of late is how these principles are interpreted, and the extent to which states and corporations actually comply with them.

As the Dresden text indicates, the *ancien régime* rested on three overarching principles, from which flowed over the years an increasingly wide range of other principles, norms and rules detailing how they were to be operationalized.

National sovereignty

As would be consistently reiterated in virtually all important ITU instruments in the years ahead, states retained absolute sovereign control over their telecommunications systems. The sovereignty principle had both internal and external dimensions. Internally, states could configure and govern their national networks and industries however they pleased as long as they played by the rules where international correspondence was concerned. Externally, international relations had to be conducted in accordance with the mutual consent of the countries involved.

Building on the Dresden precedent, the Convention and Regulations as revised over the years formalized subsidiary norms illustrating what sovereignty meant in operational terms. For example, while the right of citizens to engage in international communications was recognized, government messages were given transmission priority over private messages. Moreover, ITU members reserved the right to intercept, monitor, and stop particular transmissions that were deemed to threaten national security and public order, both of which could be defined however a government liked. Members also could suspend service on particular international routes for the same reasons. These measures extended territorial control into the realm of intangible, cross-border information flows.

But sovereignty had another meaning that would be less apparent by simply reading ITU instruments. The term was routinely invoked to justify practices that had the effect – and were widely understood to have the effect – of buttressing monopoly control in general and state monopoly control in particular. This played out in three ways. First, the fundamental political glue that held the system together was that ITU members agreed not to compete in each other's territories or undertake any other activity without the consent of the corresponding administration at the other end of the line. This not only precluded predatory behavior and distributional struggles between government administrations, but also applied to any private carriers located in a member's territory.

To clarify what this meant, the regime laid out quite elaborate operational rules for relations among members. But what if two administrations wanted to establish or allow private firms to create a bilateral relationship that deviated from the norm? This was possible under the provision for "special arrangements." The 1865 Convention held that, "The High Contracting Parties respectively reserve the right of making separately, between them, special arrangements of all kinds, on service points that are not of interest to the generality of States" including, *inter alia*, tariffs, equipment and special telegraph vocabularies.[14] Since then, this provision has served as a broad exemption from public service and related obligations to allow the development of new services prior to their full standardization, e.g. phototelegraphy, telex, automatic switching and leased circuits. It also made the participation of the United States easier to the extent that some of its carriers did not want to be "recognized," with all that entails.

Second, ITU members adopted a wide array of regime norms, rules, and decision-making procedures designed to control the activities of private international carriers. To this end, the Paris Convention of 1865 decreed that

> The High Contracting Parties pledge to impose, as far as possible, the rules of the present Convention on licensed terrestrial or submarine telegraph companies ... Not included, in any case, in the international tariff are ... The telegraphic bureaus of States and of private companies who have not to this point accepted the uniform regulatory dispositions and obligations of the present convention.[15]

Hence the PTTs took a dual approach to bringing such firms into compliance with the regime by generally imposing behavioral standards and by denying economic benefits to any *refuseniks*. The rules could not be imposed directly on non-signatory governments like the United States, but American-based carriers "were forced to transmit messages to the telegraph systems of other countries, [and so] were forced to accept the rules laid down by the Telegraph Union."[16]

Third, ITU members adopted parallel prescriptions and proscriptions to control the ways in which large corporate users of telecommunications like the airlines, banks, and news agencies could employ private leased circuits and networks. From the late nineteenth century onward, large corporations, first in North America and the United Kingdom and later in other countries, sought to have circuits set aside from the switched networks for their exclusive intra-organizational use. As direct foreign investment grew in the post-World War I era, a growing number of transnational corporations (TNCs) began to request the right to extend these circuits internationally in order to run their geographically dispersed operations. To ensure that such circuits were provided in an orderly manner that did not contradict existing arrangements or put administrations in a semi-competitive position in relation to one another, in 1927 the CCIF promulgated its landmark Recommendation No. 13, which laid down strict rules for the operation of international leased circuits. Among other things, the recommendation held that

> we have to avoid this rental causing discomfort in the general service or allowing abuse on the part of renters of circuits ... [hence] The stations so linked cannot in any case be stations normally made available to the public ... The conversations exchanged should concern exclusively the personal affairs of correspondents or those of their establishments. The lines cannot in any manner be made available to third parties.[17]

Already in 1927 we see a shared concern among PTTs that corporate circuits should in no way detract from the revenues of their regular public switched services, which led them to fix rather high tariffs on such circuits. Similarly, by stipulating that messages must directly pertain only to the business of the customer and that third-party access was prohibited, the Recommendation effectively banned the setting up of inter-corporate systems that might later evolve into a cream-skimming alternative to the public networks. Leased circuits were to be solely for intra-corporate messages, for example between a firm's home office and branch plants. In the 1930s, this language was amended to further require that any private equipment connected to the circuits be approved by the administrations at both ends and not be used in any fashion that was not explicitly provided for in the original contract. These provisions were paralleled by telegraph Recommendations adopted in the CCIT, and remained largely unchanged until the 1960s, when they became even more restrictive in some respects.

In a quasi-cartelized environment, Recommendation No. 13 and its successors meant that when corporate users sought to secure private leased circuits at low rates or use them in potentially problematic ways, the PTTs could say, in effect, "I'd like to help you, but I'm party to an international agreement which does not allow that – my hands are tied." Citing the imperative of uniform practices and the constraints of international consensus provided a rationale – albeit one that was undoubtedly transparent to the affected parties – for precluding the slightest competition and preserving PTT's mastery of their domains.

Joint service provision

The second overarching principle flowed from the first. If nations were to maintain sovereign control over mutually exclusive territorial domains, how could traffic flow from one self-contained system to the next? The answer was that services were to be "jointly provided." Under the joint service provisioning principle, outbound traffic moved to an imaginary halfway point between national networks and was then handed off to the inbound carrier for delivery and termination within its territory. The revenues from cross-border calls were to be shared by sending and receiving carriers, with a fixed amount going to any transit countries in between them. In short, end-to-end provisioning and competition was precluded unless two governments agreed on a "special arrangement."

Over the years, ITU members developed a number of methods for managing the division of revenues from joint services, and the relevant provisions in ITU instruments became progressively more elaborate and complex. Telegraph union members fixed terminal and transit charges in tables annexed to the treaties, indicating in each case whether these held for all correspondence or (less frequently) particular relations. This in effect entailed cartel-like price fixing for both customer charges and inter-carrier compensation. Outbound administrations paid transit and terminating administrations for the use of their facilities on this basis. As international cables spread and the demand for communication grew, more nations and colonial territories opted to coordinate with or join the ITU. From 1885, separate tables of charges (and at times, regulatory concepts) were developed for what were called the "European Regime" (which any nation could join) and the "Extra-European Regime." The European Regime was consistent, collaborative, and very restrictive on rates and related matters, on which the Extra-European was looser.

Outside the European Regime, two alternatives were followed. First, the British Empire (and, later, the Commonwealth) routed most of its traffic through London and kept it on British-owned facilities as far as possible in order to minimize payments to foreign transit carriers, even when this meant taking very indirect routes. A new approach was adopted after World War II in light of the colonies' new independence and their widespread nationalizations. From 1948 to 1973, the Commonwealth used a Wayleave Scheme in which networks were treated as common user systems. Terminal and transit charges were employed, but "accounting" followed an unorthodox pattern which relied on central management from London, and expenses were allocated to each carrier in proportion to its share of total revenue. The scheme maximized use of Commonwealth networks and helped developing countries finance their systems by spreading costs, but it probably did not encourage disciplined financial management on their part. The Wayleave scheme was replace in 1973 by the Commonwealth Telecommunications Financial Arrangement, under which the cost of each administration's facilities were recovered from its partners in proportion to their use, measured in units of traffic carried. Revenues were shared equally between terminal points, while transit countries were compensated separately for use of their facilities.

The second major alternative to the European Regime involved the United States. In the 1930s, AT&T developed the notion of negotiated "accounting rates," separate from collection charges (the prices paid by end customers), that would be the same in both directions and facilitate settlements based on a 50/50 division of revenues. The approach was devised with intercontinental relations in mind, and was linked to AT&T's efforts to win direct routing arrangements to points in the British Empire. The 50/50 split assumed, conveniently, that costs were comparable if not the same for both carriers in a correspondent relationship. The FCC adopted the accounting rate model for the regulation of US overseas communications, both voice and record, and agreement to it effectively became a precondition for foreign carriers seeking correspondent relations with AT&T. The PTTs also were obligated to undertake uniform settlements with all American counterparts so that they could not play one off against the other in contract negotiations.

After the TAT-1 trans-Atlantic cable was laid in 1956, and with the development of successor facilities and of direct dialing, intercontinental telephony took off and came to dwarf telex and other record services. The AT&T–FCC approach began to spread beyond intercontinental relations with the United States to other parts of the Extra-European Regime. Accordingly, from the late 1950s the CCITT began to develop Recommendations laying out elaborate rules for accounting and settlements systems. Finally, in 1968, it adopted Recommendation E. 250, "New System for Accounting in International Telephony," which served as the framework for organizing the global market until the late 1990s. In the decades to follow, the CCITT became the locus of an enormous amount of ongoing work on tariff and accounting rate issues and developed a slew of recommendations on the system's use for different services.

In sum, the joint service provision principle, and the complex norms and rules operationalizing it, established an international order in which monopolists could exchange traffic without competing against each other. Importantly, the charges were the same regardless of the route messages took, so there was no incentive for carriers to engage in circuitous routings in order to attain cheaper prices from their correspondent; distributional conflicts between national monopolies were thereby precluded.

International interconnection

The third principle required interconnection between national networks via technical standardization. This was not a simple matter, because key ITU members in the industrialized world saw the promotion of domestic manufacturers as a sovereign right. Full standardization of their networks and services would be divisive if this required choosing one manufacturer's technology over others as the basis for specifications. Hence, as a former CCITT Director has observed,

> Standardization in [the] early days was restricted to a few points in the networks. Because of manual operation, only the international operators had access to international circuits, whereas the equipment in the national network was practically not involved in international standardization.[18]

Standardization concentrated primarily on the gateways, signaling and transmission between national extensions. This minimalism left administrations and their manufacturers free to employ internationally incompatible systems within their national networks, and to use closed standards as non-tariff barriers to equipment trade. Sharply delineating between the national and international realms and applying regime rules only to the latter, states had it both ways: monopoly control *and* lucrative cross-border communication. Hence, ITU standards should be seen as situationally specific regime rules, just like the detailed accounting and settlements arrangements and restrictions on private networks, by which the higher principles of sovereignty and interconnection were balanced and operationalized.[19]

Technical standardization became an increasingly complex and demanding process in the post-World War II era. With the shift to automatic direct dialing, the development of more differentiated services, and from the 1960s the computerization of network functions, the need to standardize beyond inter-network gateways grew in tandem. Not surprisingly, the need to extend certain types of standards further into national networks, coupled with the growing competition among manufacturers for carriers' favor, often made agreement difficult to reach. Among the factors separating success from failure were the type of system involved (there was less need for full agreement on some types of customer terminals than on network equipment) and whether major players had made substantial investments in competing systems prior to undertaking coordination. In such cases, the committees might settle for oxymoronic "dual" or "multiple" standards listed together in a Report, rather than achieving a single Recommendation. Alternatively, a majority of members might agree on a single Recommendation, but important players would pursue different implementation "options" that it blessed. And in still other cases members might agree to a purportedly universal Recommendation but implement it in dissimilar ways. When competing preferences could not be reconciled, market players had to undertake complicated and costly interworking via gateway translator technologies or settle for a lack of compatibility. But in the broad sweep of ITU history, such occurrences, while significant, were more the exceptions than the rule.[20]

ITU members brought issues to the table through an exceedingly formalized and rather slow-moving process. This was in keeping with the culture of central planning preferred by PTT technocrats, as well as the European-inspired desire to ensure that everyone in the club was on board before anything important was done. The approach was only feasible because of the monopolization of telecommunications markets, which allowed members to painstakingly work out details without fear that external market forces would disrupt their plans.

The CCITT and its predecessors comprised a series of study groups which divided their ongoing work into four-year study periods. Particularly in the postwar era, this became an enormous operation involving up to eighteen study groups, each comprising at least four or five working parties, each of which involved hundreds of people and three to four meetings per year, each of which floated and worked through thousands of pages of documentation. At the outset of each study period, the study groups would define a series of Questions to be investigated over the next four years. The working parties would examine particular questions and slowly come to suggested Recommendations, which would then be taken up by the study group as a whole. All of this proceeded on the basis of consensus, with votes taken only on the most divisive issues. Then, at the end of the period, all the study groups would meet in Plenary Assemblies to formally decide on the adoption of Recommendations. Often the Questions would go unresolved, and would stay on the agenda for another four-year cycle. In fact, many important issues took decades to resolve. In sum, the CCITT process during the *ancien régime* was: slow, since final standards took at least four years, and often more; consensual, so as to maximize input from and minimize later non-compliance by leading members; reactive, as it largely involved existing national technologies brought in "bottom up" for international standardization; and power-based, as the only system specifications being considered were those advocated by the dominant carriers and manufacturers of a few industrialized countries.

Compliance

It is not surprising that, under the *ancien régime*, there were occasions where negotiations in various ITU forums stalled because the parties could not agree. But
the fundamental symmetry of interests among PTTs, a pronounced "shadow of
the future" associated with their ongoing and multi-level cooperation, and their
strong normative commitment to technocratic and multilateral problem-solving
all contributed to reducing the number of such instances. Moreover, when problems could not be solved immediately, members often left them for further
consideration and consensus building at subsequent meetings. This contributed
to the slow pace of change in both the ITU's instruments and the international
network, but it kept the coalition together.

From its early days up to the present, the ITU has lacked centralized mechanisms to monitor compliance with its instruments. In the telegraph union,
administrations and private carriers listed their terminal and transit rates for
international correspondence in an annex to the Regulations. But otherwise,
data-gathering efforts focused more on compiling carrier-supplied statistics about
such items as traffic levels on different routes, the number and type of lines laid
in national territories. The ITU has never attempted to monitor or measure
compliance with regulatory rules or technical standards per se, and indeed it
would be difficult to do so. Part of the problem is that in both the old monopoly
order and the increasingly competitive market of today, ITU members have
regarded many types of information about their policies and practices as proprietary. In neither era were carriers eager to have anything more than the
absolutely necessary degree of transparency about their operations. Similarly,
there have never been sustained initiatives to establish centralized mechanisms
for the operationalization of regime prescriptions at the international level.[21] In
general, the implementation of regime prescriptions was undertaken at the
national level.

Nevertheless, despite the lack of centralized mechanisms, most ITU members
– especially those in Europe – generally appear to have complied with the *ancien
régime*. It is possible that administrations found opportunities to cheat or at least
interpret their obligations liberally, but the available evidence suggests that they
attached real importance to following the rules. They had many reasons to do so,
three of which merit mention here. First, since it was the national carriers who
created the rules, they had professional interests and reputational stakes in implementing them, and in seeing them implemented by others. Moreover, because of
the high level of interdependent decision-making involved in managing interconnected networks and jointly provided services, non-compliant practices would be
very visible to their foreign correspondents. Second, for the same reasons, most
PTTs and RPOAs valued compliance as a way to ensure a stable and predictable
operating environment within which to undertake the capital investments and
long-term planning needed to scale up new networks and services. And third,
from a monopolist's standpoint, a strong regime helped serve a collective protectionist function *vis-à-vis* potential competitors.

In general, reactions to non-compliance involved members applying bilateral pressure on defectors. Given the lack of central monitoring, the foreign correspondents of a carrier would be the most aware of and affected by its non-compliance. The Convention provided for arbitration in the event of disputes, but there does not appear to be evidence of members using this option on telecommunications regime issues. Instead, the practice under the *ancien régime* was to simply negotiate some compromise solution directly. In extreme cases, particularly involving the cable companies in the early years, the PTTs might even threaten to terminate operating agreements.

The biggest problem was that American (and to a lesser extent, Canadian) compliance with the *ancien régime* was far more selective. The United States constantly opted to pick and choose which obligations it would accept, to press others to loosen the regulatory requirements embedded in ITU instruments, and so on. The PTTs would have preferred a different outcome, but to deal with North America they employed techniques like differential obligations to keep everyone under a nominally shared framework. Separate obligations were established for particular countries or regions which would have difficulty accepting and applying universal rules based on the European model, such as the division between the "European" and "Extra-European" accounting systems. Similarly, whereas the CCITT created "tariff groups" for Europe and the Mediterranean, Africa, Asia, and Latin America to design customized tariff and accounting principles, this was not done for North America because the United States and Canada preferred to handle such issues outside the ITU.

Moreover, even in the case of prescriptions that were supposed to be universal, countries have had the option to select their levels of conformity. Legally, ITU members may take reservations to particular provisions when signing treaties like the Convention and the Regulations. This was especially important in the case of the United States. Given the trans-Atlantic divide over tariffs and related matters, the only solution in many cases was for everyone to simply agree that the United States would play by somewhat different rules. It was simply too important that the United States be part of the planning and operation of the global network for the country to remain outside the ITU fold; better to have it abide by most of the rules than none at all.

From adaptation to transformation

Incremental challenges to the ancien régime

The information control revolution and the CCITT

While North America's partial acceptance of regime obligations required operational adjustments in the organization of international correspondence and sometimes generated friction in meetings, neither the United States nor any other player made a concerted effort to alter fundamentally the architecture of the *ancien régime*. As such, the international order that the PTTs designed remained stable and unchanged for over one hundred years. This is not to say there were no international politics or disagreements with regard to regime matters. The details of tariffs and accounting, the adaptation of technical standards and operating procedures, and a host of other challenges raised by technological progress and the expansion of the international network required the continuous elaboration of increasingly complex agreements and sometimes difficult mutual adjustments on the part of ITU members. But these activities involved change *within* the existing regime – in certain norms, a great many rules, and some decision-making procedures – rather than a change *of* the regime and its overarching principles and objectives. Instead, the most contentious international politics in the ITU revolved around the division of frequency spectrum under the international radio regime, bickering among Cold War protagonists, and the extent to which the organization should adapt itself to meet the needs of the post-colonial world. These issues took up a great deal of energy in the ITU, but they did not impact the telecommunications regime and the organization of international networks and services in any significant way.

Given the national monopolies' tight grip on the industry, it is not surprising that the first real challenge to the regime originated outside the domain of its membership and the technologies and markets they controlled. The beginning of the end arrived with the development of computer communications in the United States during the 1950s. Contractors to the Department of Defense demonstrated in the SAGE project that mainframe computers could be linked up via telecommunications lines to perform distributed data processing and file management. As the commercial computer industry blossomed, especially after International Business Machines (IBM) released System 360 in 1964, the boundary line between "in-house" computing and communications began to blur. New technological possibilities set off a learning process in which telecommunications was increasingly reconceptualized as an extension of companies' internal management information systems to be customized for competitive advantage, rather than as a plain vanilla public utility to be procured from monopoly providers on whatever terms they cared to offer. Large corporate users in the airline, financial, petroleum, automobile, and other industries began to see that datacommunications could vastly enhance the company-wide management of their operations, both domestically and internationally.

In this context, AT&T's monopolistic practices became a problem for a widening array of corporate customers. Like the PTTs abroad, AT&T restricted customers' ability to attain, configure, and use leased circuits and to attach specialized customer premise equipment (CPE) for private data networking. As such, corporate users began to complain to the FCC and demand greater flexibility, a cause which IBM and other computer firms happily joined. Similarly, users demanded the right to procure systems and services from other suppliers, while potential competitive suppliers began to step up and demand entry into the emerging market niches. From the 1960s onward, this new corporate interest configuration grew into a sort of movement that generated a steady stream of calls for the FCC to curtail AT&T control over first the emerging specialized markets, and later over the public switched telephone network (PSTN) and provision of basic services.

At the same time, technological change also led to an intellectual sea change regarding the optimal governance of telecommunications amidst what was being called the information revolution. By the mid-1960s, a growing number of economists and industry analysts were questioning the continuing applicability of the old rationales for protecting AT&T from competition, such as the theory of natural monopoly. Increasingly, telecommunications was seen by many observers as being both key to the vitality of the economy as a whole and too important to be left in the hands of a monopolist. While AT&T and its supporters could dismiss the demands of potential competitors as being driven by narrow self-interest, this was more difficult with respect to the claims of independent analysts. In short, over time the combination of corporate demands and new ideas led the FCC to reevaluate the wisdom of constraining innovation and entrepreneurship to benefit one company, and to embark on an incremental process of deregulation that eventually led to AT&T's divestiture and the establishment of a highly diverse and competitive market for communications systems and services.

In principle, the fact that its instruments sharply delineated between the domestic and international spheres and applied only to the latter could have insulated the ITU's telecommunications regime from any disruptions stemming from the US market. But, in practice, this proved impossible because US-based TNCs began to broaden their objectives. Given the increasingly global scope of their operations, corporate users and new suppliers wanted to attain from foreign PTTs at least a measure of the freedom they were gaining at home. Individually and collectively through multinational trade associations, they began to press PTTs in the industrialized countries for greater flexibility with respect to leased circuits, CPE, computerized information services, and a host of related issues that mattered to businesses but did not threaten directly the monopolists' control over PSTNs and basic services. They also worked with foreign counterparts in selected industries to raise awareness of their common interest in promoting telecommunications liberalization, and managed to gain some support in fields like banking and air transportation. Inevitably, the fact that PTTs tended to cite their need to conform with international regime instruments as a reason for not accommodating such corporate claims more fully meant that the campaign had to be taken into the ITU.

This was not an entirely new development. As early as the 1932 Plenipotentiary Conference, multinational business associations like the ICC and the IPTC had begun to complain vehemently about the Recommendations governing leased circuits, tariffs, and other issues. At subsequent WATTCs, especially the 1949 conference, they were joined by colleagues in the International Air Transportation Association (IATA) who also wanted greater freedom to attain leased circuits under more favorable terms and configure them into international private networks. What was new, though, were the stakes for all involved. With the information revolution, it was no longer simply a matter of private telegraph, telex, or telephone services, all of which were fairly homo-geneous and mature; rather, at issue was the brave new world of computerized information systems and services and specialized telecommunications services, which users and competitive suppliers wanted to design and control themselves.

ITU members had rather mixed interests in this regard. On the one hand, by accommodating corporate users and the computer industry to some extent, they could benefit directly from new sources of traffic and revenue, and laterally from increased innovation in the industry. And more generally, the PTTs' governments needed the private sector to invest and thrive for all the obvious reasons, so too much resistance would be counterproductive. On the other hand, allowing the expansion of private services layered on top of their facilities might actually deprive the PTTs of some revenues, insofar as leased circuits were tariffed at flat rates while the regular public services were tariffed on a usage-sensitive basis. More generally, the flourishing of private networks and cyberspaces and the emergence of new markets catering to them might turn out to be a Trojan horse for a wider erosion of the PTTs' control over the telecommunications environment. Administrations did not want to be consigned to the limited role of providing the facilities over which other firms provided services. Hence, designing appropriate multilateral rules that would meet the new demands without going too far would be a difficult balancing act.

This struggle between the old monopoly order and the incipient information age was primarily played out in the CCITT. In 1961 the committee established Study Group III, which was responsible for addressing all accounting and tariff questions in a new D Series of Recommendations. In each of the four-year study periods until 1988, the group and its working parties went about laying down rules for every conceivable issue associated with private leased circuits, which were then forwarded on to the quadrennial CCITT Plenary Assembly for adoption. Some of these rules were workable, if not ideal from the corporate standpoint. For example, the 1968 assembly accepted that a flat-out global ban on leased circuit access to PSTNs (which would allow customers to send messages outside of their organization at the flat rate) was impractical, if for no other reason than the United States allowed this in its territory; administrations were therefore free to decide whether to do the same, as long as the messages pertained solely to the customers' business. Similarly, the 1972 assembly decided that circuits could be used to route messages to other users outside a company, as long as the communications concerned the activity for which the circuit was leased. This removed an important regulatory barrier to inter-organizational networking, e.g. between an automobile company and its suppliers, or among the members of "closed user groups" like the SITA airline network or the SWIFT banking network.

But on the whole, the growing family of rules was fairly restrictive. For example:

- leased circuits were generally to be made available only after the needs of public services were met;

- administrations could withdraw such circuits when they deemed it to be in the public interest;
- leased circuits could be used only between fixed points for a designated purpose relating to the customer's non-telecommunications business;
- customers could not resell excess capacity;
- equipment connected to private circuits had to meet conditions specified by the administrations involved;
- switching and transmission were the exclusive functions of administrations;
- private networks were only to be allowed when administrations could not meet a customer's specialized requirements;
- administrations reserved the right to provide such networks, on an exclusive basis if they chose, and accepted no responsibility for the quality of transmissions;
- users could not change their private network facilities without the administration's consent;
- the interconnection of two or more private networks required the administration's approval;
- administrations could choose whether to authorize the interconnection of private leased circuits to public networks, subject to the consent of the other relevant administrations;
- transmissions should pertain solely to the circuit's approved purpose, and be sent only to approved public network subscribers;
- administrations could levy special charges for public network access;
- administrations should not consider financial claims resulting from failure in the public networks to which a private circuit is connected;
- administrations were not obliged to guarantee the quality of transmission to or from the public network over a leased circuit;
- private leased circuits terminating at one end in a data-processing center were to be allowed public network access only if the information was not exchanged on a store and forward basis, the data-processing center did not switch and transmit messages between users, the list of connected users was provided to the administration on demand, and the participants did not provide a telecommunications service;
- closed user groups could exceptionally attain circuits for uses not authorized under other recommendations which were not met by existing public services until such offerings became available, and the user groups could not be engaged in the telecommunications business.

US-led multinational business alliances took advantage of their advisory status to submit papers and – if they were recognized, which was at the discretion of study group and working party chairmen – make statements decrying these and related policies. Sometimes the language involved became rather ripe. In one especially floral instance, the IPTC lectured study group members that the D Series Recommendations:

tend to discourage the use of message data switching computers and the lease of private circuits. Furthermore, this discouragement would seem to stem less from any reluctance to appreciate the potentialities of private use networks as the servants of society than from a fear that their proliferation constitutes a threat to the revenues or even to the status of administrations ... the comprehensive responsibilities of administrations to society at large has impeded their ability to meet the highly specialized requirements of principal users ... [to develop] unrealistic tariffs and a maze of loosely worded Recommendations, against whose restrictive interpretation users would have little redress, is to disregard the canons of social justice and of conventional business conduct. Furthermore, it is retarding the development of telecommunications in the service of man.[22]

Similarly, representatives of the ICC, IATA, INTUG, and other groups, as well as individual companies, complained that study group members were engaging in cartel behavior and abusing their monopoly powers. But in the end, the business groups could not vote and had to sit on the sidelines while administrations made decisions.

Insofar as most PTTs and RPOAs are generally believed to have followed them most of the time, and as the international business community persistently complained about them, the Recommendations probably did raise the cost and decrease the efficiency of running internationally dispersed businesses. But at the same time, it seems reasonable to suppose that some large and influential companies were able to negotiate deals with PTTs that deviated from the rules. After all, the Recommendations were at least nominally non-binding, and in many instances it would be difficult for a carriers' counterparts to detect its defection from the coalition if the right incentives were available.

But placing restrictions on leased circuits was not the only controversial way in which CCITT members responded to the incipient pressures for private control generated by the information revolution. They also sought to strengthen their hand by developing the Integrated Services Digital Network, or ISDN. The ISDN was conceived in the 1973–6 study period as a single integrated national high-speed network that could carry all traffic regardless of its technical requirements. The vision was that with such networks in place, administrations' public networks could handle all business requirements for advanced services, potentially obviating the need to lease lines. The very term "the ISDN" had a monolithic ring to it, so corporate users dubbed the concept, "Innovations Subscribers Don't Need." Throughout the 1970s and 1980s the ISDN concept generated significant controversy, but the committee painstakingly moved forward with attempts to specify the requisite technical standards.

The spread of national liberalization

But while the CCITT was circling the wagons to fend off growing demands for greater private control, the political ground was shifting under its feet. The

United States was coming to the view that comprehensive international liberalization was in the national interest. The FCC fired an opening salvo in 1980 by announcing its intention to extend unilaterally resale and sharing from domestic to international circuits, despite the facts that almost every administration prohibited these services in accordance with the Recommendations. The CCITT Director sent the FCC a letter noting the "surprise" and "deep disappointment" within the ITU, stating further:

> It seems to me an extremely dangerous situation when one country, and what is more, the leading country with regard to the number of subscribers, the extent of its services and its telecommunications technology, can help to undermine the work of the CCITT.[23]

Many PTTs sent similar messages, some of them declaring that if the FCC proceeded, they would in turn revoke TNCs' access to leased lines. The FCC backed off, but this was just the opening battle in what would become a permanent US attack on the old order.

The Reagan Administration decided to make the promotion of international competition in telecommunications a central element of its trade strategy. The US Trade Representative (USTR) began to undertake bilateral negotiations with foreign governments with the objective of winning not only better treatment of corporate users, but also market access for US suppliers of telecommunications services and equipment. Moreover, the USTR joined forces with an emerging community of service industry specialists to argue that jointly provided telecommunications services in fact constituted trade, and as such should be covered by the General Agreement on Tariffs and Trade (GATT). The notion that international services exchange had trade-like properties first emerged in the early 1970s, and by the early 1980s the United States was pressing other governments to set trade in services rules as part of what became the 1986–94 Uruguay Round negotiations.[24] The new interest configuration in the United States supported strongly the government's position, and indeed played an important role in its formulation. The very act of viewing telecommunications as part of a larger category of services transactions to be "traded" created a strong conceptual bias toward openness, and set a new yardstick for evaluating telecommunications regulations as simple non-tariff barriers to be removed. Hence the GATT was an attractive venue in which to push for an a new multilateral framework that would deal with the economic dimensions of international correspondence, as well as a means of pressuring administrations in the ITU to reform the extant regime.

In consequence, the 1980s witnessed an unprecedented politicization of the organization of global telecommunications markets and, by extension, of international regime rules. The United Kingdom, Japan, and Canada decided early in the decade to begin privatization and liberalization in the hope of energizing their markets. But other industrialized countries' PTTs and their domestic supporters – the postal industrial complex – energetically opposed the American approach, claiming that the Americans' new discourse about "restrictive trade barriers," "abuse of dominant position," and "excessive regulation" simply reflected the interests of large American firms poised to swoop down on their presumably vulnerable markets. Many governments began to consider and sometimes enact regulatory, trade, and industrial policies for telecommunications and information that the new interest configuration damned as protectionism. Hence, the early 1980s were marked by growing discord and drift in bilateral and multilateral policy discussions. Within and without the ITU, PTT managers were aghast at being described as undemocratic cartel managers conspiring against the free market, since commercial considerations had never been an acknowledged criteria for evaluating standards and regulations. They were doing as they had always done, but were suddenly being castigated for it.

Nevertheless, by the late 1980s the PTTs' positions were becoming untenable, for at least four reasons. First, locally based corporate users, especially those in financial and other services, found themselves competing with American-based counterparts which were benefiting from the efficiencies and enhanced range of choice in systems and applications associated with liberalization. Market incentives therefore pointed to the desirability of achieving similar gains with their home PTTs, and of extending these gains to cross-border services. Further, a conceptual realignment accompanied these users' shift to more globally oriented profiles. They were coming to see themselves as having similar interests as American users in relation to states, insofar as they were more concerned with accessing the best resources than with buying nationally. Hence, the regulatory preferences, negotiating agendas and intellectual orientations of large users across the industrialized world began to converge around imported focal points, which substantially broadened the support for and impact of the efforts of INTUG, ICC and similar industry alliances.

Second, a parallel shift was occurring on the supply side of the market. The increasing globalization and differentiation of demand generated new opportunities which could be best realized in a competitive environment. Traditional telecommunications manufacturers and new entrants, whether medium-sized start-ups or large computer and electronics firms crossing market niches, could not recover the rising research and development costs of advanced CPE and network equipment without foreign sales. Potential private service suppliers could not lure customers to their new offerings unless they could provide international reach. Corporate competitiveness therefore required international liberalization. Where states were slow to change, TNCs devised novel solutions to access barriers, such as international corporate alliances and gray markets.

Third, the emerging reconceptualization of telecommunications' role in economic activity raised the question of whether PTTs should retain their exclusive jurisdictions. The spread of American-style intellectual frameworks and the growing debate about trade in services in the GATT helped to redefine how industry analysts and government officials across the industrialized worlds regarded their national monopolies. High-level politicians and trade ministers alike began to believe that liberalization would energize their economies and be in the national interest. And fourth, by 1987 the Commission of the European Communities was coming out strongly for the liberalization of the European market in the context of its broader integration program. With the Commission's conversion to the cause, European PTTs found themselves confronted with a pro-liberalization force backed by substantial legal and political authority.

In short, in the second half of the 1980s, PTTs across the industrialized world came under domestic as well as international pressure to open their markets. In the years to follow, they undertook – with varying degrees of enthusiasm – liberalization programs that typically began with specialized business-oriented systems and services, but in the 1990s would extend into the PSTNs and basic services. In parallel, the PTTs would be broken up in the 1990s, with the national telecommunications administrations separated from the postal services and ministerial policy organs. The telecommunications administrations were privatized, often with the governments retaining 51 or 49 per cent shares of the stock at the outset and then releasing more to the market over time. The newly privatized entities came to be referred to as "Public Telecommunications Operators" (PTOs) or simply, as in the United States, as "telcos." With time lags, a substantial number of developing countries would move down the same path in the years ahead. These changes in domestic conditions, which are necessarily rendered here in highly abbreviated form, would begin to alter governments' preferences regarding the international order.

Regime transformation

The WATTC-88 watershed

The CCITT was not the only ITU body to witness a struggle between the old regulatory order and the forces of liberalization and private control. A watershed event, the outcome of which in my view inaugurated the transformation of the telecommunications regime, was the 1988 WATTC in Melbourne, which was called to update the 1973 Regulations in light of the rapidly changing policy environment.[25] In the three years leading up to the meeting, the preparatory committee tasked with drafting the new agreement was deeply and bitterly divided between the partisans of sweeping liberalization, and a PTT majority that was just beginning to undergo liberalization and privatization and hence favored much more incremental and limited reforms. The PTTs inserted into the draft text new language that was seen as highly restrictive and hence heatedly opposed by the international business community and the governments of the United States, Britain and Kuwait. These players believed that the draft text represented a grand plan by the PTTs, not only to preserve their existing market positions and regulatory authority, but actually to expand them into new domains of the information economy. The critics argued that the draft text would establish new rights for administrations to apply tight regulations on any type of telecommunication service provided by any company to any customer. Specialized suppliers such as private value-added networks (VANs), and perhaps even large users who employed internal capabilities to service their geographically dispersed operations, could be forced to attain official approval for any operation. Moreover, opponents maintained that the draft opened the door to an unprecedented expansion of the regime's scope beyond telecommunications transmission to the new world of computerized information services.

The impending WATTC became a major controversy that brought the ITU to the front page of newspapers' business sections around the world. In the press and on the industry conference circuit, leading analysts depicted the WATTC process as an almost cosmic struggle between free market good and PTT evil. The organization that had always seen and depicted itself as the paragon of smooth, apolitical technical cooperation was now becoming the locus of a major struggle over the rules of the game in the global information economy. From mid-1987 to mid-1988, a worldwide pressure campaign was launched against the preparatory committee's text. The American and British governments denounced it, the former intimating that not only would it return to its old practice of not signing or abiding by the Regulations, but also that it would reevaluate entirely its participation in the ITU. At the same time, the fight focused the minds of corporate managers around the world on their common political interests, and helped solidify the transnational front to an unprecedented degree. Multinational lobbies and their domestic counterparts voiced strong opposition to the draft text. Powerful firms in the United States filed submissions with the FCC saying the United States should not sign the accord, and foreign companies whose home PTTs had supported the draft applied similar pressures on their governments. Some corporate spokespersons suggested that they would attempt to customize their CPE and leased circuits so as to bypass any new restrictions. In the face of this opposition, the PTT majority was clearly going to have to compromise, but needed a way to do so without losing all face.

A few months before the conference, Secretary General Richard Butler proposed an alternative draft that cleverly made the inevitable concessions to pro-liberalization forces without undermining administrations' existing legal positions. This was an unprecedented intervention in telecommunications regime negotiations by an ITU Secretary General; previously, the ITU's leadership generally had had little influence on the regime because governments jealously guarded their prerogatives on such matters. The "Butler Draft" underscored that sovereign choice rather than a uniform and restrictive global framework would form the basis of national policies; deleted controversial language that appeared to apply the regulations to any entity providing electronic communications and information services across borders; and added an expansive new article on "special arrangements," which held that ITU members could authorize their administrations, RPOAs, and "any other organization or person" to enter into special arrangements with counterparts abroad, subject to national laws, "for establishment of special networks, systems, or applications, including the underlying means of telecommunications transport, to meet their own international communication needs or those of others."[26] This language positioned the ability of new suppliers and users to conclude special arrangements for any type of facilities and services as a presumptive baseline from which departures would need to be justified. Of course, government approval could still be required for such arrangements, but refusal to provide it to influential companies would now be more difficult if PTTs could not hide behind a collective obligation to do so.

While 112 member governments were represented at Melbourne, most of the important decisions were taken by a small ad hoc group of mostly advanced capitalist countries working long into the night behind closed doors. Many developing countries expressed strong concerns about a document which now seemed to bless the expansion of private networks and services, but these were pushed aside into a series of non-binding resolutions and opinions that would be appended to the text. Hence, after much heated debate, the meeting concluded a new, integrated treaty – the International Telecommunication Regulations – by a majority vote assembled by pro-liberalization forces through a combination of pressure and compromise. The final text drew heavily on the Butler Draft, but it also made some concessions to administrations reluctant to embrace change. The document was technically "neutral" insofar as it required neither open markets nor strict regulation; that choice was left to individual states. But in the emerging market environment, opting not to collectively buttress or expand administrations' power made it *de facto* a liberalizing agreement.

The new Regulations largely met the demands of TNCs and governments favoring competitive supply and user control. As countries liberalized and the private sector increasingly found openings to enter markets in the years ahead, the new Regulations opened the door for operators and users of private networks to extend their operations internationally, thereby facilitating the transition to a multi-provider world. Hence, the 1990s would witness a worldwide explosion in the number and diversity of international networks and service providers that operated "special arrangements" outside the scope of the ITU's Regulations. Moreover, by adopting a formally neutral agreement, the conference helped created legal space for the GATT's Uruguay Round negotiators to establish binding trade principles that did not conflict with the ITU treaty.

In short, from a regime standpoint, WATTC-88 initiated a progressive decoupling of the traditionally linked concepts of sovereignty and national monopolies over international telecommunications. By choosing not to apply the traditional model to the emerging markets for basic and advanced services, governments in effect acknowledged that they could not retain exclusive control or hope to maintain rules that were sharply out of synch with an increasingly private sector-led marketplace. The treaty signaled the beginning of a transition to a new international regime under which global interconnection and service provisioning would involve a complex competitive mixture of public and private entities based on contractual relationships rather than administrative power.

Liberalization of the sovereignty rules

The results of the WATTC ushered in a full court press on the part of the United States, some of the increasingly pro-liberalization industrialized countries, and TNCs to relax the remaining regulatory prescriptions in ITU instruments. Invoking the "spirit of Melbourne," they now demanded that the CCITT finally remove the rigid rules on private circuits and networks that were used by PTTs to restrain corporate users and new service providers. The move came at a time when the CCITT was taking substantial heat from many sides beyond the usual suspects. In 1990 the *Financial Times* published a widely noted set of articles decrying the committee as a "cartel" or "cabal" that was stifling the development of global communications markets and ripping off consumers, a theme that was then picked up by many press outlets around the world, especially in the United States and United Kingdom. This unusual and highly critical press attention caught the eye of many government leaders who had not paid much attention to the ITU in the past, and these then took the matter up with their ministries and administrations. All this reverberated throughout the ITU and put people on the defensive. Moreover, the EC Commission's competition directorate notified regional PTTs that the D Series Recommendations appeared to be contrary to the Treaty of Rome and the 1992 single market program, and that its retention could lead to anti-trust litigation. European PTTs were thus forced to abandon a key element of the *ancien régime* of which they had been the primary architects.

After two years of negotiations, in the summer of 1991 the CCITT approved a sweeping revision of the Recommendations on leased circuits and private networks. The new texts allowed largely unfettered customer access to and control over intra-organizational circuits; accepted the attachment of private equipment to and the modification of lines, subject to easier type approval and the avoidance of technical harm to PTT facilities; opened the door to the provision of telecommunications services to third parties using private circuits; allowed the interconnection of private leased circuits and networks with each other and with public networks; and accepted the resale of excess capacity. Moreover, on prices it specified that leases should be cost-oriented and generally established on a flat-rate basis, and that any access charges must be "cost-related" and dependent on the administration's own additional expenses from providing the specific mode of interconnection or special routing requested by a customer. Changes in conditions such as cancellation or temporary withdrawal of lines were to be done only after substantial consultations. Finally, many of the restrictive sections of the old text were simply dropped from mention, e.g. the rules giving administrations exclusive control over switching, limiting communication with data-processing centers, etc. Administrations could still designate certain (public switched telephony) services as their exclusive domain, but there would no longer be specific prohibitions in the regime to cite as justifying or requiring such actions in either domestic or international planning.

Hence, with the new Regulations and Recommendations, the restrictive norms and rules governing the activities of players other than PTTs and RPOAs that had once been central to the regime were now gone. While some countries (especially in Asia and the developing world) continue to charge well above cost prices, most of the other problems TNCs encountered in the past with respect to leased circuits and private networks are receding. With the playing field thus cleared of international regulatory obstacles, private firms now had a clearer path to negotiating permissive arrangements with national administrations, and had greater incentives to invest in scaling up a dizzying array of new networks and service offerings, including in the Internet environment. This would become a factor in facilitating the globalization of firms and markets throughout the 1990s, both in telecommunications services and in other industries that use such services (e.g. automobile manufacturing, banking, and so on).

Liberalization of the interconnection rules

A similar dynamic took hold in the field of technical standardization. The spread of liberalization and the convergence of telecommunications and information systems in the 1980s greatly increased the number and diversity of firms with stakes in standardization, as well as the range of systems that needed to interconnect and interoperate. PTTs and RPOAs now had to work with more than their traditional national champion manufacturers if they wanted to generate Recommendations that would actually be accepted and implemented. Private firms began to outnumber administrations in many CCITT study groups and working parties, and they demanded the right to participate in decision-making on a more equal footing. Moreover, standards conceived in the context of monopoly control could not be imposed easily upon the market in an increasingly liberalizing environment. For example, by the time the CCITT finally got around to specifying enough of the standards necessary to make "the ISDN" a reality, American and corporate resistance had rendered the original deployment model moot. Instead, carriers would slowly roll out variably configured ISDNs as just one of many service options. Despite twenty years of work in the committee, in the end there would be rather limited demand for ISDNs in many markets, especially as more robust broadband alternatives developed in the 1990s.

Complicating things further, by the mid-1980s, the CCITT's dominance over international standardization had begun to slip away. Frustrated with the slow pace of decision-making and the PTTs' power in the CCITT, the new private carriers and competitive manufacturers increasingly launched their standards efforts in national bodies such as the American National Standards Institute (ANSI), the T1 committee of the National Exchange Carriers Association (NECA), and Corporation for Open Systems (COS) in North America, and the Technical Telecommunications Committee (TTC) in Japan; and in standards bodies like the EC's new European Telecommunications Standards Institute (ETSI) and the European Standards Commission (CEN). Moreover, dozens of new industry-run standards groups were popping up to coordinate the development of systems that were emerging outside the realm of traditional PSTN planning. To address these challenges, the CCITT's Director spearheaded a dual-edged program designed to make the committee more responsive to the demands of a liberalizing global market.

The first move was to reform the CCITT's working methods. Manufacturers, service suppliers and users all complained that the industry could not wait for the finalization of standards at the quadrennial plenary assemblies. Hence, at the 1988 assembly, the committee decided that some recommendations could be adopted quickly via balloting, as was the practice in many of the new private standards bodies. The new "accelerated procedures" allowed that, when needed, standards could be adopted if 70 per cent of CCITT members approved them within three months of the Director's circulation of a proposal. The 1988 assembly also approved a number of other measures designed to improve coordination among study groups, drop obsolete questions and recommendations, streamline documentation, and increase the use of electronic networks in the standards process.[27]

The second move was to improve coordination with external standards bodies. Despite hopeful resolutions at the 1988 assembly and WATTC endorsing its "pre-eminence" in global standardization, it was recognized the CCITT would have a somewhat different and diminished role in the making of some standards. Rather than being the origin and locus of most activity, the committee could at times serve as a sort of clearing house or central switch for a global network of standards organizations. To establish this framework, an Interregional Telecommunications Standards Conference was held in 1990. There a three-step plan was agreed under which other standards bodies would consult with the CCITT (and on radio matters, the CCIR) to set plans and priorities, engage in networked problem-solving, and submit consolidated proposals to it for possible multilateral adoption. This "upstream" flow would generate global standards for national implementation in the "downstream" stage. Although official delegates to the conference were from the CCITT, CCIR, T1, ETSI and TTC, other industry bodies organizations also were invited feed into the process. A framework of periodic meetings and electronic consultations was established to implement the plan. In the next few years, a new inter-organizational virtual body, the Global Standards Coordination meetings, evolved to help institutionalize the new architecture.

Finally, as part of a broader ITU restructuring, the 1992 Plenipotentiary Conference folded the CCITT and the CCIR into the Telecommunications Standardization Sector and Radio Sector, respectively, and gave them each corporate advisory councils. In addition, the study periods would now be reduced from four years to two so as to improve "time to market" for the production of business-critical technical standards, although on more divisive regulatory matters like accounting and tariffs the change has not resulted in greater speed.

Despite these reforms, the ITU's historical dominance of the standardization process has continued to slip in the years to follow. Hundreds of privatized carriers and other firms still participate in the ITU–T's various study groups, some of which generate dozens of new standards per year. But in many cases the concepts in play are generated by or in close consultation with other forums. To be sure, the ITU's blessing of a standard as an official multilateral agreement can be useful in signaling customers that a system will conform with other ITU approved systems, but there are other standards bodies in the world now that often have more clout in particular market segments (e.g. Internet-related products). Moreover, in an era in which networks and equipment are increasingly software defined, it is also possible in many cases to achieve interoperability without such formal agreements. In short, while the interconnection of national networks is still as important as it was in the 1860s, the rules and decision-making procedures used to achieve this have been redefined in that universal, multilateral standardization in the ITU is no longer taken to be the only, or even the primary, acceptable means to that end.

Organizational reform and new decision-making procedures

In the liberalized world of the 1990s, reforming the standards process alone would not be enough to preserve the ITU's relevance. Parallel changes in the ITU's leadership, organizational structures, working methods, and overall decision-making procedures have also been pursued. With regard to leadership, the 1989 Plenipotentiary Conference elected Finland's Pekka Tarjanne as Secretary General. Strongly supported by the United States and other powerful members, Tarjanne set a tone that differed sharply from that of his predecessors by constantly speaking of the necessity of liberalization, the benefits of moving toward a trade framework and other market friendly measures, while at the same time emphasizing that reform had to take place in a manner and at a pace that was compatible with local conditions. This was useful in that it encouraged developing country members to recognize the inevitability of change. In addition, the 1992 Plenipotentiary created a Strategic Planning Unit within the office of the Secretary General. The unit has attracted top-notch experts who have generated a slew of reports on both the changing global industry and implications for ITU members, as well as Strategic Plans and other intra-organizational initiatives designed to streamline the organization's activities.

The ITU has opened itself up to much greater private sector participation in its decision-making processes. For example, the 1989 Plenipotentiary revised the Convention to allow SIOs to participate in the consultative committees on the same footing as the RPOAs. Going further, the 1992 Plenipotentiary's reorganization gave all three sectors high-level Business Advisory Committees, and the Secretary General has his own business advisory group for overall organizational planning. Further, private firms have been given full membership voting rights in the sectors' technical committees, and the ITU is actively campaigning to recruit them to participate in (and fund) its various programs. The Secretariat even has taken to referring to the worldwide industry as the ITU's "customers" who must be given "value for money." All this represents a striking departure from the past, when the business community was viewed as a somewhat disruptive force to be grudgingly accommodated, if at all. In a privatizing world market, the ITU is now forced to woo the private sector and make it care what happens in Geneva. But the effort is having mixed success; while there are over six hundred sector members today, their level of involvement is highly variable, and many segments of the global industry still consider participating in the ITU to be either unnecessary for their operations or too frustrating to bother.

In sum, by the early 1990s, the distribution of power in global telecommunications policy had changed dramatically. The meta-dynamic was a broad shift in power from the public to the private sector, with US-based TNCs and US-originated ideas and policy discourses leading the way. In the second half of the decade, five additional forces would deepen this trend, and thereby call into question the importance of even a liberalized international regime.

From transformation to decay

External pressures on regime relevance

The international trade in services regime

The Uruguay Round trade negotiations that were launched in September 1986 concluded in December 1993. The agreements formally signed in April 1994 comprised a series of interrelated agreements among the 125 member governments of what was then the GATT. One major change they embodied was the establishment of the World Trade Organization (WTO), which among other things has a broader mandate and a stronger dispute settlement mechanism than did the GATT organization. In addition, two new treaties were added to the WTO nexus, alongside the GATT regime on trade in goods: the agreement on Trade Related Intellectual Property, and the General Agreement on Trade in Services (GATS).

International telecommunications plays a dual role under the GATS regime, which covers trade in a wide variety of services sectors. First, telecommunications is a lucrative sector in its own right, estimated to be worth about US $600 billion per year, $100 billion of which is said to involve cross-border trade. Governments undertook a range of market-access commitments in the sector, mostly on advanced or specialized "value-added" services geared toward corporate consumers. Second, the GATS framework recognizes that telecommunications is a key means of moving other types of information-embodied services – e.g. financial, management consulting, audio-visual, and advertising services – across national borders. As an infrastructure for the delivery of other services, telecommunications networks and services therefore constituted a crucial form of cross-border supply.[28]

To address the unique issues associated with this second role, WTO members added a Telecommunications Annex to the agreement which runs directly counter to the traditional thrust of ITU Regulations and Recommendations. The annex obliges governments that have made market-access commitments in various sectors – e.g. value-added telecommunications services, financial services, professional services, and so on – ensure that foreign providers of such services have access to and use of public telecommunications transport networks and services controlled by the dominant national carriers on a reasonable and nondiscriminatory basis. Moreover, governments must ensure that foreign service suppliers also have access to and use of private leased circuits, and that they can:

- purchase or lease and attach terminal or other equipment interfacing with public networks;
- interconnect private leased or owned circuits with public networks, or with circuits leased or owned by another service supplier; and
- use computer protocols of their choice, provided that this does not disrupt the provision of telecommunications transport networks and services to the public generally.

In addition, governments must ensure that foreign service suppliers can use these networks and circuits to transfer information without undue impediments within and across national borders, and that they can access information contained in data bases held in any member country. This last provision is an echo of the transborder data flow debate of the 1970s–1980s, when many companies worried that governments would for protectionist purposes limit their ability to send and access computerized information over transnational private lines.[29]

In addition, the Telecommunications Annex requires that governments apply no conditions on access and use other than is necessary to safeguard the dominant carriers' public service responsibilities, protect the technical integrity of public networks, or ensure that foreign service suppliers only provide services that have been designated open to competition in their market access commitments. However, if they meet these criteria, governments may adopt policies that: (1) restrict resale and shared use of public services; (2) require the use of specific technical interfaces and protocols for interconnection; (3) require the interoperability of services; (4) require type approval of terminal or other equipment interfacing with public networks; (5) restrict the interconnection of private leased or owned circuits with either public networks or the circuits of other service suppliers; and (6) require the registration or licensing of foreign suppliers.[30] In principle, these would seem to be potentially restrictive loopholes that governments could use to impede market access and limit the actual value of their commitments. In practice, with the liberalization of both the relevant ITU Recommendations and the wider telecommunications environment, and with the prospect that any disagreements over such actions could lead to conflicts with powerful players and into the WTO dispute settlement process, these provisions do not appear to have given rise to significant problems for foreign service suppliers.

Viewed in the context of the historical narrative provided above, the establishment of the GATS regime arguably is the biggest change in the governance of global telecommunications since the Treaty of Dresden. Never before has there been a broad-based, multilateral regime that actively promotes international competition as a way to organize the world market. The GATS establishes pro-competitive principles to which, if countries make relevant commitments, national policies must be adapted, institutionalizes mechanisms of mutual surveillance and binding dispute resolution, and sets a disciplined baseline for progressive liberalization in the future – this is almost the exact opposite of the world market envisaged and organized by the traditional telecommunications regime.

But despite its long-term significance, the immediate impact of the agreement was limited by the fact that only a few small market countries made partial market access commitments on basic telecommunications services, such as telephony, that constitute the biggest chunk of the global market. Seeking to rectify this limitation, a group of WTO governments agreed to additional negotiations designed to deepen their national schedules of commitments by encompassing basic telecommunications. After two difficult years of bargaining, on 5 February 1997 members of the Group on Basic Telecommunications (GBT) struck an agreement. The GBT deal, which came into force in February 1998, committed 69 countries (a handful more signed on subsequently) comprising approximately 93 per cent of the $600 billion per annum world market to liberalize their basic telecommunications services sectors in accordance with GATS disciplines.

Not surprisingly, critics pointed to the various qualifications embodied in the national schedules of commitments. For example, some countries retained limitations on foreign direct investment (FDI) or licensing requirements, and many developing countries opted to phase in their commitments over the next few years. Even so, that the vast majority of the world market is now subject – or soon will be – to greatly expanded competition relative to the past 150 years, and that governments have agreed to a multilateral framework under which any remaining restrictions are subject to evaluation, bargaining, and dispute resolution according to trade principles, is surely a major historical change.[31] Moreover, recognizing that liberalization is a favor they do for themselves rather than for others, some countries have actually chosen to accelerate and deepen their market opening commitments since the deal was reached.

In addition to its market access commitments, the GBT deal is profoundly significant because 57 countries endorsed a Reference Paper establishing six overarching principles for the redesign of national regulatory rules and institutions:

- *Competitive safeguards* Governments must ensure that major PTOs do not engage in anti-competitive cross-subsidization; use information gathered from competitors with trade-restricting results; or fail to make available, on a timely basis, technical information about their facilities and operations competitors need to enter the market.
- *Interconnection* PTOs must provide market entrants with interconnection at any technically feasible point in the network. Interconnection is to be offered under nondiscriminatory terms and conditions no less favorable than the provider gives its own services. Interconnection rates are to be cost-oriented,

transparent, and (where economically feasible) unbundled. A dispute mechanism administered by an independent national body is to handle disputes over interconnection terms and other issues.

- *Universal service*   Such obligations are to be administered in a transparent, nondiscriminatory, and competitively neutral manner that is no more burdensome than is required to meet the policy objectives.
- *Public availability of licensing criteria*   Where licenses are needed, information and decision-making procedures are to be transparent.
- *Independent regulators*   Regulatory bodies are to be separated from service providers and not accountable to them.
- *Allocation and use of scarce resources*   Procedures for allocating and using frequencies, numbers, and rights-of-way are to be carried out in an objective, timely, transparent, and nondiscriminatory manner.

Collectively, these principles represent a substantial departure from the old multilateral order. To note just one key example, the term "interconnection" is used here not in the traditional ITU sense of simply linking national networks via standards, but rather in the current American sense of establishing flexible and pro-competitive inter-carrier operating agreements. Under the Reference Paper a carrier has a right to extend its network directly into a foreign counterparts' network, interconnect at a point of presence, and terminate traffic there at cost-oriented rates. Or if FDI is allowed, it could opt to build or buy its own facilities within a foreign country. This is a significant shift from the CCITT's joint service model, which involved linking national circuits at an imaginary halfway point between them, counting the minutes of traffic exchanged in each direction, and multiplying this by a negotiating settlement rate that was typically far above cost. Not surprisingly, since the deal was reached there have been at least nine squabbles between US carriers and foreign PTOs over the precise terms of interconnection offered by the latter, and the US government has taken to threatening use of the WTO's dispute resolution mechanism to resolve these. But foot-dragging on the part of incumbents is to be expected in the transition to competition; the point is that the GATS establishes a framework to deal with such issues.

While WTO members failed to launch a new round of negotiations at their ministerial meeting at Seattle in November 1999, the resumption of services negotiations in 2000 is required by the Uruguay Round agreements. Although US presidential politics and other factors undoubtedly will delay new efforts to begin the round, preliminary services talks have begun. Four issues concerning telecommunications will be important to the new 'networld order'. First, and as per the above discussion, governments that have made commitments already will be pressured to clarify and actually implement them. Second, there will be a concerted push to increase the number of WTO members making commitments in line with the GBT deal, including the over thirty developing countries (and China) that are seeking to accede to the WTO. Third, governments will need to decide whether the Telecommunications Annex and the Reference Paper require revision, for example by elaborating on their broadly framed principles. Arguably, their lack of specificity invites constant battles over the terms of inter-connection, spectrum management and so on in a competitive market, and it could be unwise to leave their interpretation to dispute resolution panels. But the most ardent pro-liberalization countries may be reluctant to re-open the wording of these instruments for fear that others will insist on adding qualifications which limit their forcefulness.

Fourth, there is a looming battle on the horizon over the precise coverage of Internet service providers (ISPs) and backbone operators under the GATS. One side of the coin concerns whether existing commitments provide such firms with market access rights, in part because only a few WTO members have included specific entries to that effect in their national schedules. There are strong grounds for arguing that ISPs do enjoy market access rights unless specifically prohibited, but some countries may not be ready to accept this. This is just one of the many issues that will need to be sorted out with respect to the coverage of global electronic commerce under the WTO instruments, which is a topic that has generated a great deal of discussion in trade circles and will be central to pending negotiations.[32]

The other side of the coin, which is much more problematic, concerns whether Internet providers also have obligations under the GATS. When they were devised, governments made a conscious decision to focus the Annex and the Reference Paper on the underlying PSTNs supplied by the incumbent national administrations. Now, with the emergence of major Internet suppliers which are not PSTN operators, the European Commission and some developing countries are arguing that the obligations contained in the two instruments cover these firms as well. In effect, ISPs would be deemed to be basic telecommunications providers subject to the relevant WTO obligations. But such a change would pose difficulties for the United States, where the FCC has repeatedly refused to designate Internet access as a basic telecommunications service subject to common carrier legislative and regulatory obligations. Moreover, US-based ISPs would be vehemently opposed to such a classification, which they would decry as an effort by foreign governments to impede entry into their markets and to boost their own firms' prospects via administrative power rather than consumer choice. The solution to this definitional question also would impact the current battle over international Internet Interconnection, discussed below, which could find its way into the WTO.

Commercial development of the global Internet

The GATS was not the only major threat to the telecommunications regime to emerge from outside the ITU in the 1990s. The rapid commercial development of the global Internet represented an equal if not greater challenge to ITU members and the international rules of the game they devised. Some telcos in the industrialized world (especially in North America) were quite willing at the outset to facilitate the Internet's development, which among other things provided them with a new source of revenue in the form of leased circuit usage. But for the ITU's more traditionalist members (especially in the developing world), adjusting to the Internet required that they go through a three-stage process that was roughly akin to coming to terms with one's impending death. The first stage was denial: many dismissed the Internet as an "academic play-thing" that was similar to ham radio and would turn out to be of no real significance to the world of serious international telecommunications. The second stage was anger and resistance: the incumbent PTTs or PTOs saw the Internet as another unwelcome force for liberalization and competition, and in consequence sometimes attempted to slow and limit its development within their territories. The third stage was acceptance and accommodation: they acknowl-edged that the Internet explosion was both inevitable and irreversible, and sought to direct and channel its development in ways that would be less subver-sive to their interests.

Why did so many traditional carriers react negatively to the rise of the Internet in the early 1990s? For one thing, the Internet represented a cultural challenge to their universe. Telecommunications managers and engineers were used to planning long-term investments and roll-outs of new systems and services in a stable and predictable environment, maintaining barriers to compe-tition through their operating rules and closed technical standards, dealing with political pressures and statutory requirements, and related aspects of building and managing PSTNs. All this had meant a slow-moving bureaucratic style of professional conduct and organizational ethos at the national level, which was compounded in the ITU by the need for multilateral agreement. In sharp contrast, the computer scientists who had shaped the Internet's development operated in a very different institutional context that facilitated open-ended, rapid, and decentralized problem-solving and innovation. And as internet-working moved out of computer science circles into the larger academic environment, and later into the general population and the commercial market-place, this taste for unconstrained innovation and rapid change was picked up by an expanding and increasingly heterogeneous group of users. These players were doing things over telco facilities – like organizing Multi-User Shared Hallucinations or hacking servers – that were unfamiliar and had not been offi-cially approved through the usual endless array of documents and consultations at the ITU.

If the new players and practices seemed strange to PTT/PTO managers, the cultural gap cut the other way as well. The personalization of computing meant that users were growing accustomed to configuring information resources to suit their diverse interests. When telco practices or government policies got in their way, these became the targets of ridicule and anger by increasingly vocal and libertarian users who depicted them in global electronic forums as the actions of hopelessly out-of-touch dinosaurs. For 150 years, telcos had sought to legitimate their market dominance with claims to authority – e.g. "we're your Ma Bell or your friendly PTT, we're the experts, we know how to build and operate networks, here are the services we will offer you and the price sheet" – but now a growing range of users were not buying any of it. This problem would grow with the Internet's commercialization and the market entry of independent ISPs that relied on the telcos for leased circuits and interconnections. In this sense, the Internet helped to broaden beyond the corporate user population the range of players who were dissatisfied with the telcos and favored liberalization.

The Internet also represented a technological challenge to the telco order, in several respects. First, as a voluntary agglomeration of thousands of networks that simply agreed to use TCP/IP (Transfer Control Protocol/Internet Protocol) and related protocols and standards, the Internet demonstrated that a decentralized, user-driven architecture could be a robust way to organize networks. Second, the Internet is a packet-switched network of networks, in contrast to the telcos' circuit-switched PSTNs. While the former is optimized for data and the latter for voice, it was clear even in the early 1990s that the Internet approach to managing resources and capacity would grow over time and require some significant rethinking of network planning and service provisioning. Third, the Internet environment was the source of a number of major breakthroughs in systems, services, and applications that the PTOs probably never would have thought up and until recently generally did not provide. For example, while the PSTN operators dithered over the roll out of multimedia applications and services, non-traditional players were developing them rapidly, in a bottom-up fashion, on the Internet.

Fourth, the Internet was eroding the significance of the computer networking protocols and standards the telcos had devised. From the late 1970s the ITU had cooperated with the International Standards Organization (ISO) – which is across the street in Geneva – to develop the Open Systems Interconnection (OSI) model as the key protocol suite for computer communications. PTOs and their governmental supporters told corporate users that they would be migrating networks away from proprietary offerings like IBM's System Network Architecture as soon as OSI was ready, and then the Internet came along and upset the plan. The telcos claimed that the Internet's TCP/IP-based model was technically inferior to the OSI model under construction, refused to incorporate it into their work programs, and discouraged corporate users from adopting it in their private networks. But corporate managers apparently were unimpressed by the PTO side of what was being called a "religious war" between the two models and their respective advocates.[33] TCP/IP was already available and worked fairly well; in consequence, as one industry analyst noted: "OSI ... made little impact where it really matters – in real user networks ... What it boils down to is that TCP/IP is here, and OSI is not."[34] As early as 1992, a survey of 400 corporations showed that the still developing OSI approach was in use in less than 2 per cent of corporations' enterprise networks, whereas TCP/IP was in use in 25 per cent.[35] The latter number grew rapidly in the years to follow and rendered the OSI approach increasingly irrelevant, a fact that the telcos and their preferred manufacturers were forced to acknowledge in their product specifications.

A similar thing happened with the ITU's X.400 standard for message handling. Throughout the 1980s, PTTs had worked to make X.400 the premier, "official" electronic mail system. But some administrations implemented the standard in different ways using national technologies, so that users often experienced inadequate interoperability. Moreover, the addressing scheme was user-unfriendly; PTOs often failed to continuously upgrade the software involved and improve the quality of service, or to provide the requisite technical support; and building up from just text to supporting audio and visual data transmission had been difficult. Similarly, in typical PTT fashion, the tariffs for international messages were high, which constrained usage; in 1994, X.400 service providers reportedly charged an average of $0.70 to deliver a brief message, whereas delivery on the Internet cost $0.0007.[36] For a while many corporations adopted both services, but they later shifted their emphasis to the Internet as security and service quality improved.

Fifth, the Internet represented a new and different paradigm for the institutional organization of standardization. In contrast to the slow-moving, bureaucratic, and PTT-dominated decision-making processes of the CCITT, Internet standardization was carried out in open, flexible, and industry-run forums. The most important of these was the Internet Engineering Task Force (IETF), which was not a formal membership body but simply the name for a few hundred software engineers, who chose to participate on their own authority. The IETF approach involved a streamlined development process based on ongoing electronic coordination, thrice-yearly physical meetings, transparency, and an informal culture widely praised by its members as facilitating cooperation. Working groups were proposed, utilized, and dismantled as soon as particular standards were demonstrated to work well or if the effort was dropped, and typically lasted from 9 to 18 months. In the years to follow, many other industry-driven standards bodies would be launched in the Internet environment. While commercialization and the entry of major players into the Internet marketplace now may be changing the character of the IETF, the relevant fact here is that much of the most important work being done on computer communications has been taking place outside of the ITU and according to starkly different procedures.

Finally, the Internet also presented an economic challenge to the PTT/PTO universe. For example, the Internet allowed users to substitute very low-cost electronic mail for the telcos' tariffed services like international fax and telephony, so there was an unwanted substitution effect. Moreover, the substitution effect expanded from working simply across (i.e. electronic mail instead of phone calls) to within service categories. The Internet severely damaged the market for X.400-based electronic mail services provided over the public data networks some PTTs had developed in the 1980s, became an alternative means of sending fax traffic, and deterred the PTOs from making serious commitments to proprietary multimedia services. But the real nightmare scenario that has arisen since the mid-1990s has been the growth of Internet telephony. While a few crude applications had been around for several years, in 1995 a small Israeli company called VocalTec Inc. took a significant step forward in the development of computer-to-computer voice communications. Both parties had to be logged on at the same time and to have the proper software and equipment, and the transmission quality was substandard, but it meant that users could have international phone conversations that bypassed entirely the telcos' high collection charges and the ITU-based accounting and settlements system. To the user, this meant "free" international calling once the local telephone and ISP charges were paid.

In the years to follow, the fears of many PTOs, especially in the developing world, have been realized. In addition to computer-to-computer connections which, despite improvements, are primarily used by technophiles, there are now computer-to-telephone and telephone-to-telephone configurations which have spurred a robust and rapidly growing business market. With these configurations the service providers must obtain PoPs and pay interconnection charges to the telcos for traffic routed from or to their PSTNs, and a number of innovative mechanisms such as clearing-houses have been set up to handle the compensation. Still, such services take traffic out of the normal charging and accounting scheme. In addition, some service providers have opted to route Internet telephony calls entirely over leased or wholly owned facilities linking clients' offices. Given these considerations, many PTOs in the developing world have banned Internet telephony, although technological progress may make such restrictions difficult to maintain.

Especially in light of the pressures PTOs were already feeling due to liberalization and the Uruguay Round negotiations, considerations such as the above made the Internet's rapid rise a source of concern in ITU circles. As an ITU report later summed up the problem:

> Why is it, then, that PTOs are so worried about the Internet? The main reason is that the Internet is coming from *outside* their sphere of influence, and therefore outside their control. Unlike other telecommunications services, such as mobile communications, which have largely been provided by the PTOs themselves, or by closely allied firms, Internet services are primarily provided by firms outside the traditional telecommunications sector. Thus the Internet is seen, in some quarters, as being "subversive," and undermining the established order.[37]

Nevertheless, the Internet's burgeoning mass popularity since the World Wide Web took off in 1994 and its increasing importance to global communications and commerce made accommodation of this subversive force the only option. In the industrialized world, most telcos eagerly if belatedly plunged into the emerging markets by providing Internet access services in competition with the independent ISPs, building out broadband backbones, aggressively adapting their network architectures and service portfolios, and even supplying Internet telephony to corporate customers. But in the developing world the situation is more mixed. While many Third World PTOs (especially in the middle-income countries) have moved up the learning curve, others (especially in least-developed countries) still seem to be stuck in the anger and resistance stage in certain respects. And on both sides of the development line there are growing tensions between the PTOs and the Internet world: for example, with end users over the per-minute dial fees applied in most countries, and with independent ISPs over the price of leased circuits and the terms of interconnection.

Given the challenges and opportunities presented by the Internet, many PTOs have been looking for ways to involve the ITU in its development. From their standpoint, since the Internet rides on top of their facilities and some of its services will increasingly converge with those provided through PSTNs, it is only natural that they should play a key role in shaping its trajectory, and the ITU is the obvious forum in which to coordinate their efforts. But to their surprise, the ITU's Internet initiatives have often met less than receptive responses from the vast and diverse non-PTO universe of Internet stakeholders. Many of the firms involved, especially those in North America, are steeped in a tradition of industry coordination and self-regulation of the infrastructure and view the ITU – somewhat unfairly – as still being the same exclusive clubhouse for monopolies that it was in the past. This view has been picked up and amplified in various trade publications, industry conferences, and electronic forums where vocal critics have depicted the ITU as (take your pick) engaging in a pathetic and ultimately doomed effort to remain relevant in a post-monopoly world, launching a bureaucratic power grab for new turf, or having some secret strategy to force the Internet into the old model of centralized control.

In this highly charged environment, the ITU's first foray into the Internet world was perhaps ill chosen. It participated in an extremely controversial effort by one industry faction to establish a new system for the management of the Internet domain name system (DNS). The story of the "Global Top Level Domain Memorandum of Understanding" (gTLD-MoU) and the eventual creation of the Internet Corporation for Assigned Names and Numbers (ICANN) is told elsewhere in this volume and need not be repeated here.[38] The relevant point is that, under the gTLD-MoU, the ITU was to serve as the depository for the agreement and to appoint one of twelve members of a new policy oversight committee, a role which gave rise to responses ranging from hostility to near hysteria in many Internet circles. As a leading critic summed up the mood:

> ITU is the representative *par excellence* of the old regime in telecommunications … The gTLD-MoU, which the ITU played a major role in formulating and promoting, can be seen as an attempt to incorporate the Internet into the traditional governance model applied to the telecommunication sector.[39]

US Congressional committees held hearings in which the gTLD-MoU was depicted as an effort to transfer power over the apparently red, white, and blue DNS to "UN bureaucrats in Geneva," and the Clinton Administration made it abundantly clear that it would not accept a model in which the ITU played a central role in DNS governance. Moreover, the administration consistently invoked the specter of the DNS somehow falling into the hands of foreign governments and the ITU when urging the private sector to support the ICANN alternative to the gTLD-MoU model.

It is highly debatable whether there is a technical need for the ITU to play a key role in DNS management. The DNS is not an extension of the international telephone numbering system, and any issues raised by the future convergence of the Internet and telephony can be handled through inter-institutional coordination with organizations indigenous to the Internet environment. At the same time, it is also debatable whether the ITU serving as a depository for the gTLD-MoU by itself would have had a negative impact on the Internet's development, although the larger contours of that agreement arguably have. ICANN has followed key elements of the gTLD-MoU approach and has favored trademark holders and other well-organized interests at the expense of a more open and expansive name space, but that is another matter. While an ITU staff member represents the organization in meetings of ICANN's advisory bodies, it would be a heroic stretch to argue that this accounts for the new organizations' various procedural shortcomings and conservative policies.

The real problem was that ITU's participation in the gTLD-MoU was perceived by opponents as the organization getting a foot in the door with which to push on to an expanding role in other aspects of Internet governance. The perception that the ITU has grander designs on the Internet has been lent credence in the past few years by various statements made by the new Secretary General, and by positions taken by members in the Council and at the ITU's 1998 Plenipotentiary Conference. Given that ICANN is widely viewed as an American organization, many developing countries, and even some European governments, apparently would like to see the ITU play a leading role in the DNS and beyond, irrespective of persistent objections from the US government and large segments of the Internet business community.

To that end, since 1998 the ITU has undertaken an ambitious work program on technical standardization with respect to the interplay between the Internet and PSTNs, and has established working relations with the IETF on certain issues. ITU–T study groups have adopted new Recommendations concerning the transport of Internet Protocol (IP) signals over Asynchronous Transfer Mode technology and on performance parameters for IP networks. Moreover, work is underway on a such items as interworking between IP and circuit switched networks, multimedia applications over IP, addressing and routing, transport for IP signals, performance requirements and security, and even telecommunications issues related to electronic signatures. Critics charge that ITU–T is wandering far afield of its treaty mandate to devise standards for PSTNs; that its study groups are not competent to adopt forward-looking Recommendations on private IP-based internetworking, services, and applications; that some of the work is unnecessary, and that much of the rest can be better handled by industry standards organizations indigenous to the Internet environment; and that, in the end, it is unlikely that ITU standards on such issues will be widely adopted or influential, especially outside of the PTO realm.

Even more controversial are current efforts to establish a Recommendation on the economic organization of peering and interconnection on the Internet. Unlike the traditional joint service arrangements for telephony, the Internet historically operated on a "sender keeps all" (SKA) principle, under which outbound networks handed off traffic to peer networks without providing compensation for its carriage and termination. This model worked well when the Internet was devoted to research and education, but it has been breaking down somewhat with commercialization and the traffic boom. Today the larger ISPs typically require their smaller counterparts to pay volume-based interconnection fees, although they continue to practice SKA with each other. In parallel, ISPs around the world currently pay the full cost of connecting to the United States, through which much of their traffic is routed and in which the vast majority of the world's most heavily visited websites are located. Many PTOs and independent ISPs, especially in Australia and Asia, argue that this constitutes an unfair, forced subsidization of American ISPs and users, even if the bulk of the traffic from the United States is generated by their customers downloading American web pages and by the lack of adequate intra-regional capacity outside Europe. Accordingly, they are seeking a Recommendation that would call for mutual compensation between carriers to hand off and terminate traffic – effectively applying a telephony model to the Internet. The United States, Canada, and Great Britain are strongly opposed to such a Recommendation, and American ISPs – many of which are not involved in the ITU – may be unwilling to comply with any such regulatory rule.

In sum, the Internet has raised a range of significant challenges for ITU members and, by extension, the multilateral rules of the game they devised. It challenges the sovereignty principle by operating to a significant extent outside the domain of state authority and PTO control; by vastly increasing the cost and difficulty – probably even for participants in the ECHELON surveillance system – of acting on the norms giving members the right to monitor and stop private messages they deem threatening to national security and public order; and by greatly increasing the pressure on PTOs to actually implement and go beyond the reformed D Series Recommendations by providing low-cost leased circuits and allowing the more flexible development of private networks. The Internet challenges the joint service provision principle by simply ignoring it: international data traffic constitutes a very substantial share of global traffic – by some estimates, it has or soon will outstrip the level of PSTN telephone traffic, at least on major routes – and it is exchanged without accounting and settlements. And as for the interconnection principle, the bulk of the important work on Internet protocols and standards is being conducted outside the ITU in accordance with very different decision-making procedures. Insofar as it is becoming the central driving force in the development of global communications, the net effect of the Internet is to contribute – along with the GATS and other trends discussed below – to the progressive decoupling of the international regime and the realm it is supposed to be regulating. Whether governments and PTOs can push this genie into their bottle by passing Plenipotentiary Resolutions and ITU–T Recommendations is an open question indeed.

New market, new modes of operation

Technological change (including in the wireless field), the liberalization of national telecommunications systems, the liberalization ITU instruments like the Regulations and D Series Recommendations, the establishment of the GATS, and the rapid growth and commercialization of the Internet have collectively removed many of the long-standing barriers to entry in the international telecommunications services market. The consequences have been striking. For example, in the field of telephony alone:

> As of July 1999, over 1,700 companies worldwide were authorized to build facilities to offer international telephone service. Three years before, there were less than 500. In the fastest growing markets (the US and Western Europe), the pace is not likely to slow down. Even by conservative estimates, the world should easily have more than 2,200 international carriers by mid-2000 ... [however] the world's top 20 carriers carry about 60 percent of the traffic whereas the thousands of new carriers which have just started business since 1989 carry just 13 percent.[40]

Hence, the new international market that is developing is somewhat bifurcated, although the two halves are interdependent. On one side of the line are the major telcos, including former PTTs, that operate PSTNs, primarily in the industrialized world. For example, according to Telegeography Inc., the top ten carriers (ranked by international revenues) are, in order, AT&T, MCI Worldcom, Deutsche Telekom, British Telecom, France Telecom, Sprint, Cable & Wireless, Telecom Italia, Swisscom, and China Telecom.[41] Especially important are about two dozen international "super-carriers," that are invading national markets and forming inter-firm alliances to provide corporate users with integrated, end-to-end solutions on the most lucrative and high-volume routes.[42] In many cases they compete directly with each, even while cooperating in third markets. Given that the underlying political bargain of the *ancien régime* was that "thou shalt not compete with thy neighbor," the spectacle of, say, France Telecom battling with Deutsche Telekom would have been unimaginable little more than a decade ago.

The new strategic orientation of the major carriers has two noteworthy implications for the international telecommunications regime. First, given their size and clout in the world market, in many cases they have little need for multilateral regulations or rules, either to order their own relationships or to constrain their competitors. Indeed, insofar as they operate in multiple markets, they have an incentive to ensure that what rules there remain do not impede their ability to cut attractive deals and operate in the most competitive manner possible. In a liberalized environment, variable bilateral contracts rather than uniform multilateral restraints generally suit their purposes. Hence, while many developing countries still prefer strong and consistent regime rules to buttress their positions against potential competitors, support for that approach among the carriers that actually control the majority of traffic is dissipating.

Second, in situations where the regime rules do get in the way, technological change provides them with an enticing option: cheat, without getting caught. In recent years, a number of "new modes of operation" have arisen which allow service providers to spin traffic around the world in directions that do not conform to the traditional pattern of direct bilateral correspondence, with perhaps a transit carrier or two in between. Indeed, some of the new modes are arbitrage operations that exist precisely because of the cost distortions associated with joint service provision and accounting and settlements. Estimates vary, but new modes of operation may now account for as much as 20 per cent of global traffic.

One such mode, which is practiced by leading facilities-based carriers (especially in the United States), is refile. Refile allows an outbound carrier to reduce its settlements payments to correspondents on traffic it passes off. For example, if the combined accounting rates between country A and country B and between country B and country C are lower than the rate that has been negotiated between country A and country C, a carrier in country A may route its traffic to country C via country B. The carrier in country C receives less revenue than it would have on a direct inbound routing, but it is unable to detect that the traffic is actually originating in country A. What is noteworthy here is that refile is directly at odds with the sovereignty principle, according to which correspondence must be organized in accordance with the mutual consent of the originating and terminating countries. But treaty provisions or no, carriers do it anyway; the practice is flourishing.

On the other side of the line are the thousands of new service providers that lease from the PTOs rather than building and operating their own networks. Many of these "light" carriers are also following new modes of operation, and they have even less use for multilateral regulation. Most are based in the more liberalized national markets, especially North America and Great Britain, and have emerged outside and in competition with the PTO nexus. As such, they generally see the regime's regulatory dimensions as being overly restrictive, and view the ITU as essentially a clubhouse for semi-reformed PTTs. This distrust, coupled with the cost of participating in ITU bodies, has led many members of this parallel universe to work outside the organization, participating only to the extent necessary to prevent potentially restrictive decisions. What this means is that ITU members favoring an orderly world frequently find themselves having to react to forces emerging outside their domain, rather than proactively planning the evolution of the global network within the organization and on their own terms.

In fact, many of the light carriers exist precisely because of the high cost of delivering traffic in accordance with ITU rules. New modes like Internet telephony allow firms to provide services to customers at significantly reduced rates by avoiding the accounting and settlements system. Another new mode popular with light carriers is international simple resale (ISR). ISR is the resale of switched services using privately leased circuits that are interconnected with public networks. International leased circuits are charged for on a flat-rate basis, so the traffic they convey is not subject to the international accounting and settlements system. ISR is very attractive to new market entrants because they do not have to invest in building facilities. But even PSTN operators may opt to provide ISR. On outbound traffic, incumbent facilities-based carriers have strong incentives to bypass the system in this manner because they can levy per-minute collection charges on their customers without having to pay settlements on any surplus of minutes sent abroad. For inbound traffic there obviously is less incentive to allow ISR (given the loss of settlements revenue) unless a carrier also gains assurances that it can send back such traffic and have it terminated in its foreign correspondent's network. The FCC has prohibited "one-way bypass" and insists that ISR relationships with the United States must involve reciprocal market access. Other countries, such as the United Kingdom, Sweden, New Zealand, and Australia, have taken a more liberal approach, believing that competition and consumer interests will be promoted even if their carriers are not protected by strict reciprocity.

A more controversial new mode practiced by light carriers is call-back. Call-back is the reversal in direction of an international call to bypass high collection charges in the outbound country; it typically is provided by resellers in competition with incumbent facilities-based carriers. In the most common approach, a customer in country A calls a number in country B that has low collection rates (typically, the United States) and hangs up after a certain number of rings without being charged. Having thus been signaled, a computer at the number then "calls back" the customer and provides a dial tone that can be used to place the international call as if it actually originated in the low-cost country B. The traffic remains within the accounting and settlement system and is treated as a normal outbound call from country B to country A. Although country A carriers will receive settlements payments on the inbound traffic if there is a surplus in the relation, the loss of collections revenue is strongly objectionable to many of them.

In the mid-1990s, the developing countries waged a campaign against call-back in the ITU. They argued that, like refile, the service violates the requirement for mutual consent between corresponding carriers. However, the United States claimed that call-back is not a "service," but rather a computer application, and that as such it is compatible with ITU law. Other industrialized countries also showed no interest in a multilateral ban of some sort, so the developing countries' complaints were pushed off into non-binding plenipotentiary resolutions. Over one hundred ITU members have announced that call-back is prohibited in their territories, but the service suppliers will continue to thrive until accounting rates fall far enough to make them irrelevant.

In sum, a significant segment of the new global market is operating outside of (and because of) the international telecommunications regime. And these external pressures on the regime's relevance are now being matched by pressures within the regime-governed world of joint service provision.

Internal pressures on regime relevance

Erosion of the joint service provision rules

Perhaps nothing exemplifies the declining importance of the telecommunications regime more than the crisis of the international accounting and settlements system. As noted above, this is the ITU-defined mechanism under which a carrier in country A compensates a carrier in country B for receiving and terminating a call. Although the FCC and AT&T invented the system and won its multilateral adoption in the Recommendations in 1968, the fact that the United States liberalized its market earlier and more fully than other countries and has lower international collection charges (together with other factors) has resulted in a huge excess of outbound traffic over inbound traffic, and hence (as of 1998) an over $5 billion dollar deficit on outpayments to foreign carriers, mostly in developing countries.

The United States and its supporters fought a six-year battle in the CCITT and its successor, the ITU–T, to get changes in the relevant Recommendations and in carrier practices. In March 1992, it won agreement on a new Recommendation D. 140, Accounting Rate Principles for International Telephone Services, which embodied five key principles:

1   Accounting rates should be cost oriented and take into account relevant cost trends.
2   Each Administration should apply cost orientation to all relations on a nondiscriminatory basis.
3   Administrations should seek to achieve cost-oriented rates in an expeditious manner, recognizing that this may need to be implemented on a scheduled basis where the reduction required is significant. In the event of scheduling, Administrations should aim to agree staged reductions over a period normally of one to five years. However, the actual length of the period may depend on the extent of reduction and the level of development of the countries concerned.
4   Administration should periodically review accounting rates to ensure that they continue to reflect current cost trends.
5   Information relative to accounting rates for telephony should be made available on a voluntary basis to the ITU in an aggregated format in accordance with guidelines accompanying the Recommendation.

Over the next few years, similar language would be incorporated into the various service-specific charging and accounting Recommendations on intercontinental telephony, data services, mobile services, and so forth. But to satisfy developing countries, Recommendation D. 140 also notes that costs "depend on many factors which vary by country." This has remained a major bone of contention throughout the 1990s. In accepting cost orientation, developing countries consistently have focused their negotiating strategies on arguing that their direct costs are higher, their indirect costs should be reflected in accounting rates, and D. 140's methodological guidelines for the calculation of costs should reflect these considerations.

In bilateral consultations about operating agreements, American companies and carriers from other reform-minded countries could point to these multilateral instruments when calling for lower rates. So could governments in their dealings with each other. Nevertheless, these instruments were not legally binding, and the flexibility that had been built into the Recommendations in order to win broad support also provided some escape clauses for foot-draggers when it came to their interpretation and implementation. In the years to follow, accounting rates declined in many relations, but not far or fast enough for US carriers and the FCC. Outbound traffic from the United States continued to boom, especially in relations with a small group of developing countries. Moreover, new technologies and techniques of traffic re-origination – e.g. call-back, calling cards, and country direct services – were in many cases reversing the "normal" flow of traffic and increasing US outbound minutes, so much so that today many analysts believe they are the principle cause of the deficit's continuing growth today. Hence, when the Clinton Administration came to power in 1993, the US settlements deficit was still growing rapidly, and political pressure for stronger action was increasing.

In light of the ITU members' reluctance to move, at the behest of AT&T and MCI in particular the FCC decided that it should tell the rest of the world what it may charge to export termination services to the United States. In 1997 it issued its "Benchmark Order," which went into effect on 1 January 1998.[43] The FCC set a timetable on which US carriers must negotiate cost-based accounting and settlements rates with corresponding foreign carriers. If they are unable to do so, the FCC then specifies – on the basis of a controversial methodology – what rates American carriers may pay, these generally being about one third of the previous price. Reduced settlements income has very serious consequences for developing countries and hence has caused an enormous battle within the ITU, where again questions of comity and legality have been raised at great length but have fallen on deaf American ears.[44]

Faced with this challenge to the regime's standing and the ITU's authority, Secretary General Pekka Tarjanne took up the issue by speaking out on the need for reform of the system to fit a more competitive environment, as well as for lower accounting rates and collection charges. In September 1996, he took the unusual step of submitting a consultation document to Standardization Sector, calling on it to accelerate its work on these matters while exploring alternative payment methods. At the same time, he and his staff began to publicly criticize the FCC's unilateral approach. Accounting rate reform, they suggested, should be done on a multilateral basis and take into account the problems of developing countries.

In March 1997, Tarjanne convened a meeting of an informal expert group in an effort to regain the initiative. The FCC was invited to explain its policies, and the group countered with a call for a multilateral approach that would speed up change in a more cooperative and balanced manner. The group recommended that the Secretary General propose a global accounting rate reduction of 5 to 10 per cent per year during 1997 and 1998. Furthermore, it stated that "in all but a few cases, settlement rates should be priced below US 25 cents per minute," a figure not that far off from the FCC's proposed benchmarks. But to soften the blow, the group also stated that there should be a "soft landing" for the forty-eight least developed countries, with carriers guaranteeing certain payments to them for a transition period not to exceed five years. In tandem with these proposals, the World Bank has begun exploring options to help developing countries handle the financial shock of reduced settlement revenues.

In the end, the Expert Group's pronouncements failed to head off the growing conflict. ITU staffers believed that the FCC had indicated that it would refrain from adopting benchmarks and wait to see if multilateral reforms would ensue, but the FCC disavowed such statements. Moreover, when the relevant study group met in May 1997, developing countries decried the Expert Group's report, stating that they had been severely under-represented in the meeting that defined it, that the proposed cuts were too deep and too fast, and that it would be treated as merely one input to be considered in a broader discussion.

In consequence, the FCC went ahead with the application of the Benchmark Order, unilaterally forcing other countries' PTOs to reduce the rates at which US carriers compensate them for terminating traffic. In effect, the US unilateral move gutted the ITU's authority over the issue and rendered irrelevant both the Recommendations and those provisions of the treaty Regulations which specify that accounting rates should be set by mutual consent between corresponding carriers. While in response ITU–T has managed to rework the relevant Recommendations to allow for new forms of mutual compensation, it has not been able to agree on pricing guidelines acceptable to the United States.

Erosion of compliance

As the above discussion indicates, in sharp contrast with the dominant pattern of the past, compliance with ITU agreements is eroding on multiple fronts. For the ex-PTTs in particular, there are strong counter-pressures at work here. On the one hand, there are many privatized PTOs around the world who have invested a great deal of time and effort over many years building up the habits and mechanisms of cooperative management, and which are committed to preserving both the regime and the ITU. Moreover, the functional requirements of maintaining and progressively expanding and upgrading the global network of networks still make cooperation imperative in many cases. In short, there is a deeply embedded institutional "legacy system" in place.

On the other hand, the global market and policy environment have changed so radically that the idea of anything more than baseline uniformity of behavior is an anachronism. In an increasingly privatized and normalized market, firms tend to go their own ways as their strategies and opportunities dictate. Privately arranged contracts between buyers and sellers, and bilateral deals with the governments of countries they want to operate in, are now far more consequential for the day-to-day conduct of the international telecommunications business than anything contained in the ITU instruments. Moreover, new technologies allow PTOs and their competitors alike to bypass and operate outside the rules without any effective detection.

As in the past, the United States remains the most non-compliant member of note. Even though it has been quite successful in winning the liberalization of regime rules since the 1980s, the government still regards the ITU and its instruments as overly regulatory and anti-competitive, and hence feels justified to follow a course that is sharply at odds with its instruments. The unilateral imposition of accounting rates, refile, and arguably call-back are unambiguously violations of the treaty requirement that the provision of international services must be agreed to by the members concerned. To be sure, these and related American actions do advance the cause of international competition and are beneficial to US businesses and, to a lesser extent, the average consumer. And insofar as creeping competition forces foreign PTOs to become more efficient, rebalance their inefficient rate structures, and so on, they may eventually prove beneficial beyond US borders. But there is no doubt that they also have the effect of undermining compliance with and the credibility of regime commitments, and indeed the ITU itself.

Moreover, on the theory that "if you can't beat them, join them," PTOs and their competitors in other industrialized countries are abandoning the accounting rate system and are beginning to offer some of the new modes of operation, even – as in the case of Internet telephony – at the risk of cannibalizing their own tariff structures. In short, America's defection from the coalition provides strong incentives for others to do the same. The consequence is an increasing de-coupling of the global market and the international regime. While the big national network operators continue to coordinate within the ITU, a growing percentage of the market is in the hands of firms that are not involved in the organization and are working whenever necessary and possible outside its policy framework.

Conclusion

After 150 years of shaping the organization of the global marketplace and facilitating the expansion of networks and services, the international telecommunications regime is now on a seemingly irreversible path of decline. The ITU still plays very important roles in other aspects of global communications, most notably radio frequency spectrum regulation and technical assistance to developing countries. But today, it is the WTO that sets the multilateral rules of the game on the economic organization of global communications, and private standards bodies – especially in the Internet environment – are increasingly driving the interconnection of technologies into a seamless global information fabric. What this means for the regulation of the Global Information Society is not entirely clear yet, but one thing is certain: the traditional form of state authority over the architecture of global interconnection is a thing of the past.

Notes

* A revised version of this chapter is forthcoming as a working paper of the Carnegie Endowment for International Peace.

1 International regimes can be defined as

> sets of implicit or explicit principles, norms, rules, and decision-making procedures around which actors' expectations converge in a given area of international relations. Principles are beliefs of fact, causation and rectitude. Norms are standards of behavior defined in terms of rights and obligations. Rules are specific prescriptions or proscriptions for action. Decision-making procedures are prevailing practices for making and implementing collective choice.
>
> (Krasner 1983: 2)

The international telecommunications regime is one instance in a large set of cases wherein governments negotiate to establish multilateral "rules of the game" for issue-areas ranging from trade, monetary, and environmental policies to arms control, human rights and beyond. Hence, like domestic political institutions, regimes have been analyzed as dependent variables either singularly or on a comparative basis in terms of their institutional attributes (e.g. their scope, domain, strength, distributional biases and compliance mechanisms) and historical evolution (e.g. creation, maintenance and adaptation, transformation or decay), or of the types of collective action problems they involve.

2 For a fuller discussion of the process see William J. Drake (1994a) "Asymmetric deregulation and the transformation of the international telecommunications regime," in Eli M. Noam and Gerard Pogorel (eds) *Asymmetric Deregulation: The Dynamics of Telecommunications Policies in Europe and the United States*, Norwood: Ablex, pp. 137–203.

3 The international telecommunications regime must be distinguished from the international radio regime, the primary focus of which is the management of international radio frequency spectrum and satellite orbital slots. Perhaps because both regimes are negotiated in the ITU and are technologically and politically interrelated, some analysts have treated the principles, norms, rules and decision-making procedures relating to radio frequency spectrum as part of the telecommunications regime, rather than as a separate regime. For example, see Mark W. Zacher with Brent A. Sutton (1996) *Governing Global Networks: International Regimes for Transportation and Communications*, Cambridge: Cambridge University Press; and Peter F. Cowhey (1990) "The international telecommunications regime: the political roots of regimes for high technology," *International Organization* 44 (Spring): 169–99. However, the two regimes involve distinct functional and political problems, intellectual cultures, and sets of prescriptions and proscriptions, the details of which are largely negotiated in different bodies and enshrined in separate instruments. The one exception to this is the ITU's Convention, which is negotiated in Plenipotentiary Conferences and contains broadly framed overarching principles relevant to both regimes. In general, those pertaining to radio have not changed since they were first formulated early in the century. Moreover, they have followed distinct trajectories without affecting each other. Whereas the telecommunications regime has undergone a fundamental transformation in recent years (as is discussed below), the overarching principles and norms of the radio regime have remained largely unaltered. Or to put it another way, there has been a change of the telecommunications regime, but only change within the radio regime – that is, in its detailed rules.

4 The acronyms were based on the French language names, which in the early years were more elaborate, e.g. the CCIF was the International Consultative Committee on Long-Distance Telephone Communications.

5 On the radio regime side of the ITU's operations, the relevant bodies included the Plenipotentiary Conferences, which negotiated the Conventions; from 1932, the World Administrative Radio Conferences, which negotiated the International Radio Regulations (parallel to the WATTCs and the International Telegraph and Telephone Regulations on the telecommunications regime side); from 1932, Regional and special Administrative Radio Conferences that dealt with less than global or especially pressing issues, respectively; from 1927, the International Radio Consultative Committee (from 1994, the Radiocommunication Sector) which negotiated the Radio Recommendations (parallel to the CCITT and the International Telegraph and Telephone Recommendations on telecommunications regime side); and the International Frequency Registration Board, which from 1947 maintained a master list of frequency spectrum allocations and assignments to ensure non-interference between services.

6 See Eli M. Noam (1993) *Telecommunications in Europe*, New York: Oxford.

7 For two contrasting interpretations, see Eli M. Noam, *Telecommunications in Europe*, and Andrew Davis (1994) *Telecommunications and Politics: The Decentralized Alternative*, New York: Pinter Publishers.

8 George A. Codding, Jr (1952) *The International Telecommunication Union: An Experiment in International Cooperation*, Leiden: E.J. Brill, p. 42.

9 Anthony M. Rutkowski (1982) "The USA and the ITU: many attitudes, few policies," *Intermedia* 10 (July/September): 34.

10 These firms still controlled 89.6 per cent of the total cable length as late as 1892. Daniel R. Headrick (1991) *The Invisible Weapon: Telecommunications and International Politics, 1851–1945*, New York: Oxford University Press, p. 38.

11 Another, lesser designation, "Private Operating Agency," was established for firms that did not have common carrier obligations and were not recognized to serve as a national operator, but rather served specialized market niches on a private contractual basis outside the rules under the regime's "special arrangements" provision.

12 The State Department played a coordinating role by organizing US participation in the conferences and committees where regime issues were addressed, but AT&T typically was the major player on the delegations. As the US market became more diverse in the post-war era of deregulation, other large corporations with interests in ITU affairs also became active, thereby swelling the sizes of US delegations to the point of dwarfing those of other countries. Moreover, US delegations to treaty-related conferences frequently were led by businessmen appointed at the rank of ambassador.

13 *State Treaty Between Austria, Prussia, Bavaria and Saxony of 25 July 1850 Concerning the Establishment of the Austro-German Telegraphic Union* (translation from German in the archives of the International Telecommunication Union, Geneva): pp. 2, 3, 5, 6, 10.

14 *Documents Diplomatiques de la Conférence Télégraphique International de Paris* (1865), Paris: Imprimerie Impériale, p. 33, my translation. After the development of radio, this article was amended to include a requirement that special arrangements not cause harmful interference.

15 *Documents Diplomatiques de la Conférence Télégraphique International de Paris* (1865), Paris: Imprimerie Impériale, p. 34, my translation.

16 Codding, *The International Telecommunication Union* (1952), p. 43.

17 Comité Consultatif International des Communications Téléphoniques à grande distance (1927) *Assemblée Plénière de Côme, 5–12 Septembre 1927*, Paris: CCIF, pp. 117–19, my translation.

18 Theodor Irmer (1987) "Standardization in the changing world of telecommunications," in Economic Commission for Europe (ed.) *The Telecommunications Industry: Growth and Structural Change*, New York: United Nations, p. 45.

19 For a discussion of technical standards as international regime rules, see William J. Drake (1994b) "The transformation of international telecommunications standardization: European and global dimensions," in Charles Steinfield, Johannes Bauer and Laurence Caby (eds) *Telecommunications in Europe: Changing Policies, Services and Technologies*, Newbury Park: Sage, pp. 71–96.

20 Susanne K. Schmidt and Raymund Werle (1998) *Coordinating Technology: Studies in the International Standardization of Telecommunications*, Cambridge: MIT Press.

21 For a time in the post-World War II era, the ITU attempted to do some collective planning of international network development through a series of World Plans and Regional Plans that specified targets for the construction of lines and routing of traffic, but these produced rather mixed results.

22 International Press Telecommunications Council (1972) *Revised Drafts of Recommendations D.1 and D.2 – Contribution No. 35*, CCITT Study Group III, Geneva: ITU, p. 2.

23 Quoted in Dan Schiller (1982) *Telematics and Government*, Norwood: Ablex, p. 185.

24 For a discussion, see William J. Drake and Kalypso Nicolaïdis (1992) "Ideas, interests, and institutionalization: 'Trade in services and the Uruguay Round,'" in Peter M. Haas (ed.) *Knowledge, Power and International Policy Coordination*, a special issue of *International Organization* 45: 37–100.

25 For a detailed analysis, see William J. Drake (1988) "WATTC-88: Restructuring the International Telecommunication Regulations," *Telecommunications Policy* 12 (September): 217–33.

26 International Telecommunication Union (1988) "The International Telecommunication Regulations," *Informal Consultations, Information Paper 12*, Geneva: ITU (9 December), p. 10.

27 For details, see William J. Drake (1989) "The CCITT: time for reform?" in *Reforming the Global Network: The 1989 Plenipotentiary Conference of the International Telecommunication Union*, London: International Institute of Communications. pp. 28–43.

28 Cross-border supply (via telecommunications, postal systems and so forth) is one of four designated "modes of supply" for services under the GATS regime, the others being movement of the consumer to the producer's country, movement of a natural person producer to the consumer's country, and the "commercial presence" of producer firms in consumer countries, even by foreign direct investment.

29 The evolution and resolution of the transborder data flow debate – which was closely related to the move toward trade treatment for telecommunications and information services – is assessed in William J. Drake (1993a) "Territoriality and intangibility: transborder data flows and national sovereignty," in Kaarle Nordenstreng and Herbert I. Schiller (eds) *Beyond National Sovereignty: International Communications in the 1990s*, Norwood: Ablex, pp. 259–313.

30 World Trade Organization (1994) *The Results of the Uruguay Round of Multilateral Trade Negotiations: The Legal Texts*, pp. 359–63. For analyses of the Telecommunications Annex and related GATS instruments, see Lee Tuthill (1996) "Users' rights? The multilateral rules on access to telecommunications", *Telecommunications Policy* 20 (March): 89–99; G. Russell Pipe (1993) *Trade of Telecommunications Services: Implications of a GATT Uruguay Round Agreement for ITU and Member States*, Geneva: International Telecommunication Union (May); and (1996) *Trade Agreements on Telecommunications: Regulatory Implications – Briefing Report No. 5 of the International Telecommunication Union Regulatory Colloquium*, Geneva: ITU (March).

31 On the debate over the significance of the GBT deal, see William J. Drake and Eli M. Noam (1998) "Assessing the WTO agreement on basic telecommunications," in Gary Clyde Hufbauer and Erika Wada (eds) *Unfinished Business: Telecommunications After the Uruguay Round*, Washington, DC: Institute for International Economics, pp. 27–61; and Michael Tyler and Carol Joy (1997) *1.1.98 – Telecommunications in the New Era: Competing in the Single Market*, London: Multiplex Press.

32 For an overview, see William J. Drake and Kalypso Nicolaïdis (2000) "Global electronic commerce and the General Agreement on Trade in Services: The 'Millennium Round' and beyond," in Pierre Sauve and Robert M. Stern (eds) *GATS 2000: New Directions in Services Trade Liberalization*, Washington, DC: Brookings Institution Press, pp. 399–437.

33 For discussions, see Carl Malamud (1992) *Exploring the Internet: A Technical Travelogue*, Englewood Cliffs, NJ: Prentice Hall, and William J. Drake (1993b) "The Internet religious war," *Telecommunications Policy* 17: 643–9.

34 Thomas Wood of the Business Research Group, quoted in, Donne Pinsky (1992) "In search of open systems," *Communications Week International*, 6 July: 14.

35 Elisabeth Horwitt (1992) "TCP/IP suits them fine," *Network World*, 27 (July).

36 Kenneth Hart (1994) "Rival e-mail camps forge uneasy pact," *Communications Week International*, 14 November: 46.

37 International Telecommunication Union (1997) *Challenges to the Network: Telecoms and the Internet*, Geneva: ITU, p. 4; emphasis in the original. See also the discussion in ITU (1999) *Challenges to the Network: Internet for Development*, Geneva: ITU.

38 See, for example, the chapters by Mark Gould and Michael Froomkin in this volume.

39 Milton L. Mueller (1998) "The battle over Internet domain names: global or national TLDs?" *Telecommunications Policy* 22: 103.

40 Gregory C. Staple (ed.) (1999) *Telegeography 2000*, Washington, DC: Telegeography Inc., p. 30.

41 Figures cited in Gregory C. Staple (ed.) *Telegeography 2000*, p. 36.

42 For a discussion, see Eli M. Noam and Anjali Singhal (1996) "Supra-national regulation for supra-national telecommunications carriers?" *Telecommunications Policy* 20 (December): 769–87.

43 Federal Communications Commission (1997) *In the Matter of International Settlement Rates – Report and Order*, FCC 97–280, Docket No. 96–261, adopted 7 August 1997. Available on the World Wide Web at http://www.fcc.gov.

44 For a discussion, see Chapter 2 of William J. Drake (1999) *Towards Sustainable Competition in Global Telecommunications: From Principle to Practice – Summary Report of the Third Aspen Institute Roundtable on International Telecommunications*, Washington, DC: Aspen Institute.

9 After Seattle

Trade negotiations and the New Economy

Jonathan D. Aronson

The collapse of the Seattle meeting of trade ministers from 135 countries in November 1999 was a shock. The five-year-old World Trade Organization suddenly gained the spotlight that it craved, but not in the way that its leaders had imagined. Public protests that linked environmentalists and labor movements in an unlikely alliance grabbed the headlines while negotiators from the United States, Europe, and the developing countries deadlocked behind closed doors.

Afterwards the press portrayed the collapse as a serious setback for trade liberalization while government officials downplayed the episode as a minor setback that delayed but did not derail the process.

The first section of this essay briefly (1) reviews the background of the WTO, (2) considers the objectives of the key players going into Seattle, (3) assesses the reasons for the breakdown, and (4) suggests how to proceed towards a new round of trade negotiations. The second section focuses explicitly on what needs to be accomplished to update global trade rules in light of the rise of "the New Economy" driven by new telecommunications and information technologies.

Stumbling towards a new trade round

Background

For more than half a century trade negotiators meeting under the auspices of the General Agreement on Tariffs and Trade (GATT) struggled to promote trade liberalization through a series of ever-lengthening trade rounds. Throughout, negotiators worked to lower tariffs, improve transparency, promote national treatment for goods once they cleared customs, and guarantee most-favored-nation treatment for all members of the club.

Over time tariffs fell significantly and world trade increased dramatically. Ironically, despite all the progress towards free trade, significant trade barriers persisted and new ones, mostly non-tariff barriers, were revealed or created. GATT and its rules evolved.

Five major trends were evident. First, GATT expanded beyond tariffs and focused more of its attention on non-tariff barriers such as subsidies, standard setting, and government procurement. Second, GATT expanded its mandate to include reduction of barriers to trade in services as well as trade in goods. Third, the rise of global firms and economic globalization persuaded negotiators to address new kinds of issues such as intellectual property, competition policy, and trade-related investment issues. Labor and environmental issues are issues for the future negotiations. Fourth, the number of countries in the GATT more than doubled. Even China, after more than a decade of negotiations, stands poised to join the WTO. In parallel, the GATT which began life in a small castle in Geneva, with only about one hundred in staff, grew and was given new powers and even a new name at the end of the last trade round – the World Trade Organization (WTO). Fifth, as global trade issues impacted on national sovereignty, non-governmental organizations (NGOs) committed to protecting their own focused issues became significant players.

Goals for Seattle

Past trade rounds generally revolved around three dynamics. First, the United States, always the *demandeur,* and Europe bicker on process and content, especially about agriculture. The rest of the world watches from the sidelines, frustrated that their opinions and issues are not getting enough attention. Second, the United States in its role as the world's largest importer confronts the developing countries that always seek more access to US markets without providing what the United States sees as comparable access to their own markets. Europe sits on the sidelines, providing sympathy for the developing countries but not much in the way of concessions. Third, Japan, and to some extent Korea, sit quietly on the sidelines hoping to be ignored but knowing that in the closing stages of the negotiations they will be pressured for concessions.

Every country is a sinner when it comes to free trade. After all of the rhetoric is stripped away, every country tries to promote its own companies and interests. Each country wants to reduce import barriers that hamper their efficient industries and maintain import barriers where their industries are less efficient. It should surprise nobody that the United States, for example, advocates free trade in agriculture but is reluctant to open its own markets for textiles and steel.

This time the roles were somewhat different but the basic relationships remained the same. All the main participants proclaimed their intention to lower tariff and reduce subsidies. The European Union sought a wider-ranging agenda and was willing to consider a longer negotiation than the United States. The EU wanted the Millennial Round to take up issues such as dumping, competition policy, and investment issues. The United States was not enthusiastic. The United States wanted to concentrate mainly on market access for agriculture and services and on improving transparency and strengthening dispute settlement procedures. Both sides were nervous on how to address labor and environmental issues. Japan was largely silent as it continued to cope with its prolonged domestic economic malaise. Developing countries complained that their interests were being ignored and their exports hampered while pleading for longer transition periods before they had to open their markets completely.

In the aftermath of the collapse of the Seattle meeting US negotiators tried to put the best face on the developments. They noted that most of the issues they were concerned about would continue to be addressed in scheduled, ongoing discussions mandated by the last round of trade negotiations, while they dodged the bullet on issues they did not want on the agenda. They regretted the delay, but suggested that a battle, not the war, was lost. They recalled that in 1982 a meeting of trade ministers failed to agree to begin new trade negotiations, but that the Uruguay was successfully launched a few years later. They also reminded critics that the 1988 and 1990 Ministerial meetings failed to achieve closure, so Uruguay Round negotiations had to be extended because initial deadlines could not be met. The United States even claimed they earned points with labor for raising immigration and labor issues.

The European Union did not get the wider agenda it sought but will not have to resist the attack on its agricultural subsidies. Similarly, Japan can continue to protect its farmers. The developing countries got nothing on transition periods, customs valuations, or improved market access to industrial country markets. The WTO became more visible, but in all the wrong ways. Finally, labor unions and environmental NGOs demonstrated that they could exercise significant blocking power, if not positive results.

What went wrong?

Unlike the ministerial failure of 1982, trade ministers gathered in Seattle at a time when the US economy, and increasingly the world economy, was strong and dynamic. What happened? Five separate problems, it appears, combined to set up failure. First, the location was wrong. The United States should not have hosted the meeting and Seattle was an especially poor choice within the United States. President Clinton, bolstered by a strong economy and obsessed by his legacy, wanted the prestige of launching a new trade round. Even if the resulting negotiations were titled the Millennial Round or the Seattle Round instead of the Clinton Round, the goal was to add the round as a feather to his historical cap. Other countries saw this as yet another instance of the United States throwing its weight around and acquiesced reluctantly. The final choice of sites came down to San Diego or Seattle. Wary of protests related to immigration and labor on the Mexican border and responsive to lobbying from Boeing, Seattle became the choice. Seattle, however, is a center of environmental activism and boasted a history of strong, politicized unions. Moreover, the conference organization was chaotic.

Second, the wrong WTO Director General was presiding. For months WTO members wrangled over the selection of a new leader. Ultimately, an unhappy compromise split the term between former New Zealand Prime Minister Mike Moore, supported by the United States and most other industrial countries, and a former Thai Minister, supported by many developing countries plus Japan. Had the developing country candidate gone first the developing countries might have been more willing to begin negotiations. Moore, perhaps, would have been ready as the closer.

Third, the prolonged negotiations between the United States and China over the terms of Chinese WTO accession took time and distracted top US negotiators. When an agreement was reached less than a month before Seattle, there was not enough time left to make the high-level backroom deals needed to prepare for agreement. USTR trusted that they could pull a rabbit from the hat. They failed.

Fourth, no agreement on priorities was reached. Old issues like beef and bananas shared the same agenda as new issues like trade-related anti-competitive issues (TRAMs), e-commerce, environment and labor. Governments could not agree on what needed to be done and how to do it. Most big business favored Chinese accession, but were wary that government action would hamper their global expansion and over-regulate the Internet. Environmentalists and labor groups, fearful that global rules might undermine national sovereignty and their specific interests, were vigilant in opposing progress.

Fifth, as a result of poor planning, no agreement on priorities, and rushed preparation, too many brackets remained in the conference text. Many of the fundamental deals and compromises that needed to be resolved early were not. The distance that needed to be bridged in a short meeting, already troubled by protests, was too great.

Does it matter?

Once the ministerial meeting collapsed, governments were quick to bemoan the failure but reassure anyone who would listen that the process would nonetheless move forward. Still, the failure raises three important problems. First, progress on further liberalization of trade and strengthening of the WTO will slow. Second, and more important, the collapse put the accession of China into the WTO on a different level. The Chinese may not conform without the discipline of ongoing negotiations. Third, at a time when significant international understandings are needed with regard to the fast evolving New Economy, there will instead be delay. Yet, as the next section makes clear, the Internet and the New Economy are evolving so rapidly that by the time governments get around to the next round, it may be beyond their ability to craft and implement appropriate rules.

Trade, the Internet, and the New Economy

It was only in 1989 that commercial Internet service providers emerged, offering a wide range of private and commercial customers access to the burgeoning Internet for the first time. Today, more than 200 million users are connected, including 100 million in the United States. By 1999 about 50 per cent of US households were connected; about 25 per cent in the European Union, and about 12 per cent in Japan. Affordable voice, data, and video connections between people and machines are now the norm, not the exception. Almost any government, firm, or individual has access to more information than exists in the great of libraries on the planet.

Figures collected by the US Federal Communications Commission indicate that Internet users exploded from 3 million in 1994 to 200 million by the start of 2000, and Internet traffic was doubling every 100 days in mid-1999. The speed of delivery over the Internet backbone network is increasing even more rapidly and is projected to reach 4,800 Mbps in 2000. Between 1995 and 1999 the average online usage per user in the United States increased from 12 hours per month in 1995 to about 36 hours per month in 1999 and could double again by 2002. E-commerce experienced a similar trajectory and e-commerce revenue is projected to exceed $1 trillion by 2003. E-commerce as a percentage of US GDP was essentially zero in 1995, reached 1 per cent in 1999, and may approach 4.5 per cent as early as 2002. Business-to-business e-commerce is projected to increase far faster than business-to-consumer e-commerce. It is expected that by the year 2003 global economic commerce will reach $1.3 trillion.

Overall, three key trends will likely characterize the transformation of the world economy during the next decade. First, circuit switched voice traffic will soon be overtaken by data traffic, and data traffic will grow much faster in the future. Data, not voice, is the future. Second, wireless data is fast emerging and will likely displace wireline networks as the dominant provider of information in the future. Third, business-to-business e-commerce is growing much faster than business-to-consumer e-commerce and will increasingly serve as the basis of the New Economy.

Still, the prospect of nearly total access to global information networks and databases creates threats along with remarkable opportunities. The promise and the threat rest on the basic power of information. The Internet inevitably will create new realities, transform the way we live and work, but also destroy many aspects of society, the state, and business. As the cyberspace revolution unfolds, societal norms, state laws, and business practices and standards will need to develop flexibly at Internet time. This presents a major challenge to the regulators and international institutions that typically adapt to new circumstances much more slowly than markets. Should they do nothing, try to take control, or find some form of limited intervention that they can agree on? Presumably, the middle ground wins, but where in the middle does a solution lie?

E-commerce providers contend that self-regulation is the best course. Lawmakers and regulators are not so sure. They are struggling to figure out whether and how they should intervene to ensure that the competition is fair and robust and that everybody is connected to everybody else. The challenges to governments are global as well as national. Indeed, any serious future trade negotiations will need to reach agreements that promote rather than retard the booming global e-commerce sector.

My goal in this section is to describe how an earlier transformation of the key underlying principles, institutions, and norms of the international telecom regime were completely reworked during the 1980s and 1990s. Then, I want to build on this experience to describe some of the challenges that lie ahead to promote the common good and guard against the excesses of a global, digital, network age. The challenge is directly related to international institutions and the norms they promote and protect because Internet policy must confront the fundamental nature of cyberspace. To be truly effective, Internet policy will need to be multilateral.

The old institutions, principles, and norms of telecom

In 1990 Peter Cowhey identified the core of the old telecommunications regime. The key institution was a moribund but still powerful International Telecommunication Union. The ITU was created in 1932 by the merger of the International Telegraph Union (1865) and the International Radio Telegraph Convention of 1906. The ITU set technical standards and made sure they were compatible, allocated radio spectrum and made certain that they did not interfere with one another, provided technical assistance to poorer nations, and later gave out orbital slots. With the opening of space, the ITU was joined by Intelsat in 1964. Intelsat served both as a service provider and as its own regulator. Both organizations served as a "virtual telephone cartel" for national telephone monopolies in their member states.

The starting point of the regime was the principle that telecom service and equipment monopolies were needed to provide efficient and equitable telephone services domestically and internationally. This principle went largely unquestioned in the United States or elsewhere until an upstart, MCI, challenged AT&T's long-standing long-distance monopoly. MCI set up in Washington, DC, because it recognized that it could only win if it won regulatory and political battles first.

Three major international norms grew from the reliance on monopoly that stretched back to a 1913 deal (the Kingsbury agreement) between AT&T's Theodore Vail and the government which concerned trade regulation for monopoly status. These were: jointly provided services, standardized networks and equipment, and organized global commons.

First, *jointly provided services* were the core norm of the international telecom regime and effectively ensured that there was no competitive provision of international services. National service providers argued that international communications were, in effect, handed off from the sender to the receiving telecom monopoly at the midpoint of the transmission. Thus international traffic was an extension of the domestic market, a jointly provided service, which did not constitute trade. That made it possible for the sending monopoly to charge whatever it wanted for originating a call and then to pay a fixed fee to the receiving country. Further, companies were not allowed to route international calls via circuitous but less expensive routes. The result was that international phone calls were extremely expensive and incredibly profitable. Satellite technology might have upset the cartel, but the United States chose to leave jointly provided services unchallenged.

Second, *standardized networks and equipment* became the norm because global universal service required it. Until a phone call could be automatically transmitted from any point in the global network and received at any other point, widespread international interconnection was impossible. To accomplish this goal both service standards and equipment standards were synchronized and services and equipment were inexorably linked to one another. This norm effectively led to quasi equipment monopolies in the most developed countries and fostered cross-subsidies from national telephone companies to their equipment makers. (AT&T was unique in that it built its own equipment. It neither bought from nor sold to other monopolies.)

The third norm was the public effort to *organize a global commons* for outer space spectrum. Broadcast frequencies and orbital slots were allocated to the key participants. This norm has survived, but over time developing countries were cut in for a larger share of the pie.

The breakup of AT&T and the erosion of monopoly

By the early 1980s, AT&T's monopoly was under fire from the Department of Justice. The result is well known. AT&T kept its equipment business (at that time) but spun off its local operating companies into seven Regional Bell Operating companies. In return it was allowed, for the first time, to begin to provide new value-added services. Nobody emulated the United States model precisely, but the underlying principle of the telecom regime was undermined with the death of the old AT&T. At differing paces, in different ways, competition has spread around the globe. As competition spread within countries, the prospect for real competition on the provision of international services emerged.

The basic pro-monopoly principle of the regime domestically and internationally was opened to question and began to erode. In time, a new norm began to emerge to replace it: *Governments should limit regulatory intervention in market segments where real competition exists.* As competition spread across market segments, it forced a more economic rationalization on the pricing of telecommunications services. Cross-subsidies, which were a matter of policy, came under pressure, and extensive rate-rebalancing was undertaken. Indeed, a whole series of previously sacrosanct politically advantageous subsidies began to break down. These included

- telecom subsidized postal operations;
- business subsidized individuals;
- urban areas subsidized rural areas;
- service providers subsidized equipment makers; and, most important,
- international services subsidized long-distance services and both heavily subsidized local calls.

Two other developments helped undermine the jointly provided service and standardization norms. First, in most countries the regulator and the operator were separated, providing significant new power to the regulators to promote competition. Second, innovation flourished and new services, equipment manufacturers, and networks grew that allowed for the delivery of new services and sometimes old ones through alternative parallel networks. Although standardization remained necessary within networks, it began to break down across networks. Some convergence began to become evident.

The Empire strikes back

The United States recognized that the new principle and norms would not easily be accepted. Monopolists continued to believe that their industry was special and that they deserved to keep their lucrative monopolies even if they did not innovate and prices were high. They supported competition actively only in new service sectors and in sectors that they did not dominate. The United States served as evangelist, *demandeur*, and *provocateur*. Britain and the Westminster democracies followed the US pro-competitive example. Even Japan and developing countries from Eastern Europe, Latin America, and Asia moved to a more competitive mode in some parts of the telecom realm. Still, competition spread slowly, met significant resistance from the established oligarchy of companies, and the institutions and rules were slow to evolve.

The GATT strategy

Change in the international regime proceeded more slowly than the United States had expected. Moreover, the United States did not have the leverage to dislodge stubborn monopolists controlling the ITU and Intelsat. So they sought another strategy to recreate regime norms and institutions.

The GATT provided the best possibility. The GATT had slowly enlarged its mandates from goods to services. Trade-related services were introduced into its negotiations in the Tokyo Round in the 1970s. By the 1980s, trade in services, including telecommunications services, was on the agenda. The GATT had two great advantages. First, it provided a venue that was controlled by pro-competitive trade ministers, not monopoly-bound telecom regulators. Moreover, trade ministers almost always outrank telecom ministers. Second, it infuriated the barons of the ITU and their rulers and provoked them to reenergize their own institution. The only way for the ITU to retain its influence was to adapt and change.

The major transformation of the international norms was completed in 1997 and 1998 in two stunning blows against the monopoly control of the regime. First, in a mandated follow-up to the Uruguay Round negotiations, sixty-nine countries whose telecommunications markets are worth $570 billion annually agreed to a new pro-competitive set of rules to liberalize their telecommunications markets to varying degrees. Negotiators agreed to sweeping liberalization involving market access, the adoption of transparent, pro-competitive regulatory principles, agreement to permit foreign investment in and ownership of local telecom providers, and guarantees of market access for foreign and domestic satellite services and facilities.

Second, in a controversial move, the FCC acted unilaterally to demolish the accounting and settlement rate system that allowed national monopolies to extort monopoly rents. The United States acted for two main reasons. First, the relationship between cost of delivering service and the prices charged for services was far out of line. Second, the rules of the system and the structure of calling patterns combined to create far more minutes originating from the United States than landing there. After US long-distance carriers settled their accounts with their partners, they suffered huge deficits. By the mid-1990s, the trade deficit on communication services (now that jointly provided services were gone) had reached almost $5 billion a year. The FCC, over the protest of the ITU and most of its members, pulled the rug out from under the accounting and settlement rates system and told US carriers that they could not pay out more than a certain amount to settle their accounts. The new system is being phased in over time. International calling rates continue to decline as a result.

Internet and convergence: the New Economy

The first revamping of the telecom regime is already in need of drastic revision and expansion. Borders between nations, issues, and sectors are eroding. We are at the dawn of an age of competitive, global, digital distributed networks. Convergence is finally becoming reality. Institutions that managed global trade, money, investment, or telecommunications never were intended to manage such challenges. But should countries try to alter them to deal with new circumstances, invent new rules and international institutions, or simply get out of the way and trust in competition and the market?

The greatest missed opportunity at Seattle was the failure to begin to negotiate the international ground rules for the new information economy dominated by telecommunications and especially the Internet and e-commerce. Developments are unfolding so rapidly that the world economy as it exists when this essay is published will already be quite different from the economic situation that exists as these words are being written. Any rules negotiated in a prolonged trade round will inevitably be out of date before they come into force. The only hope is if the rules are flexible enough to evolve along with the system. But that is so complicated that critics are right to wonder whether it is worth the bother to try at all. Perhaps there will be no rules? If there are rules, what should be covered and what should be left unfettered? And is the WTO the right body for making the rules?

There will be rules. Silicon Valley abhors regulation and government intervention. Growing from the unregulated computer sector, not the regulated telecom sphere, they argue that competition and self-regulation will suffice. So far governments have largely complied, content to watch the booming expansion of the Internet. Even slight movement towards regulation has provoked vehement counterattacks by Internet groups. Moreover, when the US government has tried to intervene on content issues, as happened with the Decency Act or the clipper-chip, the policies failed. (In fairness, the Decency Act was more about politics than the Internet; most supporters found the Act politically convenient but recognized that it would almost certainly be ruled unconstitutional. It was.) Still, corporate talk of self-regulation will last only as long as it works. In areas where governments are convinced that the public is being poorly served, they will intervene. Internationally, the challenge will be greater. International institutions are not well organized to affect change. The World Bank, which should be working to aid poorer countries to overcome the digital divide, is making little headway. The ITU still is not in a position to act forcefully. ICANN, the new group to oversee the distribution of domain names, is struggling to provide some order, but only on a narrow topic. And the Millennial Trade Round is still a long way from being successfully launched. Worse, nobody has a clue about a grand vision or how to pull it off.

But what kinds of rules? The nature of the rules and the norms they should support are not clear. Where should boundaries be drawn and who and what should be covered or excluded? Right now there are too many issues in play at once. To the extent that competition can substitute for regulation, many parts of the Internet are likely to remain unregulated. At a minimum some existing rules will need to be updated.

1   Intellectual property rules, especially copyright need to be settled. Products built on intellectual property such as software and movies now are America's largest single export sector. The recent WIPO agreements began the process, but the struggle to balance the rights of innovators and users continues to rage.
2   Standard setting in the development of basic protocols and networks is likely to remain a key issue because of the need to interconnect global networks.
3   What if anything needs to be done to control content? Issues of censorship, encryption, and privacy all raise tradeoffs between security, commercial, and individual interests that need to be resolved.
4   Local, national, and international authorities ultimately will need to figure out how to handle tax issues related to e-commerce and cyberspace.

More generally, jurisdictional issues will need to be resolved to sort through whose laws apply when cyberspace and the New Economy is global, but laws and regulations remain mainly local and national. The WTO remains the most likely body for providing international agreements. In addition, the Internet raises new concerns such as the allocation of domain names and rules for working against anti-competitive behavior.

Towards next time

When Trade Ministers next meet to try to launch a new round, they are likely to succeed. To successfully complete the round will be more difficult. At least three things are different this time. First, the cast of key players is larger. Developing countries, not just the industrial countries, will be part of any deal. Moreover, global firms and NGOs, having demonstrated their political clout, will continue to be part of the process. Second, the Web is a disruptive technology that is powering the transition towards a New Economy. There will be many winners and many losers. New sectors will emerge and drive the economy; many old sectors will fade. The mix of companies that matter nationally and internationally will continue to change. Third, the world economy is now moving on Internet time. Everything is faster. Large companies alter course in a month; smaller startups in a week or less. To thrive, companies need to be nimble because there are tremendous first mover advantages in the New Economy.

Governments successfully managed to transform the telecommunications regime in a decade and a half, between 1984 and 1999. The rate of change in the economy is even faster now. For governments to have any chance at guiding the emerging whirlwind of economic change they will need to be faster and more clever than in the past. They will need to know when to act, and when not to act. They will need to understand how to act, and how not to act. They will need to balance domestic politics and national interests against international necessities. It is unclear that they will be able to rise to the challenge. It will not be a disaster if a new trade round fails; the world economy will still continue to move forward and likely will muddle through. But the opportunities that would come with success would provide more jobs and growth across the globe.

COMMENT BY DIMITRI YPSILANTI ON JONATHAN D. ARONSON, 'AFTER SEATTLE: TRADE NEGOTIATIONS AND THE NEW ECONOMY'

The Seattle Meeting of Trade Ministers had three effects. It made the World Trade Organization a household name (some may argue that it made it notorious), to some extent it legitimised a role for 'civil society' in trade issues, and by creating pressure for more transparency in the negotiation process it possibly made the task of future negotiations more difficult. As this excellent essay by Jonathan Aronson notes, the issues underlying trade negotiations have shifted significantly from the early days of the GATT. The Seattle protests were to a large part due to the past success of the GATT in significantly reducing tariff barriers and helping the process of 'globalisation' and the dominance of multinationals in the global economy against which many protestors vented their ire. As tariff barriers were eliminated and trade negotiations began to focus on non-tariff issues and horizontal questions (e.g. competition, intellectual property, and labour conditions), narrow sector specific issues were less at stake providing an opportunity for more solidarity between different lobby groups. Agriculture is perhaps the exception. But even here the issue of 'multi-functionality', that is the social and economic role of agriculture in rural areas (raised by the European Union), provided some glue to cement relationships between farm and rural lobbies and environmentalists across the globe who were not representative of large agro-business interests.

The Seattle protests also focused attention on the process used by countries in taking decisions in trade negotiations. In the past, the process of making offers and preparing schedules lacked transparency, perhaps by necessity. By definition, negotiations were a process of give and take, and negotiators kept their cards close to their chest. Furthermore, it would not have been politic for negotiators to publicly admit that they would sacrifice, for example, their steel industry to gain concessions in high technology goods.

An important impact of the failure of the Seattle Meeting will, as Aronson stresses, be the delay in reaching agreements on issues related to electronic commerce and the 'New Economy'. The essay highlights the fast pace of change in Internet and electronic commerce issues, which will clearly imply that by the time negotiations begin it will be harder to reach agreement. At the present stage of policy development in electronic commerce governments and firms are more malleable, since they are in the process of formulating policies in new areas. Once policies become embedded they become more difficult to adjust.

In emphasising the rapid growth of the information economy over the last few years, Aronson highlights the potential for changes that the Internet may have on society, business and the role of government. The speed of change in the New Economy significantly outpaces the speed at which policy decisions are taken, especially policy decisions at the international level.

At the heart of the New Economy is the communications infrastructure, and Aronson's essay provides a rapid overview of the changes which have occurred in telecommunication market structures and how telecommunications, once considered as 'non-traded' services, began to be viewed as traded services. Aronson argues that the agreement on basic telecommunications negotiated, in force for two years, is itself in need of significant revision as a result of the emergence of electronic commerce and the technological, and service changes that have taken place. This observation is correct, but the essay would have benefited if these ideas had been amplified by detailing areas and issues where further progress would be needed in enhancing the agreement on basic telecommunications.[1]

Aronson views the Seattle failure as a 'missed opportunity' in rule-making for electronic commerce. He perhaps puts too much emphasis on the WTO process, and as a result discounts processes that have already been underway for several years in other international organisations, bilaterally and through the international business community to deal with electronic commerce issues. For example, the OECD has been discussing electronic commerce since 1997 and, although not a rule-making institution, has facilitated the process in reaching a greater consensus on how certain issues should be treated.[2] Other organizations, such as UNCITRAL, WIPO and UNCTAD, have also been involved in electronic commerce related issues. More importantly, business, through a number of institutions, including the International Chamber of Commerce and the Alliance for Global Business,[3] has been trying to obtain greater consensus on a number of issues placing emphasis on self-regulation. In the area of domain names the Government Advisory Committee (GAC) has been working closely with ICANN and has made a number of recommendations to that body. Bilateral discussions, such as on privacy protection between the European Union (with a formal privacy framework) and the United States (relying on self-regulation) have also helped in moving towards greater international consensus.

Thus, while the failure to begin negotiations at the WTO on electronic commerce should not be minimised, the ongoing initiatives elsewhere are also important and will ultimately facilitate agreement at the WTO. The importance of the WTO may be in enshrining consensus in a more treaty-binding framework linked with a dispute-resolution mechanism. Ultimately the delay in WTO negotiations may be of benefit since it provides business breathing space to develop better self-regulation and to demonstrate that self-regulation can work. This is a significant challenge for business, and one that they have still not been able to come to grips with. Time is also providing us with a greater understanding of the workings of the New Economy, which allows us to be more judicious in rule-making. It needs to be recalled that one important objective in putting electronic commerce on the WTO agenda was to try and ensure that governments did not act hastily in imposing rules and regulations and taxes on the New Economy.

As Aronson notes, governments need to understand when to act as well as when not to act. Electronic commerce is at an inflection point on the growth curve and, while growing extremely rapidly, is still an immature activity. Acting hastily by imposing rules can have significant negative economic effects but, at the same time, where there is no user confidence – which may require rules – then growth can falter. The breathing space provided by the Seattle failure may thus be important in allowing for a better clarification of a number of key issues for the New Economy and should be used by governments to informally explore these issues.

Notes

1   See, for example, OECD (1999) *A Review of Market Openness and Trade in Telecommunications*, DSTI/ICCP/TISP(99)5/Final, Paris. Also available at http://www.oecd.org/dsti/sti/it/cm/index.htm.
2   See, Ypsilanti, Dimitri (1999) 'A borderless world, the OECD Ottawa Ministerial Conference and initiatives', in *info* 1(1). Also see the OECD website: http://www.oecd.org/dsti/sti/it/ec/index.htm.
3   The Alliance for Global Business is a co-ordinating mechanism of leading international business organisations created to provide private sector leadership on information society issues and electronic commerce.

Part III

International self-regulation and standard setting

10 Locating Internet governance

Lessons from the standards process

Mark Gould

As the Internet has grown, the debate about its governance and regulation has become more significant. At the same time, that debate has also become polarised, with different constituencies arguing for incommensurable solutions. The consequences of this debate are many. A system for governing the Internet could regulate access to the networks, peering agreements between network providers or 'netiquette'.[1] At its heart, however, are questions about the infrastructure. The infrastructure itself is founded on standards. Those standards, therefore, are the basic subject matter of Internet governance:

> We care about standards because of the fantastically complicated economic question of who captures the often considerable value that is created through the establishment of a standard. And we also care about standards because … they arise through the condensation of processes of social discourse … To the extent that Internet standards shape public discourse, their rule-setting function is a matter of public concern. And to the extent that the Internet serves as a medium for the agenda-setting from which a wide variety of technical standards emerge, the properties of that medium and the larger technical public sphere of which it is a part are likewise matters of political concern.
>
> (Agre 1998)

This chapter examines how various standards processes might contribute to an understanding of Internet governance, and especially the question of where that governance might be located.

What is Internet governance?

The notion of governance is not novel to the Internet. 'Internet governance' is rarely defined, however. Valuable guidance can be found in the literature on the provision of public services, and especially in the work of R.A.W. Rhodes. Noting that 'current use does not treat governance as a synonym for government', Rhodes draws on the insights provided by socio-cybernetics to arrive at an understanding of governance in a wider context. The socio-cybernetic view of governance sees it as 'the pattern or structure that emerges in a socio-political system as a "common" result or outcome of the interacting intervention efforts of all involved actors' (Kooiman 1993: 258). Further, the cybernetic nature of governance implies that the system thus governed is being steered towards a known objective. For Andrew Dunsire, the problem is how decision-makers cope with isostasy, being subjected to pressures from every side:

> the management of social isostasy, intervention to stabilise in the long run by controlled local destabilising in the short run, the deliberate tipping of the balance of one conflict or another, the rigging of a market whether economic or political or some other kind, the manipulation of group desires and energies – this kind of activity … furnishes a mechanism for guiding, influencing, biasing, loading or otherwise affecting the course or outcome of a conflict in the interests of the governors; in other words a steering mechanism.
>
> (Dunsire 1993: 31)

Whilst there may be governance without government (Rosenau and Czempiel 1992), the presence of government in a sphere of activity will tend to make regulation of that activity follow governmental goals. The diffuse nature of the Internet, and the fact that its infrastructure is almost all in private hands means that the socio-cybernetic view of governance cannot provide an accurate picture of the processes by which the network is organised and co-ordinated and by which network resources are distributed. Even when governments become involved in these processes, absent the use of their more coercive powers, they are no more powerful than are other actors.

Here Rhodes's more developed notion of governance offers some assistance. For him, 'governance is about managing networks' (Rhodes 1996: 658). These networks encompass any system involving inter-organisational links, through which services are delivered, activities managed or objectives achieved. In addition to each of these systems being autonomous, their constituent organisations are also independent of each other and self-interested. Rather than offering a compromise between the market-driven concerns of private-sector actors, and the hierarchical nature of public bureaucracies, networks provide a means by which these features of their component organisations can be accommodated. Most significantly, networks are self-organising. Unlike the socio-political systems that are the concern of the socio-cybernetic approach to governance, a self-organising network will arise out of a particular circumstance or environment. Crucially, this means that 'integrated networks resist government steering, develop their own policies and mould their environments' (Rhodes 1996: 659). For Rhodes, then, governance has four crucial elements:

1   Interdependence between organizations … Changing the boundaries of the state meant the boundaries between public, private and voluntary sectors became shifting and opaque.

2   Continuing interactions between network members, caused by the need to exchange resources and negotiate shared purposes.
3   Game-like interactions, rooted in trust and regulated by rules of the game negotiated and agreed by network participants.
4   A significant degree of autonomy from the state. Networks are not accountable to the state; they are self-organising. Although the state does not occupy a privileged sovereign position, it can indirectly and imperfectly steer networks.

(Rhodes 1996: 660)

Although this position is clearly distinct from the socio-cybernetic school, the notion that the state may play an indirect steering role is drawn from the insights provided by that approach. In considering Internet governance, one cannot ignore the fact that the policies of the United States government have been crucial in the development of the Internet. A question remains as to whether states will be content to continue not to dominate the network. Alongside that reservation, one might also question whether the processes by which the Internet is co-ordinated are mature enough to meet Rhodes's definition of a self-organising network. Michael Froomkin points out in his contribution to this volume, for example, that the trust which was a feature of early forms of Internet resource allocation, such as domain naming and Usenet newsgroup creation, have not been carried into more recent mechanisms, such as the Internet Corporation for Assigned Names and Numbers (ICANN). Most importantly for the present, it is clear that the actors involved in the various processes of Internet governance do not necessarily have the same understanding of the functions and purposes of the system. This makes it difficult to argue that their interactions are game-like or regulated by pre-agreed rules. It has been pointed out that the key to Rhodes's approach is that it requires that networks under scrutiny must be *integrated* and that 'the term "institutionalisation" can usefully be substituted for "integration" to highlight the development of routines, standard operating procedures and normative structures through which policy problems are understood, managed and resolved' (Armstrong and Bulmer 1998: 259). This chapter will show that the processes by which the architecture and resources of the Internet are managed are insufficiently institutionalised to adopt Rhodes's analysis wholesale. However, in examining the different traditions and styles of standards-setting processes, it should become apparent that whilst those processes encompass a wide variety of methods and assumptions, there are some common elements which mean that, in some areas of Internet activity, governance of some kind is beginning to come about.

A context – the DNS 'wars'

The background

For the past four years at least, there has been a continuous debate about the future of the Domain Name System (DNS). That controversy is not the primary subject of this paper, but its progress is instructive.

Broadly speaking, there are two types of top-level domain (TLD) (Postel 1994). The most numerous type is that based on the two-letter country codes listed in ISO-3166 (with a small number of exceptions). The operation of the country code TLDs (ccTLDs) is not, for the most part, a matter of global concern, although some of them have become global in nature. The other type, generic TLDs (gTLDs), were defined as being intended for specific types of organisation, and two of them were limited to use in the United States only (.mil and .gov). The internationally available TLDs are .com (intended for use by commercial entities), .net (for use in the network infrastructure), .edu (for higher education institutions), .int (for international treaty organisations and the like), and .org (a miscellaneous category). As the Internet became more popular and ownership of a domain name became a *sine qua non* of commercial activity, these categorisations began to break down. In particular, domain name registration under .com, .net and .org was not subject to scrutiny as to the proposed use of those names, and .com and .net became especially sought-after.

The DNS is not a directory system. It is simply a means of overcoming the limitations of naked IP addresses (by which every host on the Internet is identifiable). Such addresses are difficult to remember, and the ranges of addresses used by companies or other institutions do not necessarily run consecutively (which might help in identifying which addresses belong to whom). Policies for the administration of the TLDs are set by each administrator. One of the most basic decisions, for example, is whether the domain is delegated further, or whether it develops in a flat fashion directly below the top level. The global domains have tended to be administered in a flat fashion, whilst the ccTLDs have adopted a range of styles. The ccTLD has a flat structure, with entities of any type being entitled to registration directly at the second level. Conversely, the .us and .uk domains show a high degree of hierarchy and delegation. For a number of reasons, including the ease of registration in the .com domain and the relative complexity of registration under the .us TLD, most domain names registered by United States entities occur in one of the gTLDs. In addition, the root servers include detailed information about the gTLDs (Manning and Vixie 1996), which makes these domains more resilient to network disturbances. For many registrants, therefore, a domain name in the .com name-space is a *sine qua non* of their Internet presence.

Problems

A number of problems have contributed to the continuing debate over the domain name system. Some emanated from outside the system, whilst others reflected changes to the system itself. The most difficult issue is one that first arose in 1994, and still continues to be litigated. As the account of the DNS above suggests, domain names must be unique. This does not prevent a name being used at different levels or under different TLDs, but it does mean that, for instance, there can only be one domain called microsoft.com. Naturally enough, early Internet users registered many domains which were then denied to 'late-comers', since the domain registries (including Network Solutions, Inc. (NSI), the registry for the widely available gTLDs .com, .net and .org) tended to adopt a 'first come, first served' policy. For some of the commercial Internet users, this policy opened the door to breaches of their trademarks, and a cause for litigation (Yee 1997; Gigante 1997). The first such cases occurred in 1994, just a decade after the first domain names were registered (Rony and Rony 1998: 299–378). These legal disputes caused the domain registry some concern (Sbarbaro 1997). It became clear that there was a potentially unbridgeable gap between the interests of domain name holders and trademark holders. The former might have invested a good deal of time and money in creating an online presence depending on a particular name. The latter might have pre-existing rights to the same name. Worse still, the fragmented, non-exclusive nature of the trademark regime meant that there were potentially many more angry trademark holders than disappointed domain registrants. In addition, trademark protection is based on national registration, so that any mark that needs to be protected throughout the world must be registered in all the appropriate countries.

When Network Solutions became involved in domain registration at the beginning of 1993, all registrations were to be funded by the US National Science Foundation (NSF), but in September 1995 NSI was permitted to charge $50 per year for registrations in the .gov, .edu, .com, .net and .org domains. The decision to charge fees for domain registration was NSI's second blow to domain registrants. The first was the institution of a domain dispute policy in July 1995. This policy was a response to the unhappy position the registry found itself in – between domain owners and trademark holders. The policy reasserted NSI's basic 'first come, first served' allocation policy, but then required domain registrants to warrant that their chosen name would not infringe anyone else's trademark or other rights. Registrants were also required to indemnify NSI in the event of legal action arising out of allegations of such infringement. The policy's real bite, however, came in the provision that NSI would have the right to de-register a domain name if ordered to do so by a court or arbitrator. Unfortunately for NSI, its policy had the opposite effect from that intended. As NSI now had the power to suspend domains, a power which it used, the offended domain name holders started to sue NSI (Rony and Rony 1998: 379–457). Subsequent revisions of the policy did not substantively alter NSI's position, and it is still the case that trademark holders can invoke the policy to the detriment of innocent domain name holders (Oppedahl 1997a). The policy automatically prefers trademark holders to those who do not have such protection (even if they are not *using* the domain name in a way which infringes a trademark), and it fails to recognise that a similar mark might be held by more than one person (Oppedahl 1997b).

The 'domain name problem' can be summed up fairly easily. Unfortunately, it is actually a variety of different problems for different people. For potential domain registrants or users of the Internet, the problem is that the growth of the network combined with over-reliance on one or two TLDs has led to a scarcity of 'good' domains. For trademark holders (and for those who think that the DNS is a directory service), the problem is that their trademark has been registered by someone else, thereby making it more difficult to establish their Internet presence. For domain name holders, the problem is that their domain is at risk of suspension or revocation if it corresponds to a registered trademark, even if that correspondence is identical or if the use made of the domain does not infringe the rights of the trademark holder. Perhaps unsurprisingly, given that the problem is multi-faceted, the process of finding a solution has not been easy.

Arguing towards a solution?

Having identified a problem, those affected – naturally enough – sought a means of solving it. The process by which a solution was reached is not yet complete, but it already offers some insights into the way other Internet issues might be governed. It can be divided into three parts, which are roughly consecutive, although there is some overlap. The first period shows the Internet community attempting to address the issues as a technical problem – the way Internet difficulties had been resolved previously. The second sees an attempt at an international solution. The third (and probably conclusive) period has a solution brokered by the US government.

Faced with having to pay for domain names, and being subjected to NSI's dispute policy, the response of a number of Internet users was to discuss the problem as a technical matter. For many, the appropriate technical response was to establish new TLDs, so as to duplicate the opportunities for registering the same name. That was not acceptable to those who liked the fact that they had come to enjoy a degree of certainty that certain names would be found in the com domain. More significantly, those who had trademark interests indicated that they would consider such registrations to dilute their marks. Despite these objections, the e-mail discussions led to the production of an Internet-Draft. These documents form part of the process whereby standards are created for the Internet, and this one had a particular significance (Postel 1996a and 1996b), as it was written by Jon Postel – one of the original team which created the ARPANET, who had gone on to have a pivotal role in the Internet, being the major part of the Internet Assigned Numbers Authority (IANA), whose function is best described thus:

> Services like Telnet and FTP depend on the assignment of 'well-known' TCP and UDP ports for initiation of the service; and numerous options are defined with IP, TCP, and the other protocols. To coordinate the assignment of ports, values for options, and the like, the Internet has established the Internet Assigned Number Authority ... Anytime a specification permits extensions, the task of registering those extensions and assigning an appropriate extension name or number is performed by IANA.
>
> (Crocker 1993a: 53)

More significantly in the present context, IANA asserted authority over all IP addresses and domain names, and was responsible for delegating responsibility for ccTLD administration (Postel 1994). Postel's draft, therefore, carried a degree of authority that was not necessarily enjoyed by other authors (Nash 1997). The essence of his proposal was that there should be a number of new top-level domains created, which would be administered by new registries, competing with NSI. The decision as to which domains should be created and to which registries they would be allocated was to be made by an ad hoc committee.

Concurrently with the e-mail discussions and writing of Internet-Drafts, a number of meetings were held. The most noteworthy was a large workshop, which took place at Harvard over two days in September 1996.[2] Two aspects of the meeting had a lasting impact. The first was a formal presentation by Don Heath, President/CEO of ISOC, of Postel's proposals, which had been approved in principle by the Board of Trustees of the Internet Society ISOC at the IETF/INET 96 meeting in June 1996 (Shaw 1997). It was clear that this was ISOC's view of the future. The second was the presence at the meeting of Robert Shaw, an official of the International Telecommunications Union (ITU), and Albert Tramposch of the World Intellectual Property Organisation (WIPO). This meeting, like others on the same subject, involved participants from outside the technical sphere, but was predominantly composed of North Americans. The stage was set for the next stage in the progress towards a resolution of the domain name crisis.

The establishment of the International Ad Hoc Committee (IAHC) was announced in October 1996. Two members were nominated by each of ISOC, IANA and the Internet Architecture Board (IAB), and one each from the ITU, WIPO, the International Trademark Association (INTA) and the Federal Networking Council (FNC) of the United States government. Within a very short time, the committee had reached a preliminary conclusion that seven new gTLDs should be added to the root, and administered by a number of new registrars, who would share responsibility for registering names within those domains. The ultimate intention of the IAHC would be to have twenty to thirty new TLDs per year, and to include the .com, .net and .org TLDs in the shared name space. After public discussion of these proposals, the IAHC issued its final report in February 1997 (IAHC 1997).

Significantly, the IAHC starts by asserting that

> the Internet top level domain space is a public resource and is subject to the public trust. Therefore any administration, use and/or evolution of the Internet TLD space is a public policy issue and should be carried out in an open and public manner in the interests and service of the public. Appropriately, related public policy needs to openly balance and represent the interests of the current and future stakeholders in the Internet name space.

From this postulation, the IAHC inferred that domain names should be managed by an international non-profit organisation, to be located in Geneva. It also advised that twenty-eight new registrars spread equitably throughout the world should assign domain names in the seven new gTLDs. The registrars would all be governed by the same rules and would compete in terms of domain name registration times and fees. The law of the state in which a registrar was located would govern disputes. However, the IAHC also developed a complete dispute resolution system, designed in particular to deter domain name 'piracy'.

The IAHC's technical and political recommendations – the international and non-profit status of the gTLD regulation authority, reform of the existing gTLD system, and creation of new registrars in different countries – were largely positively received. The adoption of a mediation and arbitration procedure might also have been welcomed, apart from two factors. The first is that the proposal dealt only with trademark-related disputes – other challenges must still be resolved elsewhere. The second is that the actual procedure appeared to be complex and hard to implement. A fundamental weakness in the IAHC's initiative was that it was basically private in nature and lacked a legal basis in public international law. Many governments found it difficult to accept exclusion of governmental input into domain name reform affecting trademark law and national sovereignty. That, in part, accounts for the ultimate failure of the IAHC's scheme. A number of other concerns were also expressed, including the authority of WIPO, ITU, IANA and ISOC to enter into such a quasi-governmental role (Rony and Rony 1998: 534–43).

The IAHC's work was completed by the creation of a Memorandum of Understanding (known as the gTLD-MoU), which was open for signature by any interested party. IANA and ISOC were required to sign for the MoU to come into force. The United States government, amongst many others, did not sign the document. In July 1997, following a presidential directive, the Department of Commerce called for 'comments on the current and future system(s) for the registration in Internet domain names'. Tellingly, the request for comments included the statement:

> various private sector groups have proposed systems for allocating and managing generic top level domains ... The Government has not endorsed any plan at this stage but believes that it is very important to reach consensus on these policy issues as soon as possible.
>
> (Department of Commerce 1997)

This non-partisan approach meant that comments were specifically invited on a range of issues that were apparently resolved by the gTLD-MoU.

The National Telecommunications and Information Administration (NTIA), which had been given responsibility for the domain name consultation, issued a Green Paper in February 1998 (Department of Commerce 1998a). This proposed that a new US-based non-profit corporation be founded to take over various DNS-related functions of IANA. The Green Paper further proposed that the functions of registry (an essentially technical database-maintenance role) and registrar (the interface between domain name holders and the registry) be separated, and that the registrar function be opened up to competition. It was proposed that five new TLDs be created, but it was not specified what they should be (that was left to the new corporation). Finally, the trademark question was left unresolved – registries and registrars were to set their own policies. Generally, the Green Paper was a return to the principle of bottom-up Internet governance. Rather than establishing cumbersome and complex structures of regulation, as the gTLD-MoU had, the Green Paper proposed a light-handed and privatised system of self-regulation.

The model proposed by the Green Paper was not universally welcomed. The primary bone of contention was the US government's claim of authority over the domain name system (and by extension, the Internet in general). The European Union was perhaps the most concerned by this, especially as a joint EU–US statement had indicated that the two parties would work towards 'the creation of a global market-based system of registration, allocation and governance of Internet domain names which fully reflects the geographically and functionally diverse nature of the Internet' (Commission of the European Communities 1997h). The EU listed a range of issues of concern in its response to the Green Paper (Commission of the European Communities 1998b). Whilst the major problems for the EU were related to the failure to implement an international approach to the domain name issue, it was also concerned about the creation of a private monopoly over a resource which the IAHC had identified as having a public character.

Following a period of consultation, the NTIA issued a statement of policy (referred to as the White Paper) in which the proposals in the Green Paper were amended (Department of Commerce 1998b). The resulting policy was guided by the principles of stability; competition; private, bottom-up co-ordination; and representation. There would still be a new corporation, but it would be required to depend on management structures reflecting 'the functional and geographic diversity of the Internet and its users'. The split between registry and registrar functions remained, and WIPO was requested to start the development of a set of recommendations for trademark and domain name dispute resolution, for the use of the new corporation. A number of proposals for the new corporation were submitted to the NTIA, and in November 1998 the Internet Corporation for Assigned Names and Numbers (ICANN) was named as the new corporation (Department of Commerce 1998c). In some respects the process whereby ICANN was selected was similar to that used for Internet standard-setting generally, but in others it was very different. There was a great deal of discussion of a small number of alternative proposals, which were elaborated by groups or individuals with different perspectives on the problems created by the domain name crisis. The proposed bylaws and articles of incorporation of ICANN were also debated. However, the openness traditional to the Internet was absent from the processes by which ICANN defined its constitutional documents and from the final decision of the NTIA to recommend ICANN as the new corporation. It appears that the latter decision was probably influenced by the wider consensus behind ICANN, which in turn was driven by the fact that it was supported by IANA and NSI.

Now, some five years since the origin of the apparent crisis in domain naming, it would appear that little has actually changed. NSI is still the registry for the gTLDs, although it competes with other companies for the registrar business. ICANN has become the de facto authority for domain expansion and regulation. For Internet users, however, little of consequence has occurred as a direct result of four years spent discussing domain names. It is still possible to register names in the com, net and org TLDs, and the promise of more gTLDs has not yet been fulfilled. Instead (in a fairly typical fashion for the Internet), a number of ccTLDs have become substitute gTLDs. Some of these belong to smaller states or developing nations. Many of these have been taken up by international domain registration companies on behalf of the government of those states. The companies tend to offer domain registration at a low cost, often combined with additional facilities such as e-mail or web forwarding, to anyone who desires a domain name. This trend upsets the assumption made in the DNS that a ccTLD will be used primarily in that country. As a consequence it also upsets the premises on which the international consideration of rules for the gTLDs has proceeded. There is potential for conflict here between ICANN, the US government, and the national governments that have allowed 'their' TLDs to be used in this way.

Whilst the purpose of this overview of the DNS crisis is to provide a context for the rest of the paper, one issue arises that does not directly impinge on the question of standard-setting processes, but is still important. That is regulatory capture. Here, in the process of resolving of a problem with many facets (the allocation of domain names in an apparently shrinking name space), one aspect was given priority over all others. It is true that there is a problem fitting domain names to the existing trademark system, and there clearly were some instances where trademarks were being infringed by the use made of domains. Those instances could, however, have been resolved in the normal way, through the legal system. It was not necessarily appropriate to endow intellectual property with the primacy it currently has. It is not even clear that the threat of trademark piracy is as significant as it is said to be (Mueller 1999). The trademark community has managed to become part of the process of Internet governance merely as a consequence of a number of accidents of history, rather than for a technically defensible reason. This would not matter, were it not for the fact that the objectives of trademark holders are often at odds with those of the Internet technical community (amongst others).

How standards are set

The long struggle towards a resolution of the domain name crisis has illustrated the problems inherent in attempts to set rules for an expanding Internet. The rest of this chapter investigates the processes whereby standards are set in the Internet and in other areas of international communications that overlap with the Internet.

The traditional Internet standards process

It may seem a little odd to talk of a process which is still developing as 'traditional', but by comparison with the new models of decision-making introduced as part of the resolution of the DNS problems the work of the Internet standard organisations is well established, and consequently has a high level of acceptance amongst the Internet community. It has even been described as 'the best [standards development process] in the business' (Rutkowski 1995: 597). An assessment of the truth of that statement is beyond this paper. How did this paragon of standards processes come to be? If its success is measured in terms of accessibility, or efficiency, the history of the Internet does appear to contain the seeds of that success.

In 1968 the Information Processing Techniques Office (IPTO), a section of the US Department of Defense's Advanced Research Projects Agency (ARPA) started an experiment into connecting computers over a shared network that would lead to the ARPANET and, ultimately, the Internet (Hafner and Lyon 1998). Much of the work was undertaken by research students from universities around the United States. It is likely that the youthfulness of these researchers contributed directly to the informality of the discussions that led to the resolution of technical problems in the development and construction of this network. Another factor was that there were few preconditions as to the nature of the network. At an early stage, it became necessary to document those discussions, and those notes were labelled 'Request for Comments', in order to emphasise the basic rule 'that anyone could say anything and that nothing was official' (Reynolds and Postel 1987). The name stuck, and Request for Comments (or RFC) is still the title of all Internet standards. It is important, however, to stress that although all Internet standards are found in RFCs, not all RFCs are standards (Huitema *et al.* 1995; Bradner 1996).

Unsurprisingly, the original informal RFC process has given way to more formal processes, governed by a range of institutions. These have also evolved over a number of years. The initial rationale for institutionalising the process of Internet development was to co-ordinate the activities of various groups working on Internet research and development. By 1984, the Internet project had evolved to such a point that the Internet Activities Board (IAB) was created, to perform that function (Cerf 1990). The IAB was comprised of a number of task forces, and in 1986, a new one was added: Internet Engineering – the precursor to the current Internet standards development body. By 1989, the IETF had become the principal subsidiary body to the IAB. The IAB was described as 'the co-ordinating committee for Internet design, engineering and management … [It] is an independent committee of researchers and professionals with a technical interest in the health and evolution of the Internet system' (Cerf 1990). However, the IAB left much of the real standard-setting work to the IETF. Whilst the IETF determined the content of Internet standards, the IAB was responsible for their final approval.

In the early 1990s, the Internet standards process was put under great strain. In order to expand the numbering capacity of the network, the IAB promoted a solution promoted by the Open Systems Interconnection programme (a joint undertaking of the International Telephone and Telegraph Consultative Committee (CCITT) and the International Organisation for Standardisation (ISO) (Clark *et al.* 1991). The IETF was not happy with this development, especially in view of the technical and cultural differences between the OSI and Internet standards, and in July 1992 the IAB withdrew its proposal in the face of the IETF's clear opposition. At the same time, the IAB (rechartered as the Internet Architecture Board) was taken under the wing of the Internet Society (ISOC), which had been created in 1991 to secure funding for Internet standards activity to replace that from the US government.

The major part of the standards work of the IETF is done by the Working Groups (WG), which are usually created as required to address a specific problem, or to create a particular standard or guideline, and are wound up once their function is completed (Bradner 1998). They are open to any interested party. This openness in participation is complemented by an openness in communication. All communications between WG members are electronic – by means of mailing lists, discussing documents or specifications which are freely available online, or by regular face-to-face meetings. The formation of WGs is now a fairly formal process. Informal sessions at IETF meetings allow ideas to be tested before deciding whether they merit a WG. Preliminary discussions may also be held by e-mail. Participants in WG discussions are required to disclose 'any relevant … intellectual property rights' (Hovey and Bradner 1996). WG activity is co-ordinated by the Internet Engineering Steering Group (IESG). David Crocker has compared the open processes of standards development favourably with the openness of standard publication or standard ownership that are more typical of standards organisations outside the Internet (Crocker 1993b). In that analysis, the openness offered by the IETF model also improves the *quality* of standards, since it can easily be seen if a standard is being proposed by an interested party, or if, for other reasons, a proposal has failed to command wide support. Other commentators have noted, however, that the IETF model may be fragile, and threatened by the very success of its own creation (Malamud 1993: 147–9; Lehr 1995: 141).

The starting point for the standards process is publication of the proposal as an Internet-Draft (unless the specification has already been published as an RFC – perhaps as an experimental RFC). These documents are discussed for at least two weeks and no more than six months, before approval (Bradner 1996). On approval, the specification is published as a Proposed Standard RFC. Its progress along the standards track is now governed by time limits, as well as by the debates on the standard in the relevant mailing list and at IETF meetings. All Proposed Standards must remain at that level for at least six months before being reclassified as a Draft Standard. Draft Standards are left under review for at least four months before they can be considered for promotion to Standard by the IESG. Specifications that remain at the same level for two years are reviewed. If deemed to be non-viable, work on such specifications is terminated. Moribund standards are, therefore, nipped in the bud. At each stage there is an opportunity for complaints to be made against actions of the IESG. Those complaints are reviewed by the IESG and reported to the IAB. If the complainant is still dissatisfied, an appeal may be made to the IAB, which is the final arbiter as to whether the Internet standards procedures have been followed. Appeal to the Board of Trustees of ISOC is possible, but only where it is claimed that the procedures themselves are 'inadequate or insufficient to the protection of the rights of all the parties in a fair and open Internet Standards Process' (Bradner 1996). Decisions of the Board of Trustees are final in all respects.

This bare description of the process framework sheds no light on the conditions for acceptance of an Internet standard. These conditions are the distinguishing feature of the process, and are summed up in the oft-cited credo: 'We reject kings, presidents, and voting. We believe in rough consensus and running code' (Clark and Zittrain 1997). For a specification to succeed in becoming an Internet standard, it is essential to prove that it works. It is possible for a Proposed Standard to be published without presenting an implementation or operational experience, but the practical approach is felt to be 'highly desirable, and will usually represent a strong argument in favor of a Proposed Standard designation' (Bradner 1996). If a specification affects the core Internet protocols or might have a significant operational impact on the Internet, the IESG may require a practical implementation before allowing it to proceed on to the standards track. In order to progress to a Draft Standard, 'at least two independent and interoperable implementations' must be developed, together with 'sufficient successful operational experience' (Bradner 1996). This requirement means that no standard is made that cannot be used, and technical disputes are easily resolved by reference to real implementations and experience.

The second element of the credo is more unusual, but reflects the informal nature of IETF discussions. Since there are no specified members of a particular WG, and no way of delegating, electing or otherwise dictating who those members should be, voting – the normal method of resolving philosophical disputes about a specification – is not possible. It is not clear how rough consensus is reached. In some instances there seems to be more roughness than consensus (Crocker 1993a: 66). One factor (surprisingly, given the open and non-hierarchical nature of the IETF) might be the long-term relationships between Internet 'old hands' (Lehr 1995: 133–4). Those with a deeper investment in the development of the Internet than just the current specification are able to accept defeat on minor issues more readily than those for whom the immediate discussion either is their first foray into the Internet standards process or represents a significant personal investment. For the latter group, it is harder to accept that 'if I yield today, you will yield tomorrow'.

Other standards (and quasi-standards) processes

ITU

The International Telecommunications Union is the successor to the International Telegraph Union, which was established in 1865.[3] Since 1992, its functions have been carried out in three sectors. ITU–T, the telecommunications sector, took the standardisation function over from the International Telephone and Telegraph Consultative Committee (CCITT). That body had been instrumental in creating, or participating in the creation of, a number of standards which could be regarded as being in competition with standards offered by the IETF. In particular, the X.400 Message-Handling System (MHS) e-mail standard competed with the Simple Mail Transfer Protocol (SMTP), and the F.401 standard for naming and addressing for public MH services was a direct comparator with the DNS. The CCITT (and later ITU–T) provides the greatest contrast with Internet standards-setting, in both its processes and its ethos.

The basic ITU process is driven from the top. As an intergovernmental organisation, the role of the member state governments is crucial. This finds its focus in the quadrennial Plenipotentiary Conference. This is the supreme organ of the ITU and sets long-term policies for the guidance of its subordinate bodies. Participation in the meetings of the Plenipotentiary Conference is open only to the member states, the UN and its agencies, and a small number of other specified interested parties. In the interval between Plenipotentiary Conferences, the policy function is undertaken by the Council, which also facilitates implementation of the decisions made by the Union. The Council consists of representatives of forty-six member states, distributed equitably between the regions of the world. Below this level, in the telecommunication standardisation sector (ITU–T), telecommunication standardisation conferences are held every four years. These conferences are responsible for the promulgation of standards by means of Recommendations to the member states. The standards themselves are drafted by Study Groups, which are created at, and allocated work by, the standardisation conferences. These conferences therefore control the direction in which standardisation should proceed. Unlike the IETF, where technical and political issues are procedurally inseparable, the division of responsibilities between the study groups (which are supposed to resolve technical issues) and the standardisation conferences (which concentrate on political questions) means that the standards which are eventually embodied in Recommendations are more likely to depend on political machinations than are Internet standards. This is particularly likely to be true when national interests are at stake (Zacher 1996: 154–5), although participation in the standards process is open to sector members (primarily interested parties from the commercial and research worlds), who pay for the privilege (Schmidt and Werle 1998: 138–41).

In comparison with the Internet process, then, the ITU is more hierarchical and subject to political controversy. It is also, by some measures, less open. For standards organisations, the concept of openness is contested. David Crocker suggests three broad classifications of open systems: open publication, where the specification of a proprietary technology is published, but the specification itself remains under the control of the vendor (an example might be the Microsoft Windows Application Programming Interface); open ownership, such as traditional standards bodies where membership is needed to participate, but the requirements for membership are relatively straightforward; and open development, where there are no requirements for membership and the results of the development process are freely (*gratis* or at low cost) available (Crocker 1993b). Ken Krechmer offers a more sophisticated ten-fold typology, by which measure neither the IETF nor the ITU are completely open (Krechmer 1998). In particular, the IETF fails to comply with the voting model set down for US standards-setting organisations by the American National Standards Institute (ANSI 1998: Annex A.8). The ITU does not provide open access to its finished work, except on payment of a fee. For those in developing countries this fee might easily be prohibitive (Malamud 1993: 344).

The ITU and IETF also differ in their approach to the relationship between specification and implementation. The ITU process does not require that a specification be proved by being implemented, unlike the IETF, which insists on significant operational experience before recognising that a protocol has reached the 'Standard' state. One can identify three positions in the implementation cycle at which standardisation might occur (Baskin *et al.* 1998). Anticipatory standards are created before a specification or protocol has been widely tested or implemented. Participatory standards arise out of development and testing as part of the standards process. Responsive standards codify products or service that are already well established in the market. According to this categorisation, the IETF promotes only participatory standards, while the ITU often, but not always, produces anticipatory standards. Many ITU–T Recommendations follow implementations of a technology (the V.90 modem standard is a recent example, which was settled after two competing implementations of 56kb/s technology had already been on the market for some time), but they often differ enough to render the existing technology incompatible. In other instances, the standard is set over a period of years, but no widespread implementation takes place at all. The prime example of this is the X.400 standard, which lost out in the marketplace to the Internet e-mail standard, SMTP (Schmidt and Werle 1998: 229–62; Rose 1993). The success of SMTP may be attributed to a complex set of circumstances, but the complexity of the X.400 specification combined with the relatively closed nature of the standard must have played a part.

W3C

As the Internet has grown and become more pervasive, the work of the IETF has been supplemented by specialist quasi-standards organisations. Predominant amongst these is the World Wide Web Consortium (W3C). The function of W3C is to develop common protocols for the evolution of the World Wide Web, but this function does not sit squarely within the Internet. Whilst the core transport protocols of the web (Hypertext Transport Protocol, or HTTP) are Internet protocols, and are therefore developed in collaboration with the IETF, the document presentation standards (such as HTML and XML) are more widely applicable. Since these latter specifications are closely related to the ISO-8879 SGML standard, the W3C co-operates with ISO, rather than the IETF. The processes used by W3C reflect its position between the traditional standards organisations and the IETF. Most notably, although the W3C welcomes public comments on its work through various mailing lists, it is a membership organisation and the bulk of its work is conducted in working groups and activities that are open only to members. In this respect, the W3C is closer to the ITU than to the IETF.

ICANN

The most recent addition to the process of Internet governance is also the most controversial. The Internet Corporation for Assigned Names and Numbers (ICANN) has taken over the functions of the Internet Assigned Numbers Authority (IANA). The latter body exercised powers that appeared to have been delegated originally by the IAB before it became a subordinate body of the Internet Society, but the exact extent of that delegation was never clear. The IANA function was funded at least in part of the United States government, and has now been re-assigned by the Department of Commerce to ICANN. Currently, ICANN is operating under an interim board, until the details of its constitutional structure are settled. Whilst it will have powers over the numbers of the Internet (such as policies for IP address allocation, port numbers and the like), its primary concern at present is the orderly regulation of domain naming, as already described. Following the White Paper, it has instituted a system of competitive registrars for the com, net and org registry. That process has been controversial enough, but the constitution of ICANN itself has been even more problematic, as is indicated in Froomkin's chapter in this book. Concerns have been raised about the composition of the interim board (either because of the closed way in which it was selected, or because the members of the board are not felt to be well enough acquainted with the issues underlying the domain name crisis); the fact that trademark and other commercial interests are too dominant (this is probably not ICANN's fault, given the wording of the White Paper); the influence of governments on ICANN's work; and, generally, the fact that it appears that political considerations may outweigh technical issues in the decisions ICANN makes. It appears that ICANN itself is unconcerned about these allegations.

Where is the Internet heading?

The IETF process is probably not the future of Internet standard-setting. Even if it does remain in place as a standards body, it is not likely to serve as a model for Internet governance; the ICANN experience suggests that whatever the views of

the Internet community, there are important governmental or commercial interests which outweigh the traditional expectations (see also Froomkin 1999c).
There are complex reasons why this might be so. The Internet process is one
which generally lacks central control. Not only is the IETF organised in a
bottom-up fashion, but it also sets standards which are probably less well
enforced than those set by the ITU. The nature of the Internet itself is that it is a
network of networks. Each of those private networks is autonomous, and may
attempt or refuse connections as its operators see fit. There should be no expectation of universal connectivity in the Internet. This uncertainty is not a firm
basis for e-commerce, and it is likely that as the Internet becomes more infras-
tructural, the standards underpinning it will have to be formalised in some way.
In particular, the current system does not easily permit involvement in standard-
setting by those who are not yet part of the network. Conflicts may also start to
arise with patent rights asserted by participants in the process. The IETF may
start to move away from a participatory model towards an anticipatory one.
Finally, the social model of the IETF is starting to break down. As more people
become involved in its work, the influence of the 'Internet elders' is diminishing.
The long-term game which underpinned much of the IETF's early work may be
replaced with short-term behaviour.

Even if that does not happen, it is not clear that the IETF process is a suitable
model for wider governance. Any process which is intended to create detailed
technical rules will necessarily exclude those who lack expertise in the area under
scrutiny. Standards processes do not lend themselves naturally to rule-making of
a more general nature. The ultimate resolution of the domain name crisis, which
was more political and legal than technical, suggests that the application of
purely technical solutions to such problems is not particularly fruitful. The
remaining issue, then, is where global Internet governance will take place. In
that context, ICANN appears to have ushered in the kings and presidents. In a
network that is the basis of e-commerce, the model for governance is likely to be
the normal political system that governs commerce and communication outside
the Internet. However, there are too many conflicting interests and perspectives
to conclude that a self-organising network, which is necessary to Rhodes's definition of 'governance', has arisen. These conflicts include, most obviously, the
tensions between the IETF technical tradition and the bureaucratic model of
decision-making implicit in the gTLD-MoU and ICANN. There are also differences between national approaches to regulation – the US model being more
light-handed and sensitive to commercial interests, whereas the tendency in
Europe and the UN agencies is a centralising governmental one. The introduction of special interests of a non-technical nature (beginning, but not ending,
with intellectual property) will create new stresses in the structure of governance.
Finally, the question of dispute-resolution, which has been pivotal in the DNS, is
likely to become more pervasive. Should disputes be resolved by existing
processes (which are largely judicial), or should new procedures and norms be
promulgated? The current mechanisms for standard-setting are poorly positioned to deal with these questions, but one may also be legitimately concerned

that the answers provided by systems outside the Internet might not give sufficient weight to the special technical requirements of the network (Gillett and
Kapor 1997: 33). Internet governance cannot, therefore, take place in one location. Rather, a collection of mechanisms – some unique to the Internet, some
not – will jointly furnish the means by which protocols are determined, resources
allocated and networks managed.

Notes

1 For examples of the range of possible rules see Lessig (1999b).
2 Papers and other materials from this meeting are online at http://ksg
   www.harvard.edu/iip/cai/caiconf.html and most are also published in Kahin and
   Keller (1997).
3 A brief synopsis of the history of the ITU is available in Zacher (1996).

11 Semi-private international rulemaking

Lessons learned from the WIPO domain name process

A. Michael Froomkin[1]

The World Intellectual Property Organization (WIPO) domain name process was an ambitious and at least partly successful attempt to make rules about a public issue – the relationship between Internet domain names and intellectual property law – via a semi-private process. It produced a lengthy and very readable report, which advanced the debate over the regulation of domain names (WIPO 1999a). The semi-private process leading up to that report had several novel features, and perhaps as a result was not well understood by the public or even key participants. Trailblazing is never easy. The lessons learned from this experience might suggest that this particular trail is better treated as a dead end; if, however, the process is to be repeated, as seems all too likely, lessons learned from this first run can improve any future attempts at a semi-private process.

A semi-private process is a cooperative endeavor between a public body and private interests that is designed to create a body of rules enforced by some mechanism other than direct promulgation by the public body. Semi-private rulemaking should not be confused with either negotiated rulemaking or self-regulation. In negotiated rulemaking a government agency or other public body meets with representatives of the groups who will be affected by the regulation, and seeks to find agreement on rules that can then be promulgated and enforced by the government (Coglianese 1997). US law, for example, defines negotiated rulemaking as rulemaking through the use of "an advisory committee established by an agency ... to consider and discuss issues for the purpose of reaching a consensus in the development of a proposed rule" (US Code 5 USC section 562). True self-regulation excludes the participation of a public body. Thus, much of what is loosely called "self-regulation" is not in fact self-regulation. For example, US stock exchanges engage in so-called "self-regulation" but their rules are subject to approval by the US Securities and Exchange Commission.

Semi-private rulemaking melds the two: the rules may be drafted in a process superficially similar to negotiated rulemaking, but the role of the public body is different. The public body may take a direct role in the negotiations, as did WIPO, or it may act through a private proxy. Market regulation through the establishment of a government-owned market participant or by a standards body is an example of action through such a proxy. The Commerce Department's relationship with the Internet Corporation for Assigned Names and Numbers (ICANN) at times appears to have this character. Private federally chartered government corporations are a somewhat related phenomenon (Froomkin 1995a). In either case, the public body either chooses not to promulgate the rule, or lacks the jurisdiction to do so; instead, the rule is enforced by some private means. In the case of the WIPO domain name process, WIPO suggested that ICANN require the proposed rules to be included in every private contract governing the rights of registrants of the most popular types of domain names.

Although considerable scholarly attention has been paid to traditional regulation, negotiated rulemaking, to markets as regulatory devices, to other forms of so-called "self-regulation", and even to privatization of previously governmental functions, less attention has been paid to semi-private rulemaking of the kind exemplified by the WIPO process, perhaps because until now it has been relatively rare. Semi-private rulemaking may be on the increase, however, as governments and others look for flexible and credible ways to regulate transnational phenomena such as the Internet. Whatever the long-run prospects for semi-private rulemaking, experience gained in the WIPO process provides useful lessons for the emerging semi-private rulemaking processes now taking shape under the rubric of ICANN. Indeed, ICANN seems set to re-invent the wheel several times over, as it creates a bewildering profusion of subsidiary bodies (Rutkowski 1999), each of which will need to figure out its own rules of procedure.

This chapter offers a critical insider's view of the WIPO Internet domain name process. It is an "insider's" view because I was a part of the process: I was a late addition to WIPO's advisory "Experts" panel, brought in about one third of the way into the domain name process described here. Nevertheless, in some important ways I was not an insider. My addition to the panel appears to have been in response to complaints that there were no civil liberties experts included in the original advisory group. For reasons that were never made clear to me, WIPO chose not to empanel a representative of the Domain Name Rights Coalition, the advocacy group that had the most expertise and the longest track record as a counterweight to intellectual property rights holders. Instead they sought an academic, and picked one who was not, by any standard, a trademark expert, although I had both written about civil liberties in cyberspace and practiced as an arbitration lawyer. Even so, appointing an internal institutionalized representative of civil liberties issues was a noble and courageous move on WIPO's part, and I continue to hope that they do not now regret it, especially since I was very public about my views as to where both WIPO's Interim and Final Reports erred (Froomkin 1999a; Froomkin 1999b).

The WIPO experience raises broad questions about the appropriateness of public bodies engaging in creative procedures for rulemaking. As a general matter creativity of this sort should be viewed with great caution, and perhaps even alarm. In democracies, traditional public rulemaking and rule-enforcement comes hedged with valuable substantive and procedural protections for those impacted by the rules. Semi-private processes may be subject to very attenuated democratic control at best, do not need to conform to due process, and if the

WIPO process is any guide will be enforced in a way that makes it impossible to challenge the substance of the rules in any meaningful fashion (Froomkin 1999c).

All that, however, is another story: this chapter will focus on *procedure* and not on substance. Whether you agree with it or not, WIPO's Final Report is elegantly written, contains a great deal of useful information, and sets out a clear view of the issues. I was very critical of some matters of substance, but my assessment of the procedure is that WIPO did many things right, and that those things can and should be emulated in any future semi-private process. I also will argue, however, that it did a few important things wrong – most of which could be avoided in the future. In fairness, however, one should note that WIPO was working on a very difficult issue, in a politically charged environment, to a short timetable, and that the WIPO process was in many ways the first of its kind. There are costs to going first, but one of the benefits is that those who come later can learn from the experience.

There are also issues about how ICANN and others should weigh the end-product, the WIPO Final Report. External perceptions of the process may have diverged from what appeared, at least from my vantage point, to be the reality. These perceptions matter enormously in a semi-private rulemaking, because the end-product's influence relies on perceptions of a fair and encompassing process for its political legitimacy and potential adoption.

Domain names: the underlying issues

Domain names are the alphanumeric text strings to the right of an "@" in an e-mail address, or immediately following the two slashes in a World Wide Web address. By practice and convention, domain names can be mapped to a 32-bit number consisting of four octets (sets of eight binary digits) that specifies a network address and a host ID on a TCP/IP network. These are the "Internet Protocol" (IP – not to be confused with "Intellectual Property") numbers – the numbers that play a critical role in addressing all communications over the Internet, including e-mail and World Wide Web (WWW) traffic (Mockapetris 1987). They have justly been called the "human-friendly form of Internet addresses" (WIPO 1999a: para 4). Their potential "friendliness" is also the source of legal and commercial disputes: businesses have come to view their domain names as an important identifier, even a brand. And as both businesses and users increasingly have come to view domain names as having connotations that map to the world outside the Internet, rather than as arbitrary identifiers, these conflicts, often involving claims of trademark infringement or unfair competition, have become more frequent.

The Internet works the way it does because it is able to route information quickly from one machine to another. IP numbers provide the identifying information that allows an e-mail to find its destination, or a request for a web page to reach the right computer across the Internet. Unlike e-mail, web page access can be achieved with an IP number. Thus, for example, http://www.law.miami.edu is equivalent to http://129.171.187.10. However, e-mail to froomkin@129.171. 187. 10 will not reach me or anyone else. IP numbers are hard for people to remember, so the designers of the Internet introduced easier alphanumeric domain names as mnemonics. When a user types an alphanumeric Uniform Resource Locator (URL) into a web browser, the host computer must "resolve" the domain name – that is, translate it into an IP number. Both domain names and IP numbers are ordinarily unique (subject to minor exceptions if resources are interchangeable). The system by which these unique domain names and IP numbers are allocated and domain names resolved to IP numbers is a critical function on the Internet.

Currently, the large majority of domain names for Internet resources intended to be used by the public have a relationship to two organized hierarchies. (Internet-based resources for private use, such as intranets can be organized differently.) The first, very visible, hierarchy, relates to naming conventions for domain names and constrains how domain names are allocated. The second, and largely invisible, hierarchy determines the ways in which domain names are resolved into the IP numbers that actually make Internet communication possible. The two hierarchies are closely related, but not identical.

Domain naming conventions treat a domain name as having three parts: in the address www.miami.edu, for example, ".edu," the rightmost part, is the "top level domain" or TLD, while "miami" is the second-level domain (SLD), and any other parts are lumped together as third or higher-level domains. Domain names are just conventions, and a core part of the current dispute over them arises from the conflict over whether new TLDs should be added to the so-called "legacy root" – the most widely used, and thus most authoritative, list of which TLDs will actually map to IP numbers. It should be noted that in addition to the "legacy root" TLDs discussed in this article, there are a large number of "alternate" TLDs that are not acknowledged by the majority of domain name servers (DNS). There is no technical bar to their existence and anyone who knows how to tell his software to use an alternate domain name server can access both the "legacy root" and whatever alternate TLDs are supported by that name server. Thus, for example, pointing your DNS at 205.189.73.102 and 24.226.37.241 makes it possible to resolve http://lighting.faq, where a legacy DNS would only return an error message.

The legacy root is currently made up of two-letter country-code TLDs (ccTLDs), and seven three-letter generic TLDs (gTLDs). There are 243 ccTLDs, each having a two-letter country code, almost all of which are derived from ISO Standard 3166. Not every ccTLD is necessarily controlled by the government that has sovereignty over the territory associated with that country code, however. This is likely to be an area of increasing controversy, as (some) governments argue that the ccTLD associated with "their" two-letter ISO 3166 country code is somehow an appurtenance of sovereignty (ICANN Governmental Advisory Committee 1999). The ccTLDs sometimes have rules that make registration difficult or even next to impossible; as a result, the gTLDs, and especially .com, have the lion's share of the registrations. Three gTLDs are open to anyone who can afford to pay for a registration: .com, .org, and .net. Other gTLDs impose additional criteria for registration: .mil (US military), .gov (US government), .int (international organizations), .edu (institutions of higher education, .arpa (primarily used for testing purposes). Domains registered in ccTLDs and gTLDs are equally accessible from any computer on the Internet.

The registration hierarchy

The registration side of the current DNS architecture is arranged hierarchically to ensure that each domain name is unique. At least prior to the recent introduction of a "shared registry" system, which seems to have introduced some at least transitory uncertainty about whether the master file is authoritative, a master file of the registrations in each TLD was held by a single registry (Network Solutions n.d.; Rony and Rony 1999). In theory, and ignoring software glitches, having a single registry ensures that once a name is allocated to one person it cannot simultaneously be assigned to a different person. End-users seeking to obtain a unique domain name must obtain one from a registrar. A registrar can be the registry or it can be a separate entity that has an agreement with the registry for the TLD in which the domain name will appear. Before issuing a registration, the registrar queries the registry's database to make certain the name is available. If it is, it marks it as taken, and (currently) associates various contact details provided by the registrant with the record.

While one can imagine other possible system architectures, the current domain name system requires that each domain name be "unique" in the sense that it be managed by a single registrant rather than a single IP number. The registrant may associate the domain name with varying IP numbers if that will produce a desired result. For example, a busy website might have several servers, each with its own IP number, that take turns serving requests directed to a single domain name. In a different Internet, many computers controlled by different people might answer to http://www.law.tm. In that world, WWW users who entered that URL, or clicked on a link to it, would either be playing a roulette game with unpredictable results, or they would have to pass through some sort of gateway or query system so their requests could be routed to the right place. (One can spin more complex stories involving intelligent agents and artificial intelligences that seek to predict user preferences, but this only changes the odds in the roulette game.) Such a system would probably be time-consuming and frustrating, especially as the number of users sharing popular names grew. In any case, it would not be compatible with today's e-mail and other non-interactive communications mechanisms.

The DN resolution hierarchy

The resolution side of the DN system is an interdependent, distributed, hierarchical database (Rony and Rony 1998: section 3.4.2). At the top of the hierarchy lies a single data file that contains the list of the machines that have the master lists of registrations in each TLD. This is the "root zone" or "root," sometimes the "legacy root." Although there is no technical obstacle to anyone maintaining a TLD that is not listed in the legacy root, these "alternate" TLDs can only be resolved by users whose machines, or ISPs as the case may be, use a domain name server that includes this additional data or knows where to find it. A combination of consensus, lack of knowledge, and inertia among the people running the machines which administer domain name lookups, means that domain names in TLDs outside the legacy root, e.g. http://lighting.faq, cannot be accessed by the large majority of people who use the Internet unless they do some tinkering with obscure parts of their browser settings (ORSC Root Zone n.d.).

Domain names are resolved by sending queries to a set of databases linked hierarchically. The query starts at the bottom, at the name server selected by the user or her ISP. A name server is a network service that enables clients to name resources or objects and share this information with other objects in the network (Domains FAQ: section 2.3). If the data is not in the name server, the query works its way up the chain until it can be resolved. At the top of the chain is the root zone file maintained in parallel on thirteen different computers. These thirteen machines, currently identified by letters from A to M, contain a copy of the list of the TLD servers that have the full databases of registered names and their associated IP numbers. (To confuse matters, some of these machines have both a copy of the root zone file and second-level domain registration data for one or more TLDs.) Each TLD has a registry that has the authoritative master copy of the second-level domain names registered for that TLD, and the root zone file tells domain name resolving programs where to find them.

Since every Internet-related communication requires an address, and people tend to use domain names rather than IP addresses, DN lookups occur millions of times per hour. Most queries, however, do not make it to the computer holding the master list because copies are distributed to thousands of other name servers, and many local ISPs keep a cache of frequently requested or recently requested IP numbers to provide better service to their customers. If a "local" nameserver doesn't have the information needed, it can send a query up the tree, querying caches all the way, perhaps even going as high as a root server if the query involves a TLD whose address is not present in the local cache (Barkow 1996).

Domain names and trademarks

Governments issue (or, in the case of common-law trademarks, recognize) trademarks on a geographic and industry-sectoral basis. With the exception of some treaty-based registration systems that allow multiple registration in a unified process, trademarks are issued one country at a time. Further, trademarks generally are issued for one or only a few categories of goods or services at a time. Thus, a firm can trademark the word "united" for air transport, but this will not extend to moving vans unless the firm is in that business also. Trademark registrations generally require use to remain effective; while they are in effect they give the holder important rights against others who unfairly would seek to capitalize on the goodwill of the mark by confusing consumers. Equally importantly, trademarks protect consumers against those who might seek to pass off their goods as produced by the mark holder. As a general matter, however, in the US at least, trademark infringement requires commercial use by the infringer. Absent commercial use, some type of unfair competition, or a very small number of other specialized offenses (e.g. "tarnishment" of a mark by associating it with obscenity), trademark law does not make the use of the mark an offense. Thus, for example, in the United States and many other countries, parody, criticism, names of pets, and references in literature, and every other use one might make of a basic dictionary word such as "united," are all permissible uses of a word that is also trademarked for some purposes. Indeed, unless the mark falls into a very small category of "famous" marks where it is considered likely that any product which bears the mark will be associated with a single source, it generally is permissible to make commercial use of a name trademarked by another so long as it is not likely to cause customer confusion. Even some types of commercial use of famous marks are permitted, e.g. accurate comparative advertising, news reporting, and news commentary (*Avery Dennison* v. *Sumpton* (9th Cir. 1999)).

The Internet is notoriously international, and every site registered in one of the legacy root TLDs is accessible world-wide. A system that relied on geographic distance and sectoral differentiation maps badly to a borderless world in which every participant in the global network needs a unique address. For some time now, there has been a near-consensus among policy-makers interested in the Internet that the management of Internet domain names is a core issue of Internet governance. In particular, owners of trademark and related intellectual property rights have asserted that issues relating to so-called "cybersquatting" needed to be resolved before any new TLDs could be added to the legacy root. "Cybersquatting" is shorthand for the practice of registering domains that correspond to other people's trademarks in the hopes of reselling them at a (sometimes substantial) profit (*Brookfield Communications, Inc.* v. *West Coast Ent.* (9th Cir. 1998)). While there may be grounds to question whether cybersquatting is the first issue to resolve, some believe strongly that it is, and their view has dominated policy debates relating to new TLDs for the last three years or more.

Whether registration of a domain name that is identical to a trademarked term is in and of itself a trademark violation has been one controversial issue. Generally speaking, in the US at least, one does not violate a trademark right without commercial use and (absent a finding that the mark is famous) likelihood of confusion. Unless, therefore, registration is itself a commercial use, mere registration without use of a domain name cannot be a violation of trademark right. This is especially clear in the case of trademarks in common words and in terms trademarked by more than one party. On the other hand, courts in the US and in the UK have found that a person who made a practice of registering others' trademarks for potential resale was making commercial use of those trademarks and thus had committed a violation (*Panavision Int'l* v. *Toeppen* (9th Cir. 1998); *British Telecommunications* v. *One in a Million* (Court of Appeal, 1998)).

Bitter disputes arose between trademark holders and others who registered character strings identical or similar to their trademarks. In "cybersquatting" cases, the allegation was usually that the registrant was not using the domain but rather warehousing it in hopes of reselling it at a (sometimes substantial) profit. Not every string conflict, however, necessarily involved a claim of misuse of a domain and not all warehousing is necessarily a misuse. For example, firms sometimes acquire domains with the same name as a trademark they have registered even though they have no intention of using the domain. They do so in order to prevent someone else from using it and causing customer confusion. Similarly, firms and others sometimes acquire domains for future use. A firm may register a domain name before trademarking a term as part of the often-secret process of preparing a new product or campaign. In fact, these practices have given rise to some expressed concern that without new gTLDs large amounts of the attractive part of the namespace might become unavailable to users.

Conflicts also arise between multiple owners of a trademark in the same string of characters. The owners may be (1) sectorally separate (same country, but different use or different category of goods and services); or (2) geographically separate (same business, but different countries or regions within a country); or (3) both sectorally and geographically separate (*Prince PLC* v. *Prince Sports Group, Inc.* (Chancery Division 1997)). Conflicts also arise between trademark holders and persons with some other legitimate interest in a mark not deriving from a trademark. Each potential conflict tends to be aggressively pursued by trademark owners, because trademark law punishes owners who fail to police uses of their rights. An owner who fails to take action against a true infringer can soon find that the infringer has established rights of his own, and that the original mark is thus reduced in value.

Enter WIPO

WIPO is one of sixteen specialized agencies operating under the UN umbrella. It is charged with promoting "the protection of intellectual property throughout the world through cooperation among States and, where appropriate, in collaboration with any other international organization" (WIPO 1996: article 3). Currently 171 states are WIPO members (WIPO n.d. Contracting Parties of Treaties).

In a White Paper formally known as the *Statement of Policy on Management of Internet Names and Addresses* issued by the US Department of Commerce, the United States government called on WIPO to:

> initiate a balanced and transparent process, which includes the participation of trademark holders and members of the Internet community who are not trademark holders, to (1) develop recommendations for a uniform approach to resolving trademark/domain name disputes involving cyberpiracy (as opposed to conflicts between trademark holders with legitimate competing rights), (2) recommend a process for protecting famous trademarks in the generic top level domains, and (3) evaluate the effects, based on studies conducted by independent organizations, such as the National Research

Council of the National Academy of Sciences, of adding new gTLDs and related dispute resolution procedures on trademark and intellectual property holders. These findings and recommendations could be submitted to the board of the new corporation for its consideration in conjunction with its development of registry and registrar policy and the creation and introduction of new gTLDs.

(Department of Commerce 1998b)

The Department of Commerce subsequently designated ICANN as the "NewCo" referred to in the White Paper.

By the time the US government issued the domain name White Paper in 1998, WIPO was no stranger to the domain name issue. Three years earlier, in 1995, Network Solutions Inc. (NSI) and the US National Science Foundation (NSF) negotiated new terms under which NSI would continue to be the sole allocating authority for domain names in the .com, .org, and .net TLDs. This agreement allowed NSI to charge fees for registrations, signaled a new era in the commercialization of the domain space, and catalyzed a series of political maneuvers among those with interests in commercializing the Internet, or in protecting existing rights that might be affected by it (Simon n.d.). One leading organization, the International Ad Hoc Committee (IAHC), proposed to create seven new TLDs (Rony and Rony 1998: section 13.5). In the spring of 1997 the IAHC and others issued a Generic Top Level Domain Memorandum of Understanding (gTLD-MoU). Oddly, although the document is formally a private creation and the signatories are private corporations, the International Telecommunications Union (ITU) agreed to "act as the depository" of the gTLD-MoU and to promote it, as if it were an international convention. The gTLD-MoU created a twelve-person policy oversight committee (POC), with WIPO picking one member (Simon undated).

The gTLD-MOU made WIPO the sole arbitral institution charged with administering any dispute arising from intellectual-property related claims settlement policy set out in the document. WIPO's Arbitration and Mediation Center had been established in 1994, although commentators have not been completely kind to the institution, and its caseload was low (Bernstein *et al.* 1998: section 10–49). Critics of the gTLD-MoU charged that its authors and proponents were over-solicitous of trademark interests, and they claimed that WIPO, a UN body charged with the promotion and protection of intellectual property, could not be a neutral body to hear or administer disputes between trademark holders and Internet-based competitors who might not have registered trademarks. The gTLD-MoU never achieved the critical mass of agreement necessary to claim consensus, and the belief that the plan was biased in favor of established trademark interests seems to have been a significant factor in the opposition. As passions ran high, many of those who opposed the gTLD-MoU decided WIPO was in cahoots with those who sought to expand the rights of existing trademarks holders to additional world-wide rights online; even for other less dogmatic opponents, WIPO's participation in what came to be seen as a partisan proposal made it next to impossible for them to conceive of WIPO as an honest broker.

The White Paper's call to WIPO to produce a study was thus not seen by all as a reference to a neutral, disinterested, expert body. On the contrary, by the time of the White Paper, battle lines were drawn and, at least in the eyes of the faction that wished to have new TLDs added to the legacy root quickly, WIPO was strongly identified with another faction, one that opposed large numbers of new gTLDs and was very attentive to both the legitimate rights and the more ambitious claims of intellectual property holders (Kleiman *et al.* 1998). In the eyes of others, however, including the US government, WIPO was an expert body that could be asked to tackle an almost intractable problem.

WIPO responded to the US government's request for a report with the elaborate Internet domain name process that is the subject of this paper. The WIPO process began a month after the White Paper, when WIPO published *RFC 1*, its draft "terms of reference" (WIPO 1998a) and culminated in a Final Report issued 30 April 1999 (WIPO 1999a). ICANN ultimately adopted part of the suggestions in somewhat modified form (ICANN 1999a; ICANN 1999b).

Being an organ of the United Nations, responsible to all its member states rather than just the US, WIPO understandably felt empowered to define its own terms of reference rather than limit itself to the relatively narrow mandate set out in the White Paper. In its *Request for Comments 1*, WIPO set out a laundry list of possible issues it might address, and asked for comments (WIPO 1998a: paragraphs 4–5). WIPO posted these on its web page, and invited e-mailed or written comments. WIPO received sixty-plus e-mailed comments, which were publicly archived on its website and the large majority of which supported its approach. WIPO then met with its Panel of Experts (although NSI Chief Litigation Counsel Philip Sbarbaro and I were added later), and issued *RFC 2* in mid-September 1998 (WIPO 1998b).

In *RFC 2*, WIPO stated that it intended to make recommendations concerning (1) dispute prevention, (2) dispute resolution, (3) process for the protection of famous and well-known marks in the gTLDs, and (4) effects on intellectual property rights of new gTLDs (WIPO 1998b: para. 12). WIPO thus gave itself a considerably broader and more ambitious charge than the fairly narrow one proposed by the US in the White Paper.

The consultation process

The WIPO process had a number of innovative features, most notably an extensive consultation process. The process also included an advisory, if ultimately somewhat marginal, "Experts Group" that was regionally diverse (although predominantly male, and perhaps inevitably had a heavy US representation) and composed of people with varied experience, including leaders in trademark law, in Internet technology, representatives of country-code registries and, with the addition of NSI's litigation counsel, of the major gTLD registry. WIPO undertook an ambitious, hybrid, consultation exercise in which it solicited comments both via a series of internationally dispersed physical meetings and by requesting e-mailed input that was archived on its website. In hindsight, however, both parts of the consultation offer lessons for future projects.

Live consultations

The live consultations began after the publication of *RFC 2*, the final terms of reference. Between 23 August and 4 November 1998, WIPO held open meetings in eleven cities: Palo Alto, Brussels, Washington DC, Mexico City, Cape Town, Asuncion, Tokyo, Hyderabad, Budapest, Cairo, Sydney (WIPO 1998c). Unfortunately, the publicity for these meetings left something to be desired. Meetings were announced on the WIPO website, with dates set with varying degrees of advance warning but frequently less than the magic 21-day purchase period for airlines. The information was also posted to a WIPO announcement mailing list composed of a few hundred people who had previously found the website. The mailing list had just over 200 members in July 1998, about 550 at the time of the first physical consultation, and eventually grew to 1,358 by the Final Report (WIPO 1998f; WIPO 1999a: Annex III). WIPO itself may have sent official communications to the patent and trademark offices of member states, but the brunt of publicity appears to have been handled by host groups and intellectual property associations. Neither WIPO nor the host groups posted meeting announcements on the various Internet technical or legal mailing lists in which I participate. Perhaps as a result, turnout at the meetings was not on the whole very impressive. The eleven regional consultations following *RFC 2* averaged 77 persons, with a very uneven geographic distribution ranging from 30 in Cape Town to 160 in Asuncion. The six meetings following *RFC 3* averaged just under 70 people, ranging from 48 in Toronto to 117 in Dakar (WIPO 1999a: para. 28). I attended only one meeting in the first round and four of the final six meetings, but it was my strong impression that the very large majority of the speakers, and indeed the attendees, at those events were either intellectual property rights holders, their lawyers, their trade associations, or Internet service providers. There were a few representatives from user groups, but only a few.

WIPO encouraged members of the Panel of Experts to attend these meetings, paid our expenses, and placed us on stage or at the front of the room. The meetings were chaired by a WIPO staff member and structured as if attendees were directing their remarks to the panel, even though we were not in fact the drafters of the report. Members of the public were encouraged to present short prepared statements, followed by brief question and answer sessions. There usually was also a period of open discussion. Members of the Panel of Experts were encouraged to ask questions of the attendees, but we were strongly discouraged from making statements of our own. In some cases, however, we did anyway, as did the members of the WIPO staff who efficiently chaired the meetings. The format was somewhat formal, but it was good-humored and there was a fair amount of give and take between panelists and audience, and even some comments from audience members responding to each other. The overall effect, however, was much more like a hearing before an administrative agency than, say, a faculty seminar.

WIPO made audio files and transcripts of the meetings available on its website, although in most cases these did not become available until well after the actual meeting, or even after the close of the comment period. Perhaps because of the time lag, I had little sense that large numbers of attendees at one meeting were aware of, much less responding to, what persons said in earlier meetings; in this regard the presence of repeat participants from WIPO and the Panel of Experts provided most of what continuity there was.

Online consultations

WIPO's use of the Internet to further the consultative process was in some ways exemplary, in some ways poor, and in some ways timid. It was exemplary in that WIPO designed an attractive website that was easy to navigate and which contained all the critical information about the process in very readable form. Although English was the primary working language for most meetings and commentaries, WIPO-produced materials and reports were available not only in English, but also in Spanish and French. WIPO reports that the website received more than 700,000 "web hits" during the life of the process, although whether "web hits" are independent visits or page views is unclear (WIPO 1999a: Annex 3, section 4). Even taking the narrowest measure, in which the same people revisited the site repeatedly, this surely represents many thousands of independent visitors. The volume of traffic is all the more impressive as publicizing the web site does not appear to have been an especially high priority.

Furthermore, WIPO made e-mail announcements to a mailing list it created and also set up an e-mail discussion group. The utility of the mailing lists was limited, however, by the "consultative" paradigm: the ultimate authors of the WIPO report, the WIPO staff, read the list but did not post to it. There was thus very little traffic on it, and the discussions that started tended to fizzle out quickly in the absence of any sign of intellectual engagement from the management. Given that WIPO is a somewhat bureaucratic body, and a part of the UN at that, it is unsurprising that staff may have been reluctant to engage in public dialog on an ad hoc basis. In contrast, there was a private list for the advisory panel, to which WIPO staff did contribute.

WIPO also received and publicly archived e-mailed comments to each of its three requests for comments. Again, the web tools were commendably easy to use and the comments easy to read, but the discussion was essentially one-way and one-time per request for comments. Comments were directed to WIPO; most came in at or near the deadline. WIPO did not undertake to reply, and there was little dialog amongst commentators.

In general, therefore, both the meatspace and cyberspace processes worked much like an informal agency hearing process: a draft document was put out for comment, the agency held public hearings and requested written input, and then retired in private to write and issue its conclusions.

Course of discussions

After the first set of public hearings, WIPO issued its Interim Report, *RFC 3* (WIPO 1998c). The report met with a mixed reception. Some members of the intellectual property rights holding community thought it did not go far enough for them; others either approved or had various technical objections. Those who had opposed the gTLD-MoU, and others also, had a large list of objections (Froomkin 1999a). One notable objection was that, although the White Paper had asked WIPO to "develop recommendations for a uniform approach to resolving trademark/domain name disputes involving cyberpiracy" (Dept. of Commerce 1998b) the report did not include a clear definition of what had come to be known as "cybersquatting". Another very controversial issue was the special protections proposed for famous and well-known marks. Famous and well-known marks are particularly recognizable trademarks that are entitled to additional legal protection beyond the ordinary protections afforded regular trademarks (Federal Trademark Dilution Act of 1995; Paris Convention; TRIPS Agreement). Some national authorities have published lists of the marks considered famous and well-known in their jurisdictions; others leave it to their courts to decide on a case-by-case basis. Despite several years of work by an international panel convened by WIPO, however, there remains no agreed definition of what constitutes a globally famous or well-known mark, so WIPO proposed to set up a tribunal to rule on applications for this status. Marks found sufficiently famous would be entitled to additional protection against having domain names with the same or similar character strings registered in the DNS by anyone but the famous mark holder.

Process difficulties

The limited role of the Experts

WIPO empanelled an impressive, experienced, and diverse group of people to advise it. I found it a privilege to be associated with them. Nevertheless, it was unclear to me what exactly WIPO had hoped the Experts would do. Whatever that something was, it certainly was not drafting.

My first introduction to the workings of the Expert Group was a two-day meeting in Geneva, in December 1998, to discuss the Interim Report that was due to issue shortly thereafter. Unfortunately, we were provided with only minimal text in advance of our meeting – some by e-mail shortly before we left, more under the door of our hotel rooms the night before our first meeting. While our debates are confidential, I think it breaks no confidence to say that our meeting in Geneva was not a drafting session. Rather, we were invited to comment on the issues, and discussed the rather limited texts we had been given. WIPO then revised the texts very extensively, and e-mailed us the revised versions. We had only a very short turnaround, of a few days late in the holiday season, to comment by e-mail on what was, to my eye, a wholly new document.

WIPO then made some additional changes, including the insertion of new material, and on 23 December 1998 WIPO issued *RFC 3*, the Interim Report, which contained WIPO's first draft of its proposals. That report noted the Experts were not responsible for the text (WIPO 1998c: Annex I), but this fact often seemed to have been lost on attendees at the regional consultations I attended.

As noted above, several Experts attended each of the regional consultations. We then had another two-day meeting to discuss the comments on the Interim Report in Geneva in March 1999. Again, this was not a drafting session. We were promised time to review the text of the final report before it would be issued. In fact, Chapters 2–5 arrived by e-mail during what proved to the final week before publication, with the last one arriving perhaps two days before the report was issued. This made commenting in detail rather difficult. None of the Annexes in the Final Report, some of which contain critical procedural recommendations, were sent to the Experts prior to publication. Both the Interim and the Final Report were drafted privately by WIPO staff after the close of the public comment periods, and after meeting with the panel.

Mission blur

The purpose of the WIPO process was to produce a useful document. But uncertainties and varying perceptions as to the objective of the exercise – to whom the document should be useful, and for what purpose – lurked throughout the process. On the one hand, WIPO is part of the United Nations; as such it represents the nations and peoples of the world. It is thus seen by many, especially in the less-developed countries, as more than an honest broker: rather a trustee, a protector of their interests. In addition, both the White Paper and WIPO's own terms of reference spoke of a balanced and transparent process – the kind of language that suggests a search for consensus. On the other hand, WIPO exists "to promote the protection of intellectual property throughout the world." Indeed, the many thoughtful and intelligent staff members I came into contact with appeared sincerely committed to this mission from the highest of motives. The history of the gTLD-MoU further polarized WIPO's position.

The suggestions relating to famous marks, mentioned above, were the most controversial of the recommendations in the Interim Report that survived into the Final Report. Even the trademark bar appeared divided, since there is great uncertainty as to how the WIPO tribunals would work in practice, and also some worry about the effects on a mark that applied for designation as globally famous but was rejected. However, several large trademark holders felt intensely about the issue. In their view the most famous marks had been the ones most frequently victimized by cybersquatters, who counted on the expense of a court case to extort substantial ransoms before releasing domains they had registered. To these trademark holders, the introduction of new gTLDs threatened to repeat the expensive and painful experience over and over again. They were adamant that no new gTLDs open to all comers should be created until and unless someone mandated a policy that would protect famous marks. Although it certainly had a significant number of vociferous supporters, no one who observed the process could plausibly claim that WIPO's decision to keep the famous marks proposal essentially unchanged reflected a consensus on the issue, because there clearly was no consensus. Here, WIPO was clearly acting in some role more like advocate than consensus-builder, although precisely whose advocate was not explained.

Everyone involved in the process understood that the WIPO report was only advisory, and that the "NewCo" described in the White Paper (later, ICANN) would make the ultimate decision after some further process. In my opinion – and what follows is inevitably a subjective view – the advisory, intermediate, character of the report affected the deliberative dynamic in a number of subtle ways: it reduced participation, polarized positions, and removed pressure for a truly transparent process. The WIPO DNS process happened during a busy time for Internet governance. The main stage was occupied by the debates over larger issues raised by the White Paper, especially the nature and structure of the NewCo that would ultimately become ICANN. Many people without a direct financial interest in the trademark/cybersquatting issue felt, reasonably enough, that given onrushing deadlines, and limited time and resources, it was more important to focus on the fundamental structural issues being decided about NewCo, especially when it seemed clear that once NewCo was up and running they would have a chance to be heard on the intellectual property issues. This attitude was not lost on the trademark partisans within the WIPO process. It would not be surprising if the fear of being asked to make further compromises later led to a hardening of positions, since there was an evident danger that any compromise offered in the WIPO process might become an hors d'oeuvre. The result was that, even from my vantage point near the center of the WIPO process, it was not always clear to what extent various participants intended the final product to be a statement of a consensus position of all affected parties, or a consensus of the intellectual property community, or a bargaining token to be played before NewCo. Few people took the bargaining chip view, at least out loud. WIPO staff tended to suggest they were searching for a general consensus or at least an outcome fair to everyone, but at times they and other participants seemed to feel that their most effective contribution would be to forge a consensus among an IP community that was itself of several minds on the key issues, and that it would be unreasonable to expect any more under the circumstances.

WIPO process compared to other types of rulemaking

The WIPO domain name process can be usefully contrasted to international inter-governmental rulemaking via executive agreements or treaties, and also to a US federal agency notice and comment rulemaking. The WIPO process bore little resemblance to a traditional public international law-making or agreement procedure. For one thing, other than authorizing the WIPO secretariat to proceed (WIPO 1998e: #P643_157650), governments appeared in the WIPO process primarily as commentators; the Final Report was drafted by the Secretariat and forwarded to ICANN without first being approved by the WIPO General Assembly. This differs from both the treaty-making and executive-agreement processes in which, whoever may do the actual drafting, states must take a formal action to ratify and effectuate the decision.

In contrast, the WIPO process bore a substantial similarity to a US agency rulemaking, although the two processes also had critical differences. The look and feel of the experience of attending a hearing was remarkably like an US agency promulgating rules under the informal rulemaking procedures of the Administrative Procedures Act (APA). Like a US agency engaged in informal rulemaking, WIPO published proposed texts, held public hearings, invited written comments, then published its final disposition.

WIPO is, obviously, not a US federal agency, and it was under no obligation to adhere to the APA's informal notice and comment requirements. The APA's rules nonetheless provide a useful touchstone against which to compare the WIPO process, as the APA is the result of decades of evolution in a legal culture greatly concerned with procedural and substantive rights.

Despite the name, APA informal rulemaking is quite formal, although not as formal as the trial-like "formal" rulemaking. Among the most important require-ments arising from the APA or judicial glosses on it, the agency must (1) issue a notice of proposed rulemaking and publish it in the Federal Register; (2) give adequate opportunity for comments (oral hearings are usually optional but not at all uncommon); (3) consider the comments and provide reasoned responses that address every issue raised in the comments. The APA also imposes a number of duties on agencies designed to promote fairness, such as rules regulating ex parte contacts with interested parties. Once an agency issues a rule, affected parties may challenge it in court if the agency failed to follow proper procedures, or if the rule is "arbitrary and capricious," exceeds the agency's statutory mandate, or violates a constitutional guarantee such as Due Process.

Measured by this standard, several aspects of the WIPO process are problem-atic, although not all of these problems were necessarily easily foreseeable. To begin with, WIPO's publication of its draft documents on its website is both commendable and insufficient. On the one hand, there is no question that web publication is about as open and transparent as anything could be. On the other hand, there is the "purloined letter" problem – the actual as opposed to potential notice provided by publication on a web page depends entirely on whether potentially affected parties become aware that the web page is there to be read. Any ad hoc semi-private rulemaking, and especially the first one announced on any given web page, must overcome the risk that the notice provided by the open publication will fail to reach all the eyes that should see it unless accompanied by a very energetic outreach and publicity campaign. Lack of routines and formal structures also affect governments' abilities to respond, as it becomes uncertain which department(s) are "in the loop". For example, it emerged that consultation was far from perfect within the very US government which had called for the process to begin. At the 10 March WIPO consultative meeting in Washington

DC, held only days before the final comment deadline, Eric Menge of the Office of Advocacy, US Small Business Administration, stated that he had only learned of the proposals a week earlier.

More traditional, routinized, administrative and legislative procedures benefit from familiarity: interested parties know (or at least reasonably should know) how to inform themselves about potential rulemaking and legislation. It is difficult to say that affected parties reasonably should have known how to find the WIPO pages. Many obviously did, but the pool of potentially affected parties was large, distributed, and diverse. The lesson here is that outreach will be necessary until the number of affected parties who are aware of the project reaches some hard-to-define critical mass.

The notice issue also ties into the question of time limits. While WIPO's time limits for comments were tight, they were not unreasonable given that WIPO ran a single-track process, with centralized and clearly displayed information as to what was going on. Other processes, such as the current ICANN process, may need considerably more time to allow people to comment when large numbers of issues are being considered in parallel, and information about what is going on is more dispersed and fragmented.

The citizen's right to comment under the APA (5 USC section 553) has received particularly important judicial glosses: the right to comment must be meaningful, not just a formality. One cannot, for example, have a meaningful opportunity to comment if one is denied access to relevant data, or if the agency adopts a final rule that could not have been reasonably foreseen from the notice of proposed rulemaking (Kannan 1996). WIPO's willingness to make substantial changes to its interim report demonstrates both the value of taking public comment and the organization's willingness to listen. Nevertheless, at some imperfectly defined point, the introduction of new material after the close of the final comment period raises questions about the status of the final document. As the DC Circuit famously put it, a final rule should not be a "bolt from the blue" (*Shell Oil* v. *EPA* (1991)). If a final rule diverges too much from a proposed rule, an agency must engage in another round of notice and comment.

The WIPO Final Report contained a wealth of material not found in the interim draft. All the procedural sections, for example, were completely new and in my opinion fit into the "bolt" category. Similarly, although the White Paper asked WIPO to define cyberpiracy, WIPO's Interim Report contained at most a very dubious definition of cybersquatting (WIPO 1998c: section 244; Froomkin 1999b: para. 164). In contrast, the Final Report produced a substantially different and considerably superior definition (WIPO 1999a: paras 171–2). Whether the second definition was a "logical outgrowth" of the first is, I think, debatable. My point is not that WIPO erred in changing its definition – quite the contrary – but rather than the decision to do significant new work after the close of the comment period sometimes makes another round of comments necessary. As the WIPO report was only an advisory report to ICANN, and ICANN itself would need to engage in its own comment procedure, this need was perhaps less great than usual – so long as everyone was clear on what had happened. Alas, this does not appear to have been the case. Many participants in the ICANN process have cited the WIPO report not only for the force of its arguments, but as the product of a consensus-seeking process in which its ideas were subjected to searching international examination. Cries of estoppel are not, I believe, reasonable on these facts, but the ad hoc nature of semi-private rulemaking makes unproductive debate over the import of what was agreed all too likely. Professor David Post's suggestion that would-be Internet rulemakers take responsibility for documenting outreach and consensus (Post 1999) is well taken, but the WIPO experience demonstrates that documentation by the institution may not suffice. WIPO in fact did an excellent job of documenting the very elaborate series of consultations it undertook (WIPO 1999a: para. 30(i)). On its face this appears to be excellent outreach. What the numbers do not tell you, however, is how much or little WIPO publicized the meetings and website, or to whom, and how lopsided (from my admittedly partisan perspective, of course) the participation in those meetings was – especially before a very small number of observers concerned about the process mounted a campaign to broaden awareness.

The APA imposes a number of duties on agencies, including restrictions on *ex parte* contacts. Agencies engaged in informal rulemaking are not forbidden from meeting interested parties *ex parte*, but they must docket the contacts and provide a brief summary of the topics discussed (*Home Box Office* v. *FCC* (DC Cir. 1977)). No such formalities apply to the bodies managing a semi-private rulemaking, with pernicious psychological effects. Even if the process is utterly fair and above board, it becomes impossible to convince the skeptic of this. People predisposed to believe the worst of WIPO or any other body performing a similar role will be convinced that the body is consulting secretly with the wrong partisans; without some kind of transparency requirement, such rumors are impossible to squash.

The *ex parte* contacts issue is actually part of a more fundamental problem. The APA imposes no requirement that agencies draft in public. By drafting in private, therefore, WIPO acted no differently from a US agency. But agencies are formally accountable to the courts, and the President, and Congress, and through them the people, although opinions about the extent to which formal accountability translates into actual accountability differ. WIPO's staff is formally accountable to the delegates from its member states, and only through them to the peoples of the world. There is no direct judicial review of its work, although implementation in contracts creates opportunities for court action if appropriate. Private standard-setting bodies ameliorate these problems by having relatively open drafting sessions; in some, like the IETF, anyone can participate. In others, such as the American Bar Association, one has to join the organization, and in still others, such as the American Law Institute, membership is restricted, but drafting is done by committees that tend to welcome interested non-voting observer/participants. While more open drafting sessions are much slower, and would probably have produced a less elegantly written product, the gains in legitimacy attained by such openness would, I believe, be substantial.

Legitimacy comes in many forms. The easiest is consensus, but while that is easy to claim it is hard to attain, and perhaps impossible given the polarized nature of the domain name wars. Legitimacy in rulemaking comes most commonly from democratic processes, but semi-private rulemaking by its nature is largely divorced from the democratic process. A form of legitimacy comes from a right to challenge and review, but the extent to which challenges are available or appropriate in a semi-private rulemaking will vary enormously with the circumstances. In the WIPO proceedings, the issue of judicial challenge did not arise, since the final product was only advisory. Nor was there an opportunity to query the report in the WIPO General Assembly, since the report went to ICANN before being considered by that body. (Quite apart from the merits of semi-private rulemaking, there may be reasons to be concerned about the precedent set by a procedure in which the staff of a UN body can make policy so independently of member states.)

The WIPO DNS plan will probably never be subject to judicial review. ICANN is a private non-profit corporation, with (at present) no members and hence no one to challenge its decisions. The WIPO report calls for ICANN to require registrars who sell registrations in domains that form part of the legacy root to include mandatory domain name dispute resolution plan in all contracts entered into with registrants in global top-level domains. This mandatory contracts approach contrasts with the enforcement mechanisms that apply to the results of other types of rulemaking. Agency rules, whether promulgated or negotiated, have force of law and are reviewable. Self-regulatory processes, e.g. technical standards processes, rely on their intrinsic merit or market forces (including, at times, very coercive network effects) to attract adherence. Contracts fall between the two. They have force of law, but absent unconscionability are not usually reviewable. Of course, contracts differ from (some) agency rules in that in theory one always has the option not to enter into the contract – at the cost, here, of forgoing a name in the gTLD space – while one may or may not have the option to avoid the regulated conduct.

Thinking about semi-private rulemaking creates an almost irresistible compulsion to quote Winston Churchill's dictum that democracy is the worst form of government except for all the others. So far, semi-private international rulemaking looks mostly like one of those "others". There are very good reasons why societies entrust major aspects of social policy-making to elected officials, and the difficulties of the semi-private process remind one strongly of those reasons. On the other hand, there are also valid reasons to decide things without recourse to democratic institutions. True "bottom-up" methods exemplified by the better technical standards bodies are surely legitimate even if they too have their imperfections.

The legitimacy of the outcome of any given semi-private rulemaking procedure always will be difficult to gauge. The problem is compounded for international semi-private rulemaking by the relative thinness of the international public interest sector. In most democratic countries, civil society contains groups of various degrees of formality that monitor the legislative and regulatory process. Whether one can speak of an international public interest sector or international civil society is debatable; what is clear is that at best the equivalent institutions at the international level are few, and despite (or, sometimes, because of) the Internet, monitoring is difficult when meetings are far away in expensive places, or real-time-chat is at four in the morning local time. Institutions are frequently less transparent, and their linguistic and cultural diversity, not to mention their geographic spread and sometime peripatetic nature, only adds to the difficulties. One certainly cannot have confidence that no decisions will fly in "below the radar". Nor can one necessarily trust in self-proclaimed whistle-blowers: the good ones may not be heard, not everyone noisy is necessarily worth hearing, and it can be hard to sort them.

A semi-private rulemaking process poses a particularly stark choice for those who believe it to be captured by an interested faction. The process is dangerous to ignore because that increases the risk of future claims of consensus due to the absence of dissenting views. On the other hand, participating has risks also, as it increases the legitimacy of the final outcome: Proponents will say, accurately, that all sides in fact represented. After all, semi-private rulemakers have no more duty to agree with any particular viewpoint than does an agency. Neither the right nor the opportunity to be heard is a right to a veto.

A semi-private process led by a public body risks combining some of the worst features of both traditional regulation and private ordering: Opaque decision-making is easy. In some cases the process may be managed by a body acting outside its jurisdiction. The public–private blend may also insulate the process from judicial review since it falls outside the categories that courts would tend to think of as within their purview. The great challenge for semi-private rule-making, therefore, is to keep the advantages of the form, which I take to be rapid start of a process, relative rapidity of decision, and regulatory creativity, while adding in as many of the bureaucratic and Internet virtues as possible. The bureaucratic virtues include predictability, regularity, and review. The self-regulatory virtues, sometimes called Internet virtues, include openness, explanation, and sometimes excessive debate in the search for consensus.

A semi-private process may appear to offer the hope of working to a fast timetable, but this speed comes at a cost. It is no accident that the legitimacy of standards process is based on (over)full debate, and that even agency processes require a fresh round of notice and comment if the final rule begins to diverge too much from the one in the notice of proposed rulemaking.

Summary and conclusion

Regarding one critical matter, the WIPO process was a significant success: WIPO ultimately produced a clear definition of cybersquatting (abusive registrations) that, despite its flaws, was considerably superior to those before it. That definition subsequently underwent additional refinement both before the US Congress (Anticybersquatting Consumer Protection Act) and before ICANN (ICANN 1999a), but the WIPO process undoubtedly played a pivotal role in framing the issues and in moving the discussion forward. Other parts of the report, notably the recommendations relating to famous marks, were in my opinion less welcome and undoubtedly much more controversial.

Ultimately, however, the WIPO experience may be more important as a trail-blazing process than for any conclusions it reached. Lessons learned from this first run can be used to improve any future attempts at a semi-private process:

- *Beware mission blur* Everyone, not least the parties managing the process, needs to have a clear sense of goal, and of the managing institutions role in achieving it.
- *Outreach and real notice are essential* Putting up a wonderful web page is important, but it is not enough. A very significant outreach program is needed to tell potentially affected parties about a semi-private process; in most cases there will be no reason to expect them to hear about it otherwise. In addition, long lead times are needed to allow information to propagate. If there are physical meetings, they (and, to the maximum extent feasible, their agendas) need to be announced well before the 21-day deadline for cheaper airfares. Last-minute changes need to be kept to a minimum, and if group decisions will be taken at physical or virtual meetings, procedural rules may need to be worked out with some detail in advance.
- *Involvement can affect outcomes* At the risk of immodesty, it is probably fair to claim I was the most vocal, or at least verbose, critic of WIPO's interim report (Froomkin 1999a; Froomkin 1999b). By no means all of my criticisms were adopted, or even addressed, in the Final Report. Nevertheless, many were, and I came away impressed with the degree to which participants were listening to opinions with which they tended to disagree.
- *Visible intellectual engagement by the deciders promotes participation* The absence of judicial review in semi-private rulemaking might be turned into a benefit if the persons charged with writing the final rule are emboldened to engage in discussions with the public rather than have communications be essentially one-way. If there is no court breathing down your neck, the risks of saying something in public are less. Internet norms envision the deciders taking part in the give-and-take with commentators on mailing lists or similar interactive mechanisms. Without this interaction, potential commentators will be less likely to take part. Furthermore, although costly in staff time, there is more to be learned from a very interactive conversation than a small series of set piece meetings.
- *Explain and document procedures* The ad hoc nature of the process creates a greater need to explain the reasons for a decision. The explanation needs to document the outreach, the consensus if any, and the reasons. This imposes substantial costs in staff time and in reader time as well, but a detailed report like the WIPO document is nonetheless greatly preferable to something conclusory.
- *Be prepared for "swerves"* A good consultative process creates the risk of learning new things. Sometimes, often perhaps, these will require very substantial changes in existing proposals, or even wholly new ones. When that happens, another round of comments is essential, especially if the new ideas were not reasonably foreseeable from the process that preceded them.

This has negative implications for the timetable. One way to blunt this danger, therefore, is to have the decision-makers engaged in a public dialog (e.g. an archived mailing list) with interested parties. If the thinking of the deciders begins to shift towards something new, detailed discussion of the proposal in a public forum reduces the "bolt from the blue" factor.

Caveat lector

I have argued elsewhere that the greatest challenge posed by ad hoc rulemaking is figuring out when a process was sufficiently legitimate to be worthy of respect (Froomkin 1999c: 631). In this paper I have tried to suggest that although the task of running a semi-private process that is not only legitimate but demonstrably so is not trivial, there are a number of things the convening body can do to at least run a better process. Whether even those suffice to overcome the fundamentally undemocratic nature of semi-private rulemaking remains debatable.

Note

1   Professor, University of Miami School of Law, e-mail: froomkin@law.tm. As noted in the text, WIPO appointed me to its advisory panel for the domain name process. I was thus a participant in many of the events discussed in this paper.

   Some of the events discussed in this paper are in rapid flux. Unless otherwise indicated, this draft seeks to reflect events up to 26 August 1999.

Part IV

Standard setting and competition policy

12 Will the Internet remake antitrust law?

Mark Lemley[1]

I have to start out with an apology – I have a bit of a problem. I wish to discuss the subject of whether the Internet will remake antitrust law, but I have been retained by one of the parties in the *United States* v. *Microsoft* case.[2] As a result, I can't tell you about that case. It is roughly like asking someone to sit in a room for an hour and not think about a 900-pound gorilla. Nonetheless, it is fortunate in one sense because the thesis of my chapter all along would have been that the press is missing the point. There are lots of things going on at the intersection of antitrust, intellectual property, and the Internet right now that are more important than *United States* v. *Microsoft*. I will therefore take this opportunity to discuss a couple of them.

Now you have read the newspaper and you are no doubt asking: "What could be more important than *United States* v. *Microsoft*?" I want to focus on three things. The first is antitrust in standard setting by groups. This is a lurking issue. It never makes the newspaper because it is not an issue, it is not a case, it is a thousand little issues and a thousand little cases. But they are going on all around you. Every standard-setting organization all around the world has, or is, developing some set of rules regarding the treatment of intellectual property and standards. Every company in the high technology community belongs to at least one and frequently as many as sixty or a hundred different standard-setting organizations. And antitrust law, as it turns out, has inconsistent things to say about what you can and cannot do with intellectual property in a standard-setting organization. Issue number two, which is also more important than *United States* v. *Microsoft*, relates to the Intel cases and more generally the idea of refusing to license your intellectual property as an antitrust violation or something that antitrust law itself restrains. And number three relates to the question of who owns, or can own, a network standard. I will present this question not so much as one involving *US* v. *Microsoft*, but by a case going on in the Northern District of California right now called *Sun* v. *Microsoft*.[3]

Let me give you a little bit of background. I think what makes these issues so important from an Internet perspective is that the Internet is a network – it is a market governed by network effects. What do I mean by that? Well, the Internet is not like normal markets in the same way the telephone system is not like normal markets. If you are the first person in the world to own a telephone, it is useless. It might make a good doorstop but it does not do anything. If one other person buys a telephone, now it is a somewhat useful device because you can communicate with that one other person, but it is not earth-shattering. It is earth-shattering only when it is global. The value of the telephone network increases as the number of users of the network increases, because the value of the telephone network is precisely the ability it gives you to communicate with other people. And that has some dramatic implications.

For one thing, it means that the market tends toward a single, dominant standard. The optimal number of telephone networks and the optimal number of Internets is one. I could set up, if I wanted to, a new, incompatible telephone network. I could say, "Come join my telephone network – you cannot call anyone who is on the other one, but you can call anyone who is on my network." But I won't succeed. The reason I won't succeed is that the network value of all those people who are already linked to the telephone network is so enormous. The implication of this for antitrust, it seems to me, should be obvious, at least at the first order. We are not in a world where competition is good – at least competition between different telephone networks. We are in a world in which the market tends, properly, towards a single, dominant standard.

Now that does not mean there can't be competition in a network market like the Internet, a telephone network or, as we shall see, computer operating systems, which have the similar characteristic of being frequently chosen simply because everybody else uses it. There can be competition but it has got to be competition *within* a standard. This means that somehow, somewhere, competitors have got to agree on the nature of the products they will produce and then compete to produce products that will incorporate that standard.

Now we do this all the time without thinking about it. The reason your hair dryer works in your hotel room is that your hair dryer has a two-prong or three-prong adapter. But you could make a hair dryer with a 23-prong adapter or an adapter that is square. In fact, once you leave the United States you will find that the rules differ by country. But the rules almost never differ within a country because, without thinking about it, industries have converged around standards for plugging electrical devices into wall outlets. Of course, that doesn't mean that only one company makes hair dryers. There are lots of companies that make them, they just do it using a standard and the standard is an open one – it is available to anyone who wants to use it because there is no proprietary ownership or control over two-prong adapters. If I want a two-prong adapter, I can use a two-prong adapter. It is also the case, and I think this is not incidental, that it is pretty easy to figure out the two-prong adapter. The interconnection standard between a hair dryer and the wall is a lot easier to figure out than the interconnection between a computer operating system and a computer application program. Standard-setting organizations can promote all these standards by establishing this framework. But, of course, there is no such thing as a free lunch; this comes at a cost. If you build in a standard, it is hard to get out of the standard, just as it is hard to change telephone networks. It would be hard at this point to throw away the Internet and create a new information infrastructure. You lock yourself in by virtue of getting everyone to do the same thing.

Group standard setting poses some antitrust risk. The first antitrust risk is inherent in the nature of group standard setting. When you think about what group standard setting is, you realize it is a bunch of people who want to compete in a market but who are getting together in a room and saying: "All right, what products are we going to build in the future and how can we make those products similar?" If you talk to antitrust lawyers who practiced in the 1950s or 1960s and say: "Can I get together with my competitors, talk about the products I am going to build in the future, and plan our future together?" those lawyers will have apoplexy. They will say that it cannot possibly be legal. It is a cartel. And, in fact, one of the real problems is that standard-setting organizations in their structure look a lot like cartels. They might in fact be cartels in certain circumstances – you are getting together with your competitors. There are cases, notably the *Addamax* case,[4] which take standard-setting organizations and subject them to antitrust scrutiny under the rule of reason because they fear they are in fact cartels.

The second sort of antitrust problem associated with group standard setting has to do with competition. If you have a standard-setting organization, one of the things you might like to do is to promote competition by making sure that no member of the standard-setting organization in fact owns intellectual property rights in the standard. That is, no one can say: "We own this standard and so, yes, we've made a group standard-setting decision, but in fact only our company, or people we license, can use this standard." But the government has periodically gone after standard-setting groups that require members to license their intellectual property to other members of the organization. The Antitrust Division went after the European Telecommunications Standards Institute in the mid-1990s because it said that the ETSI was violating the antitrust laws by requiring people to license their intellectual property rights. The FTC went after a similar group in the case *In re American Society of Sanitary Engineers*. Furthermore, standard-setting organizations can run into trouble if they deal with an outsider who has intellectual property rights in a collective way. For the same reason they can't get together and set prices for the products they sell; they can't get together and set or negotiate prices for licenses with intellectual property owners who approach them. So antitrust imposes significant limits on the ability of standard-setting organizations to restrict intellectual property.

But it gets worse. Antitrust also does the reverse. Standards groups commonly require, not necessarily a complete waiver of intellectual property, though certain Internet groups like the IETF have done so, but they will require non-discriminatory licensing of the intellectual property that covers the standard. It turns out antitrust enforcers will also come after you if you violate this private rule by concealing from the standard-setting organization that you have an intellectual property right. Most famous here is the *Dell* case where the Federal Trade Commission enforced against Dell a representation that Dell made to a standard-setting organization that it didn't have a patented-covered standard.

Furthermore, in 1998 in *Wang* v. *Mitsubishi*,[5] the Federal Circuit suggested that if you make representations in the marketplace that a standard is open and free for all to use, you may be bound by that representation at least to the extent of not later asserting your patent against people to whom you have made the representation.

Let's leave standard-setting organizations for a minute and talk about de facto standards – standards that are created not by many companies getting together and agreeing, but by a company winning in the marketplace. For example, standards are developed when Microsoft or Intel creates a product or an architecture that simply dominates its competitors. The traditional rule for the intellectual property/antitrust interface has been that it is OK not to license your intellectual property rights to people, as long as you make that decision unilaterally and you are not trying to tie or link that decision to other considerations. That is true regardless of who you are. So, for example, Section 271(d)(4) of the patent statute[6] provides that refusal to license cannot be patent misuse, as does the *Continental Paper Bag* case[7] – a venerable US Supreme Court case. Most recently in *Data General* v. *Grumman System Support*,[8] the First Circuit looked at the cases and said it would presume that if you refuse to license your intellectual property rights to someone, even if you are a dominant player in the market, that refusal is supported by a reasonable business justification.

You may have noticed a switch here. Presumption is not the same thing as an absolute right, and several courts jumped through this loophole in 1997–8. First was the Ninth Circuit in *Image Technical Services* v. *Kodak*,[9] a case which had been going on for a long time and had already been to the Supreme Court once. Kodak had decided it wanted to abolish or cut off independent service organizations that serviced its copiers by denying them parts. Kodak was sued for antitrust violations and the Supreme Court decided the antitrust claim could proceed. Eventually the case was tried to a jury and the jury found against Kodak. Rather late in the game, it occurred to Kodak that it had patents on the parts in question and therefore could presumptively refuse to grant licenses. Therefore, Kodak reasoned, it could refuse to license their intellectual property rights and their patents on the parts to the independent service organizations. The Ninth Circuit said no, that in this circumstance, even though Kodak's refusal to license was unilateral, the court would not permit the refusal because it was pretextual. The court found that Kodak was really trying to accomplish another goal that antitrust law does not allow. In such circumstances, the court said, even a unilateral refusal to license can violate the antitrust laws.

A more recent, and much more significant, decision is the one handed down by the Northern District of Alabama in 1998 in *Intergraph* v. *Intel*.[10] Intergraph is a maker of specialized computer equipment that uses Intel chips. Intergraph sued Intel for patent infringement on some unrelated patent that related to some of Intel's technology. Intel, in response, said: "Fine, if you are going to sue us for patent infringement, we see no reason to continue dealing with you as a business entity so we're not going to give you advance copies of our Pentium II chips or technological support to build our chip architecture into your computer systems." Intergraph claimed this was an antitrust violation and the Northern District of Alabama agreed on remarkably broad grounds. The Northern District of Alabama found Intel's chip architecture – and here we are talking about the Pentium II – is an "essential facility" for antitrust purposes. What that means in the antitrust law is that this is a facility so necessary for competition in the industry that it must be made available to competitors on a reasonable and non-discriminatory basis. This means that Intel cannot deny its business consumers access to its Pentium II architecture; it can't deny them a continual supply of chips even in circumstances where chips are in short supply; it has, the court ruled, to ration the chips to companies that ask for them. Furthermore, the court found, in a highly significant result, the fact that Intel has patents on its Pentium II architecture does not change this result. Because this architecture is an essential facility, Intel has got to make it available, notwithstanding the old rule that you can refuse to license your intellectual property rights to anyone you want to.

Now think about the implications of the district court's decision in *Intergraph* v. *Intel* for a minute. If Intergraph, a customer of Intel's, is entitled to a continued supply of Pentium II chips and is entitled to the technical information necessary to build compatible products, what about Intel's competitors? AMD, on similar grounds, should be entitled to a continued supply of Intel's chips and the technical information necessary to understand and, not incidentally, reproduce the Intel chip architecture. To be sure, Intel has patents on this architecture, but that does not matter according to the court.

The facts of Intergraph also form the basis for an FTC complaint against Intel. The complaint is based on three instances in which Intel refused to license to those who sued for infringement. Cases involving not only Intergraph, but also Digital Equipment Corporation and Compaq. The FTC did not bring the case on the basis of "essential facility;" it instead tailored the sought-for relief. But the basic idea here is that the antitrust laws care about intellectual property licensing and intellectual property lawsuits.

If you think about this case for a moment you might decide it should not be of antitrust concern. It may appear to you that someone who is sued for patent infringement is responding perfectly rationally by refusing to do further business with the people who are suing them. What this case and the FTC complaint, which is currently pending, stand for, I think, is the idea that in a market in which you are the dominant player, if you are Intel, that rational response and that rule no longer apply. We may impose obligations on you as a dominant player to license and make available your intellectual property, your protected inventions, notwithstanding the fact that anyone else who did the same thing would be considered to be a reasonable business person acting in a logical, self-protecting way.

The third piece of this puzzle involves Sun and Microsoft. The background on this is the promise or hope of Java, or I suppose the fear of Java, depending on where you sit. The promise of Java is that it may open up the network that is the computer operating system. Strong, self-supporting forces have kept Microsoft's operating system dominant for so long: the idea that everyone else has a Microsoft Windows operating system so I should get one, that way I can use their computers and we can trade files; the fact that there are more application programs that work with the operating system because it is the dominant one, and so on. All of the things that lock in a network market, that drive it towards a single standard, might be circumvented. Because what Java is, in effect, is a meta-operating system. It is a piece of software – a virtual machine – that sits on top of the operating system and works across platforms. It sits between your operating system and your applications programs and allows you to run Java-compliant applications regardless of the operating system you use. If this turns out to be an effective way of running applications programs, the network effects that have supported the Microsoft operating system suddenly disappear. I do not have to buy Microsoft's operating system to run all the best application programs, all I have to do is run them through Java. I do not have to buy Microsoft's operating system in order to translate files and work on somebody else's computer, all I have to do is run them through Java. Now this does not mean that Microsoft will suddenly go out of business, but what it means is that what used to be a network market in which the dominant player had a tremendous advantage suddenly becomes a competitive market where people will buy operating systems solely on their technical merits and not on the basis of their installed base.

Microsoft, as you might expect, is not too happy with the idea that Sun will come in and introduce another layer into the computer market that will render irrelevant the installed base of the monopoly that Microsoft has. What can Microsoft do about it? One thing that Microsoft is alleged to be doing about it in the *Sun* v. *Microsoft* complaint is acting to split the Java standard. Java is an open system. It is a set of code that people can use and adapt and write to. Microsoft is a Java licensee, and has produced a version of Java which it says is optimized for Microsoft's operating system but which, not coincidentally, does not work so well with anyone else's operating system. Think about that. If you are defining a cross-platform, meta-operating system, the critical thing about it, from Sun's perspective, is that it remain cross-platform, that it really works with anybody's different operating system. If Microsoft produces a version of Java that works best with its operating system and does not work with anyone else's, this promise of Java to open up the market disappears.

Complicating this case is the fact that Sun submitted the Java protocol to the International Standards Organization (ISO) for acceptance as an international standard, and in so doing it offered to give up some of its intellectual property rights in the Sun–Java program (see following chapter by David McGowan). It agreed not to assert patents, and it agreed, to a certain extent, not to assert copyrights. Sun has sued Microsoft saying, in effect, "You are violating our intellectual property rights in the Java standard by changing it in a way that makes it incompatible." But Sun sued under trademark law. It said: "You are taking this thing and you are mutating it so that it is no longer really Java, but you are still calling it Java." Sun was able to get a preliminary injunction from the Northern District of California on contract grounds precluding Microsoft from marketing as Java or Java-compliant its version of Java that was altered in ways that did not meet the Sun protocol.

I do not know, and I do not pretend to know, what is going to happen in this market. I do not know how well Sun's Java works technically, and I do not know who will win this intellectual property case over Microsoft's efforts to split the standard. But I do want to suggest this: there is real value in opening a standard to competition. We are all better off as consumers if we can choose from five or six operating systems, all of which will do roughly the same thing and all of which will work together. Because that is the way the market has always disciplined competition. The goal of competition is to have a bunch of competitors who can battle it out. But there is at least a risk – or an opportunity depending on who you are – that if this meta-operating system pans out, we will have simply traded Microsoft for Sun; that we will end up with another company that owns intellectual property rights in a dominant standard that everyone has to use to work with their computer. It is just that the dominant standard will be Sun's Java and not the Microsoft operating system. And what I want to suggest is that if Sun wins this competition, having represented frequently and loudly to the public that Java is an open system, it perhaps ought to be estopped from later closing the system. That if you want – as you should want – to promote competition within a standard by using open systems, the only way to do that is to bind companies to their representations that their systems are in fact open.

Finally, I want you to think about putting these pieces of the puzzle together. If Intel's chip architecture is an essential facility, as the Northern District of Alabama has stated, to which everyone must have non-discriminatory access, perhaps it is possible that Microsoft, under a similar antitrust theory, will be forced to provide non-discriminatory access to its application program interfaces. Surely its facility is as essential as Intel's – indeed, they are tied together. And I have to confess that I am a little troubled about that. I am a little troubled about the district court's holding in *Intergraph*, and I am a little troubled about the idea that we will take people's intellectual property rights away from them, which, in effect, is what is going on. Taking people's intellectual property rights away, even for a good cause, could affect the intellectual property system as a whole. Nonetheless, if you don't take intellectual property rights away from people, then you need to understand the consequences of intellectual property in a network market. If I am the owner of a dominant standard and I have an intellectual property right to preclude someone using that standard or making a product compatible with that standard, then there is no question that intellectual property rights in these markets contribute to the long-term market power of some companies in the industry. That may be a good thing, I suppose, or it may be a bad thing that we have to put up with because we are afraid of what the alternative will do to the intellectual property system. But it is certainly something we have to take into account when we figure out how to design antitrust, intellectual property policy.

What do I conclude from this?

1   I think open systems are good; they are the way to promote competition in a network market. Group standard setting as a result, I think, is generally good because it is an avenue to open systems that at least holds out the possibility of competition which would otherwise not exist in the market. But group standard setting turns out to have intellectual property and antitrust problems. Group standard setting might be a vehicle to take away your intellectual property rights on the one hand, or on the other hand it may turn out to create antitrust problems.

2   The second lesson to learn, I think, is that courts in the cases I have described show an increasing willingness to apply antitrust law to limit intellectual property rights or to, in effect, order compulsory licensing even when companies act alone where they are dominant players in the market.

3   And finally, a kind of odd little conclusion that comes out of the *Sun* case: if Sun wins its suit against Microsoft and thereby keeps the system open, it will be because Sun preserved its intellectual property rights in the standard. If Sun had given away all of its intellectual property rights in the standard, it would have no cause of action against Microsoft and no way of preventing the standard from being split.

Notes

1   This is an edited transcript of a talk presented on 5 June 1999 when the author was Marrs McLean Professor of Law, University of Texas School of Law. Published in March 2000 as Professor of Law, University of California, Berkeley; of counsel, Fish and Richardson P.C. Thanks to David McGowan, my collaborator on many projects in this area.
2   *United States* v. *Microsoft Corp.*, 147 F. 3d 935 (DC Cir. 1998). This is only one of many proceedings between the parties.
3   *Sun Microsystems, Inc.* v. *Microsoft Corp.*, 21 F. Supp. 2d 1109 (ND Cal. 1999); *Sun Microsystems, Inc.* v. *Microsoft Corp.*, 999 F. Supp. 1301 (ND Cal. 1998).
4   *Addamax* v. *Open Software Foundation*, 152 F. 3d 48 (1st Cir. 1998).
5   *Wang Laboratories, Inc.* v. *Mitsubishi Electronics America*, 103 F. 3d 1571 (Fed. Cir. 1997).
6   35 USC, sec. 271(d)(4).
7   *Continental Paper Bag Co.* v. *Eastern Paper Bag Co.*, 210 US 405 (1908).
8   *Data General Corp.* v. *Grumman Systems Support Corp.*, 36 F. 3d 1147 (1st Cir. 1994).
9   *Image Technical Services* v. *Eastman Kodak Co.*, 125 F. 3d 1195 (9th Cir. 1997). Since this talk was given, the Federal Circuit has rejected the position of both the First and Ninth Circuits, holding in *In re Independent Service Organizations Antitrust Litigation*, 53 USPQ 2d 1852 (Fed. Cir. 2000) that a unilateral refusal to license a patent could never violate the antitrust laws.
10 *Intergraph Corp.* v. *Intel Corp.*, 3 F. Supp. 2d 1255 (ND Ala. 1998). Since this talk was given, the Federal Circuit reversed the district court decision in *Intergraph*. See *Intergraph* v. *Intel*, 195 F. 3d 1346 (Fed. Cir. 1999).

13 The problems of the third way

A Java case study

*David McGowan**

Standards are vitally important to computer software markets, and there are two basic ways in which standards may be created and adopted. The first is by competition among proprietary standards. Under this model, the law creates property rights in technology and assigns them to the technology's creator, who therefore has the economic incentive to promote the technology as a standard. The owner of that technology takes responsibility for developing it to a marketable stage, persuading other firms and consumers to adopt it, and improving it over time. The standard is established through the purchasing decisions in a market, rather than through the choice of a standards-setting organization.

The second model is one of cooperation among persons or firms interested in the technology. The interested parties, generally through some sort of organization, will establish bureaucratic procedures to evaluate potential standards and to choose the one the organization will endorse.[1] All else being equal, organizations operating under this model would prefer not to adopt a standard in which a firm owned intellectual property rights for which it could charge firms implementing the standard. In many cases, however, it would not be realistic to expect to discover a standard in which no one claimed intellectual property rights. So organizations will typically require firms participating in standards-setting to disclose any intellectual property rights they claim in technology being proposed for a standard, and to agree to license their technology on reasonable, nondiscriminatory terms if the standard is adopted.[2]

And, with apologies to many present governments, there is also, in theory, what one might call a third way. Here a firm might seek to have an organization formally adopt, as a standard, technology over which the firm asserted intellectual property rights that the firm intended to retain and use to maintain some degree of control over the standard.

This description is, of course, simplified. Among other things, it assumes an unrealistic world in which the standards-setting process involves new standards that begin their competition in an equal position. That is not how the world works, however. Actual standardization strategies have to take into account the state of the markets in which firms will employ the standards. Firms that wish to see a particular standard adopted, rejected, or displaced will pursue standardization strategies that complement their competitive strategy as a whole.

This essay examines the efforts of Sun Microsystems to supplant Microsoft's Windows operating system with Sun's Java technologies as the standard interface for applications running on personal computers. Part of Sun's strategy has been market-based. It has positioned its Java technologies as a middle layer of software in between Windows and applications consumers wish to use. Sun has also taken various steps to persuade developers and consumers to adopt Java, including licensing the technology and developing the Java brand. In addition to these market-based steps, Sun also sought to popularize Java by submitting it to the International Organization for Standardization (ISO) for adoption as a formal international standard.

The jury is out on whether Sun's market-based strategy will work. Its standardization strategy has failed. This essay examines Sun's standardization efforts and why they failed, and asks what we can learn from the failure. The first section, 'The Java technologies and the market structure', describes some basic economic principles and the various technologies that comprise Java. The second section discusses Sun's efforts to ensconce Java as a formal standard. The final section draws some conclusions relevant to standardization and innovation in technology.

The Java technologies and the market structure

To begin: what is Java and why should we care about it? As Sun described the technology in its pending lawsuit against Microsoft:

> Sun Microsystems is the developer and licensor of the JAVATM Technology, which comprises a standardized application programming environment that affords software developers the opportunity to create and distribute a single version of programming code that is capable of operating on many different, otherwise incompatible systems platforms and browsers.[3]

Java technologies include the Java programming language, a set of Java Application Program Interfaces (APIs), and a Java compiler, which compiles source code written in the language and using the APIs into Java bytecode. The Java bytecode runs through a Java Virtual Machine (JVM). JVMs are written for specific operating systems, such as Windows. Working with attached Java class libraries, the virtual machine translates the Java bytecode into instructions that can be executed through the operating system for which the virtual machine is written. "In essence, the Java-based program views the JVM as an operating system, and the operating system views the JVM as a traditional application."[4]

Because JVMs sit atop traditional operating systems, such as Windows, and expose Java APIs to software developers who write applications consumers may wish to use, the Java technologies comprise a possible substitute for Windows. As a Microsoft witness testified during the trial of the Justice Department's antitrust suit:

Q: And what is it you're afraid of from a paradigm shift, Mr Kempin?

A: Now, I mean in the case of Sun and Java, for instance, I fear that they would make, over time, an operating system totally obsolete, meaning they could replace it with any operating system. Because if they succeed in having developers write to their mid-layer – to their Java only – they can, in theory, take this out and there is no need – and replace it with an operating system which they might design in the future. So the operating system itself is less important.[5]

Microsoft's concern about Java can be best understood as based on the economic theory of network effects.[6] Network theory points out that the value of some things increases with the number of persons who use them. For example, setting bandwidth concerns aside, telephones are more valuable as more persons acquire them. Their function is to let people talk to one another, and each additional person acquiring a telephone is another person who can be contacted with an existing phone. Additional users confer positive externalities on existing users, leading to positive feedback effects for technology that is adopted and negative feedback effects for technologies that are not adopted. For markets for goods that derive a relatively high portion of their value from being part of a network (rather than the value they would have standing alone), these effects may play a significant role in establishing the structure of the market and the strategies firms in the market pursue.[7]

Communications networks such as the telephone or fax machines have been referred to as "actual networks." Operating system software is characterized by strong "virtual" or "market-mediated" network effects.[8] Network theory has been used to support the claim that barriers to entry in the operating system software market are high, implying a probability of monopolization and durable monopoly power. The Court of Appeals for the DC Circuit accepted this principle, in conjunction with a finding of significant economies of scale, in its opinion in the Justice Department's contempt proceeding against Microsoft.[9] The trial judge in the Justice Department's civil action against Microsoft concurred, stating as a finding of fact that:

> Consumer demand for Windows enjoys positive network effects ... the size of Windows' installed base impels ISVs [Independent Software Vendors] to write applications first and foremost to Windows, thereby ensuring a large body of applications from which consumers can choose. The large body of applications thus reinforces demand for Windows, augmenting Microsoft's dominant position and thereby perpetuating ISV incentives to write applications principally for Windows. This self-reinforcing cycle is often referred to as a "positive feedback loop."

What for Microsoft is a positive feedback loop is for would-be competitors a vicious cycle. For just as Microsoft's large market share creates incentives for ISVs to develop applications first and foremost for Windows, the small or non-existent market share of an aspiring competitor makes it prohibitively expensive for the aspirant to develop its PC operating system into an acceptable substitute for Windows. To provide a viable substitute for Windows, another PC operating system would need a large and varied enough base of compatible applications to reassure consumers that their interests in variety, choice, and currency would be met to more-or-less the same extent as if they chose Windows ...

In deciding whether to develop an application for a new operating system, an ISV's first consideration is the number of users it expects the operating system to attract. Out of this focus arises a collective-action problem: Each ISV realizes that the new operating system could attract a significant number of users if enough ISVs developed applications for it; but few ISVs want to sink resources into developing for the system until it becomes established. Since everyone is waiting for everyone else to bear the risk of early adoption, the new operating system has difficulty attracting enough applications to generate a positive feedback loop.[10]

Sun had to deal with these economic facts in developing its strategies for competing with Microsoft. Sun's strategy was to minimize the cost to consumers of adopting Java. It created Java APIs to which developers could write, and virtual machines to translate Java bytecode into code that any operating system could execute. Developers could in theory use these technologies to write cross-platform Java-based applications that would run on Windows, meaning that consumers could use these cross-platform Java applications without sacrificing the existing array of applications written for Windows. The trial court in the Microsoft civil proceeding thus appropriately characterized Java as "middleware."[11] Echoing Microsoft's witnesses, the court concluded that

> to the extent the array of applications relying solely on middleware comes to satisfy all of a user's needs, the user will not care whether there exists a large number of other applications that are directly compatible with the under- lying operating system.[12]

Sun's standard-setting efforts

Whether Java technologies will actually facilitate a transition from Windows at a cost developers and consumers find acceptable depends on the number of devel- opers and users who adopt the technologies. As one of Microsoft's counsel stated in the trial of the Justice Department's civil action, "the competition between Microsoft and Sun is competition for the hearts and minds of developers."[13] Sun's task has been to persuade developers in particular (though developers would pay attention to the probable behavior of consumers, so consumer and developer expectations are related) that Java technologies stood a decent chance of becoming the new applications interface standard. The more likely that was, the more probable it would be that developers would write to Java APIs, thus making Java more likely to become a standard, and setting the positive feedback loop on its way. And what better way to persuade developers that Java would become a standard than to have it formally adopted as one?

Sun's ISO standardization plan

On 14 March 1997 Sun submitted to Joint Technical Committee 1 (JTC 1) of the ISO and the International Electrotechnical Commission (IEC) a request for recognition as a submitter of Publicly Available Specifications (PAS) for Java.[14] In its application, Sun sought recognition for the Java "platform," which as of the date of Sun's submission consisted of "the Java language, the class file format, the bytecodes recognized by the Java Virtual Machine, and the Java APIs." As of March 1997, Sun considered the first three components of the platform to be "most mature" and "the likely first candidates for submission" as a standard, while the APIs were in varying states of maturity.[15]

Sun's PAS application reflected many things. Not the least of these was the recognition by ISO and IEC members, both in their adoption of the PAS process and their approval of Sun as a PAS submitter, that information technology moves quite rapidly (faster, in any event, than the consensus-based standardization process has moved in the past) and that proprietary products may become *de facto* standards in information technology markets. Recognition of these facts led JTC 1 to adopt a procedure for the "Transposition of Publicly Available Specifications into International Standards."[16] ISO designed the PAS process to achieve three goals: to keep standardization current in information markets, with a target of transposing text to standards in twelve months; to encourage "the contribution to international standardization of proven specifications which may be considered *de facto* standards by virtue of their wide market success;" and to provide ISO with technical expertise that might be necessary for standardization in certain technologies. Taken together, these goals fairly contemplated the introduction of privately developed, privately owned products as candidates for transformation into international standards.[17]

In the initial round of voting on Sun's application, three member nations voted to approve Sun as a PAS submitter, five voted approval with comments, and fifteen voted disapproval with comments to which Sun was allowed to respond before a second round of voting. The comments adduced from this round of voting centered on two topics of interest: whether a single firm should be allowed to submit proprietary technology under the PAS procedure and whether such a firm should be permitted to retain intellectual property rights in the proposed standard.[18] During this process, Sun and Microsoft exchanged two sets of letters addressing such issues to the United States Technical Advisory Group (US TAG) to JTC 1.[19] Sun submitted a detailed response to the comments from the first round of voting, in which it articulated its vision of the manner in which a PAS submitter could retain intellectual property rights in an international standard.[20] A second round of voting then commenced, resulting in approval of Sun as a PAS submitter in November 1997.[21]

Before proceeding to the unhappy denouement of Sun's ISO standardization efforts, it is interesting briefly to consider the arguments made on the question whether a single firm should be allowed to submit proprietary technology for adoption as a standard. One does not often see Microsoft and China allied on a question of intellectual property rights. Sun's PAS application, however, produced such an alignment.[22] Microsoft contended that no single firm should be recognized as a PAS submitter if it was submitting a technology in which it wished to retain intellectual property rights. Its argument was in part that a single firm with a proprietary product would be driven by market forces rather than the need to achieve consensus through cooperation that had been the paradigm for standardization efforts in the past.[23]

Microsoft's arguments are reflected to some degree in its comments before the second-round voting, in which Microsoft urged that US TAG adhere to its initial negative vote in part because, under Sun's proposal:

> Sun will continue to set the rules for evolution and branding of Java and asks ISO to endorse the Sun Java product and distribute Sun-authored specifications. Sun plans to maintain control over all substantive changes and enhancements to the Java technology. At the same time, Sun seeks to gain ISO as an endorser, if not advertiser, of Sun's products via the use of an "open" specification name that explicitly references Sun's proprietary implementation.[24]

Microsoft argued that these concerns demonstrated that "Sun should not be given the benefit of ISO standardization of its technologies while controlling them as proprietary products that compete with vendors like Microsoft and others."[25]

Microsoft's concerns were not dispositive as a matter of pure logic. Where information technology markets exhibit strong network effects, and are therefore likely to gravitate to a single standard with or without the help of a standards-setting organization, there is in theory no reason why a single firm should not be permitted to submit proprietary technology for adoption as a formal standard. In such markets there is relatively little risk that a standardization process would be worse than *de facto* standardization (the market could always reject the standard adopted), and the process of standardization could encourage the more rapid adoption and implementation of desirable technology. But Microsoft's concerns were not trivial either. And as a practical matter, Sun appears to have been unable to reconcile the tension Microsoft pointed out early on in the process.

The problems of maintenance and intellectual property rights

The sticking points for Sun's standardization efforts were intellectual property rights and the maintenance of the proposed Java standard. Absent some legally binding constraint, allowing a private party to own intellectual property rights in a formally adopted standard is risky. If an installed base formed around the standard, the rights holder might engage in opportunistic activity – discriminatory or unreasonable license terms for continued access, for example – taking advantage of the installed base for its own gain. If a standard was widely adopted in a network market, such conduct might impose a significant cost on users of the standard. The costs might take the form of rents extracted by the rights-holder, or of costs consumers incurred in moving to a new standard.

Sun sought to alleviate these concerns in its response to the first round comments. Sun stated that its policies with respect to patents in the Java platform were more liberal than required by ISO policy, and also stated that it would follow ISO policy or extend its then-current policy.[26] Sun acknowledged that it had used its copyright "to prevent unauthorized changes" in the Java technology, but stated that it would grant ISO "all necessary rights to print and sell copies of the International Standard without payment of copyright fees or royalties."[27]

Trademark rights presented a more complex issue. Sun's response stated unequivocally that, while it would permit use of the Java mark to describe products that utilized the Java specifications adopted by ISO, it would retain the rights to the Java marks and reserve the right to deny a license to use those marks to firms that did not satisfy its licensing criteria:

> These trademarks are used to represent that a given implementation of Java meets the strict compatibility and interoperability criteria inherent in the Java(tm) platform specifications. We expect to continue to own all of our trademark logos and names and would not expect to transfer the rights associated with them to ISO.
>
> Java(tm) is a trademark of Sun Microsystems, Inc., that describes the name of a product – a brand – not the name of the set of specifications for this ubiquitous computing platform. Sun Microsystems, Inc., invented and developed the Java(tm) product. To further the use of that product, Sun extracted the specifications and supplied those specifications to its direct licensees, and then to the general computing community, with licenses for use and implementation.
>
> Sun is not giving its products to ISO. We want to standardize the specifications that underlie those products through ISO.[28]

Thus, Sun concluded, while it was willing "to permit ISO to use the term 'Java(tm) Platform' in the name of the International Standard,"[29] it was not willing to give its Java marks to ISO in connection with adoption of Java as a standard. Sun's response instead explicitly contemplated a market in which firms might utilize the ISO standard to "build completely separate, conforming implementations of" the contemplated ISO specifications "with no commercial relationship to Sun."[30] Under this approach, such implementations would be marketed under a different brand, owned by the firm producing the implementation. Firms would thus have two choices: if they wished merely to adhere to the ISO standard, they could label their products "ISO–xxxx conformant."

Alternatively, Sun proposed that firms could enter into a licensing agreement with Sun or comply with Sun's "fair use" guidelines, and use "Java" to describe their products.[31]

Sun's guidelines permitted licensees to advertise their products as "XYZ for Java(tm),"[32] while simultaneously recognizing under the rubric of trademark "fair use"[33] that firms whose products incorporate the Java specifications may mention the Java mark in advertising so long as the reference unambiguously refers to Sun's products and does no more than accurately describe a characteristic of the firm's product.[34] At least in the United States, regardless of Sun's position before ISO or of Sun's licensing guidelines, the doctrine of non-trademark use might well permit firms other than Sun to use the name "Java" to indicate that their applications worked with Java, so long as this statement was in fact true.[35] Sun's proposal was therefore not a large sacrifice of Sun's trademark rights. Outside the scope of this doctrine, however, a firm desiring to use the Java mark would likely have to deal with Sun; Sun promised to deal with such firms on "a fair and nondiscriminatory basis on reasonable terms." Sun's response made clear, however, that a firm wishing to claim "Java" conformance rather than ISO–xxxx conformance would have to produce "complete and compatible implementations of the *current* version of the [Java] specifications" without alteration.[36]

Sun's litigation with Microsoft over the Java technologies provides an example of the sort of disputes that might arise over the use of Java technologies and the Java brand. Sun's suit was based in part on the terms of its agreements with Microsoft and in part on intellectual property law.[37] Because Sun was fighting to persuade developers that Java would become the API standard of the future, it was interested in distributing Java technologies as widely as possible to perform the greatest possible number of tasks. Toward this end, it licensed Java technologies to several firms, including Microsoft. A Java license from Sun to Microsoft might at first seem odd, given that Sun wanted Java to supplant Windows. But Microsoft distributes an enormous amount of software. From Sun's perspective, licensing Java technologies to Microsoft was one of the quickest ways to achieve widespread distribution of Java-based works. From Microsoft's perspective, obtaining the rights to use Java technologies, and to modify and adapt them in derivative works, was a way to seek to influence and perhaps control the evolution of a technology that could pose a threat to Windows.

Not surprisingly, the license agreements that tried to reconcile these conflicting interests soon gave rise to a disagreement, which in turn became a lawsuit that is still pending as of this writing.[38] In a technology license agreement, Sun gave Microsoft the rights to "make, access, use, copy, view, display, modify, adapt, and create Derivative Works" of the core Java technologies. Sun also gave Microsoft the rights to incorporate such work into Microsoft products, and to distribute the products in binary form.

In addition to these rights, however, Sun required Microsoft's derivative Java products to pass tests Sun created to ensure that those products were compatible with Sun's Java specifications. From Sun's point of view, this requirement was important to maintaining Java as a uniform, platform-independent technology. Incompatible implementations of Java would threaten developer confusion at a minimum, and possibly the fragmentation of the standard altogether.[39] Sun alleged that Microsoft altered the Java technologies in an effort to "pollute" and fragment the standard, inducing developers to write Java applications that ran only, or at least best, on Windows. In litigation with Sun, as well as with the Department of Justice, Microsoft insisted that it has the contractual right to create its own Java technologies that optimize Java for Windows.[40]

Sun also used its Java trademarks to enforce the requirement that Microsoft's Java products conform to Sun's specifications. In a trademark license agreement, Sun "granted Microsoft a license to display Sun's 'JAVA Compatible' logo on or in connection with only such products as have successfully passed Sun's" tests for conformance "and which otherwise fully comply with all other compatibility and certification requirements of the" technology license agreement.[41] Linking this requirement to its overall strategy, Sun alleged that:

> Under license from Sun, a systems manufacturer or browser developer ... is licensed to distribute products including the JAVATM Technology, *provided that those products have passed Sun's Test Suites, are otherwise fully compatible, and display the JAVA Compatible logo. The "JAVA Compatible' logo symbolizes that each product bearing the logo has to Sun's satisfaction successfully passed the Sun Test Suite accompanying the version of the JAVA Technology incorporated or emulated by that product, and otherwise complies with Sun's set of JAVA specifications and JAVA APIs,* such that programs written for the JAVATM programming environment will run successfully on that implementation and on any other JAVA Compatible implementation.[42]

From the outset, therefore, Sun used its intellectual property rights to maintain the coherence of the Java technologies and to defend against Microsoft's efforts to steer Java into a niche as a Windows development tool. Sun's use of its trademarks was interesting because those marks represent the brand to consumers and, perhaps to a lesser extent, to developers. In its efforts to increase adoption of Java and build a base of users that could create positive feedback, Sun's Java brand played on important role as a focal point for the expectations that were so important an element of Sun's competition with Microsoft.

Sun's trademarks were also important because its situation with respect to copyrights was vulnerable. The district court concluded that Sun was likely to succeed on its claim that Microsoft's modifications of the technology amounted to a breach of contract and copyright infringement, and enjoined Microsoft from shipping products it believed probably infringed Sun's copyrights. The court did not explain why it believed Microsoft had probably infringed Sun's copyrights, though Sun had argued that Microsoft's products "fail to pass the applicable compatibility test suite and that, therefore, Microsoft's distribution of these products infringes Sun's copyrights."[43] Microsoft claimed that its right to modify Java and distribute the modification in Microsoft's own products was a grant of rights distinct from the contractual requirement that these products conform to Sun's standards. The court of appeals concluded that the district court had not properly found that the Microsoft failure to pass Sun's tests amounted to infringement, rather than merely the breach of a contract term. In the view of the court of appeals, breach of a contract term did not imply copyright infringement unless the term was a condition of use or a restriction on use.[44]

On remand, the district court agreed with Microsoft that its license rights were not conditioned on or subject to its obligation to pass Sun's tests.[45] As a result, Sun did not get the benefit of the presumption of irreparable harm that accompanies a finding of probable infringement and, therefore, the district court declined to reinstate the injunction on copyright infringement grounds.[46] (The court did enjoin Microsoft based on Sun's claims under California's unfair business practices statute.) When Sun first filed suit against Microsoft, however, it had sought and obtained an injunction based on probable trademark infringement.[47] While the focus of the case later shifted to copyright and unfair competition theories of injunctive relief, Sun's initial foray using trademark law suggests that each of these rights could play an important role in maintaining the coherence of widely distributed technologies.

The collapse of Sun's ISO efforts

The legal and economic issues driving the litigation between Sun and Microsoft ran through the ISO standardization process as well. As noted above, in network markets expectations are important to competition. If the Java trademarks uniquely conveyed to the market that a product adhered strictly to the Java specifications, and if the ISO standard technology differed from the branded Java technology, then firms competing in a Java-based world might have felt substantial pressure to agree to Sun's conditions for issuing a trademark license.[48] Sun might, in other words, have been both a source of competitive products and a supervisor of competition. It is therefore understandable that Microsoft's comments to US TAG before the second round of voting accused Sun of being a fox seeking international authorization to guard the henhouse.[49]

This problem was compounded by the rapidly changing nature of technology markets and the significant cost of maintaining and distributing the Java technologies. Many of the round one comments focused on the manner in which the Java standard would be maintained over time if ISO adopted it. Sun proposed in response that it continue its own "open and inclusive" development process, and that a working group be created to address "all aspects of maintenance including: handling defect reports, writing draft technical corrigenda, writing draft amendments, and carrying out the five-year periodic review of the International Standard."[50] Sun made no mention of working group participation in approving new versions of the Java specifications, and indeed made it fairly clear that it wanted evolution of the branded technology to be within its ultimate control, reserving evolution of the ISO standard for new submissions by Sun to JTC 1.[51]

Sun's PAS application posed the risk that Sun might adopt new branded standards before JTC 1 had agreed to the parallel "ISO–xxxx conformant" standard, thereby creating a divergence between the branded technology and the ISO standard. If competitive reality compelled firms to use the Java marks, the branded standard might have remained the "true" standard in the marketplace. ISO might have blessed each version as adopted, and JTC 1 members might have had input into evolution of the branded standard, but if JTC 1 had sought changes to the "ISO-xxxx conformant" standard that were not embodied in the branded standard, such proposals would likely have carried little weight. Under those conditions, the Java standard would in effect have been a private *de facto* standard, not an ISO-determined one.[52] This problem was plainly foreshadowed by Sun's position on intellectual property rights and the maintenance-related comments of members voting to recognize Sun as a PAS submitter. The comments suggested that ISO had to control maintenance of the standard itself, while Sun referred to maintenance as the mere fixing of bugs.

After the vote to recognize Sun, JTC 1 revised its management guide to state explicitly that the maintenance of standards originating in the PAS process would be treated no differently than the maintenance of other ISO standards. The revision made clear that the normal rules "distinguish between the correction of defects and revisions of or amendments to existing Standards."[53] One might infer that Sun's insistence that maintenance of a standard referred only to "fixing … bugs and everything" did not go over well at ISO. The revised guide stated that "it is JTC 1's intention to avoid any divergence between the JTC 1 revision of a transposed PAS and a version published by the originator."[54] The revised guide therefore "invite[d] the submitter to work closely with JTC 1 in revising or amending a transposed PAS."[55]

This revision was approved by a JTC 1 resolution adopted in January, 1999. The resolution provided that "[e]xisting, approved PAS submitters' current PAS recognition status [would] not be affected" by the change,[56] but the resolution was fairly clear as to JTC 1's view of who would control the maintenance of an ISO standard, and that maintenance was not the mere fixing of bugs. In April 1999, Sun declared that its plans to have ISO adopt Java as a standard were dead and that "ISO killed them."[57] The problem, said Sun, was that "A PAS submitter must now turn over the maintenance part of a standard to ISO. That's something we've always said we wouldn't do."[58] Sun thus declared that it would pursue a different standardization strategy.

Repeating that "we typically don't leave the invention of new things to standards bodies or consortia," and that "that's typically done within the industry," Sun's next move was to the ECMA, an entity once known as the European Computer Manufacturers' Association.[59] Sun chose the ECMA on the ground that ISO typically did not involve itself in maintaining standards submitted by the ECMA.[60] Sun continued to maintain that it would obtain ISO approval, but hedged a bit by saying it would be content with ECMA approval. In late June 1999, ECMA voted to establish a technical committee to begin standardizing Java, with Microsoft voting in favor.[61] Sun was wary of Microsoft's intentions, and stated publicly that since it owned the copyright in Java it would not proceed with standardization if Microsoft sought to "load up" the standard with technology of its own.[62] A Microsoft representative questioned how Sun would treat the intellectual property rights it held in Java, while Sun affirmed that it would retain its rights in the Java brand.[63]

Sun's ECMA experience lived down to this inauspicious beginning. By November 1999, the media were reporting a falling-out between Sun and ECMA. Sun was reported to have refused to submit the Java specification to ECMA because ECMA refused to allow Sun to maintain its copyright in the specification. (ECMA was reported to have insisted that Sun submit a specification that ECMA could change, combine with other submissions, and make freely available to the public.)[64] In early December, ECMA General Secretary Jan van den Beld was quoted as saying that "[t]he ECMA copyright policy has not changed over the last 38 years" and that it was "premature to assume that ECMA will change its copyright policy because, 'if it ain't broke, don't fix it.' "[65]

With these positions firmly set, the process collapsed quickly. On 7 December 1999, Sun announced that it was withdrawing its proposal to standardize Java through ECMA. Its statement on the matter noted that ECMA lacked "formal protections for copyrights or other intellectual property."[66] In a speech on the date of withdrawal, Sun's Chief Executive Officer was quoted as saying that "[t]he problem with standards bodies is they can be influenced by the dark side", meaning "[t]hey can be very political and they need money to run and they have to listen to their constituents, which change over time."[67] Over the following weeks, ECMA considered whether to attempt to standardize Java without Sun, and open-source software advocates urged the clean-room development of an open-source version of Java.[68]

Some implications of Sun's Java standardization experience

> You can interpret these events very negatively ...
>
> It's possible to conclude that Sun has never wanted a standard.
> (Jan van den Beld, ECMA)[69]
>
> Being a *de facto* [standard] is pretty good.
> (George Paolini, Sun Microsystems)[70]

Never say never is the first rule of business, so perhaps we should not say that Java will never be adopted by an international standardization body. The odds against formal Java standardization, however, are overwhelming. And while a single case study does not amount to conclusive proof on these complex matters, the Java standardization experience provides evidence for two strongly related points. First, particularly for complex, dynamic standards such as Java or

Windows, for which innovation and maintenance are costly endeavors, there must be some way to align the costs of maintaining a standard with revenues derived from the value added by maintenance. The proprietary model achieves this alignment by awarding property rights that enable a rights-holder to exclude others from use of the standard, thereby allowing the rights-holder to charge for use, providing a source of revenues to compensate the rights-holder for the cost of innovation and maintenance.

Property rights also offer one way to defend the stability and uniformity of the standard, giving to a firm such as Sun the legal means necessary to suppress non-conforming technology that threatens to fragment the standard. Thus Sun's intellectual property rights formed the basis for its claims against Microsoft; some of those claims are straightforward assertions of those rights, while others are based on a contract by which Sun licensed those rights. As we noted at the outset, the principal alternative to this model is cooperative standard-setting, as through JTC 1 or ECMA. Needless to say, this model fared poorly in Sun's Java standardization initiatives. The tug-of-war between Sun and the standards-setting organizations over intellectual property rights was the main reason for this failure.

This raises our second point, concerning competition in the market. Sun was tied to its intellectual property rights in Java for many reasons, each of them related in one way or another to the pitched battle it has been waging with Microsoft over whose APIs would be the standard interface for applications running on personal computers. Sun had invested substantial capital in the Java technologies, and it would be easier to recoup that investment (or at least minimize losses) with intellectual property rights than without them. This may not have been much of an issue, for Sun might well have considered it worthwhile to absorb losses on Java in the hope of making them up on other technologies if Java supplanted Windows.

In addition, however, Java was an entrant technology fighting an incumbent standard in a strong virtual network market. Sun's intellectual property rights were a key to this fight. Sun's rights enabled it to disperse the technology through licensing, promote it through branding, and police the conformity of derivative works, thus defending against fragmentation of the standard. Microsoft, whose conduct with respect to Java suggests it has a keen appreciation for the economics of networks, has done its best to see that Java becomes simply a method of programming for Windows rather than a substitute for Windows. As the litigation between the two has shown, Sun's intellectual property rights are its main weapons in this fight. In the midst of such a fight, ceding those property rights to a standards-setting body in which Microsoft had a vote could not have been an appealing option.

Network theory suggests that Sun's standardization initiative may have been purely strategic from the start. In a battle for the hearts and minds of developers, the imprimatur of a standards-setting body might have been a valuable asset. It is at least possible, however, and perhaps likely, that Sun knew from the start that standards-setting organizations would demand that it relinquish many of its rights in the Java standard. It is also likely that Sun understood from the start that it had to retain ultimate control of those rights if it was to use Java to compete with Microsoft in the market. Sun's standardization initiative was part of a broader competitive strategy in a networks market, and the chances are high that Sun valued the publicity its standardization efforts generated as much if not more than the prospect of actually having Java adopted as an ISO standard.

The collective action problems Judge Jackson identified in the Microsoft trial do pose a significant challenge for firms trying to displace prevailing standards in markets characterized by strong network effects. The positive feedback between applications written for Windows and consumer use of Windows has proved a strong force and, as Judge Jackson concluded, a significant barrier to entry.[71] In such circumstances, competing against an incumbent requires fast, aggressive action designed at every step to persuade developers and consumers that the incumbent will supplant the standard. Sun's standardization efforts suggest that the demands of this model of competition strongly conflict with cooperative standards setting through organizations such as ISO.

These factors in turn suggest that the cooperative standards-setting model will be ineffective as against incumbent standards that are costly to develop and maintain, are protected by intellectual property rights wielded by a single firm, and which enjoy strong network effects. Under these conditions, property rights are more conducive to competition and innovation when held and exercised by a single rights-holder than by a standards-setting organization. Though Sun never actually gave its Java rights to such an organization, its persistent refusal to do so is strong market-based evidence in support of this conclusion.

Notes

*   Associate Professor of Law, University of Minnesota Law School (dmcgowan @tc.umn.edu). This essay is adapted (and updated) from Daniel J. Gifford and David McGowan, "A Microsoft dialog," *Antitrust Bulletin* 44: 619 (1999), and Mark A. Lemley and David McGowan, "Could Java change everything? The competitive propriety of a proprietary standard," *Antitrust Bulletin* 43: 715 (1998).

1   There is a variation on this theme, that of relatively unstructured cooperation in the development of a product but of highly concentrated control over the basic content of the standard, as with Linux, but I do not address those issues here.

2   Lemley and McGowan (1998a: 759, n. 111).

3   Second Amended Complaint of Sun Microsystems, Inc., para. 2 (available at http://java.sun.com/aboutJava/index.html). Many of the citations in this paper are to World Wide Web links that were current at the time the events described took place. Some of the links, particularly with respect to Sun's ISO initiative, may no longer work. I have hard copies of most of the cited material, which I will provide to interested persons upon request.

4   Direct testimony of James Gosling, *United States* v. *Microsoft Corp.*, no. 98–1233 (United States District Court for the District of Columbia) para. 24 (available at www.usdoj.gov/atr/cases/f2000/2049.htm).

5   Testimony of Joachim Kempin, 26 February 1999 (a.m. session), p. 35. Paul Maritz, a Microsoft Vice President for Platforms and Applications, testified to the same effect.

Sun is attempting to establish what I call the Java runtime here – that is their

foundation classes – into a collection of software that can provide most of the services of the operating system. That is what I mean by 'New OS API'.
(Testimony of Paul Maritz, 28 January 1999 (a.m. session) pp. 60–61)

We believe that Sun's Java strategy is to establish a Java development platform that will run on top of all computer operating systems, and to which all application developers will write their applications. If this strategy were successful, the Java development platform would replace Windows and all other operating systems (or reduce them to commercial insignificance).
(Direct Testimony of Robert Muglia para. 32)

Direct testimony and transcripts of live testimony for all Microsoft witnesses are available at www.Microsoft.com.

6 Mark A. Lemley and David McGowan, "Legal implications of network economic effects," *California Law Review* 86: 479 (1998).

7 Ibid., 488.

8 I follow the foundational work of Michael Katz and Carl Shapiro in this terminology. Michael L. Katz and Carl Shapiro, "Network externalities, competition, and compatibility," *American Economic Review* 75: 424 (1985). Katz and Shapiro distinguish between "direct" and "indirect" network effects, and further discuss positive consumption externalities that may arise in markets relating to durable goods. In a later article Katz and Shapiro adopt the term "virtual networks" for goods characterized by "indirect" effects. Michael L. Katz and Carl Shapiro, "Systems competition and network effects," *Journal of Economics Perspective* 8: 93, 95 (1994). Joseph Farrell and Garth Saloner articulated the same concept in discussing "a market-mediated effect, as when a complementary good (spare parts, servicing, software …) becomes cheaper and more readily available the greater the extent of the (compatible) market." Joseph Farrell and Garth Saloner, "Standardization, compatibility, and innovation," *Rand Journal of Economics* 16: 70 (1985). Professors Shapiro and Varian use the Macintosh as an example of a virtual network good in Carl Shapiro and Hal R. Varian, *Information Rules*, 13–14 (1998).

9 *United States v. Microsoft Corp.*, 147 F. 3d 935, 939 (DC Cir. 1998).

10 *United States v. Microsoft Corp.*, no. 98–1233 (United States District Court for the District of Columbia), Findings of Fact, paras 39–41 (available at http://www.usdoj.gov/atr/cases/f3800/msjudgex.htm).

11 Ibid. para. 28.

12 Ibid. para. 29.

13 The comment came during argument on an evidentiary point during the testimony of James Gosling, 3 December 1998 (a.m. session), 26.

14 Established in 1906, IEC was the pioneer organization in international standardization. ISO works closely with IEC on matters of electrotechnical standardization. A 1976 agreement between the two organizations allocates responsibility for electrical and electronic engineering to IEC; all other subject areas fall within ISO's jurisdiction. http://www.iso.ch/infoe/intro.html.

15 See http://java.sun.com/aboutJava/standardization/index.html.

16 See *Transposition of Publicly Available Specifications (PAS) into International Standards (DRAFT) – A Management Guide*, www.iso.ch/dire/jtc1/pas/html (hereinafter *Management Guide*).

17 See ibid. Section 6 of the *Management Guide* states that "[t]here are no formal conditions or restrictions as to what form the organization should take." Section 3.3 of the Annex "A" to the *Management Guide* calls for "organizations" seeking PAS recognition to respond to a number of queries regarding intellectual property rights held by the organization that relate to the proposed standard.

18 These questions were also raised by the ad hoc committee formed by the American organization voting on the proposal, the United States JTC 1 Technical Advisory

Group (US TAG). See http://www.jtc1tag.org/jt97264r.htm (minutes of meeting 4–6 June 1997).

19 Sun's responses were posted at http://java.sun.com/about-Java/standardiza-tion/april30response.html and http://java.sun.com/aboutJava/standardization//may20response.html. Microsoft submitted a detailed analysis of Sun's response to the overall comments from the first round vote (http://jtc1tag.org/jt970457.htm).

20 See http://java.sun.com/aboutJava/standardization/response1.html.

21 The vote in favor of recognizing Sun as a PAS submitter for Java was 20–2, with Italy and Switzerland abstaining. The United States and China voted against recognition. US TAG voted against recognition, with comments, in June 1997. See above, note 18 (minutes of meeting 4–6 June 1997). The minutes of the 4–6 June meeting reflect substantial discussion and multiple votes on issues relating to the application. During US TAG's meeting of 28–29 October, it considered whether to change its vote to approve Sun's application, in light of Sun's responses to comments accompanying the first ballot, comments made by US TAG members (the most extensive of which were provided by Microsoft), and comments from non-members. According to Sun, a majority of US TAG voted in favor of recognition but the vote was two short of the two-thirds majority needed to override the prior vote. Sun attributed its failure to prevail within US TAG to

> a situation where a small number of companies in the US, one of them software and three of them hardware, simply lobbied very hard – including putting pres-sure on some of their partners – to just barely escape a two-thirds majority "yes" versus the simple majority "yes" that the US did provide.
>
> (http://java.sun.com/pr/1997/nov/pr971117.tran.html, comments of Alan Baratz, President of Sun's JavaSoft division)

22 In casting its first-round vote, China commented that it "believes that standards shall be developed in an open and consensus building process consistent with ISO principles, in a non-profit unbiased standard organization. An individual shall not control such a process." China further noted that it was "disturbed by the consequence possibly incurred by the ownership of the Trademark, Distribution rights and its further mainte-nance right of an international standard by a private company." *Summary of Voting On JTC 1 N 4615*, http://java.sun.com/aboutJava/standardization/jln4833.html.

23 See http://java.sun.com/aboutJava/standardization/april30response.html (charac-terizing Microsoft's argument).

24 http://www.jtc1tag.org/jt970457.htm.

25 Ibid. The comments at the June 1997 US TAG meeting that opposed recognizing a single firm as a PAS submitter focused on the deleterious effect of such recognition on the traditional standardization process. Members (unidentified in the minutes) argued that "[c]onsensus standards development has no future if single companies are permitted to originate standards"; "[p]ermitting single companies as PAS submitters undermines the value of international standards"; and single-firm recognition "would set a precedent that consensus is not a necessary ingredient in the development of international standards" (http://www.jtc1tag.org/jt97264r.htm).

26 http://java.sun.com/aboutJava/standardization/response1.html. According to the response, Sun's patent policy was to

> automatically grant ... to users of the Java(tm) platform specifications a fully-paid, worldwide, limited license in perpetuity that allows them to create and distribute their own implementations of our specifications without paying any fees or royalties to Sun for the use of our patents that are necessary to practice the specifications.

Sun further stated that it was willing "to follow ISO/IEC patent policy or extend the terms of our current patent policy to cover implementors of the International Standard" (ibid. Section 2.2.1).

27 Ibid. Section 2.2.2.

28 Ibid. Section 2.2.3.

29 Sun's example of the name for the standard was "ISO.xxxxxx, The ISO Specification for the Java(tm) Platform" (ibid.).

30 Ibid.

31 Ibid.

32 http://java.sun.com/aboutJava/standardization/annexes.html#AnnexD (under Section 3 of Sun's Java Trademark Guidelines, however, licensees may not advertise products in a "Java for XYZ" format).

33 See *Zatarain's, Inc.* v. *Oak Grove Smokehouse, Inc.*, 698 F. 2d 786 (5th Cir. 1983) for a discussion of trademark's fair use doctrine, which differs significantly from the doctrine of the same name in copyright law.

34 http://java.sun.com/aboutJava/standardization/annexes.html#AnnexD, Section Five ("Fair Use of the Java Mark: Taglines").

35 See, e.g., *New Kids On the Block* v. *News America Publishing, Inc.*, 971 F. 2d 302 (9th Cir. 1992) (use of a mark to refer to the mark's owner while accurately describing attribute of service offered was "nominative fair use" of trademark); Robert P. Merges *et al.*, *Intellectual Property in the New Technological Age*, 1018–20 (1st edn, 1997). Courts will, however, strictly monitor the use of the word "compatible." See, e.g., *Creative Labs* v. *Cyrix Corp.*, 42 USPQ 2d 1872 (ND Cal. 1997); *Princeton Graphics Operating L.P.* v. *NEC Home Electronics*, 732 F. Supp. 1258 (SDNY 1990).

36 Ibid. (emphasis added).

37 On the question of injunctive relief, the case has thus far resulted in one decision by the Court of Appeals for the Ninth Circuit, *Sun Microsystems, Inc.* v. *Microsoft Corp.*, 188 F. 3d 1115 (9th Cir. 1999) (vacating injunction for further findings on claim of copyright infringement), and three decisions by the trial court: *Sun Microsystems, Inc.* v. *Microsoft Corp.*, 2000 WL 132711 (ND Cal. 25 January 2000) (NO. C 97–20884 RMW PVT) (refusing to reinstate injunction on grounds of copyright infringement); *Sun Microsystems, Inc.* v. *Microsoft Corp.*, 21 F. Supp. 2d 1109, 1998 Copr. L. Dec. P 27,838, 49 USPQ 2d 1245 (ND Cal., 17 Nov 1998) (NO. C 97–20884 RMW PVT) (issuing injunction based on claims of breach of contract, unfair competition, and copyright infringement); *Sun Microsystems, Inc.* v. *Microsoft Corp.*, 999 F. Supp. 1301, 46 USPQ 2d 1531 (ND Cal., 24 March 1998) (NO. C 97–20884 RMW(PVT)) (issuing injunction based on trademark claims).

38 I express no opinion on the merits of the parties' claims; the dispute is of interest here only for the light it sheds on the use of Sun's intellectual property rights.

39 The contract terms are described in the cases cited in note 37.

40 See Direct Testimony of Robert Muglia paras 47–60 (available at http://www.microsoft.com/presspass/trial/mswitness/muglia/muglia.htm). In a declaration filed in the litigation between Microsoft and Sun, Microsoft's Paul Maritz stated that,

> [t]o the extent we are not legally prohibited from doing so, Microsoft will continue to develop and promote independent Java tools enhancements which make no use of Sun's licensed Java Technology. Java is a useful programming language and Microsoft seeks to provide Windows developers who choose to use Java to write Windows programs with the best possible programming tools.
>
> (Declaration of Paul Maritz In Opposition to Sun's Motion to Reinstate November 17, 1998 Preliminary Injunction Under Cal. Bus. & Prof. Code sections 17200 *et seq.*, para. 8, available at http://www.microsoft.com/presspass/java/09–27maritz.htm.)

41   Second Amended Complaint, note 3 above, para. 65.
42   Ibid. para. 42 (emphasis added).
43   *Sun Microsystems, Inc.* v. *Microsoft Corp.*, 21 F. Supp. 2d at 1112.
44   *Sun Microsystems, Inc.* v. *Microsoft Corp.*, 188 F. 3d at 1122.
45   *Sun Microsystems, Inc.* v. *Microsoft Corp.*, 2000 WL 132711 (ND Cal. 25 January 2000) (NO. C 97–20884 RMW PVT).
46   *Sun Microsystems, Inc.* v. *Microsoft Corp.*, 2000 WL 132711 at *5. The district court did issue an injunction based on claims Sun asserted under California's unfair business practices act.
47   *Sun Microsystems, Inc.* v. *Microsoft Corp.*, 999 F. Supp. 1301, 46 USPQ 2d 1531 (ND Cal., 24 March 1998) (NO. C 97–20884 RMW(PVT)) (issuing injunction based on trademark claims).
48   As George Paolini, Director of Corporate Marketing for Sun's JavaSoft division, put it in commenting at a teleconference held after submission of Sun's response to ISO members' comments,

> [a] major distinction between Unix and Java, technology aside, is the power of the Java brand. We have been very effective in using the brand to essentially keep the industry on one platform, one Java platform. We have done this by using the brand to certify and allow the use of the brand in various substantiations [sic] for those who comply. If you don't comply, you will lose the right to use the brand. So far that has worked extremely well.
>
> (http://java.sun.com/pr/1997/sept/qa.html)

49   Microsoft's comments to US TAG before the second round of voting stated that

> By using its trademarks to control compliance with its proprietary implementation of Java, Sun would effectively control compliance with the proposed International Standard for Java while competing in the marketplace with other vendors seeking to conform to the standard. To allow a competitor to have this much control undermines the credibility of the standard.
>
> (http://www.jtc1tag.org/jt970457.htm)

50   http://java.sun.com/aboutJava/standardization/response1.html (section 2.1).
51   As Sun's Jim Mitchell explained on the teleconference accompanying Sun's submission of its response,

> Maintenance is fixing these bugs and everything, and there is a process in JTC 1 to go through that and put even those things up for voting and comment. *But if Java changes in some substantial way what we would expect to do is a new submission of the Java platform specs.*
>
> (http://java.sun.com/pr/1997/sept/qa.html, emphasis added)

Sun also contended quite strongly that

> the primary value proposition of Java is Write Once, Run Anywhere. When the entire computer industry shifts it in order to keep write one run anywhere we have to get consensus around changes. That's why we run as open a process as we do … [w]e can no more veto or do something with just one company – if we do that we have killed that right to run anywhere, so our process is open because it has to be. That's in enlightened self-interest. It's not altruism.
>
> (Ibid.)

This statement is revealing in three respects. First, it retained Sun's authority to pass judgment on changes to branded Java technology, and made clear that Sun did not propose to surrender that right as part of the ISO process; second, it characterized the value of Java as being, at least for the present, a hostage effectively precluding Sun from exercising this right in an arbitrary manner; third, it characterizes the "Write Once, Run Anywhere" attribute of Java as a "right" inhering (presumably) to the benefit of those who comply with branded specifications. Treating this right as legally enforceable might ameliorate some concerns that Sun's dual position as competitor and monitor might otherwise raise, though the right need not necessarily be embodied in antitrust law.

52 Mark Lemley and I made this point in an earlier paper. Lemley and McGowan, "Java," p. 769, note *.

53 *JTC 1 N 5746, The Transposition of Publicly Available Specifications into International Standards – A Management Guide, Revision 1 of JTC 1 3582*, section 5.2.5 (available at www.jtc1.org).

54 Ibid.

55 Ibid.

56 See JTC 1 N 5748, *Resolutions Adopted at the Thirteenth Meeting of ISO/IEC JTC 1*, 26–29 January 1999 (available at www.jtc1.org).

57 Lem Bingley, "Sun blames Microsoft as its Java standardization plans die," *IT Week*, 29 April 1999 (available at www.zdnet.com) (visited 28 February 2000).

58 Ibid.

59 Antone Gonsalves "Sun submits Java to ECMA for standardization," *PC Week Online*, 6 May 1999 (available at www.zdnet.com) (visited 28 February 2000).

60 Ibid.

61 Deborah Gage, "Java standardization process moves forward," *Sm@rt Reseller*, 29 June 1999 (available at www.zdnet.com) (visited 28 February 2000).

62 Ibid.

63 Ibid.

64 Deborah Gage, "Java standards glitch may open door for Microsoft," *Sm@r Reseller*, 19 November 1999 (available at www.zdnet.com) (visited 28 February 2000).

65 Deborah Gage, "Who really owns Java?," *Sm@rt Reseller*, 6 December 1999 (available at www.zdnet.com) (visited 28 February 2000).

66 *Sun Microsystems Withdraws JAVA 2 Platform Submission from ECMA*, 7 December 1999 (available at www.java.sun.com/pr/1999/12/pr991207–08.htm) (visited 28 February 2000).

67 Deborah Gage, "Sun drops plans to standardize Java," *Sm@rt Reseller*, 7 December 1999 (available at www.zdnet.com) (visited 28 February 2000).

68 Deborah Gage, "Java: to hell in a handbasket?" *Sm@rt Reseller*, 9 December 1999 (available at www.zdnet.com) (visited 28 February 2000).

69 Charles Babcock, "ECMA retreats from Java hard line," *Inter@ctive Week*, 22 and 28 December 1999 (available at www.zdnet.com) (visited 28 February 2000).

70 Scot Peterson, "Sun withdraws Java from standards process," *PC Week Online*, 8 December 1999) (available at www.zdnet.com) (visited 28 February 2000).

71 Findings of Fact, see note 10, paras 36–41, 45–7.

Part V

The limits of government regulation

14 China's impact on the Global Information Society

Perry Keller

'Sharing the same bed, but not the same dream'[1]

On 7 August 1999, Song Yongyi, a researcher and librarian at Dickinson College in Pennsylvania, was arrested in Beijing.[2] Song was visiting China to collect documents and other materials dating from the turbulent Cultural Revolution era (1966–76). He was initially accused of divulging state secrets, but was later charged with the lesser offence of purchasing and providing illegal intelligence to foreigners. In January 2000 he was unexpectedly released and allowed to return to the United States.

It is not very clear why was Song arrested. The Cultural Revolution is certainly a sensitive subject for Communist Party leaders, who still wish to protect the reputation of Mao as founder of the People's Republic and have their own secrets to guard. Perhaps Song's work on the historical documentation of this period disturbed a particular sensitivity. Or perhaps he was arrested to demonstrate to other Chinese scholars based abroad the hazards of using their insider's knowledge of China to support foreign-based research. Killing the chicken to frighten the monkeys (*sha ji, gei houzi kan*), or punishing one individual simply to ensure the proper behaviour of others, is often used to assist in the protection of official information in China.[3] And why was Song released, when so many other seemingly blameless individuals remain imprisoned? Perhaps the outcry in the American academic community over his treatment had some influence. It could also be that he was released as a goodwill gesture in the intricate poker game of Sino–US relations. Or it may even be that his activities were finally determined to be innocuous and his purported confession merely announced to paper over the event. I doubt these questions will ever be answered satisfactorily. Although this episode was frightening for Song Yongyi and his family, it was simply a small and hardly unusual incident in the enforcement of justice and security in China.

From a western liberal democratic perspective, much seems amiss in this system of law and administration, particularly in matters concerning freedom of expression and the free flow of information. In China, these principles are entirely overshadowed by the public order and security concerns of the Party-state. Moreover, the legal system itself is not only fragmented, inconsistent and often opaque, but is also closely woven into the fabric of Party and state authority and administration.[4] In these circumstances, how will China be integrated into the globalisation of national information societies? With 70 million households subscribing to cable television, a similar number of individuals possessing mobile phones and nearly 10 million Internet users, the country is rapidly developing its own information society. At a practical level, China's communication and information systems are already internationally integrated, given the huge volumes of voice, data and broadband content which flow across her borders every day. What has yet to occur is integration at the legal and institutional level. But, with accession to the WTO almost secured, this further step may be in sight.

The international patchwork

There is, of course, no institutional or legal *system* to underpin a global information society. As effective national control over media, communications and information networks and services has eroded, the reconciliation of public and private interests has drifted by default into the sphere of international governance. But in this sphere there is merely a patchwork of institutions and treaties loosely bound together through public and, often more importantly, private co-operative relationships and practices.[5] There is no comprehensive, coherent international legal and administrative system in which competing interests can be reconciled and chosen solutions imposed. Particular international regimes, notably the international co-ordination of intellectual property protection, are now well established. But in many other areas, the legal and administrative frameworks are flimsy and solutions are fashioned ad hoc for the short term.

It is clear that, as a matter of international law and relations, the emerging Global Information Society is principally considered to be a child of international economic law. This is firstly because the creation of the WTO in the 1990s pushed international economic law to the centre of post Cold War thinking about the constitutional foundations of international order.[6] But this also occurred as a result of changing national policies. The resurgence of liberal market economics and the policies of privatisation and de-regulation placed private enterprise at the forefront of the communication revolution. Consequently, the creation of national information societies came to be seen, at least in western economies, largely as a problem of fair competition and the protection of contract and property rights.[7] Not surprisingly, the globalisation of these developments has come to be seen in a similar light.

But the international economic law patchwork also leaves many issues unresolved. Cooperation on competition law has not moved beyond the experimental bilateral phase, and agreement on the treatment of investors is still tainted by the shambolic failed negotiation of the OECD Multilateral Agreement on Investment.[8] Within the WTO system itself, the GATT will continue to apply to trade in goods, which is of great importance to suppliers of hardware, including optic fibre, cable and a vast range of computer equipment. But the online provision of services, the essence of an information society, falls substantially within the scope of the GATS. This is a more loosely constructed instrument which requires that member states opt into trade concessions for specific service sectors.[9] In some areas, such as trade in audiovisual services, this has so far proven to be virtually impossible to achieve.[10] In telecommunications, however, the GATS has proven to be a useful foundation for further agreements on liberalisation.[11]

Within the scope of international economic law, the WIPO-based intellectual property rights regime provides the second foundational element for the construction of a global information society.[12] This regime, strengthened immeasurably through the adoption of the WTO TRIPS agreement, has proven to be an effective platform on which to mount campaigns for the domestic recognition and enforcement of intellectual property rights throughout the world. It is also a monument to the potential effectiveness of international law where there is a sufficient convergence of powerful state and private interests. By comparison, international human rights law, which forms the other foundational leg for a global information society, is less well developed. Interpretation and implementation of human rights treaties, including the International Covenant on Civil and Political Rights (ICCPR), remains largely in the hands of the state parties.[13] This is a particular problem for international matters affected by the principle of freedom of expression which attracts such a wide range of divergent views on its many potential applications.[14]

From a liberal democratic perspective, the task is to knit this international patchwork together to ensure that the Global Information Society is securely underpinned by liberal economic, political and legal values. And much has already been accomplished in this effort. In creating the WTO, the member states placed the resolution of trade disputes on a more legalised footing, hoping to satisfy the demands of some governments for a more effective and predictable system.[15] The WTO also requires that the state parties ensure there is adequate transparency, predictability and sustainability in domestic laws and administrative practices. These rudimentary moves towards the ideal of the rule of law and due process in international economic law are symbolically as well as practically important. A familiar strand in liberal thought which links the success of market economies to the rule of law and the protection of civil and political rights, notably the freedom of expression and the concept of free flow of information. Positive developments on one side of this equation raise expectations of associated progress on the other. Moreover, in the contemporary frenzy of dot.com investment and the rhetoric of new economic paradigms, new communication technologies are often assumed to be driving the liberal democratic project inexorably forward.

A different view

But this optimistic expectation tends to overlook the complexity and diversity of the real world. There are good reasons to doubt that those countries whose information societies are most advanced will continue to dominate institutional and legal development at the international level. Firstly, the apparent global embrace of market-based economics obviously cloaks a great diversity of views on the proper rules of commerce. In much of the world, for example, the certainty and predictability of commerce rests primarily on close, confidential relationships between business, financial and government elites. These are simply regarded as essential rather than illicit relationships.

Second, many governments of poorer states clearly feel compelled to become parties to international trade institutions and agreements without wholeheartedly embracing their ostensible principles. From their perspective, an open, competitive international trading system is inherently biased towards the advanced world economies. Consequently, whilst the benefits of membership outweigh those of non-participation, there will always be a desire to protect the domestic economy as much as possible from the disciplines of the international system. Third, most governments have limited capacity to implement their international obligations. Aside from the simple ineffectiveness of much civil and legal administration, governments will always have difficulty in introducing top-down changes which cut across the grain of established beliefs and practices.

All of these factors are well represented in the People's Republic of China. The country's fledgling market economy coexists with residual state planning and the protection of economic favourites, whether national or local, is routine. The vast, far-flung Party-state is fragmented, bedevilled by corruption and often hamstrung by bureaucratic rivalries. Moreover, China's leaders seem determined to test the assumption that new technologies will fatally undermine the capacity of governments to control the media and communications sectors. Despite the advent of satellite television and the Internet, the leadership remains thoroughly committed to its traditional media control policies. The central question for Chinese communications and media regulatory authorities is simply how best to assimilate these new technologies into the existing regulatory system.

A closer look at China's own emerging information society therefore provides a better view of the breadth of the issues to be negotiated in the shift towards a global information society. Social, political and economic influences will count as much as or more than technology in determining the nature of that society, and China will be a formidable partner in the process.[16] This article can do no more than focus on one of these influences: the legal and administrative system for regulating traditional and new media in China. But the deep cultural roots of this system should not be overlooked. Information control, for example, is not simply the hallmark of a Leninist state, it is also is a widely accepted social practice in China. Many Chinese people share a cultural disinclination to disclose information outside established personal and institutional networks. Nor can the Chinese regulatory system be understood without considering that most Chinese citizens know no foreign language. They live in an insulated, language-defined communications enclave that provides both a natural barrier to foreign media services and a well-defined sphere of operations for the security and censorship organs of the Party-state.

Grasping the pen and the gun

From its earliest experiences of power in the 1930s, it has been an article of faith that the Communist Party must control the pen as well as the gun and use both against its opponents.[17] It therefore remains a fundamental goal of media regulation in China that the Party should retain exclusive control over all means of mass communications so as to guide the thinking of Chinese citizens. In the early years of the People's Republic, it was relatively easy to secure this degree of control. After nationalising the production and distribution processes for newspapers, journals, books and films, control over physical points of entry through the customs service sufficed to exclude most unauthorised publications. The reception of foreign short-wave radio broadcasts was a greater challenge, although fear of discovery no doubt kept many individuals from ever attempting to listen. The government also developed the capability to jam the frequencies of undesired stations and continues to develop and use those capabilities today. The British colony of Hong Kong presented a special problem, as its local Cantonese language broadcasts could be received in the Pearl River delta region. Reception could only be stamped out during periods of political tension and close surveillance.[18]

This basic situation did not change until the 1980s. The new policies of economic reform and opening to the outside world prompted the rapid spread of a whole range of new communications technologies. The Party, firmly wedded to ideas of modernity and scientific progress, welcomed their introduction so long as the government controlled their use. However, the normalisation of Chinese society as the Party gradually relaxed its hold on the personal lives of the country's citizens also created a market for prohibited media and entertainment products and services. The import and illegal reproduction of audio cassettes established a pattern followed in rising numbers by video cassettes, compact disks and now digital video disks.

Rising prosperity also brought televisions and video recorders to millions of ordinary homes and created a market for the later introduction of satellite television.[19] More recently, the Internet has begun to have an impact on the lives of urban professionals and business people.

The Central Propaganda Department

The Communist Party's national media polices are formulated primarily within the Central Propaganda Department (CPD), an extremely powerful and secretive body close to the apex of the central Party organisation.[20] The framework for current policies was laid down in 1994 when the Party completed a major review of its cultural and information work.[21] At that time, the leadership reaffirmed the importance of retaining control over the creation and dissemination of media services and products. Aside from preventing its domestic and foreign opponents from gaining access to the Chinese public through the media, the central Party determined that it must ensure that the China's media foster patriotism, the national cultural heritage, as well as a 'socialist spiritual civilisation'.[22] The latter phrase has come to represent an opposition to liberal democratic political values as well as what might be described as 'loose morals'.

The Propaganda Department is not a state institution and its directives are issued internally to government and media bodies falling within its jurisdiction. As it therefore has no officially acknowledged role in public life, Chinese citizens and foreign organisations or individuals have no formal means of access to it. The CPD supervises the implementation of its policies through the Party's network of regional Propaganda Bureaux and through key national media organisations, such as the *People's Daily* and China Central Television (CCTV). This structure is replicated at the regional level and in all urban localities where the Party organisation controls the principal newspapers and broadcasting stations. Control can be extremely detailed and intrusive. The CPD, for example, dictates the content and layout of the front page of the *People's Daily* and also determines the content of the national television news programme.[23] The Party's control of key positions also ensures that editors, producers and managers serve at the pleasure of the Party and can be removed peremptorily when they have offended Party leaders.[24] This system of editor responsibility ensures that editors abide by the key demands of the CPD and do not press the boundaries of accepted content unless protected by powerful patrons within the Party.[25]

The Communist Party still attempts, as far as possible, to monopolise the determination of what is truth and fact and the characterisation of all significant events and circumstances.[26] Whilst the government has relaxed its grip on entertainment content in China, it remains committed to absolute control over the production and dissemination of officially reported news. According to well-established Party doctrine, the function of the Chinese news media is to operate as the mouthpiece of the Party and therefore to obey the all-embracing Party Principle (*dangxing yuanze*).[27] Under this principle, the news media are required to embrace the Party's guiding ideology, propagate the Party's programmes, and follow the Party's organisational principles and press policies. In practice, censorship varies considerably according to the issue and the prevailing political climate.[28] However, there is still a zone of total prohibition which includes any significant revelations about the workings of the Communist Party or the lives of its leaders, any direct criticism of established government policies or any supportive reference to the independence of Taiwan or any non-Chinese ethnic groups.

Bureaucratic rivalries

The Central Propaganda Department guides and supervises the work of several state bodies within the central government, including the State Administration of Radio, Film and Television (*Guangbo Dianying Dianshi Zongju*) (SARFT), the State Administration of Press and Publication (*Xinwen Chuban Shu*), and the State Council Information Office (*Guowuyuan Xinwen Bangongshi*). In Chinese administrative terms, these bodies are within the network, or *xitong*, of the Propaganda

Department. Bureaucratic networks, whether Party or state, are an essential feature of public administration in China.[29] They help to ensure that policies are implemented throughout particular economic or social sectors and can provide a basis for cross-institutional support.

Co-operation between networks is, however, often poor, and the existence of rival networks can be an enormous obstacle to efficient government. The CPD network does not, for example, include the Ministry of Information Industry (*Xinxi Chanye Bu*) (MII) which is responsible for the national regulation of telecommunications and, more recently, Internet infrastructure issues.[30] This administrative network boundary has made it difficult for Chinese authorities to deal with the gradual convergence of media and telecommunications in a comprehensive manner. During the 1998 radical re-organisation of the central government, the newly created MII was initially expected to absorb the Ministry of Radio, Film and Television. The resulting super-ministry would have claimed jurisdiction over content as well as infrastructure issues throughout the telecommunications and electronic media sectors.

But this overlap of the Party's propaganda and economic networks within a single state ministry did not succeed. The Propaganda Department is credited with saving the Ministry of Radio, Film and Television, albeit in the reduced form of a 'state administration' (the SARFT). Although its authority over television delivery systems, especially cable networks, has been largely absorbed by the MII, the SARFT continues both to guard its control over programme content issues and to expand its authority in new ways. But, at the same time, these rivalries at the central government are not necessarily replicated at the local level. The devolution of power in the economic reforms of the 1980s has given rise to powerful local Party-state authorities capable of ignoring many central government policies and edicts.

Commerce and the Party-state

Economic reform has also brought about the wholesale commercialisation of the Chinese media sector. In this new environment, media companies and units have worked aggressively to profit from advertising, sponsorship and other commercial arrangements in the face of a steady decline in state funding.[31] This commercial boom has presented the Party-state with an intense dilemma. As the Party is the owner of all key media entities and the state is the nominal owner of any non-Party companies in the traditional media sector, financial and commercial concerns have now seeped into all aspects of the regulatory process. With so many Party- and state-owned companies fighting to protect or secure a share of the burgeoning media market, content restrictions have provided an effective pretext for assaults on economic competitors. As one experienced observer has commented,

> It is difficult to see a genuine political motivation in any case where foreign or domestic competition has been excluded because of some purported

principle of socialist policy. In most of these cases the chief motivation is economic not political.[32]

This entanglement of political principles and economic interests can be seen in the State Council's 1996 order that all suppliers of business, economic and financial news, such as Dow Jones and Reuters, must provide their services through the medium of the Party-controlled New China, or Xinhua, News Agency.[33] The government attempted to secure Xinhua's position as the monopoly supplier for these commercial services and granted it a statutory power to filter content, set prices and to receive a commission. Given the evident threat to the Party's control over the production of news, the decision to bring these services within China's media control system was not surprising in political terms.[34] Nonetheless, it was surely not a coincidence that the solution chosen was to enrich the Xinhua News Agency by granting it a monopoly on the national business news market. It would appear that this move was only partly successful. It is rumoured that Xinhua has significantly scaled back its efforts to pre-censor the news stories provided by these services and is not receiving the major fees it initially demanded.[35]

Controlling the skies

The Chinese government has developed, largely through trial and error, a range of strategies and measures to deal with perceived external threats to its system of media and communications control. This system hinges on Party internal directives which guide its own media operations and reach non-Party media entities through state regulators. The Party's powers over the appointment and dismissal of editors and managers are a major guarantee of compliance. In 1994 the CPD re-stated its basic policy that there should be no private media ownership, no share-holding of media organisations and no joint ventures with foreign companies.[36] Quite separately, Party and state leaders responsible for the communications sector have imposed a similar ban on private and foreign investment in the telecommunications industry.[37] But as media companies have struggled to increase profitability they have sought new and, often, at best quasi-legal ways to raise capital. As a result, the once solid link between the media and the state has been substantially eroded.[38] Complex consultancy and management agreements have effectively delivered control of various journals, newspapers and even local cable and broadcast television operators into private hands.

Media regulation without law

Law has so far played a limited role in Chinese media and communications regulation. There is in fact no primary legislation governing the telecommunications, Internet, broadcasting, press or publishing industries. China's national legislature, the National People's Congress (the NPC), is constitutionally entrusted with the exclusive power to enact 'laws' (*falü*) but has yet to do so in the media and communications sectors.[39] There is instead an evolving legal framework based on the powers of the State Council and its ministries to adopt secondary and tertiary regulations.[40] The State Council, which is the executive arm of the central government, has recently issued comprehensive regulations governing broadcast and cable television and is rumoured to be in the process of adopting similar comprehensive administrative measures for telecommunications.[41] In addition to these framework regulations, there are hundreds of other more specific regulatory instruments concerning media content and infrastructure matters issued by various central state bodies.

Given the wealth of applicable regulations in this sector, one might wonder whether any national legislation was necessary. However, what is lacking is a legislative enactment of the rights and responsibilities of broadcasters in relation to the Party, the state or the general public. A national broadcasting law in combination with the much debated, but equally elusive, national Press Law would provide the legislative foundations for the implementation of the constitutional guarantee of freedom of expression. But there is little sign that either of these laws will be enacted soon. The vitally important Press Law project was frozen after the crushing of the Tiananmen demonstrations in 1989 and is only now showing signs of a cautious officially approved revival.[42]

This is not to suggest that the adoption of basic press or broadcasting laws by the NPC would dramatically change China's media and communications system. There are simply too many powerful political and economic interests involved in the media sector to expect any wholesale re-balancing of this system in favour of a more rights-oriented approach. However, the formal recognition of a modest degree of media freedom as well as the media's accountability to the general public would at least open a door to change which is now firmly shut. At present, media and communications law in China is not much more than a loose body of vaguely stated licensing requirements in which the underlying principles are at best implicit and always shifting with government policy.

Synergies of censorship and copyright

In the print media sector, the State Administration for Press and Publication (SAPP) operates as the primary regulator for newspaper, journal and book publishers and distributors.[43] Unlike the SARFT, however, the SAPP only became a separate state administration in 1987 and does not enjoy ministerial rank, nor does its administrative network extend down to the local level.[44] It has, however, successfully expanded its administrative authority to include the regulation of CDs and other multimedia products.[45] The central government attempts to control the print and multimedia sector through a national registration and licensing system.[46] But despite periodic crackdowns and closures of publishers and producers,[47] the black market in illicitly produced materials continues to thrive.

The control system over print products and more especially CDs and DVDs is now substantially assisted by China's new intellectual property rights regime.[48]

This legal and administrative regime has gradually developed over the past decade principally to satisfy the demands of foreign, particularly American, governments acting on behalf of their content-producing industries. Whilst the protection of intellectual property rights in China is frequently ineffective, the system has created potentially useful measures for rights holders and has brought them a degree of government support.[49] But this system, bolstered by foreign pressure and technical assistance, has also increased the power of the central government to locate and suppress illicit publication and production for its own purposes. Consequently, the demands of major foreign content producers for more effective state administration in China marks a significant early alignment of interests between foreign media companies and the Chinese central government.

The audiovisual tide

The import of foreign films for cinema release has never presented a major challenge to the Chinese government. Indeed, film imports have proven to be a useful bargaining chip in international trade negotiations. The SARFT operates a quota system for foreign films destined for cinema release and videotape sales which is currently restricted to ten films per year as selected by regulatory officials.[50] Under the terms of the Sino–US agreement on Chinese accession to the WTO, this quota will increase to twenty films per year after accession occurs. The advent of satellite television has, by comparison, threatened to rupture the entire media control regime. In its long campaign to suppress the illegal reception of foreign satellite television, the SARFT has not only battled against the efforts of individuals to acquire dishes and view prohibited channels, but has also struggled to curb the illicit activities of local broadcasters and cable operators who turn to these satellite channels as a source of free programming.[51]

In 1993 the State Council adopted Decree No. 129, the key national legal instrument concerning satellite reception.[52] This decree, entitled *Regulations Concerning the Administration of Satellite Television Broadcasting Ground Receiving Facilities*, set in place a complex licensing system covering all aspects of satellite television reception.[53] Work units must obtain separate permits for the production, import, sale, installation or use of satellite receiving equipment.[54] It also provides that permission for individuals to use such equipment, including dishes and decoders, will only be granted under exceptional circumstances.[55] The Decree established a control regime based on the familiar Chinese regulatory distinction between Chinese citizens and foreign residents. Under the 1994 implementing regulations,[56] there are two categories of satellite television: 'domestic' (*jingnei*) which any work unit may apply to receive; and 'foreign' (*jingwai*) which is reserved to higher standard hotels and residential compounds for foreigners as well as licensed educational and other units who can show a special need to receive foreign satellite television.[57] Only those 'foreign' satellite broadcasters who have entered into an agreement with SARFT can be legally received in China and these broadcasts may be peremptorily censored or suspended.[58]

Whilst satellite television controls are comparatively tight in Beijing, they are notoriously lax elsewhere. In the areas of Guangdong province adjacent to Hong Kong, national restrictions on the reception of foreign terrestrial and satellite broadcasts have been waived.[59] Moreover, many local radio, film and television authorities are not able or willing to conduct regular investigations and licence checks.[60] According to some reports, foreign broadcasts are allegedly received illegally by millions of Chinese households through their own dishes or those of their local cable network.[61] Effective country-wide enforcement of the satellite television regulations would seem to occur only during short-term nationally co-ordinated crack-downs on local broadcasters and cable operators as well as residences.[62]

The Chinese government nonetheless has many potential allies among the multinational media companies that hope to provide programming for Chinese viewers.[63] In the long term, these companies are not interested in fishing in the cracks and gaps of China's regulatory system.[64] Illicit viewing may be a welcome foot in the door, but it does not guarantee adequate or stable revenue streams. Stable revenue extraction from a large viewing audience will require government co-operation. Subscription systems require approved payment mechanisms and the legal means to suppress decoder piracy and other intellectual copyright violations. Similarly, advertising supported services do not merely require government approval or acquiescence, but also need the effective enforcement of the contractual and intellectual property rights on which the industry is based. Consequently, foreign media companies are not only seeking greater access to the media sector in China, but also effective legal and administrative protection for subscription and advertising systems. Many therefore see the central government as a potential ally as well as an adversary in their efforts to grow and profit in the Chinese media market.[65]

The national cable link-up

The SARFT has also spearheaded a national cable plan which may ultimately strengthen the central government's ability to control satellite television reception. By 1999 Chinese cable television suppliers had constructed 2.25 million km of cable transmission networks and had connected 77 million cable television subscribing households.[66] However, these cable networks were local – or at best regional – in scale and lacked interconnection. Recently the SARFT has promoted an ambitious construction programme of trunk lines which will link these pre-existing networks into a national cable system. [67]

Aside from the increased efficiency of the cable delivery system, a unified network has obvious administrative benefits for the central authorities. A national system would provide a more effective means of enforcing television content prohibitions. These are currently enforced by local radio, film and television administrations who are frequently unable or unwilling to rein in the money-spinning efforts of local network operators who flout national controls.[68] Under Beijing's current plans, local governments must retain ownership of the local cable networks, but they should also hive off operational control into separate companies.[69] This would seem to serve two objectives. Cable operators will be forced to function on a more commercial basis, and local governments will lose their direct control over the cable networks.

Guarding the gateways

China's leaders have consistently supported the introduction of Internet technology in China. They are evidently convinced that China must take swift advantage of new information and communication technologies if it is to construct its own information society and reap the economic benefits. But despite the international attention paid to Internet issues in China, Internet use is still restricted to a small urban elite, at best 11 million people in a country of 1.2 billion.[70] Therefore, whilst the Ministry of Information Industry and other ministries have failed to produce a coherent regulatory framework for the Internet, they have not yet lost the race to assimilate this technology. Nonetheless, some observers are extremely sceptical, questioning whether the government has yet understood the potential impact of the Internet.[71]

The firewall

Although the Internet goes by several popular names in China, for legal purposes it is referred to as a 'computer information network' (*jisuanji xinxi wangluo*) and it is regulated as a value-added telecommunications service. After an initial period of regulatory experimentation, the State Council acted in 1996 to formalise its control system governing the connection of Chinese computer networks to the global Internet.[72] The government's solution to the perceived dangers of the Internet was to create a tiered system of interconnection and responsibility. In this system, all access to the Internet outside China must pass through international gateways operated by China Telecom.[73] Furthermore, within China all international access must also pass through the four main public access networks, which are described in the regulations as 'interconnecting networks' (*hulian wangluo*).[74] As a final measure, Internet service or access providers, described as 'connecting networks' (*jieru wangluo*), must obtain an international connection permit if intending to provide access to the global Internet.[75] This structure is intended to ensure that all international Internet traffic entering China passes through the packet-level filtering software installed on the interconnecting networks.[76]

The 1996 regulations did not impose new content responsibilities on Internet providers or users. Work units and individuals were merely reminded of the applicability of the laws concerning state security, state secrets, obscenity and pornography.[77] This apparent laxity was remedied on the last day of 1997 when the Ministry of Public Security issued the *Regulations Concerning the Administration and Protection of the International Connection Security of Computer Information Networks*.[78] These regulations provide a much more detailed statement of how Internet users may breach criminal and other laws. According to Article 4, users should not produce, copy, examine or transmit information which incites the overthrow of the national government or the socialist system; incites the splitting of the country or damages national unity; incites ethnic hatred, ethnic discrimination or damages ethnic unity; fabricates or distorts facts, disseminates rumours or disrupts social order; publicises feudal superstition, obscenity, pornography, gambling, violence, murder, terrorism or instigates criminal acts; publicly insults other persons or fabricates facts slandering other persons; damages the reputation of the organs of government; or violates the Constitution or any laws or administrative regulations. Provided that users do not violate these broad provisions they are guaranteed freedom of communication and the right to private communication.[79]

A very wide range of websites and news groups relating to political or social issues in China are blocked, especially those in the Chinese language.[80] The BBC main website, for example, can be accessed from within China, but its Chinese language section is blocked. But whether or not these controls are effective is a contested issue.[81] Even the Chinese authorities acknowledge that the firewall can be avoided by anyone equipped with basic information about concealing message content.[82] However, officials also consider that potential violators will be deterred once they realise that their activities can be traced. And there is no doubt that the Chinese screening system does have a major impact on Chinese Internet users as many lack the knowledge and skill needed to anonymise content or are simply unwilling to run the risk of discovery.[83]

Filtering in, filtering out

The Chinese government is not just concerned that its citizens might have access to prohibited sources of information and entertainment. It is also determined to ensure that official information does not leak out through the Internet. The State Secrets Bureau (*Guojia Baomi Ju*) consequently issued regulations in 2000 to ensure that the national State Secrets Law is comprehensively applied to the Internet. This law is notoriously broad and ill defined. The term 'state secret', for example, may include any information derived from government sources which has not been officially released to the general public.[84] The new regulations provide that anyone who places material on the Internet is legally responsible for that information and that Internet access and content providers must monitor any hosted BBS, chat room or news groups to ensure that state secrets are not divulged.[85]

The government has also struck at Internet content providers (ICPs) who provide online information from unauthorised sources and thereby bypass the Party's news monopoly. By the late 1990s China-based Internet portal sites, including Sina.com and Sohu.com, had begun to provide news from foreign and non-official domestic sources. In the autumn of 1999, the Central Propaganda Department countered this development with an internal circular declaring that Chinese websites may only distribute news from authorised domestic sources and no content provider may engage in its own news-gathering activities.[86] The State Council Information Office has since been given the task of implementing this policy and it is now the licensing authority for all websites under China's jurisdiction which release news online.[87] These measures have caused many Chinese ICPs, some already under attack for alleged copyright violations by the traditional media, to retreat from the serious news market.[88]

Dilemmas of ownership

In 1999 the MII minister, Wu Jichuan, moved to close an apparent regulatory loophole which had allowed foreign investors to take a major role in the creation of Internet content providers and Internet service providers (ISPs) operating in China. For example, Dow Jones is one of Sohu.com's investors and Pat Robertson, the American tele-evangelist, has an important stake in the Zhaodaola search portal.[89] This situation was in marked contrast to the rigorous restrictions on direct foreign involvement in the operation of television stations or cable networks as well as the entire telecommunications sector.[90] In this sector, the efforts of Chinese and foreign companies to collaborate in the margins of legality have lead to spectacular retribution and recriminations.[91]

In 1998, the State Council announced the invalidity of more than a billion US dollars' worth of complex agreements made by China Unicom, the struggling state-owned secondary telecommunications company. Unicom and its foreign partners sought to avoid the prohibition on foreign direct investment by creating joint ventures between foreign and Chinese parties and then using these ostensibly 'Chinese' vehicles to enter into further joint ventures with Unicom (hence the name 'Chinese-Chinese-foreign' or *zhong-zhong-wai* investments). Unicom, now under the control of the MII, is currently settling the protracted dissolution of these contracts.

Consequently, there was widespread concern amongst investors in the Internet industry when Wu declared that the telecommunications foreign investment ban also applied to ICPs and ISPs.[92] However, the subsequent conclusion of Sino–US agreement on China's accession to the WTO has already had an impact on official attitudes towards foreign investment in these companies. Under this agreement, once China joins the WTO foreign investors will be able to hold up to 49 per cent foreign ownership in any telecommunication services, and in value-added services, which include ICPs and ISPs, this will rise to 50 per cent after two years.[93] The government's emphasis has now shifted from the withdrawal of foreign money from ICP/ISPs to the ad hoc control of those investment agreements, including proposed initial public offerings on the NASDAQ exchange.[94] But whether these precise percentages will make any difference in practice is open to doubt. The primary obligations of the WTO cannot assure foreign parties more than national treatment, and in China this means equal access to an opaque, highly discretionary regulatory regime.

China and the Global Information Society

The many regulatory uncertainties clouding the development of the Internet in China neatly illustrate some of the country's basic rule of law problems. The Chinese government takes a highly instrumental view of law and does not see a problem in setting aside legal provisions which frustrate the leadership's policy decisions.[95] Officials also prefer to deal with new developments on an ad hoc basis and to introduce legal measures only after a sufficient period of experimentation. Consequently the highly fluid Internet sector is not likely to see comprehensive legislation soon. But at the same time, Chinese entrepreneurs are busy creating Internet companies and making investments. They are well used to a system in which personal relations with government officials and other decision-makers have long substituted for the existence of non-discriminatory administrative rules and procedures.[96] For insiders, there is sufficient predictability to engage in business. The risks may be higher, but so are the potential rewards, which are funded in part by those who lack the right connections

There is no reason to believe that China's assumption of further international legal obligations will bring about any fundamental change in the nature of Chinese society or government, although many are hopeful that WTO membership will provide a much needed external impetus for change.[97] However, the obstacles to the development of a more transparent and impartial system of government in China are extraordinary. There is even some question as to whether the Chinese central government has sufficient control over regional and local authorities to bring about meaningful legal and administrative reform.[98] Frequent and rigorous recourse to the WTO panel procedure will not alter this situation.

Notes

1   *Tong chuang yi meng.*
2   Eckholm, E. (2000) 'China's arrest of Pennsylvania librarian alarms scholars', *New York Times*, www.nytimes.com, 13 January.
3   Woodman, S. and Yu, P. (1999) 'Killing the chicken to frighten the monkeys: the use of state security in the control of freedom of expression in China', in Coliver, S. Hoffman, P. and Bowen, S. (eds) *Secrecy and Liberty: National Security, Freedom of Expression and Access to Information*, Dortmund: Martinus Nijhoff.
4   On China's legal system, see, generally, Lubman, S. (1999) *Bird in a Cage: Legal Reform in China after Mao*, Palo Alto: Stanford University Press. See also, Alford, W. (1999) 'A second Great Wall? China's post-Cultural Revolution project of legal construction', *Cultural Dynamics*11(2) (July): 193, and Peerenboom, R. (1999) 'Ruling the country in accordance with law: reflections on the rule and the role of law in contemporary China', *Cultural Dynamics*11(3): 315.
5   See Picciotto, S. (1996) 'The regulatory criss-cross: interaction between jurisdictions and the construction of global regulatory networks', in Bratton, W., McCahery, J., Picciotto, S., and Scott. C. (eds) *International Regulatory Competition and Coordination*, Oxford: Clarendon, pp. 89–123. See also Picciotto, S., (1996–7) 'Networks in international economic integration: fragmented states and the dilemmas of neo-liberalism', *Northwestern Journal of International Law and Business* 17(1014–56): 1019.

6 Trachtman, J.P. (1996) 'The international economic law revolution', *University of Pennsylvania Journal of International Economic Law*, 17: 33.
7 See, for example, Hitchens, L.P. (1996) 'Identifying European audiovisual policy in the dawn of the Information Society', *Yearbook of Media and Entertainment Law*, Oxford: Clarendon, p. 45. See also Commission of the European Communities (1997e) *Green Paper on the Convergence of the Telecommunications, Media and Information Technology Sectors, and the Implications for Regulation* COM(97) 623.
8 de Jonquières, G. (1998) 'Retreat over OECD Pact on Investment', *Financial Times* 21 October, p. 5.
9 Hoekman, B. and Kostecki, M. (1996) *The Political Economy of the World Trading System: From GATT to WTO*, Oxford: OUP.
10 World Trade Organisation (1998) *Audiovisual Services: Background Note by the Secretariat*, S/C/W/40, 15 June.
11 Harwood, J.H., Lake, W.T., and Sohn, D.M. (1997) 'Competition in international telecommunications services', *Columbia Law Review* 97: 874–904.
12 See, for example, Commission of the European Communities Ministerial Declaration (1997) 'Global information networks: realising the potential', European Ministerial Conference at Bonn 6–8 July, paras 30–34.
13 China is now a signatory to the ICCPR and its companion treaty the International Covenant on Economic, Social and Cultural Rights but has yet to ratify either instrument. It is a testament to the flexibility of the ICCPR that the Chinese government can contemplate becoming a party without major changes to its system of law and state administration.
14 ICCPR. Art. 19.
15 Hoekman and Kostecki, n. 9 above.
16 See Winston, B. (1998) *Media, Technology and Society: A History*, London: Routledge, and Flichy, P. (1995) *Dynamics of Modern Communication*, London: Sage.
17 Lynch, D. (1999) *After the Propaganda State: Media, Politics and 'Thought Work' in Reformed China*, Palo Alto: Stanford University Press, ch. 2; see also Schoenhals, M. (1992) *Doing Things with Words in Chinese Politics*, Berkeley Institute of East Asian Studies.
18 Writer's interview, Beijing, 1999.
19 Lynch, n. 17 above, p. 82.
20 Zhao, Y. (1998) *Media, Market and Democracy in China*, Urbana: University of Illinois Press, p. 19. Although its Chinese name has not changed, the Propaganda Department (*Zhongyang Xuanchuan Bu*) has recently described itself in English as the Information or Publicity Department of the CCP.
21 Lynch, n. 17 above, p. 179.
22 Lynch, ibid., p. 187.
23 Writer's interviews, Beijing, 1999.
24 Lynch, n. 17 above, p. 141.
25 Lynch, ibid., p. 67. In January 2000, for example, the editor of the popular weekly *Nanfang Zhoubao* (*Southern Weekend*) was removed, apparently after the paper's investigative reports and liberal editorial policy fell foul of conservative factions in the Party. See, 'Editor's firing may signal media clamp', *South China Morning Post*, 26 January 2000, www.scmp.com.
26 Li, M. (1997) 'Guidance of public opinion and strict control over the media', *Inside Mainland China*, June: 21.
27 Zhao, n. 20 above, p. 19.
28 See Harding, J. (1999b) 'China relaxes red tape on the written word', *Financial Times*, 10 December, p. 14. But in periods of political tension, scrutiny of foreign imports is tightened and import percentages are reduced. Chan, J.M. (1994), 'Media internationalization in China: processes and tensions', *Journal of Communication* 44(3) (Summer): 81.

29 See, K. Lieberthal (1996) *Governing China: From Revolution Through Reform*, New York: W.W. Norton.

30 Lynch, n. 17 above, p. 35.

31 Lynch, ibid., 42–3. Zhao Yuezhi also comments that: 'the Party still refuses to recognise commercialisation as an explicit policy objective' (Zhao, n. 20 above, p. 176).

32 Writer's interviews, Beijing, 1998.

33 State Administration of Press and Publications (1996) *Administrative Procedures concerning the Distribution of Economic Information within China by Foreign News Agencies and their Subordinate Information Organisations*.

34 Zhao, n. 20 above, pp. 176–7.

35 Writer's interviews, Beijing, 1999.

36 Zhao, n. 20 above, p. 176.

37 Ministry of Foreign Trade and Economic Cooperation (20 June 1995) *Interim Provisions for Guidance for Foreign Investment*.

38 See generally, with particular reference to the concluding chapter, Zhao, n. 20 above.

39 Article 62, Constitution of the PRC.

40 See Keller, P. (1994) 'Sources of order in Chinese law', *American Journal of Comparative Law* 42: 711.

41 State Council (1997) *Regulations on Radio and Television Management*.

42 The Legislation Commission (*Fazhi gongzuo weiyuanhui*) of the NPC Standing Committee has sponsored some research but actual drafting has apparently yet to resume. 'Freedom of expression' is a sensitive issue for scholarly research in China and rarely appears in Chinese academic legal literature. Work on broadcasting or Internet regulation is also scarce and tends to be descriptive rather than analytical. See, for example, 'Luelun Wangluoshang Jisuanji Fanzui yu Duice', *Faxue Pinglun* 1998(1): 83. However, there is undoubtedly general support for the adoption of a Press Law. See, for example, Zhang Ximing (1999) 'Shiba Nian Fengyu Jiancheng, Xinwen Fa Hu zhi Nanchu', in Liu Zhifeng (ed.) *Zhongguo Zhengzhi Tizhi Gaige Wenti Baogao*, Beijing: Zhongguo Dianying Chubanshe, p. 265.

43 Although there are currently over 2,000 newspapers in China with a combined circulation of 26 billion, many of these are only two-page tabloid-sized, weekly or monthly publications.

44 Lynch, n. 32 above, pp. 158–9; see also Liang Wei (1996) 'Shukan Shichang Guanli zhi Wo Jian', *Fazhi yu Jingji* 4: 11.

45 see Lee, A. (1996) 'Developments in the audio-visual market in the PRC', *ICCLR* 9: 331.

46 On the press and publishing sector, see Lynch, n. 17 above, pp. 156–9; see also Stevenson-Yang, A. (1998) 'Word games', *China Business Review*, May–June: 42.

47 See, 'China announces major restructuring of press and industry publications', *Press and Publications News (Xinwen Chuban Bao)* 30 November 1999, www.chinaonline.com, and 'China's newspaper publishing industry leaner and meaner', China News Agency (*Zhongxinshe*) 26 January 2000, www.chinaonline.com.

48 Lee, A.(1996), 'Developments in the audio-visual market in the PRC', *ICCLR* 9: 331.

49 For a critical overview, see P. Potter and M. Oksenberg (1999) 'A patchwork of IPR protections', *China Business Review* January–February: 8. See also Alford, W. (1995) *To Steal a Book is an Elegant Offense: Intellectual Property Law in Chinese Civilization*, Stanford: Stanford University Press, who argues that, despite apparent Chinese government compliance, western-inspired intellectual property laws have not transplanted easily into the Chinese social and cultural context.

50 On the demand for foreign films and television programmes in China, see Atkinson, L., (1997) 'What's entertainment', *China Business Review*, March–April.

51 Lynch, n. 17 above, p. 182.

52 For a full analysis of this Regulation and its accompanying Implementing Regulation, see Yan, M. (1998) 'Protection of free flow of information and regulation of transfrontier television', D. Phil. thesis, University of Essex, ch. 11.

53 Its provisions have since been supplemented through other regulations, including the State Council's omnibus (1997) *Regulations on Radio and Television Management.*

54 *Regulations Concerning the Administration of Satellite Television Broadcasting Ground Receiving Facilities*, Art. 3.

55 *Regulations*, ibid., Art. 9.

56 Yan, n. 52 above, p. 328.

57 *Regulations Concerning the Administration of Satellite Ground Receiving Facilities Used to Receive Television Programmes Transmitted by Foreign Satellites*, Art. 4.

58 See, for example, the suspension in February 2000 of AOL–TimeWarner's TNT and Cartoon Network channels from the list of approved foreign satellite channels: Schwankert, S. (2000) 'Bugs Bunny, Porky Pig barred from China', *Virtual China News*, 7 February, www.virtualchina.com.

59 Writer's interview, Beijing, 1999.

60 Lynch, n. 17 above, p. 142. Beijing has gone to some lengths to make enforcement workable. In 1996, for example, three domestic Chinese satellite television broadcasters were ordered by MFRT to move from Asiasat1 to Asiasat2. It was then possible to determine who was illegally tuning in to Star TV by looking at angle of the dish (Zhao, n. 20 above, p. 177).

61 Wang, X. (1999) 'Satellite TV crackdown a rerun of 1994', *South China Morning Post*, 10 May, Business Section, p. 4.

62 Wang, ibid.

63 Yan, n. 52 above, p. 401. The Phoenix satellite television channel provides a prominent example. Phoenix is 45 per cent owned by News Corporation and 55 per cent owned by two mainland companies, and enjoys an informal agreement with the Bureau of Radio, Film and Television in Guangdong which allows its inclusion into Guangdong cable networks. The SARFT has no objection to its programming, but is concerned that if it is allowed to operate legally on a national basis, any other foreign operation based in Hong Kong will demand similar access to the cable networks (writer's interview, Beijing, 1999). However, during the May 1999 national crackdown on illicit reception of satellite signals Phoenix was also pulled from cable networks across China; Kynge, J. (1999) 'Beijing pulls plug on foreign TV broadcasts', *Financial Times*, 6 May, p. 6.

64 Phoenix Channel has so far led foreign penetration, claiming to have 40 million regular viewers.

65 The efforts of Rupert Murdoch and News Corporation executives to woo the Chinese leadership have been well covered in the press. See, for example, Vines, S. (1998), 'Murdoch moves forward in China', *Independent*, 20 November, p. 19, and Poole, T. (1998) 'Chinese thank Murdoch for "objectivity" ', *Independent*, 12 December, p.18.

66 State Council (1999) *Notice on Reinforcing the Management and Construction of Radio and Cable TV Networks*, October.

67 Rothman, W. and Barker, J. (1999) 'Cable connections', *China Business Review*, May–June: 20.

68 Lynch, n. 15 above, ch. 5.

69 State Council *Notice*, n. 62 above.

70 Dougan, D. (1999) *Scaling the Great Wall of E-Commerce*, Washington: Cyber Century Forum (see, www.virtualchina.com).

71 Qiu, J.L. (1999/2000) 'Virtual censorship in China: keeping the gate between the cyberspaces', *International Journal of Communications Law and Policy* 4 (Winter), www.ijclp.org, 2.

72 State Council (February 1996, amended May 1997) *Provisional Regulations on the Administration of International Interconnection of Computer Information Networks*. For an overview of the Internet control system, see *China Law and Practice*, December 1998.

73 *Provisional Regulations*, ibid., Article 6.

74 *Provisional Regulations*, n. 72 above, Article 7. The four interconnecting networks are ChinaNET (owned previously by the Ministry of Posts and Telecommunications and now by the MII); CERNET (owned by the State Education Commission); GBNET or China GBN (owned previously by the Ministry of Electronic Industry and its partners and now by the MII); and CSTNet (owned by the Chinese Academy of Social Sciences). These networks may be joined by UNINET (owned by the MMI telecommunications company, China Unicom).

75 *Provisional Regulations*, n. 72 above, Article 9.

76 For a description of the type of content filtering or blocking used in China, see McCrea, P., Smart, B., and Andrews, M. (1998) *Blocking Content on the Internet: a Technical Perspective*, Report prepared for the National Office for the Information Economy, Australia, June. See also United States Embassy Report (1998) *New PRC Internet Regulation*, January, www.redfish.com/USEmbassy-China.

77 *Provisional Regulations*, n. 72 above, Article 13.

78 Issued by the Public Security Ministry, 30 December 1997.

79 *Provisional Regulations*, n. 72 above, Article 7.

80 Lawrence, S., and Brookes, A. (1999) 'Missing links', *Far Eastern Economic Review* 4 March: 13.

81 Landler, M. (2000) 'Investors ask if Beijing can enforce all its new Internet rules', *New York Times*, 31 January, www.nytimes.com.

82 United States Embassy Report, n. 76 above.

83 In January 1999, the Public Security Ministry, MII, Ministry of Culture and the State Administration of Industry and Commerce issued regulations tightening up controls on Internet cafés. These regulations delegate responsibility to proprietors to prevent customers from 'participating in any online activities considered harmful to state security, social stability or other people's interests'.

84 Woodman and Yu, n. 3 above.

85 State Secrets Bureau (2000) *State Secrecy Protection Regulations for Computer Information Systems on the Internet*, 25 January. See Rosenthal, E. (1999) 'Web sites bloom in China, and are weeded', *New York Times*, 23 December, www.nytimes.com. See also Gesteland, L. (2000a) 'Internet censored further in China', 26 January, www.chinaonline.com.

86 See Chen, G. (2000b) 'China Internet: government tightens controls, clamps down on news', www.chinaonline.com. see also Chen, G. (1999) 'China's booming Internet sector: open or closed to foreign investment?' 8 October, www.chinaonline.com.

87 Gesteland, L. (2000b) 'China's ICPs need approval, license before posting news', 18 February, www.chinaonline.com.

88 Fravel, T. (2000) 'The bureaucrats battle over the Internet in China', *Virtual China News*, 18 February, www.virtualchina.com.

89 Harding, J. (1999a) 'Yahoo! forms alliance to create website in China', *Financial Times*, 27 September.

90 Ministry of Posts and Telecommunications (1993) *Interim Administrative Measures on Examination and Approval regarding the Operation of Liberalised Telecommunication Businesses*.

91 See Warwick, M. (1998) 'Access Denied', *Communication International*, November: 6.

92 Chen, G. (1999) 'China's booming Internet sector: open or closed to foreign investment?' *ChinaOnline News*, 8 October, www.Chinaonline.com.

93 White House Office of Public Liaison (1999), *Summary of US–China WTO Agreement*, 17 November.

94 Xing Fan (2000) 'Foreign investment in China's Internet business: forbidden, forgiven, forced open', 20 February, www.chinaonline.com; see also Chen, G. (2000a) 'Foreign

participation in China's Internet sector remains a major issue for 2000', 20 January, www.chinaonline.com.

95 Keller, n. 40 above; Lubman, n. 4 above.
96 Potter, P. (2000) 'Guanxi and the PRC legal system: from contradiction to comple-mentarity', Wilson Center for Scholars' Seminar on *Civil Society in China*, 9 February, www.chinaonline.com. See also Cai D. (1999) 'Development of the Chinese legal system since 1979 and its current crisis and transformation', *Cultural Dynamics* 11(2): 135.
97 See, for example, Groombridge, M. and Barfield, C. (1999) *Tiger by the Tail: China and the World Trade Organisation*, New York: AEI Press.
98 Lubman, n.4 above, p. 316.

15 Freedom versus access rights in a European context

*Ad van Loon**

During the last decade of the twentieth century, discussions in Europe focused on how to guarantee pluralism in the traditional media (press, radio and television). As a result, four different systems to safeguard and promote pluralism in the media sector can now be identified in Europe:

1   through subsidies, programme prescriptions, quality requirements, frequency distribution, maintenance of public broadcasting systems, etc.;
2   restrictions on media ownership and control;
3   restrictions on audience reach (in the UK: 'share of voice'), i.e. the audience share which a single owner or controller of media outlets is allowed to control with all its media outlets in a relevant audience market;
4   restrictions linked to the control by media undertakings over essential resources (such as financial means or infrastructure).[1]

'Mixed' – hybrid – systems to safeguard and promote pluralism in the media sector also appear. The first question which arises, however, is what exactly is one trying to safeguard and promote: what is meant by a state of pluralism in the media sector? A second question is how this desire of European states to safeguard and promote pluralism in the media sector relates to the fundamental right of everyone to freedom of expression without interference by public authorities. This fundamental right is guaranteed by the Council of Europe and all of its member states,[2] as it is laid down in the European Convention for the Protection of Human Rights and Fundamental Freedoms (ECHR). A third question to be asked is how national policies to safeguard and promote media pluralism, which are in line with fundamental rights requirements, relate to general European law requirements for those fifteen Council of Europe members (of a total forty-one) which are members of the European Union (henceforth EU law). A fourth and last question which will be dealt with is whether the existing methods of safeguarding and promoting pluralism in the (traditional) media sectors are capable of guaranteeing pluralism in the changing technological and economic environment of the Global Information Society.

Council of Europe: defining pluralism

In January 1999, after ten years of discussions, the Committee of Ministers of the Council of Europe came to the conclusion that 'media pluralism' should be understood as

> diversity of media supply, reflected, for example, in the existence of a *plurality of independent and autonomous media* (generally called structural pluralism) as well as a *diversity of media types and contents (views and opinions) made available to the public*.[3]

Pluralism, according to the Council of Europe, 'is about diversity in the media that is available to the public, which does not always coincide with what is actually consumed'.[4] Furthermore, still according to the Council of Europe, the concept of pluralism is comprised of two features:

- political pluralism;
- cultural pluralism.

The first, political pluralism, is about the need, in the interest of democracy, for a wide range of political opinions and viewpoints to be represented in the media. If any single voice within the media, with the power to propagate a single political viewpoint, were to become too dominant, this would be a threat to democracy. The second, cultural pluralism, is about the need for a variety of cultures which reflect the diversity within society to find expression in and to find themselves represented in the media. Thus, the objectives of promoting and safeguarding pluralism in the media sector are seen, by the Council of Europe and its forty-one member states, as a justification for their media policies. They regard their media policies as instrumental to safeguarding and promoting democratic values.

Fundamental right to freedom of expression

How do policies to safeguard and promote pluralism in the media sector relate to the fundamental right of everyone to freedom of expression without interference by public authorities? This fundamental right is guaranteed by the Council of Europe and all of its member states, as it is laid down in the ECHR; it can be enforced by the European Court of Human Rights.

There is no single and clear definition of the concept of 'freedom of expression'; often it includes the freedom to receive and impart information and ideas. All democratic states have a notion of the freedom of expression, one way or another, embodied in their legal system. The right to freedom of expression is, in principle, a freedom right protecting individuals from state intervention. However, in the Europe of the Council of Europe it is generally accepted that this freedom right also has a social aspect: all democratic states have an obligation to secure an adequate protection of this freedom right for everyone.[5] Therefore, the ECHR and the European Court of Human Rights allow certain restrictions to this freedom right: for example, in the interest of protection of the legitimate rights of others. In cases where the right of others to be heard or to be properly informed is infringed by certain individuals or groups in society, a state has the right (or even the obligation) to take measures to ensure that other individuals or groups whose rights have been infringed can effectively use their fundamental rights. However, according to paragraph 2 of Article 10 ECHR as interpreted by the European Court of Human Rights, any such state measures can only be taken if they:

- are laid down by law (i.e. they have to be so clear, for persons to whom they are addressed, that these persons can attune their behaviour to the requirements);
- are as such capable of reaching the objective aimed at; and,
- do not go beyond what is absolutely necessary to reach the objective aimed at (i.e. no less far-reaching methods to reach the same objective should be available).

These requirements apply to all interferences with media freedoms by public authorities in all member states of the Council of Europe.

In an attempt to assist its member states in taking the right measures, i.e. without infringing the fundamental rights of the ECHR, the Committee of Ministers of the Council of Europe adopted Recommendation 99[1], in which it informed the member states on possible measures to promote pluralism. This was done in January 1999, as indicated above, after ten years of intergovernmental discussions and consultations. As regards ownership structures in the traditional media sectors (i.e. broadcasting and press), the Recommendation calls upon the member states of the Council of Europe to examine the possibility of defining thresholds in their laws or authorisation, licensing or similar procedures, to limit the influence which a single commercial company or group may have in one or more media sectors. Such thresholds may, according to the text of the Recommendation, take the form of a maximum audience share, be based on the revenue/turnover of commercial media companies or impose capital share limits in commercial media enterprises. Furthermore, member states are called upon to consider the possibility of creating specific media authorities invested with powers to act against mergers or other concentration operations that threaten media pluralism or investing existing regulatory bodies for the broadcasting sector with such powers. In the event member states would not consider this appropriate, it is recommended that the general competition authorities pay particular attention to media pluralism when reviewing mergers or other concentration operations in the media sector. Where vertical integration (i.e. the control of key elements of production, broadcasting, distribution and related activities by a single company or group) may be detrimental to pluralism, it is recommended that member states consider the adoption of specific measures to prevent this. Apart from a call to member states to take measures with regard to ownership relations in the media sector, the Recommendation calls upon the member states to prevent that the broadcasting sector becomes the victim of the rapidly expanding telecommunications sector by taking sufficient account of the interests of the broadcasting sector, when redistributing the frequency spectrum or allocating other communication resources as a result of digitisation. Moreover, member states are asked to guarantee fair, transparent and non-discriminatory access to systems and services that are essential for digital broadcasting, providing for impartiality for basic navigation systems and empowering regulatory authorities to prevent abuses. Apart from all that has been mentioned above, member states are asked to consider to what extent they can include, in the licensing conditions for broadcasters, provisions which require that a certain volume of original programmes, in particular as regards news and current affairs, is produced or commissioned by broadcasters.

The Recommendation emphasises the importance of preserving a pluralistic local radio and television landscape and instructs the member states to ensure in particular that networking, understood as the centralised provision of programmes and related services, does not endanger pluralism. In addition, a set of measures is recommended to maintain public service broadcasting and to allow it to develop. Especially, member states are given into consideration to maintain 'must carry' rules for cable networks[6] and to envisage similar rules for other distribution means and delivery platforms (i.e. packages of digital programme services). Finally, the Recommendation suggests a number of (financial) support measures for both existing and newly established print and broadcast media, in particular at the regional and local levels; criteria are developed for granting such support (objectivity; impartiality; transparency; independent control; periodic reconsideration).

European Union (EU) and national pluralism law

Fifteen European states participate in a European Union which other European states will join soon. Within the framework of this European Union, three European Communities operate with common organs which have been given supranational powers. As a consequence, states participating in the European Union are subject to a body of EU law, the implementation of which is ensured by a supranational court: the Court of Justice of the European Communities (ECJ). Within the framework of the European Community (one of the three communities referred to above), participating European states formulated as one of the objectives that, between themselves, an internal market should be established characterised by the abolition of obstacles to the free movement of goods, persons, services and capital.[7] EU law plays a role whenever national rules or policies provide obstacles to the realisation of these freedom of movement rights in cases where they (may) hamper the establishment or functioning of this internal market.

National rules to safeguard and promote media pluralism may directly or indirectly create such obstacles. The fifteen states of the European Union all have their own national rules to safeguard and promote media pluralism. In the past, this has already been reason enough for European interference: the mere fact that transnational market players in Europe have to obey different rules in different member states may be seen as hampering their freedom of movement. Of all possible measures to safeguard and promote media pluralism one can think of, only the (types of) measures which the Council of Europe considers possible under its fudamental rights framework (see above) will be considered below. There is no point in considering (types of) rules which will eventually turn out to violate the fundamental rights protected by the ECHR, since they would eventually be set aside by the European Court of Human Rights.

Under EU law, member states remain free to apply more detailed or stricter rules to legal or natural persons under their jurisdiction. Therefore, measures to protect pluralism in the media sector in the form of thresholds on audience reach, revenue/turnover or capital share, as recommended by the Committee of Ministers of the Council of Europe, do not violate EU law as long as they favour legal or natural persons from other member states. This will normally not be the case. In addition, however, member states may, under certain circumstances, apply the stricter rules which they impose on legal or natural persons under their jurisdiction also to legal or natural persons from other member states. This is possible if

1   the restrictions on the freedom of movement which result from the stricter rules imposed by a member state do not discriminate between its nationals and nationals from other member states;
2   moreover, the stricter measures imposed by a member state must not have been the subject of harmonisation at the European level; and,
3   they must have been taken in order to protect a general interest.

On 25 July 1991, in two broadcasting cases concerning the Netherlands, the ECJ decided explicitly that cultural policies in the broadcasting field may, under certain circumstances:

> constitute an overriding requirement relating to the general interest which justifies a restriction on the freedom to provide services. The maintenance of the pluralism which that Dutch policy seeks to safeguard is connected with freedom of expression, as protected by Article 10 of the European Convention on Human Rights and Fundamental Freedoms, which is one of the fundamental rights guaranteed by the Community legal order.[8]

However, the ECJ also emphasises that, in addition to the criteria set out above,

4   the measures taken should as such be capable of protecting the general interest it wishes to protect;

5   other methods to protect that same interest but which are less far-reaching should not be available; and,

6   they should not go beyond what is absolutely necessary to protect the general interest concerned.[9]

Finally, the stricter rules imposed by a member state cannot be imposed upon a service provider which is established in another member state if the requirements embodied in these stricter rules are already satisfied by the rules imposed on those persons in the member state in which this service provider is established. [10]

   In its 1992 Green Paper on Pluralism and Media Concentration[11] and a follow-up 1994 paper,[12] the European Commission (henceforth the Commission) analysed the necessity and the possibilities of a common European approach with regard to media concentration developments. On 26 September 1995,[13] Commissioner Mario Monti, who was at that time charged with internal market issues, announced that it was his intention to submit to his collegues in the Commission a draft proposal for a Directive on the co-ordination of national rules concerning media ownership relations. The reasons he quoted for this were the following:

- given the multiplication of transfrontier media activities, the risks of circumvention of national laws would increase which would make these laws ineffective and might thus provoke serious conflicts between national authorities;
- the need to create a level playing field so that media undertakings who seek to develop themselves and to invest across frontiers, notably with a view to the development of new informations society services, can benefit from the opportunities offered by an area without frontiers to promote the growth and the competitiveness of the European media industry;
- the fact that different member states had launched projects to modernise their national rules on media ownership and media activities and the fear that that might result into a refragmentation of the internal market.

Although concrete proposals were never published,[14] sources in Brussels' inner circle revealed that the proposed co-ordination would first and foremost have meant 'liberalisation' of existing national rules and regulations:[15] the Commission wanted to dismantle national rules in this field which it considered archaic and outdated. In particular, the Commission wanted to abolish national restrictions on capital share and voting rights in media undertakings as well as restrictions on the number of media outlets a single legal or natural person or group of legal or natural persons could control. Media concentrations below a certain threshold would no longer have been subject to the rules which limit ownership of or control over media undertakings in order to safeguard pluralism and diversity in what was offered. The Commission did not intend to interfere with national measures which tried to protect pluralism by any other means, which meant that the member states could have continued to impose their content-related prescriptions. The co-ordinated anti-concentration rules would have been applicable to the television and radio sectors as well as to 'cross-media ownership' sectors in which a combination of press, radio and/or television undertakings would have been controlled. Ownership relations in the press sector and in new services sectors (such as Internet and 'video-on-demand' services) would have been excluded from measures restricting ownership.[16]

Initially, the drafters of the proposal for a Directive thought of the following measures to be taken in cases where fixed thresholds would be crossed:

- witholding of permission for the concentration operation concerned;
- no renewal of the broadcasting licence;
- prohibition of taking over another existing broadcasting licence;
- prohibition of establishment of new undertakings.

Later on, a flexibility clause was introduced, which would have given member states the right to grant permission for concentration operations above the fixed thresholds upon the condition that such permission would be accompanied by measures to safeguard pluralism and diversity. One of such measures could be, for example, an obligation to make broadcasting time available to independent third parties.[17] The thresholds considered, but never actually proposed, were:

- in the case of monomedia ownership relations (i.e. either radio or television outlets): a maximum share in audience reach (i.e. viewers or listeners) of 30 per cent;
- in the case of 'cross-media ownership' relations the average share of audience reach spread over the types of media involved would have had to be calculated and for those relations, a threshold would apply of 10 per cent of this average share.

Therefore, if a media owner's newspapers would reach 10 per cent of the relevant readers market, their radio broadcasts 5 per cent of the relevant listeners market and television broadcasts 6 per cent of the relevant viewers market, their share in audience reach would have been $10 + 5 + 6 = 21$ per cent. This result would have been divided by the number of media types controlled by the owner: i.e. three in this case, the result of which would have been 7 per cent concentration (21 divided by 3). This result would have been below the fixed threshold of 10 per cent and would therefore have been unproblematic from the point of view of concentration control. Such a system would have required the national authorities to make an analysis of the size of the different media markets.

In 1989, the Council adopted a 'Regulation on the control of concentrations between undertakings',[18] 'to permit effective control of all concentrations from the point of view of their effect on the structure of competition in the Community and to be the only instrument applicable to such concentrations'. Under this Regulation, EU member states may no longer apply their national competition rules, if they have such rules, to concentrations with a Community dimension *unless* the Regulation makes provision thereof. Thus, the relevant powers of national authorities are limited to cases where, failing intervention by the Commission, effective competition is likely to be significantly impeded within the territory of a member state and where the competition interests of that member state cannot be sufficiently protected otherwise than by the Regulation. Furthermore, the Regulation stipulates that in cases where the Commission does not or cannot intervene, Member States may take appropriate measures to protect *legitimate interests* other than those pursued by the Regulation provided that such measures are compatible with the general principles and other provisions of Community law. 'Plurality of the media' is explicitly mentioned as such a legitimate interest. So far, however, there has been only one case in which reference was made to this Article in a concentration control decision by the Commission.[19] The Commission recognised that the proposed transaction involved issues such as the accurate presentation of news and free expression of opinion and that therefore, the national authorities could still review the transaction with a view of protecting the legitimate interest of media plurality. However, the Commission warns that in doing so, the national authorities should refer to the annex of the Merger Regulation, which stipulates in regard to Article 21(3) that:

> In application of the principle of necessity or efficacy and the rule of proportionality, measures which may be taken by Member States must satisfy the criterion of appropriateness for the objective and must be limited to the minimum of action necessary to ensure protection of the legitimate interest in question. The Member States must therefore choose, where alternatives exist, the measure which is objectively the least restrictive to achieve the end pursued.

The Commission insisted that it should be kept informed of any conditions which the national authorities might deem it appropriate to attach to the transaction (marginal control).

Measures to encourage pluralism

A number of further non-merger measures also have an effect on pluralism. I consider nine in turn: national rules to prevent vertical integration; frequency distribution policies; framework proposals for telecommunications and electronic commerce infrastructure and services; access rights to essential facilities; programme requirements; programme networking; public broadcasting systems; state aid.

National rules to prevent vertical integration

Another method recommended by the Council of Europe to safeguard and promote media pluralism at the level of its member states is the prevention of vertical integration (i.e. the control of key elements of production, broadcasting, distribution and related activities by a single company or group). However, such national rules may violate EU law. Vertical integrations are taken into account in the Commission's concentration control decisions.[20] In the case of Nordic Satellite Distribution, for example, the company, which was about to acquire a dominant position on the market for satellite TV transponder services suitable for Nordic viewers, would also have had links with an important broadcaster of Nordic TV channels and distributor of satellite TV channels to direct-to-home households. Moreover, through the links to the parents as cable operators, it would have been in a position to foreclose other satellite operators from leasing transponder services to broadcasters.

In the *RTL/ Veronica/Endemol*[30] decision of 20 September 1995, the Commission stated that a structural link between a TV broadcaster and print media dealing *inter alia* with TV-related features can be used to promote the TV programmes of the broadcasters. This may occur, despite the existence of statutes on editorial independence, since experience shows that ownership of print media tends to influence the general orientations of the media. Furthermore, there can be direct co-operation between broadcasters and print media owners which are linked.

On the whole, however, it is the Commission's policy to prevent the development of dominant positions through the horizontal integration of media undertakings in order to allow vertical integration. The Commission sees vertical integration as a means for European undertakings to develop in such a way that they can confront the growing competition from vertically integrated companies from outside the European Union.

Frequency distribution policies

Rules to prevent the broadcasting sector becoming the victim of the rapidly expanding telecommunications sector by taking sufficient account of the interests of the broadcasting sector, when redistributing the frequency spectrum or allocating other communication resources as a result of digitisation, are another means seen by the Council of Europe to safeguard and promote media pluralism. Traditionally, European states are free to assign and license the radio spectrum. Technological and regulatory changes have lead to an increased demand for radio spectrum use in Europe; for example, as a consequence of the introduction of private broadcasting, of mobile phone systems and of wireless multimedia services. Radio spectrum has rapidly become a valuable economic resource and the individual states which traditionally own and control this scarce resource are confronted with new challenges: how to divide this scarce resource in such a way that consumers and market players derive the maximum economic and social benefit from it. As the Commission indicates, this requires from states to choose between commercial and non-commercial users as well as between applicants wishing to provide similar services. For this, they have introduced new mechanisms, such as auctions (valuation by the highest bidder) and administrative pricing (administration driven valuation).[21]

European states which are to decide on the distribution of scarce goods like the radio spectrum over interested parties should always keep in mind the general requirements of EU law. This means that they should not discriminate between their own nationals and nationals of other EU states and that they should not distort competition by giving undue privileged treatment to public or publicly financed organisations which may compete with private market players. Transparency, non-discrimination and equality of access are keywords in this matter.

A common framework for general authorisations and individual licences in the field of telecommunications services

In 1997, the EU member states agreed a common framework for general authorisations and individual licences in the field of telecommunications services as they adopted a 'Licensing Directive'.[22] This directive allows administrations to charge additional fees above those covering additional costs where operators use frequency bands of the radio spectrum in which scarcity can be shown. The idea is that this would enhance efficiency in the use of radio spectrum. The Commission, however, indicated that it considers it 'desirable that any fees charged by regulatory authorities should have an objectively demonstrable effect on the efficiency of radio spectrum use, rather than being used simply to fund public budgets.'[23] The Commission also indicated that although administrative pricing and auctioning of radio spectrum could be a means to ensure efficient use of radio spectrum, there was, at the same time, a need to clarify in which sectors 'such systems should or should not apply, so as to preserve other general principles while ensuring broadly comparable access to frequencies'.

Towards a common framework for electronic communications infrastructure and associated services

Satellite broadcasters and other providers of pan-European services indicated to the Commission that the introduction of new services at EU level is hampered by diverging national assignment and licensing practices; to prevent this, they argue, the harmonisation of national rules is not enough, since they would still have to acquire separate licences in every individual state. Therefore, the Commission announced measures to facilitate pan-European service provision in the form of a new regulatory framework for electronic communications infrastructure and associated services.[24] One of the main objectives of this new regulatory framework is to ensure the effective management of scarce resources, in particular radio spectrum. The common framework will be technology neutral and will cover all broadcast networks (terrestrial, satellite and cable). The licensing of broadcasters, insofar as the licensing provisions regulate content (i.e. programme prescriptions), is not covered by the proposed new framework; licensing with a view to content regulation will remain a prerogative of the member states (subject to their fundamental rights obligations). Moreover, EU law allows member states to choose the system on which basis they want to assign and license radio spectrum (i.e. broadcast infrastructure) as long as they, in exercising their powers, do not violate basic principles of EU law (such as non-discrimination and competition).

Access rights to essential facilities

Recommendation 99[1] (henceforth 99[1]), in order to safeguard and promote media pluralism, asked the member states to guarantee fair, transparent and non-discriminatory access to systems and services that are essential for digital broadcasting, providing for impartiality for basic navigation systems and empowering regulatory authorities to prevent abuses. Especially, member states are to consider maintaining 'must carry' rules for cable networks and to envisage similar rules for other distribution means and delivery platforms (i.e. packages of digital programme services). Such policies are not new for the EU states. Fair, transparent and non-discriminatory access to systems and services that are essential for digital broadcasting, providing for impartiality for basic navigation systems are already required on the basis of EU law and it is already the Commission's policy to prevent abuses.

If an undertaking controls access to distribution systems, typically associated with the TV set-top 'black box' decoder (conditional access systems – CAS) but also with control of the cable system, competitors depend on this undertaking for the distribution of their services and it would be difficult for them to get access. Under EU law, therefore, 'gateway' monopolies are to be prevented,[25] even if they offer an open encryption system.[26]

Programme requirements

Recommendation 99[1] states that, in order to protect media pluralism, the member states include, in their licensing conditions for broadcasters, provisions which require that a certain volume of original programmes, in particular as regards news and current affairs, is produced or commissioned by broadcasters. However, such programme requirements may indirectly have an impact on trade between the EU states and may therefore be subject to EU law requirements. For example, a requirement in an EU state that a minimum percentage of the programmes broadcast by a broadcaster must have been originally produced in the national language of the state concerned, may be considered as harmful for the freedom of movement of (broadcasting) services, especially if the geographical area in which the language concerned is spoken is relatively small: if, for example, the Netherlands would introduce such a requirement, only producers in the Netherlands and possibly the Flemish Community of Belgium would be able to profit from the requirement. France has in fact introduced such a requirement: in France, 60 per cent of the programmes broadcast by French broadcasters must have been originally produced in the French language. The

French language area within Europe is, however, much bigger than the Dutch language area and there are many producers outside France which can produce programmes in the French language.

Despite all this, even if such a programme requirement would have an impact on the functioning of the internal market, this might nevertheless be justifiable under EU law on the basis of the argument that the restriction on the freedom of movement is based on the general interest of protecting media pluralism (see above). The latter, however, is no longer possible if such programme require-ments have been the subject of harmonisation at the EU level. At the EU level, national laws, regulations and administrative actions concerning the pursuit of television broadcasting activities, have been harmonised by means of the 'Television without Frontiers' Directive.[27] This directive contains minimum rules for television broadcasting services. Consequently, EU states can no longer argue that at the national level, stricter rules which apply indiscriminately to national and foreign broadcasting services, in the areas which are harmonised by the directive, are necessary for general interest reasons.[28] The EU state in which a television broadcasting service is established is under the obligation to ensure that the minimum requirements of the directive are respected by the broad-casting services which come under its jurisdiction.[29] An individual state retains the right to impose stricter requirements, but only upon domestic broadcasting services.

Programme networking

Recommendation 99[1] also states that the member states ensure in particular that networking, understood as the centralised provision of programmes and related services, does not endanger pluralism. It is certainly true that the centralised provision of programmes and related services may undermine the local or regional character of broadcasting services. There is nothing under EU law which prohibits national licensing policies requiring (a minimum of) regional or local content from broadcasting services. As indicated above, the EU 'Television without Frontiers' Directive provides a minimum harmonisation of national rules concerning the pursuit of television broadcasting services, but an individual state retains the right to impose stricter requirements upon domestic broadcasting services; therefore, states retain the right to prohibit networking arrangements between their national or regional broadcasting services.

Public broadcasting systems

Recommendation 99[1] states that measures should be taken to maintain public service broadcasting and to allow it to develop. In this regard, a problem under EU law might arise in cases where public broadcasters would compete with private broadcasters, for example for broadcasting rights or for advertising revenues. However, as the Commission indicated in one of its merger deci-sions, the fact that public broadcasters – unlike private broadcasters – have a

guaranteed source of revenue from the licence fees does not necessarily constitute a competitive advantage, not even if the public broadcasters gain additional
revenues from the broadcasting of advertising: the level of staff, and hence over-
head costs of public broadcasters are much higher than those of private
broadcasters and, at the same time, the constraints on the public broadcasters
resulting from their public mission and their organisational structure would
render it much more difficult for them to provide a programme environment on
a permanent basis which is particularly attractive for the advertising industry.
Nevertheless, in cases of mixed financing of public broadcasters by public and
private means (especially from advertising revenues), the Commission may
sooner or later come to the conclusion that in a particular case, there is unfair
competition.[31]

State aid

Support measures for both existing and newly established print and broadcast
media, in particular at the regional and local levels, are recommended by 99[1]
as means to safeguard and promote media pluralism. The Council of Europe
Committee of Ministers developed criteria for granting such support (objectivity;
impartiality; transparency; independent control; periodic reconsideration).

If the public means provided for the financing of public broadcasters would
be regarded as state aid, there would be a problem under EU law for the reason
that state aid is only possible if notified to and accepted by the Commission.
However, given past decisions by the Commission, the case law of the ECJ and a
protocol attached to the Treaty of Amsterdam 1997, it seems unlikely that
providing public financing for public broadcasters will be regarded as illegal state
aid. Moreover, it has been the Commission's policy to authorise national state aid
measures if these measures favour the industry. Despite this, the Commission
sees to it that the support measures do not excessively affect interstate trade and
that the terms under which a right to state aid is granted do not discriminate
against citizens of other member states. Making the granting of aid dependent
on the nationality of the person asking support is deemed to be discriminating,
as the Greeks experienced in 1988 because of their system of support for their
national film industry.[32]

Many European states have some system of aid to the press. In general terms,
the Commission permits this, while mainly press publications are published in
different member states without being in competition with each other.[33] This is
because of language and cultural barriers. However, the support must be limited
in time, necessary and proportional to the said economic and cultural objective.
Under the Treaty on European Union 1993 signed at Maastricht, state aid
measures to promote culture and heritage conservation are explicitly permitted
where such measures do not affect trading conditions and competition in the
Community to an extent that is contrary to the common interest. This is, in fact,
a codification of policies already introduced by the Commission and the ECJ.

Pluralism in the changing technological and economic environment

The Committee of Ministers noted in 99[1] that the establishment of dominant positions and the development of media concentrations might be furthered by the technological convergence between the broadcasting, telecommunications and ICT sectors. Furthermore, it noted that there are bottlenecks in the area of new communication technologies and services such as control over CAS for digital television services. The Commission, in its merger decisions, already decided on a number of occasions that proprietary CAS should be open to other, competing service providers so that consumers do not need to buy separate systems for each digital programme package which they want to receive.[34]

New digital technologies make it possible for private undertakings to control access by the public to media services and consequently also access by the public to what is being broadcast by these media services. There is a risk that this may lead to 'gateway monopolies'. Private undertakings which have the possibility to determine (by means of CAS) who will have access to a certain set of programmes, and under which conditions, have a competitive advantage over other suppliers of media services who also have an interest in reaching a certain audience, albeit perhaps for different non-commercial reasons (especially governments, political parties, etc.). There is a risk that the new private CAS may be monopolized.[35]

New digital technologies also make it possible to put an end to the scarcity of radio spectrum frequencies. On each frequency which is used for the analogue broadcasting of a programme service, at least ten digital programme broadcasting services can be offered together with a number of radio programme services and other (multimedia- and data-) services. Furthermore, it will soon be possible, thanks to the development of a new generation of mobile wireless communication systems for the supply of broadband multimedia services (UMTS), to offer, through a normal telephone line, all kinds of multimedia services (including television programme services) Internet and other services based upon the Internet Protocol (IP) and the capacity of fibre optics cables will increase dramatically over the years to come.

Recent Council of Europe developments on media pluralism and access

As one of the consequences of the developments outlined above, the discussions on how to protect media pluralism are gradually shifting in the direction of problems such as:

- What constitutes broadcasting nowadays?
- Will licensing policies in the near future, once frequency scarcity belongs to the past, still be justifiable?

- What is to be done with the diversity in mutually incompatible private CAS which have come to development in Europe?
- Which rules should be imposed on the control over subscriber management systems (i.e. the computer system which manages subscriptions, invoicing, telephone-answering, statistics, etc.) and over subscriber access systems (i.e. software which makes it possible to provide or withdraw access to or from subscribers to pay-TV services);
- Should a cable operator have the right to un-bundle programme packages offered by a broadcasting service provider?[36]
- Which consequences follow for programme services which have not been included in the marketing package of the major players in the market?

Not a single European country has yet come to a final conclusion with regard to these new questions. Therefore, the Council of Europe assigned a 'Group of Specialists on media pluralism' with the task of examining the overall impact of the new communications and information technologies and services on media pluralism. In so doing, the group will:

1   analyse, in particular, to what extent the strategies and alliances developed between the traditional media and other undertakings in the communications, information and telecommunications sectors have an impact on media pluralism as a result of:
    (a)   the technological convergence of broadcasting, telecommunications and informatics,
    (b)   the globalisation of the markets, the networks and the activities of enterprises,
    (c)   the economic and social impact of the Global Information Society, in particular on the consumption of the products of the traditional media by the public;
2   examine the question of the acquisition and exercise of exclusivity rights by the media in the digital environment;
3   study the preconditions for analogue switch-off from the point of view of media pluralism;
4   analyse the different regulatory regimes which might be appropriate to ensure an adequate level of media pluralism.

On the basis of its analysis, the Group of Specialists is to formulate proposals for policy, legal or other measures which it considers necessary or desirable, whether at the national level or at the level of the Council of Europe, to secure media pluralism in the Global Information Society.

A further group was established which is studying the legal consequences of the development of digital distribution of traditional as well as different types of new communication and information services. The latter group is to advise on the necessity of adjusting existing legal frameworks and will make proposals for policy or legal instruments which are capable of guaranteeing effectively everyone's fundamental right to freedom of expression in this changing environment. The group is specifically examining

1   what would be the most appropriate legal framework and the most appropriate procedures for the future establishment of broadcasting services and new communication and information services, as well as the question of the possible need for a monitoring or regulatory authority, its competencies and monitoring tools;
2   the possible need for regulating the establishment of digital gateways, especially by means of specific requirements for CAS and electronic programme guides for digital television or for search and navigation instruments for online services;
3   the possibility of applying national rules and regulations and problems as regards the determination of a country's jurisdiction in a transfrontier context.

In conclusion, what will be seen in the near future is that the discussion on how to safeguard and promote media pluralism in order to protect the democratic process will shift from discussions on how to safeguard and promote pluralism in traditional media (TV, radio and press) to how to prevent gateway monopolies, and to whether or not operators of digital platforms should be made subject to 'must-carry rules' in order to provide access for all. Rebalancing freedom versus access rights is the main challenge of policymakers in the Global Information Society.

Notes

*   Co-ordinator of International Research at the Institute for Information Law at the University of Amsterdam, Senior Co-ordinator Public and Regulatory Affairs at VECAI (the association of cable networks in the Netherlands) and adjunct Professor of Law at the New York Law School.
1   In Italy, for example, natural or legal persons or groups of natural or legal persons which have obtained a licence for either a national terrestrial broadcasting service, including the public broadcasting organisations, or for national encrypted television services broadcasting via terrestrial transmitters, are not allowed to collect more than 30 per cent of the total financial means which are available for all national television services broadcast via terrestrial transmitters together. The total available financial means include the means available from the collection of a licence fee to finance the public broadcasting system; revenues from the broadcasting of national and local advertising messages, teleshopping and programme sponsoring; contracts with public authorities (like, for example, the agreement between the public broadcaster RAI and the Italian parliament concerning the broadcasting of informative programmes on parliamentary matters and the live transmissions of parliamentary debates); pay-TV services; and the expenditure of media bureaux (which buy advertising space from different media outlets and sell this space to advertisers or their agencies).
2   The Council of Europe is an intergovernmental organisation which was established in 1949 and which currently has forty-one member states. The seat of the organisation is Strasbourg (France).

3 Council of Europe (1999) *Explanatory Memorandum to Recommendation no. R (99) 1 on Measures to Promote Media Pluralism*, paras 3 and 4.

4 Ibid.

5 See, for example: Council of Europe (1998) *Recommendations and Declarations of the Committee of Ministers in the Media Field*, DH-MM (98) 2; Council of Europe (1997) *Recommendations and Resolutions adopted by the Parliamentary Assembly of the Council of Europe in the Media Field*, DH-MM (97) 3; Council of Europe (1998) European Ministerial Conferences on Mass Media Policy: Texts adopted', DH-MM (98) 4; and the decisions by the European Court of Human Rights concerning Article 10, http://www.dhcour.coe.fr.

6 In the US referred to as 'cable systems'.

7 Article 3 (c) EC.

8 Case 4/73 *Nold* v. *Commission* [1974] ECR 491, paragraph 13; Case 353/89 of 25 July 1991, *Commission* v. *Kingdom of the Netherlands* [1991] ECR I-4069; Case 288/89 of 25 July 1991, *Stichting Collectieve Antennevoorziening Gouda and others* v. *Commissariaat voor de Media* [1991] ECR I-4007.

9 'The application of national provisions to providers of services established in other Member States must be such as to guarantee the achievement of the intended aim and not go beyond that which is necessary in order to achieve it. Therefore it must not be possible to achieve the same result by less restrictive rules.'

10 See also: Commission of the European Communities, *Commission Communication on services of general interest in Europe*, 11 September 1996, COM(96)443 final.

11 *Pluralism and Media Concentration in the Internal Market. An Assessment of the Need for Community Action*, Commission Green Paper, Brussels 23 December 1992, COM(92)480 final.

12 *Follow-up to the consultation process relating to the Green Paper on 'Pluralism and Media Concentration in the Internal Market – An assessment of the need for Community action'*, Brussels 5 October 1994, COM(94) 353 final.

13 See: Decision in case NN 141/95, 'IRIS – Legal Observations of the European Audiovisual Observatory', 1995–9: 12.

14 Eventually, Commissioner Monti's proposals turned out not to be feasible from a political point of view. Despite the fact that the Commission considered his proposals on a number of occasions, it never came to a formal proposal by the Commission. This seems to have been the result of effective lobbying against such a proposal by European publishers led by the British Granada/BSkyB consortium.

15 See: 'IRIS – Legal Observation of the European Audiovisual Observatory': 1995–9: 12.

16 The informal proposals which circulated, by the way, did not refer to 'owners' of media undertakings but rather to 'controllers'. According to the Commission, whether or not a legal or natural person or a group of legal or natural persons controlled an undertaking, could be assessed on the basis of the 'Commission Notice on the concept of concentration under Council Regulation (EEC) no. 4064/89 on the control of concentrations between undertakings' (*OJEC* of 2 March 1998 no. C 66: 5–13.). According to this notice, taking control may occur on a legal or a *de facto* basis. National authorities would have had to make an analysis on a case-by-case basis to determine which legal or natural persons or groups of legal or natural persons were in control over media outlets involved in a concentration operation. For this, they could have based themselves upon the guidelines given by this Commission notice.

17 As is actually a possible measure under German broadcasting law.

18 Council Regulation (EEC) no. 4064/89 of 21 December 1989 'on the control of concentrations between undertakings', *OJEC* of 30 December 1989 no. L 395: 1; 'Corrigendum to Council Regulation (EEC) no. 4064/89 of 21 December 1989 on the control of concentrations between undertakings', *OJEC* of 30 December 1990 no. L 395; 'Council Regulation (EC) no. 1310/97 of 30 June 1997 amending

Regulation (EEC) no. 4064/89 on the control of concentrations between undertakings', *OJEC* of 9 July 1997 no. L 180.

19 Case no. IV/M.423 – *Newspaper Publishing*, 13 March 1994.

20 Case no. IV/M.202 – *Thorn EMI/ Virgin Music*, 27 April 1992; Case no. IV/M.489 – *Bertelsmann/News International/Vox*, 6 September 1994; Zaak nr. IV/M.490 – *Nordic Satellite Distribution*, 19 July 1995, *PbEG* of 2 March 1996, no. L 53: 20–40; Zaak nr. IV/M.553 – *RTL/ Veronica/Endemol*, 20 September 1995, *PbEG* of 5 June 1996 no. L 134: 32–52; Affaire N IV/M.999 – *CLT-UFA/Havas Intermédiation*, 26 February 1998; Case no. IV/M.1219 – *Seagram/Polygram*, 21 September 1998.

21 *Towards a new framework for Electronic Communications infrastructure and associated services – The 1999 Communications Review*, Communication from the Commission to the European Parliament, the Council, the Economic and Social Committee and the Committee of the Regions, COM (1999) 539 final.

22 'Directive 97/13/EC of the European Parliament and of the Council of 10 April 1997 on a common framework for general authorizations and individual licences in the field of telecommunications services', *OJEC* 1997 no. L 117: 15.

23 *Towards a new framework for Electronic Communications Infrastructure and associated services. The 1999 Communications Review*; Communication from the Commission to the European Parliament, the Council, the Economic and Social Committee and the Committee of the Regions, COM (1999) 539: 35–6.

24 Ibid.

25 Case no. IV/M.490 – *Nordic Satellite Distribution*, 19 July 1995, *OJEC* 02 March 1996 Nr. L 053: 20–40; Case no. IV/M.993 – *Bertelsmann/Kirch/Premiere*, 27 May 1998, IP/98/477; Case no. IV/M.1027 – *Deutsche Telekom/Betaresearch*, 27 May 1998, IP/98/477; Case no. IV/M.856 – *British Telecom/MCI (II)*, 14 May 1997. *OJEC* 8.12.1997 nr. L 336: 1–15.

26 In an open encryption system, decoders are available from many sources and the consumer can, with the same decoder, receive TV channels in different open systems by using different smart cards. Any broadcaster for a minor payment can acquire the right from the owner to use such an open system; in a closed encryption system, only broadcasters signing an agreement with the owner of the system are allowed to encrypt in this system. Such an agreement includes a right for a particular oper- ator to administrate the subscriber management system and, thus, prevents other operators from using the system. The households would have to buy or rent addit- ional decoders if they want to receive TV channels which are encrypted in other systems.

27 'Council Directive 89/552/EEC of 3 October 1989 on the co-ordination of certain provisions laid down by Law, Regulation or Administrative Action in Member States concerning the pursuit of television broadcasting activities', *OJEC* of 17 October 1989 no. L 298:23–30 as amended by 'Directive 97/36/EC of the European Parliament and of the Council of 30 June 1997 amending Council Directive 89/552/EEC on the co-ordination of certain provisions laid down by law, regulation or administrative action in Member States concerning the pursuit of television broad-casting activities', *OJEC* of 30 July 1997 no. L 202 : 60–71.

28 The directive does not harmonise all aspects of television broadcasting services. The harmonisation concerns the promotion of distribution and production of television programmes in the way that member states shall ensure where practicable and by appropriate means, that broadcasters reserve for European works; television adver-tising and sponsoring; the protection of minors; the right of reply. The directive stipulates that member states shall not restrict retransmissions on their territory of television broadcasts from other member states for reasons which fall within the fields coordinated by this directive.

It remains possible to restrict retransmissions of television broadcasts from other member states for reasons which do not fall within the fields coordinated by this directive. Such restrictions should then result from the desire to protect a general interest; they should not discriminate between the state's own nationals and those from other EU states, etc. The protection of copyright, frequency distribution, policies and access rules are examples of fields which are not coordinated by the directive, although in the meantime, especially in the field of copyright law but also in the field of access, separate directives have been adopted or are under preparation.

29 The criteria to decide which member state has jurisdiction over which television broadcaster are laid down in Paragraph 3 of Article 2 of the revised directive. Paragraph 4 of Article 2 stipulates in which cases a member state is deemed to have jurisdiction over a television broadcaster to which the criteria of the third paragraph are not applicable. Finally, paragraph 5 stipulates that if the question as to which member state has jurisdiction cannot be determined in accordance with paragraphs 3 and 4, the competent member state shall be that in which the broadcaster is established within the meaning of Articles 52 and following of the EC Treaty.

30 Case no. IV/M.553 – *RTL/ Veronica/ Endemol*, 20 September 1995, *OJEC* of 5 June 1996 no. L 134: 32–52.

31 When broadcasters financed wholly or partially by public means are also very active in merchandising and publishing, they may come into conflict with private sector publishers. The BBC, for example, came into conflict with major publishers because it uses its airtime to promote magazines published by its subsidiary BBC Enterprises Ltd. The publishers reckoned that there was unfair competition, since the BBC has the possibility of promoting its own publications in its radio and television programmes (and is at the same time not allowed to promote publications from other publishers (see: Monopolies and Mergers Commission (1992) *Television Broadcasting Services. A report on the publishing, in the course of supplying a television broadcasting service, of goods supplied by the broadcaster*, Cm 2035, London: HMSO).

32 'Dec. of 21 December 1988 on aid granted by the Greek Government to the film industry for the production of Greek films', *OJEC* of 20 July 1989, no. L 208: 38–41. See also: 'Notice pursuant to Article 93 (3) of Council Regulation No 17 concerning a notification in case no. IV/31.734 – Film purchases by German television stations', *OJEC* of 3 March 1989, no. C 54: 3.

33 See: 'The answer of the Commission of the European Communities to Written Questions – no. 753/76 on aid to the press by Mr Guerlin on 6 January 1977', *OJEC* no. C 64:24; 'no. 2541/87 on postage rates applying to newspapers by Mr Roberto Cicciomessere, Mrs Emma Bonino and Mr Marco Pannella on 2 March 1988', *OJEC* no. C 263: 26–7. See also: 'l'Application des règles de concurrence communautaires au secteur audiovisuel', speech delivered by Monique Aubel, chief administrator at the Commission of the European Communities – Directorate General IV, during the 'Journées internationales d'IDATE' in Montpellier, November 1990.

34 *Nordic Satellite Distribution*; *Bertelsmann/ Kirch/ Premiere*; *Deutsche Telekom/ BetaResearch*; *British Telecom/ MCI(II)*.

35 This has been attempted in Germany by Leo Kirch and in Spain by *Canal plus*. In Spain, the attempt resulted in government interference: the government determined which type of decoder should be used. However, *Canal plus* successfully complained about this government interference: the European Commission informed the Spanish government that it would not accept such interference for the reason that the chosen decoder system was the system used by a provider which was in direct competition with *Canal plus*: the Spanish telecommunication company *Telefonica*.

36 *An approach towards a possible Commission Recommendation on 'Unbundled Access to the Local Loop'*, European Commission, DG XIII, Information Society Working Document on Unbundled Access to the Local Loop, 9 February 2000, http://europa.eu.int/comm /information_society/policy/telecom/localloop/pdf/ working_en.pdf.

16 Pluralism, guidance and the new media

Thomas Gibbons

There is a sentiment being consolidated in discussion of new forms of media that the removal of problems that bottlenecks pose for media pluralism will satisfy democratic concerns about the function of the media. Elimination of bottlenecks, it is said, will provide an environment where such pluralism can flourish and thereby ensure that a wide range of materials can be made available to audiences and readerships. In this chapter, I will argue that, on the contrary, if the democratic potential of the media – or, indeed, communications more generally – is really valued, then the creation or preservation of some kinds of bottlenecks will be essential. That is because the securing of media pluralism is only a necessary but not sufficient condition for realising such democratic potential. The constriction in the flow of information that 'bottleneck' implies is not itself the issue. Rather, it is the uses to which the constriction may be put that raise the significant questions for regulatory design. Furthermore, the fact that these issues have generally been explored in relation to the more traditional mass media does not make them less relevant in the developing global information setting.

Democracy and the media

The democratic potential of the media has had a significant influence on media regulation policy. One of the more powerful justifications for giving special protection to freedom of speech is that it enables electorates to discuss governments' policies and actions and render them accountable, by providing the greatest opportunity for differing points of view to be aired and by encouraging sufficient information to be available for making policy choices. From the speaker's perspective, the media can provide platforms for communicating points of view more effectively to a large readership or audience and they can also offer opportunities for direct dialogue with other speakers. Since access to the media is relatively limited, however, it is principally the audience (for present purposes, including readerships) that appreciates their democratic value (Barendt 1985: 23–6). In a direct way, the media provide an information resource and they provide a means of accessing speakers' messages and policy discussion. More indirectly, the media may choose to adopt a 'watchdog' role in which they act on behalf of citizens to bring politicians to account (see McQuail 1996; Curran 1996; Keane 1991). Generally, the free speech principle supports a presumption that the democratic interests of both speakers and audiences are best served by not regulating the media, either through restraints over content or by special controls over their economic arrangements. In that way, it may be said, the greatest opportunities are provided for encouraging a free flow of information and opinion. There are, however, two reasons advanced to suggest that the presumption may be overcome, each directed at conflicts that may arise between speakers and audiences. One is that freedom of speech itself entails that a basic amount of information should be available – for speakers to speak about. On this view, a right to be informed is considered necessary to enhance the worth of any speaker's statements and is regarded as justifying some restriction on media content if that makes room for a wider variety of fact and opinion. There are hints of such an approach in some European and United States constitutional doctrine (Craufurd Smith 1997: 152–64). However, unless the speaker's freedom is considered sacrosanct, it seems unnecessary to reconcile two opposing themes within one principle. Instead, some kinds of free speech interest may be considered more important than others. A second reason for regulation in this context is that it may actually advance one of the objectives that the free speech principle aims to secure – democratic discussion and participation – to ensure that the audience can choose freely from a wide variety of sources.

A separate principle of media pluralism, therefore, recognises that journalists and broadcasters control an important cultural and political resource and suggests that the free speech interests of the audience should be given priority when assessing the use to which the media are put (Gibbons 1998: 30). It reflects a belief that democratic participation will not be promoted by mere non-interference with media controllers. That will simply give them the liberty to dominate the means of communication, at the expense of other citizens. Media pluralism requires regulation to ensure that there is a 'multiplicity of voices' (Fiss 1987; Lichtenberg 1987) available to the audience. At the least, this will provide an information resource and, ideally, it may encourage the media to serve as a forum for public debate. For some commentators, the media are well placed to take on the function of a 'public sphere' where there is free, equal and fully informed discussion without domination by particular groups or the state (Curran 1996; Garnham 1986 and this volume; Scannell 1989). But the media are already a central component of modern, complex democracies, channelling ideas and opinions in parallel with formal constitutional arrangements. It is important, therefore, that they promulgate a sufficient range of views, to reduce the chance of significant ideas being eclipsed by those of more powerful voices. Insofar as individuals use the media as the principal sources of information external to their own experience, it is necessary to ensure that media sources do not exclude alternative sources. For the democratic reason of promoting media pluralism, then, it may be justifiable to restrict the speech of editors, journalists or media controllers. In fact, the European Court of Human Rights has recognised as much in holding that, although Article 10 (safeguarding freedom of expression) does not insist on regulation to promote media pluralism, where a government decides that such measures will be introduced, they may be regarded as a legitimate restriction on the free speech of those who might otherwise have used the media (*Informationsverein Lentia* v. *Austria* (1994) *European Human Rights Reports* 17: 93).

Whatever the status of media pluralism, it should not be assumed that its relevance is confined to pure information. Plurality is especially important in the field of news and current affairs (Goldberg *et al.* 1998: 19) but it applies equally to entertainment (Hoffman-Riem 1996: 298). While democratic debate is especially dependent on the priorities identified by politicians in their immediate political agendas, any kind of knowledge that is relevant to policy-making will raise pluralist concerns. This will include social and cultural material and, importantly, extends beyond the intellectual sphere to popular culture. Whatever prompts comment or action is central to political argument and democratic participation. Extending the audience's access to such material information is therefore to be encouraged.

Variations on media pluralism

Although the concept of media pluralism is widely accepted to be a major manifestation of the democratic interest in the media, there is less agreement about the appropriate way to incorporate it into media practice. One approach is known as external pluralism. It involves plurality or diversity (the expressions are typically interchanged) in the source of material. This means that such material is supplied by a variety of programme or information producers, editors or owners. External pluralism is achieved, therefore, by creating structural safeguards to encourage the system, taken as a whole, to provide a range of different services. One way of implementing such a structure is to rely on general competition law and regulation to ensure that there are no barriers to entering media markets and to prevent dominant suppliers from abusing their position or monopolising media markets. Such a market model does not require content to be generated or published, and speakers are not forced into speaking. However, it is assumed that, given sufficient demand for media products, the environment will induce many suppliers to come forward. An alternative way of implementing external pluralism is to impose special rules on media ownership and control. Underlying this model, there is a concern that market pressures for mergers and consolidation will lead to a degree of concentration that is acceptable under competition rules but which places too much power, for democratic healthiness, in the hands of those who control channels for communication. Neither model can, however, guarantee that diversity of source will reflect diversity of content and, where that is considered important, a second approach may be adopted.

This other approach is known as internal pluralism. It reflects plurality or diversity of content more directly, requiring the substance of each media outlet's material to reflect a range of opinions and subject matter. Internal pluralism is a response to the needs of the whole audience or readership of each media entity, attempting to cater for the tastes and interests of all the individuals that comprise it. The structure of external pluralism does not prevent individual consumers from receiving most of their information from one provider. With internal pluralism, however, 'each broadcaster's programming palette gives coverage to the broad spectrum of positions and information important to society, that is, integrates these positions and information into its overall programming. The recipient is therefore offered a pluralistically balanced communications menu' (Hoffman-Riem 1996: 284). In Europe, public service broadcasting, with its objective of universality, has been a significant way of implementing such internal pluralism and the public broadcasters' responsibility for securing pluralism (Craufurd Smith 1997: 151–65) has been recognised in Italian and French constitutional law. Most notably, however, the German constitutional court has recognised the fundamental importance of mass communication for the free formation of public opinion and has required positive guarantees that citizens are provided with sufficient information to make social, cultural and political judgments. The existence of the German public service broadcasters is constitutionally protected, therefore, at least for so long as private broadcasters do not provide a comparable comprehensive range of programming (Barendt 1993: 58). This kind of thinking has also influenced the development of media policy in the United Kingdom where it has been accepted that the BBC's public service functions should be preserved alongside the gradual deregulation of other parts of the sector (Home Office 1988: para. 3.2; Department of National Heritage 1995: para. 1.4).

For all that it reflects an important role for the media, however, the use of the term 'media pluralism' appears only to have gained prominence in the debates about deregulation in Europe that started in the 1980s and quickly developed in the 1990s. Although the kind of diversity that has come to be associated with pluralism was first articulated by the Annan committee, in the United Kingdom, in the late 1970s (Gibbons 1998: 59), and in Italian and German doctrine around the same time (Craufurd Smith 1997: 151–65 ; Barendt 1993: 58), it was in policy-making responses to the expansion of commercial broadcasting that the idea of media pluralism began to be articulated more fully. This may have been because governments and media companies were being forced to reappraise any contribution that public service broadcasting might be making to society. I suggest, however, that media pluralism was not promoted for the purpose of supporting a more democratic role for the media, as might be supposed from its content. Instead, the idea was adopted as a transitional concept that conveniently assisted a shift from public service dominance to a market approach. The broad strategy was to identify the pluralistic aspects of public service and then to claim that they could be provided as effectively through competition. If it could be demonstrated that deregulation would not adversely affect the democratic potential of the media, there would be less need to make out a special case for public service broadcasting. Crucially, internal pluralism came to be regarded as nothing more than the public sector alternative to external pluralism, which was taken to be the market-based solution to pluralist concerns. This has had important implications, because it has encouraged the framing of the discussion about democratic regulation of the media as a reasonable difference of opinion about two different ways of achieving the same goal. In the fast-moving world of the new media, the enhanced diversity that is brought by new content, delivery platforms and digital technology appears actually to correct any problems of market failure that might have existed previously.

Media guidance and pluralism

However it is implemented, the advantages of pluralism for a democratic media are readily apparent. Yet it is misleading to think that media pluralism has been sufficient, either theoretically or historically, to satisfy democratic demands on the media. It is worth stressing, again, that a diversity of media sources will not necessarily produce a wide range of media content. But even a stronger version of pluralism, one that attempts more directly to secure a broad range of material for citizens' evaluation and choice, will be inadequate. The most that pluralism can do is to make the media available as an information resource. The larger that resource becomes, the more Herculean the task that the citizen has to undertake to keep abreast of all relevant data and to relate different parts of it to one another. The problem is not, however, simply that of 'information overload', whereby the sheer magnitude of material induces a helplessness and inability to act. Certainly, that would be unhealthy for democracy but it would be equally undesirable if the individual's attempts to manage his or her information needs led to a one-sided appreciation of the issues surrounding any policy question. For individuals to participate more fully in the democratic process, they require guidance about the context of information and ideas and the relationship between that subject matter and questions about which they wish to form judgments. A basic element of the democratic concept is that there should be *engagement* between policy choices. This applies to all conceptions of democracy, whether there is minimal citizen participation, such as Schumpeterian, at one end of a spectrum, or more direct involvement in debate and decision-making at the other, such as deliberative (Gutmann and Thompson 1996). Whatever the form, the media have an important role to play, whether they contribute to the simple focusing of issues that is required to cast a vote, even in the minimalist conception, or, quite literally, provide a forum for such engagement to take place. It is important to note that guidance of this kind is not the same, however, as editorialising or interpreting events for the audience, both of which entail media intervention in the substance of policy discussion. Rather, it is the facilitative role of the media that is being stressed here, in providing a range of material that can be compared and contrasted on the same platform and related to itself. It is a role that, in its public service manifestation, has been described as 'integration programming' (Hoffman-Riem 1996: 284).

It may be asked why individuals should feel entitled to have the media perform this function for them in a democracy. Responsible citizens, it might be said, will take responsibility for seeking out sufficient information for them to arrive at an appropriate conclusion. Furthermore, advanced democracies tend to adopt sophisticated methods of representative government so as to reduce the burdens of direct decision-making on citizens. The response to such objections depends on the assumption that the media are no longer optional extras but are constitutive parts of the modern societies and the democratic process (Thompson 1995). When audiences have no realistic 'reasonable' prospect of finding alternative views very easily or cheaply, they do not have the opportunity to exercise their democratic responsibilities adequately unless the media themselves provide it. In addition, there may be welfare gains in requiring material to be made more easily available rather than forcing individuals to look for it. Not least, it may be important to have information made available without it being requested where such requests depend on knowing of its existence. Furthermore, in relation to representative government, citizens will continue to require an informed basis for calling their politicians to account and for choosing to redefine the political agenda. In respect of media guidance, the question is what realistic opportunities exist for the citizen to discover alternative perspectives.

Historically, the guiding function of the media has been most strongly associated with public service broadcasting in European systems. Although such systems were established in a tradition of state responsibility for (or interference in) communications, there is a strong strand of democratic reasoning in their continued justification. This emphasises some of the early rationales for public service broadcasting, such as universality and trusteeship of the airwaves for the general public, together with a keen awareness of the political power of the media, reflected in notions such as impartiality and balance (see Gibbons 1998: 55–64). However, accompanying the emergence of the idea of media pluralism, described earlier, the democratic dimension of public service broadcasting has only come to the fore in more recent discussion of media regulation policy, prompted mainly by the challenges that the new media have made to its previously protected position. Its democratic potential became more appreciated as pressures to deregulate prompted re-assessment of earlier, more paternalistic, rationales. This does not render that democratic dimension less valid, of course. While it has been associated with some distrust of the capacity of the market model to generate a sufficient range of ideas for democratic consideration, it is based on positive benefits of the guiding function of the media. As Hoffman-Riem has put it,

> Clearly, faith in market forces is blanketed not only by fear of market failure but also by the view that too much is being asked of viewers if they are expected to consume all competing programs in order to achieve a balanced supply of information.
>
> (Hoffman-Riem 1996: 299)

Unfortunately, this insight has not been carried forward in discussion of broader, contemporary media policy. In regarding external pluralism as the counterpart of internal pluralism, the guiding role of the media that is reflected in – but that is not the same as – internal pluralism has been overlooked. The implication is that the democratic potential dimension of the media will not be fulfilled merely through the enhanced diversity of source that is likely to emerge in the new media environment.

The implications for new media

The term 'new media' is a convenient way of describing a set of developing media characteristics that may be distinguished from features of the traditional press and broadcasting sectors. It represents a proliferation of cable and satellite channels, a movement from free-to-air to subscription services, the provision of some interactivity between providers and consumers and, increasingly, a convergence between delivery platforms induced by digitalisation of content. Significantly, the segmenting of media markets and the creation of market-based relationships accompany these tendencies. In principle, audiences will be able to choose the combinations of content, scheduling and method of delivery that they prefer. Implicitly, it is assumed there will be access to a diversity of content over differing platforms, ranging across broadcasting, telecommunications and the Internet.

In this new environment, there will continue to be a need to encourage the democratic potential of the media by maintaining media pluralism as a policy objective. Individuals will continue to require opportunities to discover a variety of contents and the trend to convergence will not lessen the importance of that objective. However, I have suggested elsewhere (Gibbons 1999) that the current special rules about media ownership will no longer be suitable to achieve it. The regulatory response will need to address the fact that, with convergence of platforms, the focus of value will move up the chain towards production of content. Distribution systems, being more or less converged, will not be capable of maintaining a premium over their rivals, so that the key issues will become conditional access to such distribution systems and to the creation of content or acquisition of rights. In such a scenario, the regulatory aim will be to ensure that too few providers do not dominate the supply of programme and information content. A regime analogous to competition regulation would be most appropriate here, but one that used behaviour (conduct) based analysis to determine the audience's experience of diversity of source. Such a regime would not, of course, necessarily produce such diversity and it could be supplemented with quota requirements to encourage a variety of strands of material to be available. However, although the provision of public service broadcasting and Internet services would enhance pluralism, it would not be appropriate to rely on them, partly because they contain only one particular view of diversity and partly because they will not necessarily be wanted or received by all sectors of the audience.

This latter point reflects possible difficulties in securing pluralism but it also highlights the drawback of relying on a pluralism regime alone to encourage democratic participation through new forms of media. The very diversity of such media is actually a potential barrier to participation. Audiences are likely to become increasingly segmented and separated from other audiences, so that opportunities for engagement are increasingly curtailed. This may happen where individuals subscribe to only one, mass-appeal channel. Its revenue-driven theme will not cater for minority or niche interests but its competitive edge over rivals will make it an attractive economic proposition for the consumer. Alternatively, individuals may subscribe to one or more niche channels that specialise in a relatively narrow theme. The prospect of individuals knowing of the existence of much of the material more widely available, let alone surveying it, is highly unlikely.

Trends in new media may, consequently, shift their role away from the democratic. The opportunities that are opened up for almost unlimited access – less so in the case of programming channels but quite possible in the case of the Internet – give the impression of enhancing democracy because they allow everybody a voice. But what they would really do is to correct a libertarian deficit in the old media, whereby freedom to speak was effectively curtailed by limitations on access to the media. They would not address the democratic deficit that arises when voices cannot be heard in circumstances where that matters for decision-making. If it is acknowledged that some form of deliberative democracy (Gutmann and Thompson 1996) is better than more indirect ways of representing individuals' interests, it is implicit that citizens should have the opportunity to talk to one another.

In the age of new media, the question is how far that talking should take place in or through the media. Prior to the development of broadcasting, the press and publishing industries tended to supplement the formal arrangements for democratic debate. But contemporary media are much more active in setting agendas and enabling politicians to engage with each other. If the new media do herald an era of 'electronic publishing' (Home Office 1986: para. 131), it will be more than a different technological slant on an old practice. It may be that at least some parts of the media are well placed to take on the function of a 'public sphere' whether it manifests itself as a forum – ideally, for free, equal and fully informed discussion without domination by particular groups or the state – or whether it represents no more than a common point of access for discovering others' perspectives. In either case, a public space would be established, virtual rather than physical, where information could be exchanged and discussed. Not only would that enhance democratic experience, it would also bring the benefits of shared knowledge that make cultural cohesion possible (Gibbons 1998: 62). Indeed, the multiplicity of channels and other outlets in the new media make it all the more urgent that such a public space should be maintained (Price 1995b: 67). Clearly, if such a virtual space were to exist, it would be important to provide signposts to its location and provide a map of its layout. Whether or not it exists, however – and there may be reservations about allowing the media to rival parliamentary institutions – the same multiplicity of channels and outlets would necessitate guidance for individuals to the democratic information resources that the media supply. The issue, then, is whether – and how – regulation should be used to carve out such space in the new media.

Regulatory possibilities

A strong theme in recent discussion of media policy has been the belief that, because the more recent digital technology will absorb the earlier analogue, it will render older forms of regulation less relevant to new forms of media. In particular, the democratic interest in preserving media pluralism has been given a low profile. It has tended to be assumed, at the European level, that the thrust of policy reform will be to deregulate to a level where only competition law might constrain the new media (Commission of the European Communities 1997e: 1). In the United Kingdom, it has also been implied that the more that services come to resemble telecommunications rather than broadcasting, and especially if delivered over the Internet, the less regulation there should be (Department of Trade and Industry 1998). These sentiments are being driven by a technological determinism, on the one hand, and a jurisdictional pessimism, on the other. It is assumed that, since material can be bundled into discrete elements which can be marketed separately and which audiences can choose to obtain, the functions of the media will come to resemble any other consumer product. It is also assumed that, since communications now have such a prominent global character, regulatory enforcement will be almost impossible. The technological assumptions do not withstand much examination, because the public interest in media activity is not rendered less relevant by the media's form. The jurisdictional problems are more acute, however, and lend support to a greater willingness to adopt self-regulation as a way forward. In relation to the democratic potential of the media, I have suggested that there are persuasive reasons why that should be preserved and I have already indicated the possibilities that exist for preserving some degree of media pluralism. In this section, I consider possible ways of maintaining a guiding function for the media.

One approach would be to rely on public service provision, whether in broadcasting or on the Internet. Existing public service provision goes beyond a guiding function, aspiring as it does to taking responsibility for culture, minority interest and educational material. But it also plays a significant role in providing a balanced range of knowledge and providing informed analysis of issues in current affairs, arts and science. The need for this kind of provision is not restricted to programming services, since the capacity to interpret and make sense of the new world of information is also evident in so-called cyberspace. The value to the consumer of such provision is obvious from the high hit rate for the BBC's public website, BBC Online. But there is a public benefit in having such a common, shared fund of knowledge that can be employed by citizens in making fully informed choices, and that justifies public funding for the service. Nevertheless, to rely on the existence of public service provision is inadequate as a means of ensuring that media users will receive guidance about what is available. First, not everybody may use it. In the world of new media, public services will be one option to be chosen or ignored amongst many. However good they are at guiding audiences, they can only assist if they are themselves signposted. Second, public service provision typically entails a degree of editorial selection and mediation of content that may be worthy and desirable but may be more than is required to inform the citizen.

A better approach is to concentrate on the bottlenecks that will exist in the new media. Such bottlenecks represent the key points in the digital purchase and distribution of programming and information and, as such, they determine how access to the new media is achieved. Examples are set-top boxes that enable programming or information to be received by the consumer, subscriber management systems that deal with payment and authorisation to receive such material, and encryption services that may apply to the other two (see Marsden 2000b; Goldberg *et al.* 1998: 20, 307). Where access to programming and information is conditional – when access to digital services is restricted on the basis of technology and subscription – the companies that control that process are very significant 'gatekeepers' for the whole digital broadcasting industry. For regulatory policy, therefore, there is a general competition interest in ensuring that the gatekeepers do not gain complete control over access. Since the aim of such policy is to encourage a diversity of providers to be accessible to the consumer, it happens to coincide with the democratic interest in maintaining media pluralism through a diversity of source. Consequently, solving the problem of conditional access has been regarded as the solution to any media pluralism difficulties that may arise in the new media. Naturally, measures that have been adopted have concentrated on the supply end of the market, preventing restrictions on the potential availability of sources. Thus, the United Kingdom's conditional access guidelines (OFTEL 1997b), reflecting the European Directive on Television Standards (Commission of the European Communities 1995c), require that the provision of technical conditional access services in relation to television services should be offered on a 'fair, reasonable and non-discriminatory' basis. They also contain various provisions intended to secure fair trading, circulation of technical information whilst protecting commercial confidentiality, and the encouragement of a common interface to allow different systems to inter-operate (Gibbons 1998: 237).

Nevertheless, for the reasons mentioned earlier, such regulation can do no more than offer favourable conditions for an external form of media pluralism to develop. For the fuller democratic interest in guidance about the kind of information that will thereby become available, the focus must be on the consumer side of bottlenecks. In programming services, this means that the democratic significance of electronic programme guides (EPGs) should not be ignored. These perform a function similar to programme listings, in simply showing what is available, but they may also provide a means to access the material. Rather like a web-style interface, the list – or menu – may enable the choice of an item to activate directly a connection to the service and may also enable automatic payment by electronic subscription. In such cases, as is most likely, EPGs would also be conditional access systems. There are obviously many opportunities for unfair and anti-competitive practices to develop and these might be manifested, for example, in the order in which programmes are listed, the prominence given to brands or logos, the information supplied about programmes and the way that menus may be layered into different sub-menus. All these would be capable of affecting the viewer's choice, and adversely so if they highlighted or marginalised particular kinds of programming. Again, it is possible to see the problem as one of restricting the viewer's choice, of making some types of information effectively unavailable, and the code issued by the United Kingdom's Independent Television Commission (the ITC) has provisions that mirror the conditional access prohibitions on restricting, distorting or preventing competition (ITC 1997). But the code goes much further in requiring that free-to-air broadcasts, such as those of the BBC or Channels 3, 4 or 5, should be displayed on EPG menus in an easily accessible form which does not discriminate in favour of pay television services. Furthermore, due prominence should be given to public service channels, access to which should be no more difficult than other channels, and viewers should be able to obtain them without additional equipment or agreements and without being routed through pages containing details of pay services.

These kinds of provision offer a starting point to deal with issues of guidance but they are not entirely adequate because they do not supply a proper map of the kind of material that is available. Just as it is insufficient to rely on public service broadcasting itself, so it is insufficient merely to point to its existence in the hope that the problems of making sense of all the other media will be thereby compensated. The guidance function of the media requires a more interventionist undertaking to organise information flows for the viewer's benefit. This entails intelligent linking and cross-referencing between information sources and themes, rather than simple listing. Although programming services in the new media may not yet give much scope for such organisation, the value of guidance about Internet content is already apparent. Indeed, in a sense, its worth is not an issue for many Internet content providers who already structure the material they provide in terms of 'channels' or other themed groupings of material on 'portal' websites. It is the criteria for organising that material which may give rise to democratic concerns. When some sites are given priority over others, especially in return for payment, the user may be diverted from large portions of relevant information. It is not an answer to say that possible biases in portal sites can be corrected by a judicious use of search engines, because they can exacerbate the problem, whether by generating large, unmanageable and unsorted lists of links, or by suggesting spuriously related links. For the new media, programming or Internet, to fulfil a democratic function the significant point of constriction in the system – the EPGs and the portal sites – must take some responsibility for positively guiding the audience or users. The aim is to prevent individuals from gaining their information from a few sources, either because they are locked into one outlet/subscription or because they are seduced by other elements of the package. The ideal is to prevent bias or distortion by alerting the audience or user to other perspectives, so that they may look at matters from another point of view. Some sites already perform such a function, good examples being BBC Online or the Guardian Unlimited Network. A conditional access approach is not the solution because it takes effect at the point of supply, and therefore initial choice, whereas the democratic policy is to open up further choices.

Some objections will be made to this proposal to develop the EPG model as a basis for providing guidance in the new media. One is that it will be an interference with the free speech and property interests of content providers. The response is that the interference will be fairly minimal, but justified in the democratic interest. If the anxiety is about the compulsory nature of such guidance, the development of self-regulation may be an option to consider. Another objection is that not every provider should be subject to an obligation to provide guidance. This may be so in relation to small-scale operators. But where there is significant traffic channelled through an EPG or portal site, that would be sufficient to trigger a duty to provide a balanced set of choices. Yet another objection is that the provision of guidance amounts to editing, albeit minor, and that this creates other 'gateway' problems, familiar in the journalism literature (Schudson 1996), of selection and agenda-setting. This is true, and not to be glossed over as trivial, but the point is that existing arrangements for organising information flows are likely to give rise to even greater selection problems. Finally, it might be objected that this kind of regulation would not work in the new media precisely because their global character will render enforcement difficult or impossible. Again, without underestimating the problem, it may be replied that most programming will be physically connected to jurisdictions where, if the democratic policy is accepted, enforcement will be feasible. The greater difficulty is with the Internet because users may choose portal sites from anywhere on the web. Obviously, the point of first connection provides the opportunity to present an opening menu of information and that may point to the democratic obligation falling on the Internet service provider. However, in that case, if guidance is considered to entail editing, that might have to be given immunity to protect against actions for legal liability in respect of content.

Whatever the complexity of regulating for the new media, that in itself is not a ground for failing to consider whether the basis for dealing with the older media still applies. The values that justified such special treatment are primarily democratic and they are not rendered less relevant because the technology and the industry are developing so rapidly. Such change makes media policy vulnerable to the commercial demands of progress but that is just the situation where the social functions of the media should be considered more carefully. I have suggested that it is the very expansion of new forms of media that demonstrates the need for guidance to be more urgent. Fortunately, the solid tradition of media participation in democracy provides a basis for devising new ways of meeting that need.

17 Five challenges for regulating the Global Information Society

*Pamela Samuelson**

Introduction

Information technology (IT) is unquestionably having a profound effect on many aspects of the social, cultural, economic, and legal systems of planet Earth.[1] IT has enabled significant advances in global communications technologies, particularly the Internet, that make it more possible than ever before to contemplate the development of a Global Information Society.[2] Such a society may offer many benefits to humankind, but constructing policies to enable and promote this information society presents significant challenges. Among the most difficult questions now confronting legal decision-makers are these: Can existing laws successfully be applied to activities occurring via new communications media such as the Internet? Can existing law be adapted to regulate these activities? Are existing laws outmoded or inadequate? Are completely new laws needed to deal with Internet and other information technology developments?

Experience thus far addressing these questions in the European Union (EU) and United States (US) suggests that existing law can sometimes be applied with relative ease to Internet activities and that existing law can sometimes be adapted to reach Internet activities.[3] However, in some instances, new laws seem to be needed. When old laws do not fit and cannot easily be adapted, it may be necessary to go back to first principles and consider how to accomplish societal objectives in the new context of the Internet. Decisions about the law of the Internet, whether carried out by judges, legislatures, or regulators, will have an important impact on the kind of information economy that will emerge. The EU is to be commended for realizing that regulating the Internet is about more than information infrastructure and economics.[4] Deciding how to regulate the Internet is also about constructing an information society in which social and cultural values can be preserved. This article will offer some suggestions about how regulators might more wisely make policy choices to promote a Global Information Society.

Five challenges for policy-makers

For the first decade or so after the development of computer networks and related communications technologies, there was little need for policy-makers to pay attention to activities taking place there. Back then, the user community was, for the most part, a relatively homogenous group of researchers at universities and commercial laboratories who tended to use the networks to communicate the results of their work or work-in-progress and not to cause trouble.[5] Once networking and other technologies evolved to the point that ordinary people could easily use the network, and once the National Science Foundation lifted the earlier ban on commercial activities on the networks, policy-makers came to realize that they would have to decide how to regulate this new medium of communication.[6] They face at least five key policy challenges today:

1   whether they can apply or adapt existing laws and policies to the regulation of Internet activities, or whether new laws or policies are needed to regulate Internet conduct;
2   how to formulate a reasonable and proportional response when new regulation is needed;
3   how to craft laws that will be flexible enough to adapt to rapidly changing circumstances;
4   how to preserve fundamental human values in the face of economic or technological pressures tending to undermine them; and
5   how to coordinate with other nations in Internet law and policy-making so that there is a consistent legal environment on a global basis.[7]

Examples of each challenge will be discussed below.

Old law or new law?

Many examples illustrate the dilemma policy-makers now face in considering whether they can apply existing laws or need to adopt new laws. In this age of convergence of communications technologies,[8] in which the content being delivered (e.g. voice, video, text) is no longer confined to a particular delivery infrastructure (e.g. copper wires or fiber-optic cable, co-axial cable, airwaves), policy-makers must decide, first, whether to regulate at all, and second, what specific kind of regulation is appropriate. Convergence makes this second choice particularly problematic, as regulators are faced, not just with a choice between an old law and a new law, but with a choice between multiple existing regulatory forms.

Consider, for example, Internet "streaming" of video or audio signals.[9] When a content provider streams video and/or audio over the Internet, should it be treated like a television broadcaster, a radio broadcaster, or a passive content provider? Should the choice depend on whether this streaming service is offered over the existing telecommunications infrastructure, over cable lines, or via a new wireless technology? To date, the US Federal Communications Commission (FCC) has responded to these challenges with a "hands-off" approach, declining to graft the regulatory regimes of realspace on to their cyberspace analogs.[10]

The FCC maintains that its refusal to force new Internet services into old communications regulation categories has fostered the development of new Internet business models, and has increased public participation in the Internet by lowering the cost of content and service delivery.[11]

Competition law (and its American counterpart, antitrust law) provides another example of the conflict between old ways of regulating and new ways of doing business. Microsoft founder Bill Gates, for example, believes that US antitrust rules are outmoded in the digital age.[12] Such laws may, in his view, have been needed to regulate manufacturing industries because monopolists or cartels in those industries could restrict output, control prices, and exclude competitors.[13] But in the digital age, anyone can write an operating system program and sell it in competition with Microsoft, and may the best competitor win! The US Justice Department and judge overseeing the lawsuit filed by the Justice Department to challenge Microsoft's business practices have a different opinion about the viability of competition law in the information age.[14] Judge Jackson has found that Microsoft possessed monopoly power in the market for Intel-compatible PC operating systems, power which it used to maintain barriers to entry to new competitors.[15] Antitrust law will no doubt need to adapt to some degree to take into account considerations such as those that arise when a firm technologically ties its products so as to disadvantage a competitor,[16] or to respond to the presence of strong network effects, which are common in digital networked environments and may create intractable barriers to entry to the online marketplace.[17] But the general view in the US is that antitrust and competition law continues to be viable in the digital age, and can successfully be adapted to deal with software and Internet companies.

Copyright law also poses challenges to the regulation of digital content and networked environments.[18] Although some commentators have suggested that copyright law is outmoded in the Internet environment,[19] the general view in the US and the EU is that copyright law can be applied and adapted to protect expressive works in digital form.[20] Both the EU and the US are adopting or have adopted legislation in an effort to ensure that copyright law keeps pace with technological change.[21]

The EU has decided that at least one new intellectual property law is needed to respond to challenges of the information age. It has directed member states of the EU to enact *sui generis* (of its own kind) legislation to provide intellectual property protection for the contents of databases.[22] The *sui generis* right gives those who have made substantial investment in collecting or maintaining a database an exclusive right to control unauthorized extractions and uses of "more than an insubstantial part" of the database.[23] The EU has sought to persuade other nations to enact similar legislation.[24] Some have objected to an EU-style *sui generis* legal regime for databases because it would seem to grant exclusive rights in the data in databases and unduly impede the free flow of information and innovation.[25] The US and Japan are among the countries now exploring an alternative approach to database protection that might adapt unfair competition principles to protect databases against market-destructive appropriations.[26] To appropriately tailor unfair competition principles to the needs of the database industry may also require new legislation.

Like database protection, the issue of safeguarding the privacy of personal information has generated varied responses from nations around the globe. The EU has been at the forefront of the legislative response to this issue: its Personal Data Directive implements a comprehensive regime which mandates that individuals be protected against unauthorized gathering and processing of personal information.[27] Other countries, including Canada, seem to agree that greater legal protection of personal data is necessary.[28] However, the US has been resisting this policy initiative and urging self-regulation by industry as a better alternative.[29]

Proportionality

Once it is clear that new legislation is needed, a second challenge for policy-makers is to adopt a reasonably proportionate response to resolve the problems. Even when correct in concluding that some new legal protection may be desirable, legal decision-makers are not always as careful as they should be about adopting a legislative "cure" that fits the dysfunction it aims to fix. Sometimes overreaction is due to legal decision-makers having oversimplified the nature of the problem, singling out a single cause, for example, when the problem may have multiple causes. Sometimes overreaction may arise when legal decision-makers are unclear about what an effective approach would be.

Consider, for example, the problem of indecent speech on the Internet. To protect children against harmful exposures to indecent material on the Internet, the US Congress enacted the Communications Decency Act[30] which the US Supreme Court eventually ruled was unconstitutional in *Reno* v. *ACLU*.[31] The Supreme Court had no quarrel with the idea that protecting children against obscene and indecent speech was an important governmental interest. However, it decided that the CDA provisions at issue in that case were not narrowly tailored to achieve that legitimate interest.[32] The provisions were so broad that they interfered with the free speech rights of adults to engage in frank discussions on the Internet that might include some statements that would be indecent as to children. The Supreme Court said that Congress could not constitutionally reduce the level of discourse on the Internet to that suitable for small children.[33] In the aftermath of this decision, the US Congress passed the Child Online Protection Act (COPA) to regulate the distribution of material "harmful to children" on commercial websites.[34] This too has been challenged as unconstitutionally overbroad.[35]

The predominant view in the US is that both the European database directive and the personal data protection directive are examples of disproportionately overprotective legislation that would better be handled with more limited measures.[36] Giving database makers exclusive rights to control extractions of data may, for example, unduly impede legitimate businesses that make use of data generated by another firm. Internet search engines, for example, rely on indexes created by analyzing the contents of websites, which inevitably involves the extraction of data from websites and the reuse of these data in constructing the indexes. American commentators tend to criticize the European directive on personal data protection as overbroad, unnecessary in many instances in which firms have incentives to protect personal data, and unsuitable to the emerging technological environment in which data and data processors are widely distributed rather than being situated in one place, as was true in the mainframe computer era on which the data protection regulations seem to be based.[37]

One reason that the Clinton administration's policy document, *A Framework for Global Electronic Commerce*, proposed that regulation should be "predictable, minimalist, consistent, and simple" was to avoid disproportionate legislative actions likely to create more problems than they can solve.[38] The wise approach may be to adopt a minimalist approach first, and only if experience proves that more regulation is needed should one amend the law to deal with the residual abuses.

Flexibility

More difficult to achieve than proportionality is the challenge of developing legal norms capable of adaptation to a rapidly changing technological and business environment. Yet another reason to enact laws that are "predictable, minimalist, consistent and simple" is that such laws may be more flexible and adaptable than those that are more complex and ambitious. Not even the most visionary of computer scientists can predict how technology will evolve, how this evolution will affect business organizations, and how innovative entrepreneurs will use information technology to transform their businesses and invent new business models. How, then, can legal decision-makers expect to devise laws that will promote the new economy?

One strategy for building adaptability into law is to devise laws that are as "technology-neutral" as possible. For a legislature to adopt, for example, a digital signature law that endorses a particular technology may be a mistake for at least two reasons: first, because such a law is likely to become outmoded as technology evolves; and second, because such a law may unwittingly tilt the market so as to benefit certain developers to the detriment of competitors who offer a different solution, as well as the public who might have preferred that other technology if given a chance.[39]

Another strategy may be to construct laws that are simple and minimalist in character. Compare, for example, the Uniform Electronic Transactions Act (UETA) and the Uniform Computer Information Transactions Act (UCITA), two proactive state legislative initiatives aimed at regulating electronic commerce.[40] UETA validates contracts entered into electronically, and validates electronic signatures.[41] That is, if a state's laws require a "signature" for contracts to be valid, UETA says that an electronic signature will suffice.[42] UCITA establishes rules for commercial transactions in computer-readable information. It too validates electronic contracts, but contains some differing and more complicated standards for formation of electronic information contracts (in contrast to transactions involving other subject matter).[43]

Of the two laws, I predict UETA will be more successful over time. This is in part because it is predictable, minimalist, consistent, and simple, and in part because it does not endorse any particular technological approach. UCITA is very complex, difficult to predict in important ways, and very ambitious in the wide range of activities and subject matter it aims to regulate. In addition, it gives special advantages to those who choose certain technological approaches over others.[44] Its electronic contracting rules are, moreover, inconsistent with those of UETA. This will almost certainly create confusion, particularly when a transaction involves both computer information covered by UCITA (e.g. software) and goods covered by UETA (e.g. a computer).

A third thing to watch for is making legislation in advance of technological developments. UCITA, for example, contains rules about contracts made by "electronic agents" (i.e. computer programs that a person can program to seek out information or resources of a particular kind and negotiate contracts with other electronic agents through the exchange of electronic messages).[45] Many companies are working on developing electronic agents; however, this technology is still very immature and it is not yet clear that electronic agents will be a significant force in electronic commerce. One might argue that UCITA does a service by adopting rules that will validate electronic agent contracting, or one might argue that the law should wait until commercial practice with use of electronic agents provides a firmer basis on which to make judgments about how the law should be configured to deal with this new phenomenon.

One of the foremost scholars of commercial law has observed that commercial law rules should be "accurate" (i.e. reflective of the way commercial transactions are actually conducted), not "original" (i.e. invented by a smart law professor, perhaps out of his imagination).[46] As laudable as it may be to aspire to make commercial law rules accurate (as well as making them simple and technology neutral), the reality today is that rapid change may require evolving rules to deal with an evolving business marketplace. Simpler rules are more likely than complex rules to be adaptable to changing circumstances. Both UETA and UCITA should be studied carefully by policy-makers outside the US because it is quite likely that US companies and officials will eventually try to persuade other countries to adopt similar laws to promote electronic commerce.[47]

Preserving values

Technological and economic developments have made it more difficult to ensure that certain societal values, such as those favoring privacy, innovation, and freedom of expression, will continue to be preserved. Computer- and Internet-based technologies, for example, threaten privacy because they make it very inexpensive and easy to collect and process information about individuals.[48] These technologies allow the gathering of data in a manner that is often invisible to the individual concerned. These data can then be automatically compiled and cross-correlated with data on the individuals derived from different sources (a practice known as "data mining") to amass virtual libraries of personal data.

When an Internet user visits a commercial website, for example, the host of that website can use technology to glean information about the individual based on what the individual does at the site and how his browser is set. It can also plant "cookies" (identifying digital information) on the user's computer so that the host site can more easily keep track of who is (re)visiting its site.[49] Upon a second visit, the host system will check the user's cookies file to determine if the user has been there before and may add new cookies to the file. With usage-, browser-, and cookie-based information, sites can compile profiles of users.[50] The economic pressure on data privacy arises from the fact that compilations of personal data can be very valuable. Many firms exploit user data not only by using it to market new products to the users, but they may also sell user data to other firms seeking to sell their products or services to people with certain characteristics.[51]

In a valiant effort to counteract technological and economic pressures on individual privacy, the EU has developed a comprehensive set of rules to protect personal data against unauthorized reuses or processing by private sector entities.[52] These rules derive in part from previously issued guidelines such as those published by the Organization for Economic Cooperation and Development (OECD).[53] Although the US purports to support the OECD privacy guidelines, information industry organizations in the US have thus far blocked new privacy legislation, except as to online gathering of information from children.[54] While some commentators predict that technology (e.g. anonymizing browsers) can help to solve the cyberspace privacy problem,[55] others believe the law will have to play a role.[56] The law might, for example, need to require the use of anonymizing technologies to protect intellectual privacy in the future.[57]

Another information policy area in which preservation of social values is at stake is encryption policy.[58] A recent lawsuit, *Bernstein v. United States*, seeks to protect and even extend societal free speech values.[59] Bernstein is a computer scientist who wrote an encryption program which he wanted to share with his students and colleagues and post on his website. The US government has insisted that these acts would "export" a "munition" in violation of US export control laws.[60] Bernstein challenged the constitutionality of these laws as applied to his software, claiming that he has free speech rights under the First Amendment to the Constitution to express himself by writing and sharing his encryption software with others.[61] So far the courts have agreed with him (although an appellate decision was later withdrawn and the case has now been remanded to the trial court to consider the implications of the government's recent liberalization of encryption regulations).[62] Outside the United States as well as inside, the possible role of encryption in protecting the privacy of electronic correspondence means that encryption policies should be especially important to those countries, such as the members of the EU, who value privacy as a fundamental human right.[63]

A third policy area posing preservation of societal value challenges is the struggle over preserving fair use rights when copyright owners use technical protection systems to guard digital versions of their works from unauthorized copying.[64] Some, including this author, interpret the US Digital Millennium Copyright Act (DMCA) as allowing circumvention of a technical protection system in order to engage in fair use,[65] although it is less clear whether fair use circumventors have an implied right to make software necessary to accomplish fair use circumventions.[66] However, one recent decision takes the view that fair use does not apply in cases involving anti-circumvention regulations because the purpose of the DMCA is to prevent the circumvention of technical protection measures and has nothing to do with guarding against copyright infringement.[67]

A similar struggle is occurring over fair use rights and contract law. One of the most contentious issues in the US debate over UCITA has been whether courts should enforce terms of mass-market licenses when the terms prohibit activities that would otherwise be considered fair uses under US copyright law. UCITA seems to presume that such terms are enforceable, but some commentators believe that copyright policy should override contract law in this situation.[68] Behind both of these struggles are concerns about preserving the public sphere, in which information is accessible to all, and in which learning, speech and thought can occur without the threat of private control or censorship.

Transnational cooperation

One obvious fact about the Internet is the global character of its reach. While it is unquestionably true that a great deal of trade is international, the physicality of tangible goods, such as automobiles, vacuum cleaners, and television sets, makes it easy to apply territorially based rules to them. German law, for example, can easily be applied to a transaction involving bicycles that takes place entirely on German soil, but what law applies if unlawful information (e.g. pornography or copyright infringement) is uploaded to a computer in Germany and downloaded in the US or in Belgium? If two electronic agents, one representing a German client and one representing a US client, "meet" in cyberspace, exchange messages, and the US electronic agent thinks a contract has been formed, whose law will be used to judge the validity and terms of the contract? It is well known that laws vary from nation to nation on such issues. Variations in national laws may interfere with the growth of electronic commerce, as well as other desired objectives. The question is: how can nations work together to find enough common ground on the private law of the Internet to promote e-commerce and other beneficial exchanges of information?

As desirable as complete harmonization of laws may seem in the abstract, achieving harmonization is likely to be a tediously slow process. Consider, for example, that almost a decade of meetings preceded the diplomatic conference which produced the WIPO Copyright Treaty adapting copyright rules as to digital works.[69] When harmonization is infeasible (or perhaps as a step toward harmonization) nations may agree on policy guidelines to inform the legal rules nations eventually develop. The OECD has been active in promoting this form of international cooperation.[70] Guidelines may not lead to uniformity, however, in part because countries that endorse guidelines sometimes do not actually implement them.[71] Guidelines may also be implemented in inconsistent ways. Yet even inconsistent implementations of rules based on guidelines may be better than the chaos of complete disharmony.

Differences in national culture and legal traditions may make it difficult to attain consensus on the fine details of legal rules on an international basis. Nevertheless, numerous international efforts, such as those undertaken by the United Nations Commission on International Trade Law (UNCITRAL), offer some promise for evolving harmonized rules to promote electronic commerce over the Internet.[72]

Another way to achieve harmony on a global scale may be for one nation to propose legal rules that it urges other nations to adopt. This may be a faster path to harmonization than the laborious consensus process that typifies treaty making. Both the US and the EU have used this approach to international lawmaking for the Internet, in particular as to global electronic commerce. The US White Paper on Intellectual Property and the National Information Infrastructure, for example, proposed digital copyright rules virtually identical to the treaty proposals the Administration submitted to WIPO at more or less the same time.[73] The Clinton Administration's proposed rules became the baseline for discussion, even if they were ultimately transformed in the course of the US legislative and international treaty-making process.[74]

The EU has sought to persuade other nations to adopt its database and personal data protection regimes through the "stick" of reciprocity-based rules. The EU will not protect the databases of non-EU nationals unless other countries adopt the same or a very similar law.[75] And unless other nations provide what the EU considers to be "adequate" protection to personal data, the EU has announced its intent to stop transnational data flows into and out of the offending country. Reciprocity-based provisions as a means to achieve harmonization have been the subject of heated debate, much of it emanating from the US.[76] The EU has, of course, a legitimate interest in attempting to ensure that the objectives of its laws will not be subverted by computer processing of personal data outside its borders. However, reciprocity-based rules may not be an appropriate way to induce other countries to follow the lead of one country's law.[77] An "adequacy" approach may enable countries to develop their own means to achieve the same results.[78]

Perhaps nations should work towards achieving "policy interoperability" (that is, agreeing on goals a policy should achieve, while recognizing that nations may adopt somewhat different policy means to implement the goals). Policy interoperability, rather than reciprocity, may be especially important to those countries who seek to preserve the uniqueness of their social values within the framework of thriving global e-commerce. Policy interoperability also allows room for flexible approaches that can be tailored to the unique economic needs of each nation, while simultaneously avoiding the threat that incompatible national regulatory regimes will derail the unique benefits of convergence and globalization that the Internet offers. In addition, policy interoperability may foster a cooperative environment in which countries feel that their international obligations enhance, rather than erode, their valid national interests. Such an environment is less likely to lead countries to turn to the World Trade Organization (WTO) to determine whether attempts to force regulatory reciprocity represent non-tariff barriers to trade and are in violation of international trade agreements.[79] As some commentators have observed, it is not clear that settling such disputes before an organization concerned solely with international trade would result in policies that reflect the complex set of concerns that will create a livable Global Information Society.[80]

Despite the many international initiatives to develop international consensus on the law of the Internet,[81] some dangers clearly lurk in the international arena. Some arise from the ability of major multinational firms to engage in what Michael Froomkin describes as "regulatory arbitrage," in which firms play some nations off against others as a way to get acceptance of rules that the multinational firm prefers.[82] Also dangerous are potential races to the bottom (that is, contests over which nation will adopt the least restrictive rules and attract the most commercial activity as a result), or races to the top (who can adopt the toughest rules that will become a baseline for applying pressure to get international adoption by others).[83] Much as countries may wish to take some time to think through what laws should be used to regulate the Internet, there is a sense of urgency about putting in place a legal and policy infrastructure to promote electronic commerce and other exchanges of information via the Internet. The fear is that those who wait too long will be left behind in the global information economy. Perhaps this fear can have constructive consequences in motivating countries to work together to achieve the minimum level of consensus needed for electronic commerce to flourish.

Conclusion

The Internet has generated considerable interest, not only among the millions of people who use it every day, but also among legal policy-makers. The law of the Internet is still in the process of evolving. While ever more legal rules are being applied, adapted, and adopted to govern activities occurring via the Internet, there is every reason to expect that additional legal rules will need to be formulated (and reformulated) as technology advances to enable previously unimaginable activities, including new business models for producing and distributing products and services.

Information may be the principal commodity of an information economy in an information age, but policy-makers need to realize that information is not just a commodity. It is also an essential input to innovation, knowledge creation, education, and social and political discourse. If information is commodified too much, these social values may be impaired. Policy-makers need to realize that the information policies they adopt now in relation to the Internet will have profound effects on the information society that will result from these actions.

Lawyers and legal scholars can help to formulate information policies that will produce an information society that we would actually like to live in.

Notes

* Professor of Information Management and of Law, University of California at Berkeley. This chapter is based on a presentation given at a conference on Communications Regulation in the Global Information Society held at the University of Warwick in June of 1999. Thanks to Chris Marsden for organizing such an excellent conference and thanks to Leah Theriault for excellent work in bringing this paper to fruition.

1 See, e.g. Manuel Castells (1996) *The Rise of the Network Society*.

2 See, e.g. *Europe and the Global Information Society: Recommendations to the European Council*, available at http://www2.echo.lu/eudocs/en/bangemann.html.

3 See below.

4 See, e.g. Commission of the European Communities (1997e) *Green Paper on the Convergence of the Telecommunications, Media and Information Technology Sectors, and the Implications for Regulation Towards an Information Society Approach*, COM (97)623 (December); cf. Information Infrastructure Task Force (1993) *The National Information Infrastructure: An Agenda for Action* (December) (emphasizing infrastructure and economic issues).

5 See, e.g. Barry A. Leiner *et al.*, *A Brief History of the Internet*, available at http://www.isoc.org/internet/history/brief.html (last modified 20 February 1998); but see Katie Hafner and John Markoff (1995) *Cyberpunk: Outlaws and Hackers on the Computer Frontier* (well before the inception of the Internet, computer enthusiasts known as hackers engaged in disruptive and quasi-criminal behavior in networked environments).

6 See, e.g. Lawrence Lessig (1999b) *Code and Other Laws of Cyberspace*.

7 These five challenges were first discussed in Pamela Samuelson (1999a) "A new kind of privacy? Regulating uses of personal data in the global information economy," *California Law Review* 87: 751 (reviewing Paul M. Schwartz and Joel R. Reidenberg (1996) *Data Privacy Law: A Study of United States Data Protection* and Peter P. Swire and Robert E. Litan (1998) *None of Your Business: World Data Flows, Electronic Commerce and the European Privacy Directive*). They have also been elaborated upon in Pamela Samuelson (forthcoming, 2000) *Internet Law and Policy: A US Perspective*, delivered at the Japanese–American Society for Legal Studies Symposium on Internet and Private Law held at Sendai, Japan, on 26 September 1999.

8 See generally, Computer Science and Technology Board, National Research Council (1995) *Keeping the US Computer and Communications Industry Competitive: Convergence of Computing, Communications, and Entertainment*.

9 See, e.g. Lisa Napoli (1999) "Webcast audiences aren't just sitting there, survey finds," *New York Times*, 29 June, http://www.nytimes.com/library/tech/99/06/cyber/articles/29radio.html; Lawrie Mifflin (1999) "Watch the tube or watch the computer?" *New York Times*, 1 February, http://www.nytimes.com/library/tech/99/02 /biztech/articles/01tube.html.

10 See Jason Oxman, Counsel for Advanced Communications (1999) *The FCC and the Unregulation of the Internet*, (working paper, July) available at http://www.fcc.gov/opp/workingp.html.

11 Ibid.

12 Bill Gates (1998) "*US v. Microsoft*: We're defending our right to innovate," *Wall Street Journal*, 20 May, http://www.microsoft.com/presspass/doj/5–20wsjoped.htm.

13 See, e.g. Stanley J. Liebowitz and Stephen E. Margolis (1999) *Winners, Losers and Microsoft: Competition and Antitrust in High Technology*. (Traditional antitrust concepts do

not map well to the software market – despite having overwhelming market share, Microsoft was actually the driving force behind *decreasing* software prices.)

14 See Plaintiff's Complaint at 49, *US* v. *Microsoft*, 65 F. Supp.2d 1 (DDC 1999) (no. Civ. 98–1232 (TPJ), Civ. 98–1233 (TPJ)) available at http://www.usdoj.gov /atr/cases/f1700/1763.htm. For more comprehensive coverage of the Department of Justice's case, see generally, http://www.usdoj.gov/atr/cases/ms_index.htm.

15 For Judge Jackson's findings of fact, see Court's Findings of Fact, *US* v. *Microsoft*, 65 F. Supp. 2d 1 (DDC 1999) (no. Civ. 98–1232 (TPJ), Civ. 98–1233 (TPJ)) available at http://www.microsoft.com/presspass/trial/c-fof/.

16 See, e.g. Brief of Professor Lawrence Lessig as *Amicus Curiae* at 6–8, *US* v. *Microsoft*, 65 F. Supp. 2d 1 (DDC 1999) (no. Civ. 98–1232 (TPJ), Civ. 98–1233 (TPJ)) available at http://cyber.law.harvard.edu/works/lessig/AB/abd9.doc.html.

17 Network externalities occur when the value of choosing a specific product increases as the number of consumers already using that product increases. Network externalities are particularly common in the digitized environment because of the importance of interoperable systems. For an explanation of network externalities, see Mark Lemley and David McGowan (1998b) "Legal implications of network economic effects," *California Law Review* 86: 479.

18 For a comprehensive overview of these challenges, see e.g. US Government Committee on Intellectual Property Rights in the Emerging Information Infrastructure, National Research Council (1999) *The Digital Dilemma: Intellectual Property in the Information Age* (hereinafter *Digital Dilemma*).

19 John Perry Barlow (1994) "The new economy of ideas," *WIRED* 2.03, available at http://metalab.unc.edu/wxyc/legal/economy.ideas.html.

20 See e.g. Information Infrastructure Task Force Working Group on Intellectual Property Rights, *Intellectual Property and the National Information Infrastructure: The Report of the Working Group on Intellectual Property Rights*, available at http://www.uspto.gov/web /offices/com/doc/ipnii/; *Digital Dilemma*, as note 18 above, at 239:

> Intellectual property will surely survive the digital age. It is clear, however, that major adaptations will have to take place to ensure sufficient protection for content creators and rights holders, thereby helping to ensure that an extensive and diverse supply of IP is available to the public.

Commission of the European Communities (1995a) *Green Paper on Copyright and Related Rights in the Information Society* COM(95)382 (July).

21 The US Congress has enacted legislation to implement the provisions of the WIPO Copyright Treaty, adopted by the Diplomatic Conference on 20 December 1996, WIPO Doc. CRNR/DC/94 (23 December 1996) (hereinafter WIPO Copyright Treaty). See Digital Millennium Copyright Act, Pub. L. no. 105–304, 112 Stat. 2860 (1998). The EU response to the WIPO Copyright Treaty can be found in its draft copyright directive: *Amended Proposal for a European Parliament and Council Directive on the Harmonization of Certain Aspects of Copyright and Related Rights in the Information Society*, COM(1999)250 (May 1999).

22 European Parliament and Council Directive 96/9/EC of 11 March 1996 on the Legal Protection of Databases, *OJEC* (L 77) 20 (hereinafter *Database Directive*).

23 *Database Directive*, note 22 above, Art. 7.

24 *Database Directive*, note 22 above. The EU has been trying to persuade the international community to adopt its database regime ever since the WIPO diplomatic conference in Geneva, in December of 1996: *Proposal Submitted by the European Community and Its Member States for the Sixth Session of the Committee of Experts on a Possible Protocol to the Berne Convention*, WIPO Doc. BCP/CE/VI/13 (1 February 1996). See Pamela Samuelson (1997) "The US digital agenda at WIPO," *Virginia Journal of International Law* 37: 369 (for an account of this effort (hereinafter "Digital agenda").

25 J.H. Reichman and Pamela Samuelson (1997) "Intellectual property rights in data?" 50 *Vanderbilt Law Review* 51: 84–95.

26 There are currently two database protection measures before the US Congress: the Collections of Information Antipiracy Act, H.R. 354, 106th Cong. (1999); and the Consumer and Investor Access to Information Act of 1999, H.R. 1858, 106th Cong. (1999).

27 European Parliament and Council Directive 95/46/EC of 24 October 1995 *on the Protection of Individuals with Regard to the Processing of Personal Data and on the Free Movement of Such Data, OJEC* (L 281) 31 (hereinafter *Personal Data Directive*).

28 The Canadian privacy legislation has not yet passed, but was amended by the House of Commons on 7 February 2000 after Third Reading in the Senate. See the Personal Information Protection and Electronic Documents Act, Bill C-6, 2nd session 36th parl. (1999). Information on this legislation is available at http://e-com.ic.gc.ca/english/privacy/632d1.html#privup. The legislation is designed to promote e-commerce by protecting online privacy.

29 See, e.g. Joel R. Reidenberg (1999) "Restoring Americans' privacy in electronic commerce," *Berkeley Technical Law Journal* 14: 771; Peter P. Swire and Robert E. Litan (1998) *None of Your Business: World Data Flows, Electronic Commerce, and the European Privacy Directive*.

30 Communications Decency Act of 1996, 47 USCA section 223 (Supp. 1997).

31 117 S.Ct. 2329 (1997).

32 Ibid. at 2348.

33 Ibid. at 2346.

34 Child Online Protection Act, Pub. L. no. 105–277, 112 Stat. 2681–736 (1998).

35 *American Civil Liberties Union* v. *Reno*, 31 F. Supp. 2d 473 (EDPa. 1999) (granting preliminary injunction blocking enforcement of the law).

36 *Database Directive*, note 22 above; *Personal Data Directive*, note 27 above.

37 See, e.g. Swire and Litan, note 29 above, at 50.

38 See William J. Clinton and Albert Gore, Jr (1997) *A Framework for Global Electronic Commerce 3*, available at http://www.iitf.nist.gov/eleccomm/ecomm.htm (hereinafter *Framework*).

39 See, e.g. Jane K. Winn (1998) "Open systems, free markets, and regulation of Internet commerce," *Tulane Law Review* 72: 1177.

40 Uniform Computer Information Transactions Act (final draft as of 1 November 1999) available at http://www.law.upenn.edu/bll/ulc/ucita/ucitanc.htm (hereinafter UCITA); Uniform Electronic Transactions Act (1999) available at http://www.law.upenn.edu/bll/ulc/fnact99/1990s/ueta99.htm (hereinafter UETA).

41 UETA, note 40 above, section 7.

42 Ibid., section 7(d).

43 UCITA, note 40 above, section 103(b) (explaining the applicability of the Act to "computer information transactions" when those transactions also involve other subject matter). See also section 103(d) (listing specific transactions and subject matter that are excluded from the Act).

44 See, e.g. Amelia H. Boss (1999) "Searching for security in the law of electronic commerce," *Nova Law Review* 23: 585.

45 See Michael Froomkin (1998) "Article 2B as legal software for electronic contracting – operating system or Trojan horse?" *Berkeley Technology Law Journal* 13: 1023 (1998).

46 Grant Gilmore (1951) "On the difficulties of codifying commercial law," *Yale Law Journal* 57: 1341. For a comprehensive overview of the many problems with UCITA, see generally: Symposium "Intellectual property and contract law in the Information Age: the impact of Article 2B of the Uniform Commercial Code on the future of transactions in information and electronic commerce," *Berkeley Technology Law Journal* 13: 809 (1998) and *California Law Review* 87: 1 (1999).

47 See e.g. Pamela Samuelson and Kurt Opsahl (1999) "Licensing information in the global information market: freedom of contract meets public policy," *European Intellectual Property Review* 21: 386.

48 See, e.g. Jerry Kang (1998) "Information privacy in cyberspace transactions," *Stanford Law Review* 50: 1193, 1198–99.

49 Ibid. at 1227–8.

50 See e.g. Opening Remarks of FTC Chairman Robert Pitofsky, Public Workshop on Online Profiling, 8 November 1999, available at http://www.ftc.gov/opa /1999/9911/onlinepitofsky.htm.

51 Ibid. See also, National Telecom. and Info. Admin., US Dept Of Commerce (1995) *Privacy and the NII: Safeguarding Telecommunications-Related Information* 15–16 (Appendix A on business of marketing profiles).

52 *Personal Data Directive*, note 27 above.

53 See, e.g. Paul M. Schwartz and Joel R. Reidenberg (1996) *Data Privacy Law: A Study Of United States Data Protection* (detailing origins of the EU personal data directive); Graham Greenleaf (1996) "Stopping surveillance: beyond 'efficiency' and the OECD," *PLPR* 3: 148, available at http://www2.austlii.edu.au/itlaw/articles/efficiency.html (*Personal Data Directive* grew out of the OECD Privacy Guidelines and the Council of Europe Privacy Convention).

54 Children's Online Privacy Protection Act of 1998, Pub. L. no. 105–277, 112 Stat. 2681–728 (1998).

55 See, e.g. "Developments in the law – the law of cyberspace," *Harvard Law Review* 112: 1574, 1644–1648 (1999), available at http://www.harvardlawreview.org/issues/ download/5-99-DEVO.pdf.

56 See, e.g. Reidenberg, note 29 above.

57 See, e.g. Julie E. Cohen (1996) "The right to read anonymously: a closer look at copyright management in cyberspace," *Connecticut Law Review* 28: 981 (suggesting that the law may need to require anonymizing features in copyright management systems).

58 Michael Froomkin (1995b) "The metaphor is the key: cryptography, the clipper chip, and the Constitution," *University of Pennsylvania Law Review* 143: 709.

59 176 F.3d 1132 (9th Cir. 1999).

60 Export Administration Regulations, 15 CFR Pts. 730–74.

61 Bernstein, note 59 above, at 1139–41 (discussing the status of encryption software as "speech").

62 *Bernstein* v. *US Dept. of State*, 974 F. Supp. 1288 (ND Cal. 1997), aff'd, 176 F.3d 1132 (9th Cir. 1999), reh'g granted, withdrawn, 192 F. 3d 1308 (9th Cir. 1999). The rehearing en banc was later withdrawn in favor of rehearing by the original panel in the dispute.

63 See e.g. Convention for the Protection of Human Rights and Fundamental Freedoms, 4 November 1950, art. 8(1), Europ. T.S. no. 5, available at http://www.coe.fr/eng/legaltxt/5e.htm ("Everyone has the right to respect for his private and family life, his home and his correspondence"). The Convention has forty-one ratifications and entered into force on 3 September 1953.

64 See, e.g. "Digital agenda", note 24 above.

65 See Pamela Samuelson (1999b) "Intellectual property and the digital economy: why the anti-circumvention regulations need to be revised," *Berkeley Technology Law Journal* 14: 519, 538–43.

66 Ibid. at 547–57.

67 *Universal City Studios Inc.* v. *Reimerdes*, no. 00 Civ. 0277 (LAK) (SDNY 2 February 2000).

68 See UCITA, note 40 above, section 105; Mark A. Lemley (1999b) "Beyond preemption: the law and policy of intellectual property licensing," *California Law Review* 87: 111 (suggesting that contractual overrides to fair use rights should sometimes be considered a misuse of copyright).

69 See, e.g. "Digital agenda," note 24 above, at 375.

70 See, e.g. *Cryptography Policy: The Guidelines and the Issues, The OECD Cryptography Policy Guidelines and the Report on Background and Issues of Cryptography Policy*, March 1997, OECD Doc. OCDE/GD(97)204; and OECD (1980) *Recommendations of the Council Concerning Guidelines Governing the Protection of Privacy and Transborder Flows of Personal Data*, OECD Doc. C58 (final) (1 October 1980), reprinted in *International Legal Matters* 20: 422 (1981), available at http://www.oecd.org/dsti/sti/it/secur/prod/PRIV-EN.htm (hereinafter OECD Guidelines).

71 See, e.g. Reidenberg, note 29 above, at 773–4 (the Clinton Administration has cited the OECD Guidelines, note 70 above, as the basis for all American privacy laws, but American legislators have refused to implement comprehensive or meaningful standards).

72 Boss, note 44 above.

73 See, e.g. "Digital agenda", note 24 above.

74 Ibid.

75 *Database Directive*, note 22 above, Art. 11 and Declaration (56).

76 See, e.g. Swire and Litan, note 29 above.

77 Charles R. McManis (1996) "Taking TRIPS on the information superhighway: international intellectual property protection and emerging computer technology," *Villanova Law Review* 41: 207.

78 If the EU could be persuaded that US firms would effectively self-regulate, it wouldn't matter if the US did not implement a legislative solution, because adequate protection would still exist.

79 Swire and Litan, note 29 above, at 190–94.

80 Swire and Litan, note 29 above, at 194.

81 See, e.g. US Government Working Group on Electronic Commerce (1998) *First Annual Report*, at iii–iv and 5–8, available at http://www.doc.gov/ecommerce/E-comm.pdf (referring to international meetings and working groups on e-commerce policy).

82 See A. Michael Froomkin (1997) "The Internet as a source of regulatory arbitrage," in Brian Kahin and Charles Nessen (eds) *Borders in Cyberspace*, abstract available at http://personal.law.miami.edu/~froomkin/articles/arbitr.htm.

83 An example of the latter is the Clinton Administration's effort to persuade other countries to adopt the anti-circumvention rules of the DMCA as an appropriate implementation of the WIPO Copyright Treaty.

Bibliography

Aaron, Ambassador David L. (1999) Seattle, Washington, http://www.usia.gov/topical-/econ/wto99/ec1112.htm (12 November 1999).

Addamax v. Open Software Foundation, 152 F. 3d 48 (1st Cir. 1998).

Administrative Procedures Act, 5 USC, section 551.

Agre, Phil (1998) 'The Internet and public discourse', *First Monday*, 3(3). Online. Available http: www.firstmonday.dk/issues/issue3_3/agre/index.html (5 February 2000).

Aharoni (ed.) (1993) *Coalitions and Competition: The Globalization of Professional Business Services*, London: Routledge.

Alford, W. (1995) *To Steal a Book is an Elegant Offense: Intellectual Property Law in Chinese Civilisation*, Stanford: Stanford University Press.

Alford, W. (1999) 'A second Great Wall? China's post-Cultural Revolution project of legal construction', *Cultural Dynamics* 11(2) (July): 193.

America Links Up, http://www.americalinksup.org (14 July 1999).

America Online, http://www.aol.com (14 July 1999).

American Civil Liberties Union v. Reno, 31 F. Supp. 2d 473 (ED Pa. 1999).

American National Standards Institute (ANSI) (1998) *Procedures for the Development and Coordination of American National Standards*.

Anticybersquatting Consumer Protection Act, PL 106113, 29 November 1999, 113 Stat 1501, Section 3001.

Armstrong, Kenneth and Bulmer, Simon (1998) *The Governance of the Single European Market*, Manchester: Manchester University Press.

Atkinson, L. (1997) 'What's entertainment?', *China Business Review* March–April.

Aubel, Monique (1990) 'l'Application des règles de concurrence communautaires au secteur audiovisuel', speech delivered during the 'Journées internationales d'IDATE' in Montpellier, November.

Australian Broadcasting Authority (ABA) (1997) *The Internet and Some International Regulatory Issues Relating to Content*, Sydney: ABA. Online at http://www.aba.gov.au (20 February 2000).

*Avery Dennison Corp. v. Sumpton*189 F. 3d 868 (9th Cir. 1999) (online: laws .findlaw.com-/9th/9855810.html).

Ayres, Ian and Braithwaite, John (1992) *Responsive Regulation: Transcending the Deregulation Debate*, Oxford: Oxford University Press.

Babcock, C. (1999) 'ECMA retreats from Java hard line', *Inter@ctive Week*, 22 and 28 December (available at www.zdnet.com, visited 28 February 2000)

Baldwin, R. and Cave, M. (1999) *Understanding Regulation*, Oxford: Oxford University Press.

Baldwin, R., Scott, C. and Hood, C. (eds) (1998) *A Reader on Regulation*, Oxford: Oxford University Press.

Bangemann, Martin (1997a) 'A new world order for global telecommunications – the need for an international charter', Telecom Inter@ctive 97, International Telecommunications Union, Geneva 8 September (www.ispo.cec/be/infosec/promo/speech/geneva.html).

Bangemann, Martin (1997b) 'Europe and the Information Society: the policy response to globalisation and convergence', speech presented in Venice, 18 September (available at www.ispo.cec.be/infosoc/promo/speech/venice.html).

Bangemann, M. (1999) 'Which rules for the online world? The European Union contribution', *info* 1(1): 11–15.

Bangemann, M. *et al.* (1994) *Europe and the Global Information Society, The Report of the High Level Group* (available at http://www.ispo.cec.be/infosoc/backg/bangeman).

Barendt, E. (1985) *Freedom of Speech*, Oxford: Clarendon Press.

Barendt, E. (1993) *Broadcasting Law: A Comparative Study*, Oxford: Clarendon Press.

Barkow, T. (1996) 'The Domain Name System', *WIRED* 4.09 (online: www.wired.com/wired/archive/4.09/geek.html) (31 January 2000).

Barlow, J.P. (1994) 'The new economy of ideas', *WIRED* 2.03 (online: metalab.unc.edu/wxyc/legal/economy.ideas.html).

Barshefsky, Ambassador Charlene (1999) *Services in the New Round*, Senate Banking Committee, Washington DC, 2 November (at http://www.usia.gov/topical/econ/wto99/se1102.htm).

Barton, John H. (1997) 'The balance between intellectual property rights and competition: paradigms in the information sector', *European Competition Law Review* 7: 440–45.

Baskin, E. *et al.* (1998) 'The six dimensions of standards: contribution towards a theory of standardization' in Lefebre, L.A. *et al.* (eds) *Management of Technology, Sustainable Development and Eco-Efficiency*, Amsterdam: Elsevier.

Beesley, M (1981) *Liberalisation of the Use of the British Telecommunications Network: Report to the Secretary of State*, London: HMSO.

Beltrame, F. (1996) 'Harmonising media ownership rules: problems and prospects', *Utilities Law Review* 7: 172.

Bender, Gunnar (1998) *Bavaria v. Felix Somm: The Pornography Conviction of the Former CompuServe Manager* (http://www.digital-law.net/IJCLP/1_1998 /ijclp_webdoc_14_1_1998.html).

Benhabib, Seyla (1992) *Situating the Self: Gender, Community and Postmodernism in Contemporary Ethics*, Oxford: Polity Press.

Benkler, Y. (1996) *Rules of the Road for the Information Superhighway: Electronic Communications and the Law*, St Paul, Minn.: West Publishing.

Benkler, Y. (1998) 'Communications infrastructure regulation and the distribution of control over content', in C. Blackman and P. Nihoul (eds) *Convergence between Telecommunications and Other Media: How Should Regulation Adapt?*, Amsterdam: Elsevier (special issue of *Telecommunications Policy*).

Berners Lee, Tim, with Fischetti, Mark (1999) *Weaving the Web: The Original Design and Ultimate Destiny of the World Wide Web by Its Inventor*, London: HarperCollins (at http://www.harpercollins.com/catalog/redir.aspl?0062515861).

Bernstein v. *US Dept. of State*, 974 F. Supp. 1288 (ND Cal. 1997), *aff'd*, 176 F. 3d 1132 (9th Cir. 1999), *reh'g granted, withdrawn*, 192 F. 3d 1308 (9th Cir. 1999).

Bernstein, R. *et al.* (1998) *Handbook of Arbitration Practice*, 3rd edn, London: Sweet and Maxwell.

BIAC/OECD Internet Forum on Content Self-Regulation, http://www.oecd.org/dsti/sti/it/index.html (14 July 1999).

Birt, J. (1999) 'The BBC beyond 2000', *Communication Technology Decisions* 1 (Autumn/Winter): 124–7. London: IIC.

Black, J. (1996) 'Constitutionalising self-regulation', *Modern Law Review* 59: 24–56.

Blackman, C. (1999) *A Messy Future for Standards*, at http://www.law.warwick.ac.uk/lawschool/confs/commsreg/plenary3.html.

Blackman, C. and Nihoul, P. (eds) (1998) *Convergence between Telecommunications and Other Media: How Should Regulation Adapt?*, Amsterdam: Elsevier (special edition of *Telecommunications Policy* 22(3)).

Boddewyn, J.J. (1988) *Advertising Self-Regulation and Outside Participation: A Multinational Comparison*, New York: Quorum.

Boddewyn, J.J. (1991) *The Case of Self Regulation*, New York: IAA.

Boss, Amelia H. (1999) 'Searching for security in the law of electronic commerce', *Nova Law Review* 23: 585.

Bradner, S. (1996) *The Internet Standards Process – Revision 3*, RFC 2026. Online (available http: www.ietf.org/rfc/rfc2026.txt) (5 February 2000).

Bradner, S. (1998) *IETF Working Group Guidelines and Procedures*, RFC 2418. Online (available http: www.ietf.org/rfc/rfc2418.txt) (5 February 2000).

Braithwaite, J. (1982) 'Enforced self regulation: a new strategy for corporate crime', *Michigan Law Review* 80: 1466–507.

Braithwaite, J. (1993) 'Responsive regulation in Australia', in P. Grabosky and J. Braithwaite (eds) *Regulation and Australia's Future*, Canberra: Australian Institute of Criminology.

Brands, H. and Evan, T. (1999) *The Law and Regulations of Telecommunications Carriers*, London: Artech House.

Bratton, W., McCahery, J., Picciotto, S., and Scott. C. (eds) (1996) *International Regulatory Competition and Coordination*, Oxford: Clarendon Press.

Braun, Phillip and Schaal, Andreas (1998) *Federalism, the Nation State and the Global Network: The Case of German Communications Policy* http://ksgwww.harvard.edu/iip/iicompol/Papers/Braun-Schaal.html.

Breyer, S. (1982) *Regulation and its Reform*, Cambridge, MA: Harvard University Press.

British Telecommunications v. *One in a Million Ltd* (Court of Appeal, Civil Division, 23 July 1998) online www.nic.uk/news/oiam-appeal-judgement.html.

Brohmer, J. and Ukrow, J. (1999) *Die Selbstkontrolle im Medienbereich in Europa: Eine Rechtsvergleichende Untersuchung*, Dordrecht, Boston: Martinus Nijhoff Publishers.

Brookfield Communications, Inc. v. *West Coast Ent. Corp.*, 174 F. 3d 1036 (9th Cir. 1998) (online: laws.findlaw.com/9th/9856918.html).

Burk, Dan L. (1999) 'Virtual exit in the Global Information Economy', *Chicago Kent Law Review* 73(4): 943–95.

Cai D. (1999) 'Development of the Chinese legal system since 1979 and its current crisis and transformation', *Cultural Dynamics* 11(2): 135.

Campbell, A.J. (1999) 'Self-regulation and the media', *Federal Communications Law Journal* 51: 711–72.

Canadian Association of Internet Providers, http://www.caip.ca/caipcode.html (14 July 1999).

Canberra Times (1998) 'Senator Harradine launching child protection week', 13 September.

Carnoy, Martin, Castells, Manuel, Cohen, Stephen S. and Cardoso, Fernando Henrique (1993) *The New Global Economy in the Information Age; Reflections on Our Changing World*, London: Macmillan.

Case 4/73 *Nold* v. *Commission [1974]* ECR 491.

Case 288/89 of 25 July 1991, *Stichting Collectieve Antennevoorziening Gouda and others* v. *Commissariaat voor de Media [1991]* ECR I-4007.

Case 353/89 of 25 July 1991, *Commission* v. *Kingdom of the Netherlands [1991]* ECR I-4069.

Case no. IV/M.202, *Thorn EMI/ Virgin Music*, 27 April 1992.

Case no. IV/M.423, *Newspaper Publishing*, 13 March 1994.

Case no. IV/M.489, *Bertelsmann/News International/Vox*, 6 September 1994.

Case NN 141/95, 'IRIS – Legal Observations of the European Audiovisual Observatory', 1996–10: 8.

Case no. IV/M.490, *Nordic Satellite Distribution*, 19 July 1995, *OJEC* of 2 March 1996, L 53: 20–40.

Case no. IV/M.553, *RTL/Veronica/Endemol*, 20 September 1995, *OJEC* of 5 June 1996, L 134: 32–52.

Case no. IV/M.856, *British Telecom/MCI (II)*, 14 May 1997, *OJEC* of 8 December 1997, L 336: 1–15.

Case no. IV/M.999, *CLT–UFA/ Havas Intermédiation*, 26 February 1998.

Case no. IV/M.993, *Bertelsmann/Kirch/Premiere*, 27 May 1998, IP/98/477.

Case no. IV/M.1027, *Deutsche Telekom/Betaresearch*, 27 May 1998, IP/98/477.

Case no. IV/M.1219, *Seagram/Polygram*, 21 September 1998.

Case T-95/96 *Gestevision Telecinco SA* v. *Commission of the European Communities [1998]*, ECR II-0000 – Court of First Instance of the European Communities, 15 September 1998.

Castells, M. (1996) *The Rise of the Network Society*, Oxford: Blackwell.

Cave, M. (1997) 'Regulating digital television in a convergent world', *Telecommunications Policy* 21(7), Special Issue, *The Economics Regulation of Pay Broadcasting*: 575–96.

Cave, M. and Cowie, C. (1996) 'Regulating conditional access in European pay broadcasting', *Communications and Strategies* 23(3): 119, IDATE: Montpelier.

Cave, M. and Cowie, C. (1998) 'Not only conditional access. Towards a better regulatory approach to digital TV', *Communications and Strategies* 30(2): 77–101.

Cawley, R. (1997) 'European aspects of the regulation of pay television', *Telecommunications Policy* 21(7): 677–91.

Cerf, V. (1990) *The Internet Activities Board*, RFC 1160. Online. Available http: www.ietf.org/rfc/rfc1160.txt (5 February 2000).

Chan, J.M. (1994), 'Media internationalization in China: processes and tensions', *Journal of Communication* 44(3): 81.

Chen, G. (1999) *China's Booming Internet Sector: Open or Closed to Foreign Investment?* www.chinaonline.com (8 October 1999).

Chen, G. (2000a) *Foreign Participation in China's Internet Sector Remains a Major Issue for 2000*, www.chinaonline.com (20 January 2000).

Chen, G. (2000b) *China Internet: Government Tightens Controls, Clamps Down on News*, www.chinaonline.com.

Children's Online Privacy Protection Act (1998) Pub. L. no. 105–277, 112 Stat. 2681–728.

China News Agency (*Zhongxinshe*) (2000) *China's Newspaper Publishing Industry Leaner and Meaner*, www.chinaonline.com (26 January 2000).

Chissick M. and Kelman A. (1999) *Electronic Commerce – Law and Practice*, London: Sweet and Maxwell.

Clark *et al.* (1991) *Towards the Future Internet Architecture*, RFC 1287. Online. Available http: www.ietf.org/rfc/rfc1287.txt (5 February 2000).

Clark, D. and Zittrain J. (1997) *Transcript of Dialogue between J. Zittrain and D. Clark*. Online. Available http: cyber.harvard.edu/fallsem97/trans/clark/ (5 February 2000).

Clinton, William J. and Gore, Albert, Jr (1997) *A Framework for Global Electronic Commerce* at www.ecommerce.gov/framewrk.htm.

Codding, George A., Jr (1952) *The International Telecommunication Union: An Experiment in International Cooperation* Leiden: E.J. Brill.

Coglianese, C. (1997) 'Assessing consensus: the promise and performance of negotiated rulemaking', *Duke Law Journal*, 46: 1255.

Cohen, Julie E. (1996) 'The right to read anonymously: a closer look at copyright management in cyberspace', *Connecticut Law Review* 28: 981.

Coliver, S., Hoffman, P. and Bowen, S. (eds) (1999) *Secrecy and Liberty: National Security, Freedom of Expression and Access to Information*, Dortmund: Martinus Nijhoff.

Collections of Information Antipiracy Act (1999), H.R. 354, 106th Cong.

Collins, R. (1998) 'Public service and the media economy. European trends in the late 1990s', *Gazette* 60(5): 363–76.

Collins, R. and Murroni, C. (1995) *New Issues in Universal Service Obligation*, London: Institute for Public Policy Research.

Collins, R. and Murroni, C. (1996) *New Media, New Policies*, Cambridge: Polity Press.

Commission of the European Communities (1977) 'To Written Questions – no. 753/76 on aid to the press by Mr Guerlin on 6 January 1977', *OJEC* C 64: 24.

Commission of the European Communities (1987) 'To Written Questions – no. 2541/87 on postage rates applying to newspapers by Mr Roberto Cicciomessere, Mrs Emma Bonino and Mr Marco Pannella on 2 March 1988', *OJEC* C 263: 26–7.

Commission of the European Communities (1989a) 'Commission Decision of 21 December 1988 on aid granted by the Greek Government to the film industry for the production of Greek films', *OJEC* of 20 July 1989, L 208: 38–41.

Commission of the European Communities (1989b) 'Council Regulation Corrigendum to Council Regulation (EEC) no. 4064/89 of 21 December 1989 on the control of concentrations between undertakings', *OJEC* of 21 September 1990, L 257: 13, Commission of the European Communities, Brussels.

Commission of the European Communities (1989c) 'Council Regulation (EEC) no. 4064/89 of 21 December 1989 on the control of concentrations between undertakings', *OJEC* of 30 December 1989, L 395: 1–12; Commission of the European Communities, Brussels.

Commission of the European Communities (1992) *Pluralism and Media Concentration in the Internal Market. An assessment of the need for Community action*, Commission Green Paper, Brussels, 23 December 1992, COM(92) 480 final.

Commission of the European Communities (1994a) *Follow-up to the Consultation Process Relating to the Green Paper on 'Pluralism and Media Concentration in the Internal Market – An assessment of the need for Community action'*, Brussels, 5 October 1994, COM(94) 353 final.

Commission of the European Communities (1994b) *Europe and the Global Information Society: Recommendations to the European Council*, available at www2.echo.lu/eudocs/en/bangemann.html.

Commission of the European Communities (1995a) *Green Paper on Copyright and Related Rights in the Information Society*, COM(95) 382, July.

Commission of the European Communities (1995b) 'Directive 95/46/EC of 24 October 1995 of the European Parliament and of the Council on the protection of individuals with regard to the processing of personal data and on the free movement of such data', *OJEC* L 281: 31.

Commission of the European Communities (1995c) 'Directive 95/47/EC of 24 October 1995 of the European Parliament and the Council on the use of standards for the transmission of television signals', *OJEC* L 281.

Commission of the European Communities (1996a) *Proposal Submitted by the European Community and Its Member States for the Sixth Session of the Committee of Experts on a Possible Protocol to the Berne Convention*, WIPO Doc., 1 February, BCP/CE/VI/13.

Commission of the European Communities (1996b) 'Directive 96/9/EC of 11 March 1996 of the European Parliament and of the Council on the legal protection of databases', *OJEC* L 77: 20.

Commission of the European Communities (1996c) *Commission Communication on Services of General Interest in Europe*, 11 September COM(96) 443 final.

Commission of the European Communities (1996d) *Green Paper on the Protection of Minors and Human Dignity*, COM (96) 483 final.

Commission of the European Communities (1997a) 'Directive 97/13/EC of 10 April 1997 of the European Parliament and of the Council on a common framework for general authorizations and individual licences in the field of telecommunications services', *OJEC* L 117: 15.

Commission of the European Communities (1997b) 'Directive 97/36/EC of 30 June 1997 of the European Parliament and of the Council amending Council Directive 89/552/EEC on the coordination of certain provisions laid down by law, regulation or administrative action in Member States concerning the pursuit of television broadcasting activities', *OJEC* of 30 July 1997, L 202: 60–71.

Commission of the European Communities (1997c) 'Council Regulation (EC) no. 1310/97 of 30 June 1997 amending Regulation (EEC) no. 4064/89 on the control of concentrations between undertakings', *OJEC* of 9 July 1997, L 180: 1–6. Commission of the European Communities, Brussels.

Commission of the European Communities (1997d) Ministerial Declaration, *Global Information Networks: Realising the Potential*, European Ministerial Conference at Bonn, 6–8 July.

Commission of the European Communities (1997e) *Green Paper on the Convergence of the Telecommunications, Media and Information Technology Sectors, and the Implications for Regulation: Towards an Information Society Approach*, COM(97) 623. http: www.ispo.cec.be/convergencegp/97623en.doc (14 July 1999).

Commission of the European Communities (1997f) *Follow-up to the Green Paper on the Protection of Minors and Human Dignity in Audiovisual and Information Services*, COM (97) 570, final. http: europa.eu.int/comm/dg10/avpolicy/new_srv/comlv-en.html (14 July 1999).

Commission of the European Communities (1997g) 'Directive 89/552/EEC of 3 October 1989 on the coordination of certain provisions laid down by Law, Regulation or Administrative Action in Member States concerning the pursuit of television broadcasting activities [*OJEC* of 17 October 1989, L 298: 23–30] as amended by Directive 97/36/EC of the European Parliament and of the Council of 30 June 1997 amending Council Directive 89/552/EEC on the coordination of certain provisions laid down by law, regulation or administrative action in Member States concerning the pursuit of television broadcasting activities', *OJEC* of 30 July 1997, L 202 : 60–71.

Commission of the European Communities (1997h) *Joint EU–US Statement on Electronic Commerce*. Online. Available http: www.qlinks.net/comdocs/eu-us.htm (5 February 2000); *Bulletin of the EU* 12–97, point 1.3.98.

Commission of the European Communities (1998a) Working document: 'Judging industry self-regulation: when does it make a meaningful contribution to the level of data protection in a third country?' Adopted by the Working Party on 14 January 1998, DG XV D/5057/97.

Commission of the European Communities (1998b) *Internet Governance: Reply of the European Community and its Member States to the US Green Paper*. Online. Available: www.ispo.cec.be/eif/policy/govreply.html (5 February 2000); *Bulletin of the EU* 1/2–1998, point 1.3.199.

Commission of the European Communities (1998c) 'Commission Notice on the concept of concentration under Council Regulation (EEC) no. 4064/89 on the control of concentrations between undertakings', *OJEC* of 2 March 1998, C 66: 5–13.

Commission of the European Communities (1999a) *Towards a New Framework for Electronic Communications Infrastructure and Associated Services – The 1999 Communications Review*, Communication from the Commission to the European Parliament, the Council, the Economic and Social Committee and the Committee of the Regions, COM (1999) 539 final.

Commission of the European Communities (1999b) (draft directive) *Amended Proposal for a European Parliament and Council Directive on the Harmonization of Certain Aspects of Copyright and Related Rights in the Information Society*, COM(1999) 250 (May).

Commission of the European Communities (2000a) *An Approach Towards a Possible Commission Recommendation on 'Unbundled Access to the Local Loop'*, European Commission, DG XIII, Information Society working document on unbundled access to the local loop, europa.eu.int/comm/information_society/policy/telecom/localloop/pdf/working_en.pdf (9 February 2000).

Commission of the European Communities (2000b) *Green Paper on the Protection of Minors and Human Dignity in Audiovisual and Information Services*, http: www2.echo.lu/legal/en/internet/gpen-c.htm (20 February 2000).

Commission of the European Communities Council of Ministers (1998): 'Recommendation 98/560/EC on the development of the competitiveness of the European audiovisual and information services industry by promoting national frameworks aimed at achieving a comparable and effective level of protection of minors and human dignity', *OJEC* of 7 October 1998, L 270: 0048.

Commonwealth of Australia (1998) *A Strategic Framework for the Information Economy: Identifying Priorities for Action*, December: 4.

Communications Decency Act (1996) Pub. L. no. 104–104, Section 502, USCCAN (110 Stat.) 56, 133 (to be codified at 47 USC Section 223).

Consumer and Investor Access to Information Act (1999) H.R. 1858, 106th Cong.

Continental Paper Bag Co. v. Eastern Paper Bag Co., 210 US 405 (1908).

Cook, C.J. and Kerse, C.S. (1996) *EC Merger Control*, 2nd edn, London: Sweet and Maxwell.

Council of Europe (1950) *Convention for the Protection of Human Rights and Fundamental Freedoms*, 4 November 1950, art. 8(1), Europ. T.S. no. 5, Strasbourg: Council of Europe, at www.coe.fr/eng/legaltxt/5e.htm.

Council of Europe (1997) *Recommendations and Resolutions adopted by the Parliamentary Assembly of the Council of Europe in the Media Field*, DH-MM (97) 3, Strasbourg: Council of Europe.

Council of Europe (1998) *Recommendations and Declarations of the Committee of Ministers in the Media Field*, DH-MM (98) 2, Strasbourg: Council of Europe.

Council of Europe (1998) *European Ministerial Conferences on mass media policy: Texts adopted*, DH-MM (98) 4, Strasbourg: Council of Europe.

Council of Europe (1999) *Explanatory Memorandum to Recommendation no. R (99) 1 of the Committee of Ministers of the Council of Europe on Measures to Promote Media Pluralism*, Strasbourg: Council of Europe.

Cowhey, Peter F. (1990) 'The international telecommunications regime: the political roots of regimes for high technology', *International Organization* 44 (Spring): 169–99.

Cowie, C and Marsden, C. (1999) 'Convergence: navigating through digital pay-TV bottlenecks', *info* 1(1): 53–66.

Craufurd Smith R. (1997) *Broadcasting Law and Fundamental Rights*, Oxford: Clarendon Press.

Creative Labs v. *Cyrix Corp.*, 42 USPQ 2d 1872 (ND Cal. 1997).

Crocker, David H. (1993a) 'Evolving the system', in D.C. Lynch and M.T. Rose (eds) *Internet System Handbook*, Reading MA: Addison-Wesley.

Crocker, David H. (1993b) 'Making standards the IETF way', *StandardView* 1(1) (September): 48–56. Online. Available http: info.isoc.org/papers/standards/crocker-on-standards.html (5 February 2000).

Curran J. (1996) 'Mass media and democracy revisited', in J. Curran and M. Gurevitch (eds) *Mass Media and Society*, 2nd edn, London: Edward Arnold, 81–119.

Curwen, P. (1999) 'Telcos take over the world?' *info* 1(3): 239–51.

Cyber Rights and Cyber Liberties (14 July 1999) http://www.cyber-rights.org/isps/somm-dec.html.

Data General Corp. v. *Grumman Systems Support Corp.*, 36 F. 3d 1147 (1st Cir. 1994).

David, P. and Shurmer, M. (1996) 'Formal standards setting for global communications and information services: towards an institutional regime transformation?' *Telecommunications Policy* 20(10): 789–816.

Davis, Andrew (1994) *Telecommunications and Politics: The Decentralised Alternative*, New York: Pinter Publishers.

Decision of 15 September 1989 relating to a proceeding under Article 85 of the EEC Treaty (IV/31.734 – Film purchases by German television stations), *OJEC* of 3 October 1989, L 284: 36–44.

Dehousse, F. and Van den Hende, L. (1997) 'La place des services publics dans la conférence intergouvernementale', in M. Dony (ed.) *Les services publics et l'Europe: entre concurrence et droit des usagers*, Bruxelles : Université libre de Bruxelles.

de Jonquières, G. (1998) 'Retreat over OECD pact on investment', *Financial Times*, 21 October: 5.

de Long, J.B. and Froomkin, A.M. (1998) *The Next Economy?*, at http://econ161.Berkeley.EDU/Econ_Articles/newecon.htm.

Department of Commerce (1997) *Notice, Request for Comments on the Registration and Administration of Internet Domain Names*, 62 Fed. Reg. 35896.

Department of Commerce (1998a) *Improvement of Technical Management of Internet Names and Addresses*, 63 Fed. Reg. 8825 (1998) (to be codified at 15 C.F.R. chap. XXIII).

Department of Commerce (1998b) 'Statement of Policy on Management of Internet Names and Addresses', *Federal Register* 63 (10 June): 31741. Online. www.ntia.doc.gov/ntiahome/domainname/6_5_98dns.htm.

Department of Commerce (1998c) *Memorandum of Understanding between the US Department of Commerce and Internet Corporation for Assigned Names and Numbers*. At www.ntia.doc.gov/ntiahome/domainname/icann-memorandum.htm (5 February 2000).

Department of Commerce, National Telecommunications and Information Administration (1995) *Privacy and the NII: Safeguarding Telecommunications-Related Information* 15–16.

Department of National Heritage (1995) *Media Ownership: The Government's Proposals*, Cm. 2872, London: HMSO.

Department of Trade and Industry (1999) 'Building confidence in electronic commerce: a consultation document', *International Context* 6 (5 March).

Department of Trade and Industry and Department of Culture, Media and Sport (1998) *Regulating Communications: Approaching Convergence in the Information Age*, Cm. 4022, London: HMSO.

Department of Trade and Industry and the Home Office (1999): *Review of the Internet Watch Foundation*, London: KPMG and Denton Hall, www.kpmgiwf.org/ (visited 14 July 1999).

Department of Trade and Industry, Communications and Information Industries, http: www2.dti.gov.uk/cii/iwfreview/iwfreview1.html (19 February 2000).

Digital Millennium Copyright Act (1998), Pub. L. no. 105–304, 112 Stat. 2860.

Documents Diplomatiques de la Conférence Télégraphique International de Paris (1865) Paris: Imprimerie Impériale.

Dore, R. and Berger, S. (eds) (1995) *National Diversity and Global Capitalism*, Ithaca and London: Cornell University Press.

Dougan, D. (1999) *Scaling the Great Wall of E-Commerce*, Washington: Cyber Century Forum (see www.virtualchina.com).

Doyle, C. (1997) 'Self regulation and statutory regulation,' *Business Strategy Review*, 8(3): 35–42.

Doyle, G. (1998) *Media Consolidation in Europe: The Impact on Pluralism*, study prepared on behalf on the Committee of Experts on Media Concentrations and Pluralism, MM-CM (97) 12, Directorate of Human Rights, Council of Europe.

Drake, William J. (1988) 'WATTC-88: restructuring the international telecommunication regulations', *Telecommunications Policy* 12 September: 217–33.

Drake, William J. (1989) 'The CCITT: time for reform?' in *Reforming the Global Network: The 1989 Plenipotentiary Conference of the International Telecommunication Union*, London: International Institute of Communications.

Drake, William J. (1993a) 'Territoriality and intangibility: transborder data flows and national sovereignty', in Kaarle Nordenstreng and Herbert I. Schiller (eds) *Beyond National Sovereignty: International Communications in the 1990s*, Norwood: Ablex.

Drake, William J. (1993b) 'The Internet religious war', *Telecommunications Policy* 17 (December): 643–9.

Drake, William J. (1994a) 'Asymmetric deregulation and the transformation of the international tTelecommunications regime', in Eli M. Noam and Gerard Pogorel (eds) *Asymmetric Deregulation: The Dynamics of Telecommunications Policies in Europe and the United States*, Norwood: Ablex.

Drake, William J. (1994b) 'The transformation of international telecommunications standardization: European and global dimensions', in Charles Steinfield, Johannes Bauer and Laurence Caby (eds) *Telecommunications in Europe: Changing Policies, Services and Technologies*, Newbury Park: Sage.

Drake, William J. (1999) *Towards Sustainable Competition in Global Telecommunications: From Principle to Practice – Summary Report of the Third Aspen Institute Roundtable on International Telecommunications*, Washington DC: Aspen Institute.

Drake, William J. and Nicolaïdis, K. (1992) 'Ideas, interests, and institutionalization: "Trade in services and the Uruguay Round"', in Peter M. Haas (ed.) *Knowledge, Power and International Policy Coordination*, a special issue of *International Organization* 45 (Winter): 37–100.

Drake, William J. and Noam, Eli M. (1998) 'Assessing the WTO agreement on basic telecommunications', in Gary Clyde Hufbauer and Erika Wada (eds) *Unfinished Business: Telecommunications After the Uruguay Round*, Washington, DC: Institute for International Economics.

Dunning, J. (1993) 'The internationalisation of the production of services: some general and specific explanations', in Y. Aharoni (ed.) *Coalitions and Competition: The Globalization of Professional Business Services*, Routledge: London.

Dunsire, Andrew (1993) 'Modes of governance', in J. Kooiman (ed.) *Modern Governance*, London: Sage.

Eckholm, E. (2000) 'China's arrest of Pennsylvania librarian alarms scholars', *New York Times*, 13 January, www.nytimes.com.

Economist (1997) 'Persecuting Bill', 20 December: 18.

Electronic Network Consortium, http://www.nmda.or.jp/enc/guideline.html (14 July 1999).

Elias, Norbert (1978) *The civilizing process (Vol. 1): The history of manners; (Vol. 2): State formation and civilization*, translated from the German by Edmund Jephcott (1982), Oxford: Blackwell.

Ellickson R.C. (1991) *Order Without Law – How Neighbours Settle Disputes*, Cambridge, MA: Harvard University Press.

European ISP Association, http://www.euroispa.org (14 July 1999).

Export Administration Regulations, 15 C.F.R. Pts. 730–74.

Fair, P. (1999) 'Chairman of the Internet Industry Association', *Canberra Times*, 13.

Farrell, J. and Saloner, G. (1985) 'Standardization, compatibility, and innovation', *Rand Journal of Economics* 16: 70.

Faxue Pinglun (1998) 'Luelun Wangluoshang Jisuanji Fanzui yu Duice' 1: 83.

Federal Communications Commission (1997) *In the Matter of International Settlement Rates – Report and Order*, Federal Communications Commission 97–280, Docket 96–261, adopted 7 August 1997. Available at http://www.fcc.gov.

Federal Government Commissioner for Cultural Affairs and the Media (1999) *Conclusions of the Experts' Seminar on Media Self Regulation*, Saarbrücken: EMR.

Federal Trademark Dilution Act of 1995, Pub. L. no. 104–98, 109 Stat. 985 (1996) (codified at Lanham Act 43(c), 15 USC section 1125(c)) .

Financial Times (1997) 'WTO urged to act on competition rules', 20 July: 6.

Fiss, O. (1987) 'Why the state?' *Harvard Law Review* 100: 781–94.

Flichy, P. (1995) *Dynamics of Modern Communication*, London: Sage.

Florida ISP Association, http://www.fispa.org./fispa_code.html (14 July 1999).

Florini, A.M. (2000) 'Who does what? Collective action and the changing nature of authority', Chapter 1 in R. Higgott, G. Underhill and A. Bieler (eds) *Non-State Actors and Authority in the Global System*, Routledge: London.

Fraser, N. (1997) *Justice Interruptus*, London: Routledge.

Fravel, T. (2000) 'The bureaucrats battle over the Internet in China', *Virtual China News*, 18 February, www.virtualchina.com.

Freedman, J.O. (1978) *Crisis and Legitimacy in the Administrative Process: A Historical Perspective*, Cambridge: Cambridge University Press.

Froomkin, A.M., (1995a) 'Reinventing the government corporation', *Illinois Law Review* 543, online: www.law.miami.edu/~froomkin/articles/reinvent.htm.

Froomkin, A.M. (1995b) 'The metaphor is the key: cryptography, the clipper chip, and the Constitution', *University of Pennsylvania Law Review* 143: 709.

Froomkin A. M. (1997) 'The Internet as a source of regulatory arbitrage', in B. Kahin and C. Nesson (eds) *Borders in Cyberspace: Information Policy and the Global Information Infrastructure*, MIT Press: Cambridge; abstract available at personal.law.miami. edu/~froomkin/articles/arbitr.htm.

Froomkin, A.M. (1998) 'Article 2B as legal software for electronic contracting – operating system or Trojan horse?' *Berkeley Technology Law Journal* 13: 1023.

Froomkin, A.M. (1999a) *A Critique of WIPO's RFC 3*, online: www.law. miami.edu/~amf/critique.htm.

Froomkin, A.M. (1999b) *Commentary on WIPO's The Management of Internet Names and Addresses: Intellectual Property Issues*, online: www.law.miami.edu/~amf/commentary.htm.

Froomkin, A.M. (1999c) 'Of governments and governance,' *Berkeley Technology Law Journal* 14(2): 617–33, online: www.law.miami.edu/~froomkin/articles/governance.htm.

Gage, D. (1999a) 'Who really owns Java?' *Sm@rt Resller*, 19 November, available at www.zdnet.com (visited 28 February 2000).

Gage, D. (1999b) 'Sun drops plans to standardize Java', *Sm@rt Resller*, 7 December, available at www.zdnet.com (visited 28 February 2000).

Gage, D. (1999c) 'Java: to hell in a handbasket?', *Sm@rt Resller*, 9 December, available at www.zdnet.com (visited 28 February 2000).

Gage, D. (1999d) 'Java standardization process moves forward', *Sm@rt Resller*, 29 June, available at www.zdnet.com (visited 28 February 2000).

Gage, D. (1999e) 'Java standards glitch may open door for Microsoft', *Sm@rt Resller*, 19 November, available at www.zdnet.com (visited 28 February 2000).

Garnham, N. (1986) 'The media and the public sphere' in P. Golding *et al.* (eds) *Communicating Politics*, Leicester: Leicester University Press.

Garnham, N. (1994) 'The broadcasting market', *Political Quarterly*, 65(1) (January): 11–19.

Gates, W. (1998) '*US* v. *Microsoft*: We're defending our right to innovate', *Wall Street Journal*, 20 May, www.microsoft.com/presspass/doj/5–20wsjoped.htm.

GATT/World Trade Organisation (1993) *Agreement on Trade-Related Aspects of Intellectual Property Rights*, GATT Doc. MTN/FA IA1C (15 December).

Gesteland, L. (2000a) *Internet Censored Further in China*, www.chinaonline.com (26 January 2000).

Gesteland, L. (2000b) *China's ICPs Need Approval, License before Posting News*, www.chinaonline.com (18 February 2000).

GetNetWise, http://www.GetNetWise.org (19 February 2000).

Gibbons, T. (1998) *Regulating the Media*, 2nd edn, London: Sweet and Maxwell.

Gibbons, T. (1999) 'Concentrations of ownership and control', in C. Marsden and S. Verhulst (eds) *Convergence in European Digital TV Regulation*, London: Blackstone Press.

Gidari, A. (1998) *Observations on the State of Self-Regulation of the Internet. The Ministerial Conference of the OECD. A Borderless World: Realising the Potential for Global Electronic Commerce*, Ottawa, Canada: Internet Law and Policy Forum.

Gifford, Daniel J. and McGowan, David (1999) 'A Microsoft dialog', *Antitrust Bulletin* 44: 619.

Gigante, Alexander (1997) ' "Domain-ia": The growing tension between the domain name system and trademark law', in B. Kahin and J.H. Keller (eds) *Coordinating the Internet*, Cambridge, MA: MIT Press.

Gilhooly, D. (1998) *The Twilight of Telecommunications: Towards the Global Information Infrastructure*, paper presented to Global Information Infrastructure Commission Annual Forum, 12 October, at http://www.gii.org/events/ann4GDandTL.htm.

Gillett, Sharon Eisner and Kapor, Mitchell (1997) 'The self-governing Internet: coordination by design' in B. Kahin and J.H. Keller (eds) *Coordinating the Internet*, Cambridge, MA: MIT Press.

Gillett, Sharon Eisner and Vogelsang, Ingo (1999) *Competition, Regulation and Convergence: Current Trends in Telecommunications Policy Research*, Mahwah NJ: Lawrence Erlbaum Associates.

Gilmore, G. (1951) 'On the difficulties of codifying commercial law', *Yale Law Journal* 57: 1341.

Global Business Dialogue, http://www.gbd.org/ (20 February 2000).

Goldberg D., Prosser, T. and Verhulst, S. (1998) *Regulating the Changing Media*, Oxford: Clarendon Press.

Goldsmith, Jack L. (1998) 'Against cyberanarchy', *University of Chicago Law Review*, 65: 1199–250.

Gonsalves, Antone and Peterson, S. (1999) 'Sun pulls plug on Java standardization efforts', *PC Week Online*, 13 December, available at www.zdnet.com (visited 28 February 2000).

Gosling, James, Direct Testimony, *US v. Microsoft Corp.*, no. 98–1233 (US District Court for the District of Columbia) para. 24 (available at www.usdoj.gov/atr/cases/f2000/2049.htm).

Graham, A. (1995) 'Exchange rates and gatekeepers', pp. 38–49 in T. Congdon *et al.*, *The Cross Media Revolution: Ownership and Control*, Luton: John Libbey.

Graham, A. (1999) 'Broadcasting policy in the multimedia age', pp. 17–46. in A. Graham *et al. Public Purposes in Broadcasting*, Luton: University of Luton Press.

Graham, A. and Davies, G. (1997) *Broadcasting Society and Policy in the Multimedia Age*, Luton: John Libbey.

Grant W. (ed.) (1985) *The Political Economy of Corporatism*, London: Macmillan.

Gray, J. (1995) *Enlightenment's Wake*, Routledge: London.

Greenleaf, G. (1996) 'Stopping surveillance: beyond "efficiency" and the OECD', *PLPR* 3: 148, available at www2.austlii.edu.au/itlaw/articles/efficiency.html.

Grindley, P., Salant, D. and Waverman, L. (1999) *Standards WARS: The Use of Standard Setting as a Means of Facilitating Cartels in Third Generation Wireless Telecommunications Standard Setting*, at http://www.ijclp.org/3_webdoc_2_3_1999.html.

Groombridge, M. and Barfield, C. (1999) *Tiger by the Tail: China and the World Trade Organisation*, New York: AEI Press.

Gunningham, N., Grabosky, P. and Sinclair, P. (1998) *Smart Regulation – Designing Environmental Policy*, Oxford: Clarendon Press.

Gutmann, A. and Thompson, D. (1996) *Democracy and Disagreement*, Cambridge, MA: The Belknap Press of Harvard University Press.

Guttman, Louis (1994) *Louis Guttman on Theory and Methodology: Selected Writings*, Aldershot: Dartmouth.

Haag, M. and Golsing, L. (1997) 'Universal service in the European Union telecommunications sector', in H. Kubicek, W. Dutton and R. Williams (ed.) *The Social Shaping of Information Superhighways, European and American Roads to the Information Society*, Frankfurt: Campus Verlag; New York: St Martin's Press.

Hafner, K. and Lyon, Matthew (1998) *Where Wizards Stay Up Late: The Origins of the Internet*, New York: Touchstone.

Hafner, K. and Markoff, J. (1995) *Cyberpunk: Outlaws and Hackers on the Computer Frontier*.

Harcourt, A. (1998) 'Regulation of European media markets: approaches of the European Court of Justice and the Commission's Merger Task Force', *Utilities Law Review* 9(6): 276–91.

Harding, J. (1999a) 'Yahoo! forms alliance to create website in China', *Financial Times*, 27 September.

Harding, J. (1999b) 'China relaxes red tape on the written word', *Financial Times*, 10 December: 14.

Hart, K. (1994) 'Rival e-mail camps forge uneasy pact,' *Communications Week International*, 14 November: 46.

Harvard Law Review (1999) 'Developments in the law – the law of cyberspace', *Harvard Law Review* 112, available at www.harvardlawreview.org/issues/download/5–99 DEVO.pdf.

Harwood, J.H., Lake W.T. and Sohn, D.M. (1997) 'Competition in international telecommunications services', *Columbia Law Review* 97: 874–904.

Hawkins, K. and Hutter, B.M. (1993) 'The response of business to social regulation in England and Wales: an enforcement perspective', *Law and Policy*, 15: 199.

Headrick, Daniel R. (1991) *The Invisible Weapon: Telecommunications and International Politics, 1851–1945*, New York: Oxford University Press.

Held, D., McGrew, A., Goldblatt, D. and Perraton, J. (1999) *Global Transformations: Politics, Economics and Culture*, Cambridge: Polity Press.

Henderson, Hazel (1998) 'Viewing "the new economy" from diverse forecasting perspectives', *Futures*, 30(4): 267–75.

Hewitt, P. (2000) Seminar to Harvard Information Infrastructure Project 1999–2000, 15 March, Cambridge, MA.

Higgott R., Underhill, G. and Bieler, A. (eds) (2000) *Non-State Actors and Authority in the Global System*, London: Routledge.

Hirschman A. (1970) *Exit, Voice and Loyalty – Responses to Decline in Firms, Organisations and States*, Cambridge, MA: Harvard University Press.

Hitchens, L.P. (1994) 'Media ownership and control: a European approach', *Modern Law Review* 57(4): 585–601.

Hitchens, L.P. (1996) 'Identifying European audiovisual policy in the dawn of the information society', *Yearbook of Media and Entertainment Law*, Oxford: Clarendon.

Hodges, Michael and Turner, Louis (1992) *Global Shakeout*, London: Century Business.

Hoekman, B. and Kostecki, M. (1996) *The Political Economy of the World Trading System: From GATT to WTO*, Oxford: Oxford University Press.

Hoffmann-Riem, W. (1996) *Regulating Media*, New York: Guilford.

Holznagel, Bernd (1998) 'European Audiovisual Conference – results from Working Group III', *International Journal of Communications Law and Policy* 1(1) at www.digital-law.net/IJCLP/final/current/ijclp_webdoc_9_1_1998.html.

Home Box Office, Inc. v. *FCC*, 567 F. 2d 9, 51–57 (DC Cir. 1977) (per curiam), cert. denied, 434 US 829 (1978).

Home Office (1986) *Committee on Financing the BBC* (Peacock), Cmnd. 9824, London: HMSO.

Home Office (1988) *Broadcasting in the 90s: Competition, Choice and Quality*, Cm. 517, London: HMSO.

Hong Kong ISP Association, http://www.hkispa.org.hk/ (14 July 1999).

Horwitt, E. (1992) 'TCP/IP suits them fine,' *Network World*, 27 July.

House of Commons (1998) Session 1997–98, *Culture Media and Sport Committee Fourth Report: The Multi-Media Revolution*, London. HMSO.

Hovey, R. and Bradner, S. (1996) *The Organizations Involved in the IETF Standards Process*, RFC 2028. Online at www.ietf.org/rfc/rfc2028.txt (5 February 2000).

Huitema, C. *et al.* (1995) *Not All RFCs are Standards*, RFC 1796. Online. Available http: www.ietf.org/rfc/rfc1796.txt (5 February 2000).

Huyse, L. and Parmentier, S. (1990) 'Decoding codes: the dialogue between consumers and suppliers through codes of conduct in the European Community', *Journal of Consumer Policy* 13: 260–87.

ICANN (1999a) *Uniform Domain Name Dispute Resolution Policy*, online www.icann. org/udrp/udrp.htm.

ICANN (1999b) *Rules for Uniform Domain Name Dispute Resolution Policy*, online www.icann.org/udrp/udrp-rules-24oct99.htm.

ICANN Governmental Advisory Committee (1999c) Online communique. cyber.law.harvard.edu/icann/santiago/archive/GAC-Comminuque-mtg3.html.

Image Technical Services v. *Eastman Kodak Co.*, 125 F. 3d 1195 (9th Cir. 1997).

In re Independent Service Organizations Antitrust Litigation, 53 USPQ 2d 1852 (Fed. Cir. 2000).

Independent Television Commission (1997) *Code of Conduct on Electronic Programme Guides*, London: ITC.

Independent Television Commission (2000) *Internet Regulation: The Way Forward?* London: ITC.

Information Infrastructure Task Force (1993) *The National Information Infrastructure: An Agenda For Action*, Washington: GPO.

Information Infrastructure Task Force (n.d.) *Working Group on Intellectual Property Rights, Intellectual Property and the National Information Infrastructure: The Report of the Working Group on Intellectual Property Rights*, available at www.Uspto.Gov/Web/Offices/Com/Doc/Ipnii/.

Information Technology Association of America *Task Force on Internet Use*, http: www.itaa.org (3 March 2000).

Informationsverein Lentia v. *Austria* (1994) *European Human Rights Reports* 17: 93.

Intellectual Property and Contract Law in the Information Age: The Impact of Article 2B of the Uniform Commercial Code on the Future of Transactions in Information and Electronic Commerce, *California Law Review* 87(1) (1999) Symposium.

Intergraph v. *Intel*, 195 F. 3d 1346 (Fed. Cir. 1999).

Intergraph Corp. v. *Intel Corp.*, 3 F. Supp. 2d 1255 (ND Ala. 1998).

International Ad Hoc Committee (IAHC) (1997) *Final Report of the International Ad Hoc Committee: Recommendations for Administration and Management of gTLDs*, at www.iahc.org/draft-iahc-recommend-00.html (5 February 2000).

International Air Transportation Association (1970) *Airline Leased Circuit Requirements – Contribution no. 15*, CCITT Study Group III, Geneva: ITU, July, p. 3.

International Chamber of Commerce (1971) *Customer Private Networks – Contribution no. 26* CCITT Study Group III, Geneva: ITU, July, p. 3.

International Press Telecommunications Council (1972) *Revised Drafts of Recommendations D.1 and D.2 – Contribution no. 35*, CCITT Study Group III, Geneva: ITU, March, p. 2.

International Standards Organisation (2000) *Transposition of Publicly Available Specifications (PAS) into International Standards (DRAFT) – A Management Guide*, www.iso.ch /dire/jtc1/pas/html.

International Telecommunication Union (1982) *International Telecommunication Convention: Final Protocol, Additional Protocols, Optional Additional Protocols, Resolutions, Recommendation and Opinions – Nairobi 1982*, Geneva: ITU.

International Telecommunication Union (1988) *The International Telecommunication Regulations*, Informal Consultations, Information Paper 12, Geneva: ITU, 9 December.

International Telecommunication Union (1996)*Trade Agreements on Telecommunications: Regulatory Implications – Briefing Report 5 of the International Telecommunication Union Regulatory Colloquium*, Geneva: ITU, March.

International Telecommunication Union (1997) *Challenges to the Network: Telecoms and the Internet*, Geneva: ITU.

International Telecommunication Union/CCICT (1927) *Assemblée Plénière de Côme, 5–12 Septembre 1927*, Paris: CCIF.

International Telecommunication Union/CCITT (1969) *IVth Plenary Assembly, Mar del Plata, 23 September–25 October 1968 – White Book, Volume II-A*, Geneva: ITU.

International Telecommunication Union/CCITT (1977) *Sixth Plenary Assembly, Geneva, 27 September–8 October 1976 – Orange Book, Volume II.1*, Geneva: ITU.

Internet Access Australia, http://www.iia.net.au (14 July 1999).

Internet Education Foundation, http://www.neted.org (14 July 1999).

Internet Law and Policy Forum, http://www.ilpf.org/selfreg/selfreg/htm (3 March 2000).

Internet Watch Foundation, *Rating Legal Material*, http://www.internetwatch.org.uk /rating/rating.htm (visited 19 February 2000).

Irmer, Theodor (1987) 'Standardization in the changing world of telecommunications', in Economic Commission for Europe, *The Telecommunications Industry: Growth and Structural Change*, New York: United Nations.

Irving, L. (1997) *Introduction to Privacy and Self-Regulation in the Information Age*, National Telecommunications Information Administration, available at http://www.ntia. doc.gov/reports/privacy/privacy_rpt.htm.

ISPA UK, http://www.ispa.org.uk (20 February 2000).

IT Week (1999) 'Sun blames Microsoft as its Java standardization plans die', 29 April, available at www.zdnet.com (visited 28 February 2000).

Jackson, John (1993) *The World Trading System: Law and Policy of International Economic Relations*, Cambridge, MA: MIT Press.

Jackson, John (1995) Paper given at Institute of Advanced Legal Studies, London, Tuesday 9 May 1995.

Jacobson, Harold K. (1973) 'The ITU: a potpourri of bureaucrats and industrialists', in Robert W. Cox and H.K. Jacobson (eds) *The Anatomy of Influence: Decision-Making in International Organizations*, New Haven: Yale University Press.

Jayasuriya, K. (1999) 'Globalization, law and the transformation of sovereignty: the emergence of global regulatory governance', *Global Legal Studies Journal* 6: 425–55.

JTC 1 Technical Advisory Group (1997a) www.jtc1tag.org/jt970457.htm.

JTC 1 Technical Advisory Group (1997b) www.jtc1tag.org/jt97264r.htm (minutes of meeting of 4–6 June 1997).

JTC 1 Technical Advisory Group (1999a) *JTC 1 N 5746. The Transposition of Publicly Available Specifications into International Standards – A Management Guide*, Revision 1 of JTC 1 3582, section 5.2.5 (available at www.jtc1.org).

JTC 1 Technical Advisory Group (1999b) *JTC 1 N 5748. Resolutions Adopted at the Thirteenth Meeting of ISO/IEC JTC 1, 26–29 January 1999* (available at www.jtc1.org).

Kahin, B. and Abbate, J. (eds) (1995) *Standards Policy for Information Infrastructure*, Cambridge, MA: MIT Press.

Kahin, B. and Keller, J.H. (eds) (1997) *Coordinating the Internet*, Cambridge, MA: MIT Press.

Kahin, B. and Nesson C. (eds) (1997) *Borders in Cyberspace: Information Policy and the Global Information Infrastructure*, Cambridge, MA: MIT Press.

Kang, J. (1998) 'Information privacy in cyberspace transactions', *Stanford Law Review* 50: 1193–99.

Kannan, P. (1996) 'The logical outgrowth doctrine in rulemaking', *Administrative Law Review* 48: 213.

Kant, Immanuel (1970) *Kant's Political Writings*, Cambridge: Cambridge University Press.

Katz, Michael L. and Shapiro, Carl (1985) 'Network externalities, competition, and compatibility', *American Economics Review* 75: 424.

Katz, Michael L. and Shapiro, Carl (1994) 'Systems competition and network effects', *Journal of Economic Perspectives* 8: 93–5.

Keane, J. (1991) *Media and Democracy*, Cambridge: Polity Press.

Keller, P. (1994) 'Sources of order in Chinese law', *American Journal of Comparative Law* 42: 711.

Kleiman, K. *et al.* (1998) *Comments on RFC 1*, online wipo2.wipo.int/dns_comments /0055.html.

Kooiman, Jan (1993) 'Findings, speculations and recommendations', in J. Kooiman (ed.) *Modern Governance*, London: Sage.

Krechmer, Ken (1998) *The Principles of Open Standards*, online. Available http: www.ses-standards.org/library/krechmer.pdf (5 February 2000).

Kynge, J. (1999) 'Beijing pulls plug on foreign TV broadcasts', *Financial Times*, 6 May: 6.

Landler, M. (2000) 'Investors ask if Beijing can enforce all its new Internet rules', *New York Times*, 31 January, www.nytimes.com.

Lawrence, S. and Brookes, A. (1999) 'Missing links' *Far Eastern Economic Review* 4 March: 13.

Lee, A. (1996) 'Developments in the audio-visual market in the PRC', *ICCLR* 9: 331.

Lehr, William (1995) 'Compatibility standards and interoperability: lessons from the Internet', in B. Kahin and J. Abbate (eds) *Standards Policy for Information Infrastructure*, Cambridge, MA: MIT Press.

Leiner, Barry A. *et al.* (1998) *A Brief History of the Internet*, available at www.isoc.org/internet/history/brief.html (last modified 20 February 1998).

Lemley, Mark A. (1999a) 'Standardizing government standard setting policy for electronic commerce', *Berkeley Technology Law Journal* 14(2): 745–58.

Lemley, Mark A. (1999b) 'Beyond preemption: the law and policy of intellectual property licensing', *California Law Review* 87: 111.

Lemley, Mark A. and McGowan, D. (1998a) 'Could Java change everything? The competitive propriety of a proprietary standard', *Antitrust Bulletin* 43: 715.

Lemley, Mark A. and McGowan, D. (1998b) 'Legal implications of network economic effects', *California Law Review* 86: 479.

Lemley, M., Menell, P.S., Merges, R.P. and Samuelson, P. (forthcoming 2000) *Software and Internet Law*, New York: Aspen Law and Business.

Lessig, L. (1997) 'The constitution of code: limitations on choice-based critiques of cyberspace regulation', *CommLaw Conspectus* 5: 181.

Lessig, L. (1998) 'The New Chicago School', *Journal of Legal Studies* 27(II): 661–91.

Lessig, L. (1999a) Brief as *Amicus Curiae*, *US* v. *Microsoft*, 65 F. Supp. 2d 1 (DDC 1999) (no. Civ. 98–1232 (TPJ), Civ. 98–1233 (TPJ) at cyber.law.harvard.edu/works/lessig /AB/abd9.doc.html.

Lessig, L. (1999b) *Code and Other Laws of Cyberspace*, New York: Basic Books.

Lessig, L. (1999c) 'The limits in open code: regulatory standards and the future of the Net', *Berkeley Technology Law Journal* 14(2): 759–70.

Lessig. L. (1999d) *Architecting Innovation* at http://www.thestandard.com/article/display/ 0,1151,7430,00.html (14 November 1999).

Levy, Brian and Spiller, Pablo (1994) 'The institutional foundations of regulatory commitment: a comparative analysis of telecommunications regulation', *Journal of Law, Economics and Organisation* 10(2): 201–46.

Levy, D.A.L. (1997a) 'Regulating digital broadcasting in Europe: the limits of policy convergence', *West European Politics* 20(4): 24–42.

Levy, D.A.L. (1997b) 'The regulation of digital conditional access systems. A case study in European policy making', *Telecommunications Policy* 21(7): 661–76.

Li, M. (1997) 'Guidance of public opinion and strict control over the media', *Inside Mainland China* June: 21.

Liang Wei (1996) 'Shukan Shichang Guanli zhi Wo Jian', *Fazhi yu Jingji* 4: 11.

Lichtenberg J. (1987) 'Foundations and limits of freedom of the press', *Philosophy and Public Affairs* 16: 329–55.

Lieberthal, K. (1996) *Governing China: From Revolution Through Reform*, New York: W.W. Norton.

Liebowitz, S.J. and Margolis, S.E. (1999) *Winners, Losers and Microsoft: Competition and Antitrust in High Technology*, Oakland, CA: Independent Institute.

Lindblom, C. (1977) *Politics and Markets: The World's Political-Economic Systems*, New York: Basic Books.

Littlechild, S. (1983) *Regulation of British Telecommunications' Profitability: Report to the Secretary of State*, London: HMSO.

Liu Zhifeng (ed.) (1999) *Zhongguo Zhengzhi Tizhi Gaige Wenti Baogao*, Beijing: Zhongguo Dianying Chubanshe.

London Internet Exchange Ltd, http://www.linx.net (20 February 2000).

Love, J. (1999) 'Democracy, privatization and the governance of cyberspace: An alternative view of the OECD meeting on electronic commerce', *info* 1(1): 15–22.

Lubman, S. (1999) *Bird in a Cage: Legal Reform in China after Mao*, Palo Alto: Stanford University Press.

Lynch, D. (1999) *After the Propaganda State: Media, Politics and 'Thought Work' in Reformed China*, Palo Alto: Stanford University Press.

McCahery, J., Bratton, W.W., Picciotto, S., and Scott, C. (eds) (1996) *International Regulatory Competition and Coordination*, Oxford: Oxford University Press.

MacCormick, Neil (1993) 'Beyond the sovereign state', *Modern Law Review* 56(1): 8.

McCrea, P., Smart, B., and Andrews, M. (1998) *Blocking Content on the Internet: a Technical Perspective*, Report prepared for the National Office for the Information Economy, Australia, June.

McDowell, S.D. and Maitland, C. (1998) 'Developing television ratings in Canada and the US: the perils and promises of self-regulation', in M.E. Price (ed.) *The V-Chip Debate*, New York: LEA.

MacIntyre, Alasdair (1981) *After Virtue: A Study in Moral Theory*, London: Duckworth.

MacIntyre, Alasdair (1988) *Whose Justice? Which Rationality?* London: Duckworth.

McManis, Charles R. (1996) 'Taking TRIPS on the information superhighway: international intellectual property protection and emerging computer technology', *Villanova Law Review* 41: 207.

McQuail, D. (1996) 'Mass media in the public interest', in J. Curran and M. Gurevitch (eds) *Mass Media and Society*, 2nd edn, London: Edward Arnold.

Malamud, Carl (1992) *Exploring the Internet: A Technical Travelogue*, Englewood Cliffs, NJ: Prentice Hall.

Malamud, Carl (1993) *Exploring the Internet: A Technical Travelogue*, Englewood Cliffs NJ: Prentice-Hall.

Manning, B. and Vixie, P. (1996) *Operational Criteria for Root Name Servers*, RFC 2010. Online. Available http: www.ietf.org/rfc/rfc2010.txt (5 February 2000).

Mansell, Robin E. (1993) *The New Telecommunications: A Political Economy of Network Evolution* London: Sage.

Maritz, Paul (1998) *Declaration of Paul Maritz in Opposition to Sun's Motion to Reinstate November 17, 1998 Preliminary Injunction Under Cal. Bus. and Prof. Code sections 17200*, available at www.microsoft.com/presspass/java/09–27maritz.htm.

Marsden, C. (2000a) 'Not so special? Media pluralism merges with competition and industrial policy', *info* 2(1).

Marsden, C. (2000b) *Pluralism in the Multi-channel Market: Suggestions for Regulatory Scrutiny* at www.ijclp.org/4_2000/ijclp_webdoc_5_4_2000.html, study prepared on behalf on the Committee of Specialists on Media Pluralism, MM-S-PL 1999–12 Final, Directorate of Human Rights, Council of Europe.

Marsden, C. (2000c) 'The European digital convergence paradigm: from structural regulation to behavioral competition law?' in Erik Bohlin *et al.* (eds) *Convergence in Communications and Beyond*, Amsterdam: Elsevier Science.

Marsden C. and Verhulst, S. (eds) (1999) *Convergence in European Digital TV Regulation*, London: Blackstone Press.

Mathieson, C. (2000) 'FTSE review pushes trackers into tech stocks', *The Times*, 'Times 2' cover story, 8 March: 29.

Mayer-Schonberger, V. and Foster, T.E. (1997) 'A regulatory web: free speech and the global information infrastructure', in B. Kahin and C. Nesson (eds) *Borders in Cyberspace: Information Policy and the Global Information Infrastructure*, Cambridge, MA: MIT Press.

Melody, W.H. (1994) 'The information society: implications for economic institutions and market theory', in C.N. Murphy (ed.) *The Global Political Economy of Communication*, Basingstoke: Macmillan.

Merges, Robert P., Menell, Peter S. and Lemley, Mark A.(1997) *Intellectual Property in the New Technological Age*, 1st edn, New York: Aspen Law and Business.

Michalski, Wolfgang (1999) *21st Century Technologies: A Future of Promise*, OECD Observer no. 217/218, Summer 1999 at http://www.oecdobserver.-org/news/fullstory. php3?aid=48.

Mifflin, Lawrie (1999) 'Watch the tube or watch the computer?' *New York Times*, 1 February, www.nytimes.com/library/tech/99/02/biztech/articles/01tube.html.

Mockapetris, P. (1987) *RFC 1034, Domain names – concepts and facilities*, online: www.ietf.org/rfc/rfc1034.txt.

Moe, Terry M. (1997) 'The positive theory of public bureaucracy', in Dennis C. Mueller (ed.) *Perspectives on Public Choice: A Handbook*, Cambridge: Cambridge University Press.

Monopolies and Mergers Commission (1992) *Television Broadcasting Services. A report on the publishing, in the course of supplying a television broadcasting service, of goods supplied by the broadcaster*, Cm 2035, London: HMSO.

Muchlinski, P. (1996) 'A case of Czech beer: competition and competitiveness in the transitional economies', *Modern Law Review* 59(5): 658–74.

Mueller, Dennis C. (ed.) (1997) *Perspectives on Public Choice: A Handbook*, Cambridge: Cambridge University Press.

Mueller, Milton L. (1998) 'The battle over Internet domain names: global or national TLDs?' *Telecommunications Policy* 22: 103.

Mueller, Milton L. (1999) 'Trademarks and domain names: property rights and institutional evolution in cyberspace', in S.E. Gillett and I. Vogelsang (eds) *Competition*,

Regulation and Convergence: Current Trends in Telecommunications Policy Research, Mahwah NJ: Lawrence Erlbaum Associates.

Mueller, Milton L. (2000) *Technology and Institutional Innovation: Internet Domain Names*, mimeo.

Muglia, Robert (1998) Testimony: www.microsoft.com/presspass/trial/mswitness /muglia/muglia.htm.

Murphy, C.N. (1994) *The Global Political Economy of Communication*, Macmillan: Basingstoke.

Napoli, L. (1999) 'Webcast audiences aren't just sitting there, survey finds', *New York Times*, 29 June, www.nytimes.com/library/tech/99/06/cyber/articles/29radio.html.

Nash, David B. (1997) 'Orderly expansion of the international top-level domains: concurrent trademark users need a way out of the Internet trademark quagmire', *John Marshall Journal of Computer and Information Law* 15: 521–45.

National Consumer Council (1986): *Self Regulation of Business and the Professions: An NCC Background Paper*, London: NCC.

National Telecommunications Information Administration (1997) *Privacy and Self Regulation in the Information Age, Introduction*, www.ntia.doc.gov/reports/privacy/privacy _rpt.htm, and http://ntia.doc.gov/ntiahome/privacy/privacy/index.html (20 February 2000).

Negotiated Rulemaking Act of 1990, 5 USC section 561.

Network Solutions (2000, undated) *Shared Registration System Overview*, online www.nsiregistry.com/ docu ments/SRS_Overview_02.pdf.

New Kids on the Block v. *News America Publishing, Inc.*, 971 F. 2d 302 (9th Cir. 1992).

Nihoul, P. (1998) 'Les services d'intérêt général dans le traité d'Amsterdam', in Y. Lejeune (ed.) *Le traité d'Amsterdam: espoirs et déceptions*, Bruxelles: Bruylant.

Nihoul, P. (1999) *Droit européen des télécommunications – L'organisation des marchés*, Bruxelles: Larcier.

Noam, Eli M. (1986) 'Telecommunications policy on both sides of the Atlantic: divergence and outlook', in Marcellus S. Snow (ed.) *Marketplace for Telecommunications: Regulation and Deregulation in Industrialized Democracies*, New York: Longman.

Noam, Eli M. (1993) *Telecommunications in Europe*, New York: Oxford University Press.

Noam, Eli M. and Pogorel, G. (eds) (1994) *Asymmetric Deregulation: The Dynamics of Telecommunications Policies in Europe and the United States*, Norwood: Ablex.

Noam, Eli M. and Singhal, A. (1996) 'Supra-national regulation for supra-national telecommunications carriers?' *Telecommunications Policy* 20 December: 769–87.

Nobre-Correia, Jean-Marie (1995) 'Luxembourg: local, regional, national or transnational?', Chapter 9 in Miguel de Moragas Spa and Carmelo Garitaonandia (eds) *Decentralization in the Global Era: Television in the Regions, Nationalities and Small Countries of the European Union*, London: John Libbey.

Nolan, D. (1997) 'Bottlenecks in pay television. Impact on market development in Europe', *Telecommunications Policy* 21(7): 597–610.

North, Douglass C. (1990) *Institutions, Institutional Change and Economic Performance*, Cambridge: Cambridge University Press.

OECD (1980) *Recommendations of the Council Concerning Guidelines Governing the Protection of Privacy and Transborder Flows of Personal Data*, OECD Doc. C58 (final) (Oct. 1, 1980), reprinted in *International Legal Matters* 20: 422 (1981), Paris: OECD, available at www.oecd.org/dsti/sti/it/secur/prod/PRIV-EN.htm.

OECD (1997a) *Cryptography Policy: The Guidelines and the Issues, the OECD Cryptography Policy Guidelines and the Report on Background and Issues of Cryptography Policy*, March 1997, OECD Doc. OCDE/GD(97)204; Paris: OECD.

OECD (1997b) *Approaches to Content on the Internet*, DSTI/ICCP (97), S. 10. Paris: OECD.

OECD (1997c) *Co-operative Approaches to Regulation*, Public Management Occasional Papers no. 18, Paris: OECD.

OECD (1998) *Working Party on the Information Economy: The Economics of Self-Regulation on the Internet*, DSTI/ICCP/IE (98) 7, 6. Paris: OECD.

OECD (1999a) *A Review of Market Openness and Trade in Telecommunications*, DSTI/ICCP/TISP(99)5/Final, Paris: OECD. Also available at http://www.oecd.org /dsti/sti/it/cm/index.htm.

OECD (1999b) *OECD Science, Technology and Industry Scoreboard 1999*, Paris: OECD.

OECD (1999c) *Recent Trends in Foreign Direct Investment*, Paris: OECD.

OECD, http: www.oecd.org/subject/ecommerce/ (20 February 2000).

OECD/Business Industry Advisory Committee, *Internet Forum on Content Self Regulation*, http: www.oecd.org/dsti/sti/it/index.html (14 July 1999).

OFTEL (1997a) *Beyond the Telephone the Television and the PC – Regulation of the Electronic Communications Industry*, OFTEL submission to the House of Commons Select Committee on Culture Media and Sport Inquiry into Audio-visual Communications and the Regulation of Broadcasting. In Appendices to the Minutes of Evidence of the Committee's Report (HC 520-III) and on OFTEL's website: www.oftel.gov.uk.

OFTEL (1997b) *The Regulation of Conditional Access for Digital Television Services*, London: OFTEL.

OFTEL (2000a) OFTEL strategy statement: *Achieving the best deal for telecoms consumers*, London: OFTEL, January.

OFTEL (2000b) *Price Control Review: OFTEL's initial views on future retail price and network charge controls*, London: OFTEL, March.

Ogus, A. (1992) 'Self-regulation', in B. Boukaert and G. DeGeest (eds) *Bibliography of Law and Economics*, Dordrecht, Boston: Kluwer Academic.

Ogus, A. (1995) 'Rethinking self-regulation', *Oxford Journal of Legal Studies* 15: 97–108.

Ohmae, Kenichi (1990) *The Borderless World: Power and Strategy in the Interlinked Economy*, London: Collins.

Oppedahl, Carl (1997a) 'Trademark disputes and domain names', in B. Kahin and J.H. Keller (eds) *Coordinating the Internet*, Cambridge, MA: MIT Press.

Oppedahl, Carl (1997b) 'Remedies in domain name lawsuits: how is a domain name like a cow?' *John Marshall Journal of Computer and Information Law* 15: 437–64.

Oreja, Marcelino (1999) Seminar on Self-regulation in the Media (jointly organised by the German Presidency of the European Union and the European Commission).

ORSC Root Zone (undated) *How To Use New Domain Names*, online: support.open-rsc.org/How_To/.

Oxman, J. (1999) *The FCC and the Unregulation of the Internet*, available at www.fcc .gov/opp/workingp.html (July 1999).

Panavision International, L.P. v. *Toeppen*, 141 F. 3d 1316 (9th Cir. 1998). Online laws.findlaw.com/9th/9755467.html.

Paris Convention for the Protection of Industrial Property, opened for signature 20 March 1883, as amended at Stockholm, 14 July 1967, 21 UST 1630, 828 UNTS 305.

PC Week Online (1999) 'Sun submits Java to ECMA for standardization', 6 May, available at www.zdnet.com (visited 28 February 2000).

Peacock, A. (chair) (1986) *Report of the Committee on Financing the BBC*, Cmnd 9824. London: HMSO.

Peerenboom, R. (1999) 'Ruling the country in accordance with law: reflections on the rule and the role of law in contemporary China', *Cultural Dynamics* 11(3): 315.

Personal Information Protection and Electronic Documents Act (1999) Bill C-6, 2nd session 36th parl. at ecom.ic.gc.ca/english/privacy/632d1.html#privup.

Peterson, Scott (1999) 'Sun withdraws Java from standards process', *PC Week Online*, 8 December, available at www.zdnet.com (visited 28 February 2000).

Picciotto, S. (1996) 'The regulatory criss-cross: interaction between jurisdictions and the construction of global regulatory networks', in W. Bratton, J. McCahery, S. Picciotto, and C. Scott (eds) *International Regulatory Competition and Coordination*, Oxford: Clarendon Press.

Picciotto, S. (1996–7) 'Networks in international economic integration: fragmented states and the dilemmas of neo-liberalism', *Northwestern Journal of International Law and Business*, 17: 1014–56.

Pinsky, D. (1992) 'In search of open systems', *Communications Week International*, 6 (July): 14.

Pipe, G. Russell (1993)*Trade of Telecommunications Services: Implications of a GATT Uruguay Round Agreement for ITU and Member States*, Geneva: International Telecommunication Union, May.

Pitofsky, Robert (1998) *Self-Regulation and Anti-Trust*, http: www.ftc.gov/OPA/1998 /9802/SE;FREG.html (visited 14 July 1999).

Pitofsky, R. (1999) *Opening Remarks: Public Workshop on Online Profiling*, 8 November 1999, available at www.ftc.gov/opa/1999/9911/onlinepitofsky.htm.

Poole, T. (1998) 'Chinese thank Murdoch for "objectivity" ', *Independent* 12 December: 18.

Portnoy, B. (2000) 'Alliance capitalism as industrial order: exploring new forms of inter-firm competition in the globalising economy', in R. Higgott, G. Underhill and A. Bieler (eds) *Non-State Actors and Authority in the Global System*, London: Routledge.

Posner, R.A. (1984) 'Theories of economic regulation', *Bell Journal of Economics and Management Science* 5: 335.

Posner, R.A. (1998) 'Social norms, social meaning and economic analysis of law: a comment', *Journal of Legal Studies* 27(II): 553–65.

Post, D. (1999) *ICANN and the Consensus of the Internet Community*, online www.icannwatch.org/archives/essays/935183341.shtml.

Postel, J. (1994) *Domain Name System Structure and Delegation*, RFC 1591, March. Online. Available http: www.ietf.org/rfc/rfc1591.txt (5 February 2000).

Postel, J. (1996a) *New Registries and the Delegation of International Top Level Domains*, online. Available http: newdom.vrx.net/archive/draft-postel-iana-itld-admin-01.txt (dated June 1996, accessed 20 May 1999).

Postel, J. (1996b) *New Registries and the Delegation of International Top Level Domains*, online. Available http: sunsite.doc.ic.ac.uk/pub/rfc/draft-postel-iana-itld-admin-02.txt (5 February 2000).

Potter, P. (2000) *Guanxi and the PRC Legal System: From Contradiction to Complementarity*, Wilson Center for Scholars' Seminar on Civil Society in China, www.chinaonline.com (9 February 2000).

Potter, P. and M. Oksenberg (1999) 'A patchwork of IPR protections', *The China Business Review* January–February: 8.

Pratt, Andy C. (1999) *Making digital spaces: a constructivist critique of the network society*, mimeo.

Press and Publications News (*Xinwen Chuban Bao*) (1999) *China Announces Major Restructuring of Press and Industry Publications*, www.chinaonline.com (30 November 1999).

Price M. (1995a) 'Free expression and digital dreams: the open and closed terrain of speech', *Critical Inquiry* 22: 64–89.

Price, M. (1995b) *Television, The Public Sphere and National Identity*, Oxford: Oxford University Press.

Prince PLC v. *Prince Sports Group, Inc.* (Chancery Division 30 July 1997), [1998] FSR 21.

Princeton Graphics Operating L.P. v. *NEC Home Electronics*, 732 F. Supp. 1258 (SDNY 1990).

Prosser, T. (1997) Presentation to SPTL Media Law Section, Warwick, 16 September, mimeo.

Prosser, T. (1998) *Law and the Regulators*, Oxford: Clarendon Press.

Qiu, J.L., (1999/2000) 'Virtual censorship in China: keeping the gate between the cyberspaces', *International Journal of Communications Law and Policy*, 4 (Winter): www.ijclp.org, 2.

Quah, D. (1996) *Discarding Non-stick Frying Pans for Economic Growth*, http://econ.lse.ac.uk/staff/dquah/currmnu1.html#nfp.

Rapp, J. (1996) 'Public service or universal service?', *Telecommunications Policy*, 391.

Rawls, J. (1971) *A Theory of Justice*, Oxford: Oxford University Press.

Rees, J. (1988) *Reforming the Workplace, A Study of Self Regulation in Occupational Safety*, Philadelphia: University of Pennsylvania Press.

Rees, J. and Gunningham, N. (1997) 'Industry self-regulation: an institutional perspective', *Law and Policy*, 19(4): 363–414.

Reichman J.H. and Samuelson, P. (1997) 'Intellectual property rights in data?', *Vanderbilt Law Review* 51: 84–95.

Reidenberg J. (1996) 'Governing networks and rule-making in cyberspace', *Emory Law Review* 45, adapted for B. Kahin and C. Nesson (eds) (1997) *Borders in Cyberspace: Information Policy and the Global Information Infrastructure*, Cambridge: MIT Press.

Reidenberg, J. (1999) 'Restoring Americans' privacy in electronic commerce', *Berkeley Technology Law Journal* 14(2): 771–92.

Reno v. *ACLU* (1997) 117 S. Ct. 2329.

Reno v. *ACLU* (1999), 31 F. Supp 2d 473.

Reynolds, J. and Postel, J. (1987) *The Request for Comments Reference Guide*, RFC 1000. Online. Available http: www.ietf.org/rfc/rfc1000.txt (5 February 2000).

Rhodes, R.A.W. (1996) 'The new governance: governing without government', *Political Studies* 44: 652–67.

Rony, E. and Rony, P. (1998) *The Domain Name Handbook*, Emeryville, CA: R&D Books.

Rony, E. and Rony, P. (1999) *ICANN-accredited Registrars*, online www.domainhandbook.com/registrars.html.

Rose, Marshall T. (1993) *The Internet Message: Closing the Book with Internet Mail*, Englewood Cliffs, NJ: Prentice-Hall.

Rosenau, J.N. and Czempiel, E.-O. (eds) (1992) *Governance Without Government: Order and Change in World Politics*, Cambridge: Cambridge University Press.

Rosenthal, E. (1999) 'Web sites bloom in China, and are weeded', *New York Times*, 23 December, www.nytimes.com.

Rothman, W. and Barker, J. (1999) 'Cable connections', *China Business Review*, May–June: 20.

Rousseau, J.-J. (1968) *The Social Contract (Du contrat social)*, Harmondsworth: Penguin.

Rutkowski, A. M. (1982) 'The USA and the ITU: many attitudes, few policies', *Intermedia* 10 July/September: 34.

Rutkowski, A. M. (1995) 'Today's cooperative competitive standards environment and the Internet standards-making model', in B. Kahin and J. Abbate (eds) *Standards Policy for Information Infrastructure*, Cambridge, MA: MIT Press.

Rutkowski, A.M. (1999) *After ICANN-GAC* at www.wia.org/icann/after_icann-gac.htm.

Safe Surfin', http://www.safesurfin.com/ (14 July 1999).

Saltzer, Jerome W., Reed, David P. and Clark, David D. (1984) 'End-to-end arguments in system design', *ACM Transactions in Computer Systems* 2(4): 277–88.

Samuelson, P. (1997) 'The US digital agenda at WIPO', *Virginia Journal of International Law* 37: 369.

Samuelson, P. (1999a) 'A new kind of privacy? Regulating uses of personal data in the global information economy', *California Law Review* 87: 751.

Samuelson P. (1999b) 'Intellectual property and the digital economy: why the anti-circumvention regulations need to be revised', *Berkeley Technology Law Journal* 14: 519–43.

Samuelson, P. (forthcoming 2000) 'Internet law and policy: a US perspective', delivered at the Japanese–American Society for Legal Studies Symposium on Internet and Private Law held at Sendai, Japan, on 26 September 1999.

Samuelson P. and Opsahl, K. (1999) 'Licensing information in the global information market: freedom of contract meets public policy', *European Intellectual Property Review* 21: 386.

Sauter W. (1997) *Competition Law and Industrial Policy in the EU*, Oxford: Clarendon Press.

Sbarbaro, Philip L. (1997) 'Network solutions and domain name disputes: a reply to Carl Oppedahl', in B. Kahin and J.H. Keller (eds) *Coordinating the Internet*, Cambridge, MA: MIT Press.

Scannell P. (1989) 'Public service broadcasting and modern public life', *Media, Culture and Society* 11: 135–66.

Schiller, D. (1982) *Telematics and Government*, Norwood: Ablex.

Schiller, D. (1999) 'Deep impact: the web and the changing media economy', *info* 1(1): 35–52.

Schmidt, Susanne K. and Werle, Raymund (1998) *Coordinating Technology: Studies in the International Standardization of Telecommunications*, Cambridge, MA: MIT Press.

Schmitter, P.C. (1985) 'Neo-corporatism and the state', in W. Grant (ed.) *The Political Economy of Corporatism*, London: Macmillan.

Schneider, V. (1997) 'Different roads to the information society: comparing the US and the European approaches form a comparative public policy perspective', in H. Kubicek, W.H. Dutton and R. Williams (eds) (1997) *The Social Shaping of Information Superhighways*, Cambridge, MA: MIT Press.

Schoenhals, M. (1992) *Doing Things with Words in Chinese Politics*, Institute of East Asian Studies.

Schudson, M. (1996) 'The sociology of news production revisited', in J. Curran and M. Gurevitch (eds) *Mass Media and Society* (2nd edn) London: Edward Arnold.

Schwankert, S. (2000) 'Bugs Bunny, Porky Pig barred from China', *Virtual China News* , 7 February, www.virtualchina.com.

Schwartz, Paul M. and Reidenberg, J.R. (1996) *Data Privacy Law: A Study of US Data Protection*, Brussels: European Commission.

Shapiro, C. and Varian, H.R. (1998) *Information Rules: A Strategic Guide to the Network Economy*, Cambridge, MA.; Harvard Business School Press.

Shaw, Robert (1997) 'Internet domain names: whose domain is this?' in B. Kahin and J.H. Keller (eds) *Coordinating the Internet*, Cambridge, MA: MIT Press.

Shelanski, H. (1999) 'The speed gap: broadband infrastructure and electronic commerce', *Berkeley Technology Law Journal* 14(2): 721–44.

Shell Oil Co. v. *EPA*, 950 F. 2d 741, 750 (DC Cir. 1991).

Siftung-Bertelsmann,   http://www.stiftung.bertelsmann.de/internetcontent/english/frameset_home.htm (20 February 2000).

Simon, C. (undated) *Overview of the DNS Controversy*, online www.flywheel.com/ircw /overview.html.

Sinclair, D. (1997) 'Self regulation versus command and control? Beyond false dichotomies', *Law and Policy*, 19(4): 529–59.

Singapore Broadcasting Authority, http://www.sba.gov.sg/netreg/code.html (14 July 1999).

Soete, L. (1997) *Building the European Information Society for Us All*, final policy report of the High Level Group. Brussels: DGV, Social Policy Directorate General.

South China Morning Post (2000) *Editor's Firing May Signal Media Clamp*, www.scmp.com (26 January 2000).

Spa, M. de M. and Garitaonandia, C. (eds) (1995) *Decentralization in the Global Era: Television in the Regions, Nationalities and Small Countries of the European Union*, London: John Libbey.

Spar, D.L. (1996) 'Ruling commerce in the networld', *Journal of Computer-Mediated Communication* 2: 1.

Spar, D.L. (1999) 'Cyberrules: problems and prospects for on-line commerce', in B. Compaine and W. Read (eds) *The Information Resources Policy Handbook – Research for the Information Age*, Cambridge, MA: MIT Press.

Staple, Gregory C. (ed.) (1999) *Telegeography 2000*, Washington, DC: Telegeography Inc.

State Treaty between Austria, Prussia, Bavaria and Saxony of 25 July 1850 Concerning the Establishment of the Austro-German Telegraphic Union (1850), Archives of the International Telecommunication Union, Geneva.

Stevenson-Yang, A. (1998) 'Word games', *China Business Review*, May–June: 42.

Strange, S. (1998) *What Theory? The Theory in Mad Money* (November) www.warwick.ac.uk/fac/soc/CSGR/wpapers/wp1898.PDF (visited 10 June 1999).

Sun Microsystems, Inc. (1997) *Comments of Alan Baratz, President of Sun's JavaSoft division*, java.sun.com/pr/1997/nov/pr971117.tran.html.

Sun Microsystems, Inc. (n.d.) *Summary of Voting on JTC 1 N 4615*, java.sun.com/about-Java/standardization/jln4833.html.

Sun Microsystems, Inc. v. *Microsoft Corp.*, 999 F. Supp. 1301, 46 USPQ 2d 1531 (ND Cal., 24 March 1998) (NO. C 97–20884 RMW(PVT)).

Sun Microsystems, Inc. v. *Microsoft Corp.*, 21 F. Supp.2d 1109, 1998 Copr. L. Dec. P 27,838, 49 USPQ 2d 1245 (ND Cal., 17 November 1998) (NO. C 97–20884 RMW PVT).

Sun Microsystems, Inc. v. *Microsoft Corp*, 188 F. 3d 1115 (9th Cir. 1999).

Sun Microsystems, Inc. v. *Microsoft Corp.*, 2000 WL 132711 (ND Cal. 25 January 2000) (NO. C 97–20884 RMW PVT).

Swire, Peter P. and Litan, Robert E. (1997) *Internet Governance: Towards Voluntary Multilateralism* delivered at the meeting of signatories of the gTLD MoU, Geneva, 29 April 1997 (available at http://www.itu.int).

Swire, Peter P. and Litan, Robert E. (1998) *None of Your Business: World Data Flows, Electronic Commerce, and the European Privacy Directive*, Tarjanne: Pekka.

Taylor, Charles (1994) *Multiculturalism: Examining the Politics of Recognition*, Princeton: Princeton University Press.

Telecomm Services Association, http://www.telesa.or.jp/e_guide/e_guido1.html (14 July 1999).

Telecommunications Act of 1996, Pub. L. no. 104–104.

Texas ISP Association, http://www.tispa.org./bylaws.html (14 July 1999).

Thompson, J.B. (1995) *The Media and Modernity*, Cambridge: Polity Press.

Trachtman, J.P. (1996) 'The international economic law revolution', *University of Pennsylvania Journal of International Economic Law*, 17: 33.

Turque, W. (2000) *Inventing Al Gore*, New York: Houghton Mifflin; extract in 'Thank you, Dad', *Sunday Times*, 'News Review', 6 March.

Tuthill, Lee (1996) 'Users' rights? The multilateral rules on access to telecommunications', *Telecommunications Policy* 20 (March): 89–99.

Tyler, Michael and Joy, Carol (1997) *1.1.98 – Telecommunications in the New Era: Competing in the Single Market*, London: Multiplex Press.

Ukrow, J. (1999) *Self Regulation in the Media Sector and European Community Law*, Saarbrücken: EMR.

UNCTAD (1998) *World Investment Report 1998: Trends and Determinants*, Geneva: UNCTAD.

Uniform Computer Information Transactions Act (1999) final draft, as of 1 November 1999, available at www.law.upenn.edu/bll/ulc/ucita/ucitanc.htm.

Uniform Electronic Transactions Act (1999) at www.law.upenn.edu/bll/ulc/fnact99 /1990s/ueta99.htm.

United Nations (1996) General Assembly Resolution 51/162 of 16 December 1996 at http://www.un.or.at/uncitral/en-index.htm.

Universal City Studios Inc. v. *Reimerdes*, no. 00 Civ. 0277 (LAK) (SDNY 2 February 2000).

US Embassy Report (1998) *New PRC Internet Regulation*, January, www.redfish.com/ USEmbassy-China.

US Government Committee on Intellectual Property Rights in the Emerging Information Infrastructure, National Research Council (1999) *The Digital Dilemma: Intellectual Property in the Information Age*, Washington: GPO.

US Government Working Group on Electronic Commerce (1998) *First Annual Report*, available at www.doc.gov/ecommerce/E-comm.pdf.

US v. *Microsoft Corp.*, 147 F. 3d 935, 939 (DC Cir. 1998).

US v. *Microsoft Corp.*, no. 98–1233 (US District Court for the District of Columbia), Findings of Fact, paras 39–41. Available at www.usdoj.gov/atr/cases/f3800/msjudgex.htm.

US v. *Microsoft*, 65 F. Supp. 2d 1 (DDC 1999) no. Civ. 98–1232 (TPJ), Civ. 98–1233 (TPJ)) Plaintiff's Complaint at 49, available at www.usdoj.gov/atr/cases/f1700/1763.htm.

van Loon, Ad (1998) 'Die Rolle des Europarates und der EU in bezug auf die europäischen Rundfunkfinanzierungssysteme', in R. Pethig and S. Blind (eds), *Fernsehfinanzierung: ökonomische, rechtliche und ästetische Perspektiven*, Wiesbaden: Westdeutscher Verlag, Opladen.

Vines, S. (1998) 'Murdoch moves forward in China', *Independent*, 20 November: 19.

Volkmer, I. (1997) 'Universalism and particularism: the problem of cultural sovereignty and global information flow', in B. Kahin and C. Nesson (eds) *Borders in Cyberspace: Information Policy and the Global Information Infrastructure*, Cambridge, MA: MIT Press.

Wacks, R. (1997) 'Privacy in cyberspace: personal information, free speech and the Internet', in: P. Birks (ed.) *Privacy and Loyalty*, Oxford: Clarendon Press.

Walter, A. (2000) 'Globalisation and policy convergence: the case of direct investment rules', in R. Higgott, G. Underhill and A. Bieler (eds) *Non-State Actors and Authority in the Global System*, London: Routledge.

Wang Laboratories, Inc. v. *Mitsubishi Electronics America*, 103 F. 3d 1571 (Fed. Cir. 1997).

Wang, X. (1999) 'Satellite TV crackdown a rerun of 1994', *South China Morning Post*, Business Section, 10 May: 4.

Warwick, M. (1998) 'Access denied', *Communication International*, November: 6.

Watson Brown, Adam (1999) *Industry Consortia and the Changing Roles of Standards Bodies and Regulators*, 325 IPTS Report, Institute of Prospective Technology Studies, Seville, Spain, also through DGXIII, at http://www.jrc.es/pages/f-report.en.html.

Weiler, J.H.H. (1991) 'The transformation of Europe', *Yale Law Journal* 100: 2405.

Weiler, J.H.H. (1993) 'Journey to an unknown destination: a retrospective and prospective of the European Court of Justice in the arena of political integration', *Journal of Common Market Studies* 31: 417.

Weiler, J.H.H. (1994) 'A quiet revolution: the ECJ and its interlocutors', *Comparative Political Studies* 17: 510.

Weiler, J.H.H. (1999) *The Constitution of Europe*, Cambridge: Cambridge University Press.

Werbach, K. (1997) *Digital Tornado: The Internet and Telecommunications Policy*, Federal Communications Commission Office of Plans and Policies Working Paper 29, Washington: FCC.

Whish, R. and Wood, Diane (1993) *Merger Cases in the Real World*, Paris: OECD.

White House Office of Public Liaison (1999) *Summary of US–China WTO Agreement*, Washington DC: WTO, 17 November.

Whitehead, Phillip (1997) *Draft Report on the Commission Green Paper on the Protection of Minors and Human Dignity in Audiovisual and Information Services* (COM[96]0483 – C4–0621/96) PE 221.804 of 24 April 1997.

Winn, Jane K. (1998) 'Open systems, free markets, and regulation of Internet commerce', *Tulane Law Review* 72: 1177.

Winston, B. (1998) *Media, Technology and Society: A History*, London: Routledge.

WIPO (1967) *Convention Establishing the World Intellectual Property Organization*, 14 July as amended. Online www.wipo.int/eng/iplex/wo_wip0_.htm.

WIPO (1996) *Copyright Treaty, adopted by the Diplomatic Conference on 20 December 1996*, WIPO Doc. CRNR/DC/94, 23 December.

WIPO (1998a) *RFC 1, Request for Comments on Terms of Reference, Procedures and Timetable for the WIPO Internet Domain Name Process*. Online http://ecommerce.wipo.int/domains /process/eng/rfc.html.

WIPO (1998b) *RFC 2, Request for Comments on Issues Addressed in the WIPO Internet Domain Name Process*. Online ecommerce.wipo.int/domains/process/eng/rfc_2.html.

WIPO (1998c) *RFC 3, Interim Report of the WIPO Internet Domain Name Process*. Online ecommerce.wipo.int/domains/process/eng/rfc_3.html.

WIPO (1998d) *A/33/8 – General Report adopted by the Assemblies of the Member States*, 15 September. Online www.wipo.int/eng/document/govbody-/wo_gb_ab/a33_8–14. htm#P643_157650.

WIPO (1998e) *Consultations – First Series*. Online ecommerce.wipo.int/domains/process /eng/consult.html.

WIPO (1998f) *Palo Alto meeting transcript*. Online ftp://wipo2.wipo.int/pub/process/eng/ sf-transcript-en.rtf.

WIPO (1999a) *Final Report of the WIPO Internet Domain Name Process* (Geneva). Online wipo2.wipo.int/process/eng/final_report.html.

WIPO (1999b) *Consultations – Second Series*. Online ecommerce.wipo.int/domains/process /eng/consult2.html.

WIPO (1999c) *Process Timetable*. Online ecommerce.wipo.int/domains/process/eng/ timetable.html.

WIPO (n.d.) *Contracting Parties of Treaties Administered by WIPO*. Online www. wipo.int/eng/ ratific/c-wipo.htm.

Woodman, S. and Yu, P. (1999) 'Killing the chicken to frighten the monkeys: the use of state security in the control of freedom of expression in China', in S. Coliver, P. Hoffman and S. Bowen (eds) (1999) *Secrecy and Liberty: National Security, Freedom of Expression and Access to Information*, Dortmund: Martinus Nijhoff.

Woolcock, S. (1996) 'Competition amongst forms of corporate governance in the European Community: the case of Britain', in R. Dore and S. Berger (eds) *National Diversity and Global Capitalism*, Ithaca and London: Cornell University Press.

World Trade Organisation (1994) *The Results of the Uruguay Round of Multilateral Trade Negotiations: The Legal Texts*, World Trade Organisation.

World Trade Organisation (1998) *Audiovisual Services: Background Note by the Secretariat*, S/C/W/40, 15 June.

Xing Fan (2000) *Foreign Investment in China's Internet Business: Forbidden, Forgiven, Forced Open*, www.chinaonline.com (20 February 2000).

Yan, M. (1998) 'Protection of free flow of information and regulation of trans-frontier television', D. Phil. thesis, University of Essex.

Yee, Kenton K. (1997) 'Location.location.location: a snapshot of Internet addresses as evolving property', *Journal of Information, Law and Technology* 1: elj.warwick.ac.uk/jilt/intprop/97_1yee/.

Ypsilanti, D. (1999) 'A borderless world: the OECD Ottawa Ministerial Conference and initiatives in electronic commerce', *info* 1(1): 23–34.

Zacher, Mark W. with Sutton, Brent A. (1996) *Governing Global Networks: International Regimes for Transportation and Communications*, Cambridge: Cambridge University Press.

Zatarain's, Inc. v. Oak Grove Smokehouse, Inc. (1983) 698 F. 2d 786 5th Cir.

zdnet (1999) *Sun Microsystems Withdraws JAVA 2 Platform Submission from ECMA*, 7 December, available at www.java.sun.com/pr/1999/12/pr991207–08.htm (visited 28 February 2000).

Zhang Ximing (1999) 'Shiba Nian Fengyu Jiancheng, Xinwen Fa Hu zhi Nanchu', in Liu Zhifeng (ed.) *Zhongguo Zhengzhi Tizhi Gaige Wenti Baogao*, Beijing: Zhongguo Dianying Chubanshe.

Zhao, Y. (1998) *Media, Market and Democracy in China*, Urbana: University of Illinois Press.

Index

Aaron, David L. 12
accountability 61, 228, 304
Administrative Procedures Act (APA), US 226–8
advertising 67, 69, 296–7
Agre, Phil 193
Agreement on Basic Telecoms (ABT) 30
Alliance for Global Business 189
American Bar Association 228
American Law Institute 228
American Society of Sanitary Engineers 237
American Telegraph and Telephone (AT&T) 11, 19, 29, 129–31, 136, 141–2, 170–1, 183–4
Amsterdam Treaty (1997) 297
Annan Committee 307
anti-foundationalism 51
antitrust law 235–42, 318; see also competition law
AOL (company) 8–11, 29, 63, 65
Arendt, Hannah 50–2
ARPANET 4, 198, 203
Asian financial crisis 32
Australia 62, 69–70, 74, 128, 166
autonomy of the individual 51–2, 55
Ayres, Ian 2

Bangemann Report (1994) 5
Barshefsky, Charlene 12
BBC see British Broadcasting Corporation
BBC Online 312, 315
Beesley Report (1981) 109
Benhabib, Seyla 54–5
Benkler, Yochai 83
Bentham, Jeremy 56
Berners-Lee, Tim 4
Bernstein v. *United States* 322
Bertelsman (company) 30

Boddewyn, J.J. 67–9
Boeing (company) 180
bounded rationality 18
Braithwaite, John 2, 64
brands, protection of *see* trademark protection
Brent Spar oil platform 32
British Broadcasting Corporation (BBC) 47, 277, 307, 312, 314
British Commonwealth telecommunications networks 136
British Interactive Broadcasting 15
British Telecommunications (company) 29, 73, 93–105 *passim*
broadcasting 109, 113–14, 118, 120, 288, 293–300; programme requirements 295–6, 307; *see also* public service broadcasting
BSkyB 9, 104
Butler, Richard 149–50

Cable & Wireless 129, 131
call-back 169, 171, 173
Canada 70, 73–4, 128, 130, 140, 166, 319
Carnoy, Martin 8
cartels 237, 318
categorical imperative 52
CCIT *see* International Consultative Committee on Telegraph
CCITT *see* Consultative Committee on International Telegraph and Telephone
CCIF *see* International Consultative Committee on Telephone
censorship, private and public 63–4
Centre for the Study of Globalization and Regionalisation xiii
children, protection of 71–6, 319
China 28, 33, 158, 179, 181, 248, 265–6, 268–79; Central Propaganda

Department (CPD) 269–72, 277; State
    Administration of Radio, Film and
    Television (SARFT) 270–1, 273–5
Cisco Systems 8
Clinton, Bill, President 47, 180
Clinton Administration 164, 171, 320, 324
Clinton Round *see* Millennial Round
codes of practice 62, 72, 74–5
'command and control' regimes 59
commodification of information 325
Commonwealth Telecommunications
    Financial Arrangement 136
communitarianism 53–5
communities, rules and norms created by
    83
Compaq (company) 239
competition: between and within standards
    236, 243; effects of 87; limits to 108; in
    network markets 242
Competition Act (UK, 1998) 105–6
competition law 17–18, 84–5, 93, 96,
    104–7, 122–3, 318; *see also* antitrust law
compliance, erosion of 172–3
Compuserve (company) 14
computer-aided design and manufacture 7
concentration (economic, social, political
    and legal) 82; *see also* media, the;
    mergers
connectivity 111, 209
Consultative Committee on International
    Telegraph and Telephone (CCITT)
    127–8, 136–7, 140, 145–6, 170, 204,
    206; study groups and working parties
    of 138, 143–5, 152–4
consumer groups 82
consumer welfare 123
Continental Paper Bag case 238
convergence in communication
    technologies 118–23, 186, 298, 310,
    317
copyright 318, 322–4
Council of Europe 26–7, 34, 285–7, 289,
    292–3, 297, 299
Cowhey, Peter 183
Crocker, David 198, 204, 206–7
Cultural Revolution 265
Curwen, P. 11
'cybersquatting' 217–18, 223–7, 230; *see
    also* trademark protection

Data General v. *Grumman System Support* case
    238
database protection 318–20, 324

De Long, J.B. 110
Decency Act (US) 186–7
Dell (company) 237
democratic deficit 24, 64, 311
democratic process 229, 232, 270, 308,
    311; *see also* media, the: democratic
    potential of
Diana, Princess of Wales 47
Digital Equipment Corporation 239
Digital Millennium Copyright Act, US 323
digital technology 6–8, 12, 24, 298
discourse ethics 49–51, 54–5
dispersion of decision-making power 82
Domain Name Rights Coalition 212
domain name system (DNS) 164–5,
    195–202 *passim*, 208–9, 212–19, 223
dominant standards 236, 240–42
Dow Jones (company) 272, 278
Dresden, Treaty of (1850) 125, 132–3, 156
'dumbing down' 45–6
Dunsire, Andrew 194
duopoly 93–7
Durkheim, Emile 56

economic theory, limitations of 109–10
economies of density 118–19
edge-to-edge interoperability 119
egalitarian principles 50
election expenses 80
electronic commerce (e-commerce) 5, 8–9,
    16–17, 25, 27, 31, 181–2, 189–90, 209,
    323–4; businesses' and customers' views
    of 79–80; regulation of 12, 79; UK
    White Paper on (1999) 12
electronic mail 161–2
electronic programme guides (EPGs)
    313–15
electronic signatures and contracts 320
Elias, Norbert 56
elitism 46–7
Ellickson, Robert C. 83
encryption policy 322
Energis (company) 94
'enlarged thinking' 51–2
Enlightenment, the 49, 51
entry barriers: in market for PC operating
    systems 245, 318; in the media 306; in
    telecommunications 167
Ericsson (company) 30
EuroISPA 69, 73
European Commission 9, 17, 67, 73, 148,
    151, 159, 201, 292–4, 297–8;
    Communications Review (1999) 104,

106–7; Green Paper on Pluralism and Media Concentration 290
European Computer Manufacturers' Association (ECMA) 253–5
European Convention for the Protection of Human Rights (ECHR) 27, 285–7, 289
European Court of Human Rights 286–7, 289, 305
European Court of Justice (ECJ) 288–9, 297
European single market 151
European Standards Commission (CEN) 152
European Telecommunications Standards Institute (ETSI) 152, 237
European Union 5, 12, 19–20, 22–3, 27, 34, 71, 81–2, 179–80, 189–90, 316, 322, 324; Advanced Television Services Directive 103–4, 107; law of 107, 203–4, 285, 288–9, 291–6, 313, 319; *see also* European Commission
externalities 110–12, 245

fairness 110
Federal Communications Commission (FCC) 141–2, 146, 170–2, 182, 185–6, 317
Federal Trade Commission (FTC) 237, 239
feminism 46
filtering software 72, 74–6, 276
Financial Times 151
fixed and variable costs 119–20
Florida Internet Service Providers Association 74
foreign direct investment (FDI) 10–11, 29, 157–8, 278
Forrester Research 9
Foucault, Michel 56
foundationalism 51
France 295–6, 307
Fraser, Nancy 44, 53
free movement of goods, persons, services and capital 288–9, 295–6
free-rider problem 63
freedom of expression 48, 63, 285–7, 289, 292, 299–300, 304–6, 322
Freeserve (company) 13, 17

G7 conference (Brussels, 1995) 6
Garnham, N. 110
Gates, Bill 318
General Agreement on Tariffs and Trade (GATT) 146–7, 150, 155, 178–9, 185, 188, 266
General Agreement on Trade in Services (GATS) 155–9, 166, 266–7
Germany 307
GetNetWise 72
Gidari, Albert 69
Global Business Dialogue on e-commerce (GBDe) 27
Global Top Level Domain Memorandum of Understanding (gTLD-MoU) 164–5, 200–1, 209, 219, 223–4
globalisation 2–3, 12, 15, 179
Gore, Al 4–5
Graham, A. 110
Greece 297
gross domestic product, contributions to 7, 9, 182
Group on Basic Telecommunications 157–8
gTLD-MoU *see* Global Top Level Domain Memorandum of Understanding
Guardian Unlimited Network 315

Habermas, Jurgen 34, 43–6, 51, 53
Heath, Don 199
Hegel, G.W.F. 50, 53, 55–6
Held, D. 2
Henderson, Hazel 13
Hirschman, A. 23
'hit or flop' phenomenon 110
Hoffmann-Riem, W. 59, 309
Hong Kong 11, 74–5, 129, 269
hotlines 72–3
Hotmail 17
human rights 27, 267, 285–7, 289, 305
Huyse, L. 58–9
hyperglobalization 2–3

IBM (company) 8, 19, 30, 141, 161
identity politics 50, 53–4
Image Technical Services v. *Kodak* case 238
incremental cost base 98–100
Independent Television Commission 314
individuals, rules created by 84
Information Processing Techniques Office 203
information society: definition of 1–2; usefulness of term 43
infrastructure of electronic communication 294
Integrated Services Digital Network (ISDN) 145, 152

Intel (company) 8, 235, 241; Pentium II microprocessor 2, 238–9
intellectual property, licensing of 237–9, 242–4, 250
Intelsat 183, 185
Intergraph v. *Intel* case 238–9, 241
International Air Transportation Association 142
International Chamber of Commerce 189
International Consultative Committee on Telegraph (CCIT) 126–8, 135
International Consultative Committee on Telephone (CCIF) 126–8, 134
international economic law 266–7
International Electrotechnical Commission 247
international relations 23
international simple resale (ISR) 168–9
International Standards Organization (ISO) 16, 161, 204, 208, 240, 244, 247–9, 252–3, 256
International Telecommunications Regulations 150
International Telecommunications Union (ITU) 26–7, 30, 124–30, 133–8, 169–73, 183, 185–7, 199, 206–9, 219; declining significance of 141–56 *passim*, 162, 168; and the Internet 160–6
International Telegraph and Telephone (IT&T) 129, 131
Internet, the: access to 1, 10, 14, 16–17, 28–30, 83, 114, 159, 163, 181–2; architecture of 14, 64; attractions of 18; browsers for 123; businesses' use of 9; categories of content 71; in China 266, 276–9; closure of network 16; commercial development of 159–61; content control for 59, 111–12, 114, 186–7; creation of 4–5; and globalization 2, 12; governance of 31, 193–5, 198, 201, 208–10, 217, 225; government policy on 182–3; impact of 117–18, 121, 123; law of 316, 323–5; regulation of 2, 12–14, 16, 31, 48, 57–62 *passim*, 65–75, 121, 186–7, 316–18; skills needed for use of 114; standard-setting for 30–2, 162, 193, 202–8; 'streaming' on 317; substitute for all existing media 109, 114; in the United States 13–14; World Wide Web 71
Internet Architecture (formerly Activities) Board (IAB) 199, 203–5, 208

Internet Assigned Numbers Authority (IANA) 198–201, 208
Internet Content Rating for Europe (INCORE) 73
Internet Corporation for Assigned Names and Numbers (ICANN) 4, 27, 30–1, 164–5, 187, 189, 195, 201–2, 208–13, 219, 225–30
Internet Engineering Task Force (IETF) 4, 162, 165, 203–9, 228, 237
Internet Hotline Providers in Europe (INHOPE) 73
Internet Protocol (IP) 165, 298
Internet service providers (ISPs) 159–66 *passim*, 278, 315
Internet Service Providers' Association (ISPA) 69
Internet telephony 162–3, 168, 173
Internet time 10, 188
Internet Watch Foundation (IWF) 70–1, 73
interoperability 119
Interregional Telecommunications Standards Conference (1990) 153
ISDN *see* Integrated Services Digital Network
isostasy 194
Italy 307

Japan 71, 74, 128, 179–80, 185, 318
Java technologies 16, 18, 30, 239–41, 243–56
Jayasuriya, K. 21–2

Kant, Immanuel 34, 44, 49–53, 55
Kodak (company) 238
Korea 179
KPMG (company) 71
Krechmer, Ken 207

law: minimalist approach to 320; 'industrial' vision of 79; *see also* European Union: law of; Internet, the: law of
learning skills, need for 86–7
Lessig, Lawrence 4–5, 14, 19–20, 31–2, 83
Levy, Brian 24
liberal values 53–5
liberalization: of the media 113, 290; of telecommunications regimes 124–5, 146–57, 160–1, 167, 185; of trade 10–11, 178, 181
libertarianism 5

licence conditions 96–7, 105, 108, 113, 249–52
licensing of intellectual property 237–9, 242–4, 250
light carriers 168–9
Lindblom, C. 21
Littlechild Report (1983) 109
London Internet Exchange (LINX) 69
Lucent (company) 30

Maastricht Treaty (1993) 297
McCahery, J. 22, 24
MacCormick, Neil 21
Magaziner Report (1997) 5
markets and market failure 17–20, 25, 56, 59, 108, 110, 121–2, 308–9
MCI (company) 171, 183
media, the: concentration in 206, 290–2; control of (in China) 268–72; democratic potential of 304–15; judging the performance of 44, 48; ownership 287–8, 310; pluralism in 285–300, 304–13; privileging of some genres 45; regulation of 45–6, 305–9, 312; reporting by 46–8; role of 53; state aid for 297
MediaOne (company) 11, 29
Melody, W.H. 24
Menge, Eric 227
Mercury (company) 93–7
mergers 11, 17
merger and acquisition (M&A) 10–11
Michalski, Wolfgang 6
Microsoft (company) 8, 16, 18–19, 27, 73, 122, 238, 243–56, 318; case against Sun Microsystems 235, 239–42; *see also* Windows software
Millennial Round of trade negotiations 31, 179–80, 187
Mitsubishi (company) 238
mobile telephony 9, 29–30, 163
modernity 49, 54
Moni, Mario 290
monopoly 133, 142, 150, 183–5, 295, 298, 300
Moore, Mike 180
Motorola (company) 30
MS-DOS operating system 15–16, 18
MSN (company) 65
Muchlinski, P. 23–4
multimedia applications and services 161–2
Murdoch, Rupert 47

NASDAQ exchange 278
NASDAQ index 8
NEC (company) 30
Netherlands 289, 295–6
'netiquette' 65
network effects 118–19, 235–6, 240, 245, 248, 255–6, 318
Network Solutions Inc. (NSI) 197–202 *passim*, 219
New Institutional Economics 24
New Zealand 93
Noam, Eli 128
Nokia (company) 30
non-governmental organizations (NGOs) 179–80, 187–8
Nordic Satellite Distribution 293
North, Douglas 15, 21, 24
NTL (company) 29

Office of Fair Trading 105
Office of Telecommunications (OFTEL) 94–107
Ogoni people 32
Ogus, A. 69–70
Olivetti (company) 11
open standards 4, 15, 236, 238, 241–2
open systems, classifications of 206–7
Open Systems Interconnection (OSI) 161, 204
operating systems *see* MS-DOS; Windows
Organization for Economic Cooperation and Development (OECD) 11–12, 27, 31, 189, 266, 322–3

Pacific Century Cyber Works 11
Paolini, George 254
Paris, Treaty and Convention of (1865) 125–6, 132, 134
Parmentier, S. 58–9
Peacock Report (1986) 109
peer networks 165–6
Pitofsky, Robert 64
Plato 53
pluralism: external and internal to the media 306–7; political and cultural 286, 309–10, 313; *see also* media, the
policy interoperability 324–5
pornography 32, 70–1, 276
portal sites 314–15
Portnoy, B. 15
Posner, Richard 19
Post, David 228
Postel, Jon 198–9

post-modernity 54
Press Complaints Commission 65
price controls 94–102, 106–7
pricing: anti-competitive 106–7, 135;
    discriminatory 120–3; usage-dependent
    99
privacy 47–8, 55–6, 87, 106, 319, 322
privatization 148
protection of minors 71–6, 319
protectionism 147
public and private, distinction between
    45–8, 55–6
public choice theory 20–1
'public reason' 51–2, 54
public service broadcasting 307–9, 312–14
public sphere, the 34, 43–55, 311, 323

Quah, D. 6–7
Quayle, J. Danforth 4

'race to the bottom' 14, 19, 27, 325
radio: allocation of spectrum for 293–5,
    298; international regime for 126, 141;
    local 288
Rawls, John 110–11
Reagan Administration 146
reciprocity provisions 324–5
Recommendation D. 140 170–1
refile 168–9, 173
refusal to supply 84–5
regime rules 167–8
'regionalisation thesis' 3
regulation 59–62, 80, 83–7; *see also*
    Internet, the; self-regulation;
    telecommunications
regulatory arbitrage 14, 19–21, 27, 325
regulatory capture 202
regulatory failure 121
regulatory lag 14
Reidenberg, J. 19
Requests for Comments (RFCs) 203–4
Reuters (company) 8, 272
rhetoric, use of 44, 46
Rhodes, R.A.W. 193–5, 209
Robertson, Pat 278
Rome, Treaty of 151
Rousseau, Jean-Jacques 49–50, 53, 56
'RPI–X' formula 101–2
RTL/ Veronica/ Endemol decision 293
Rutkowski, A.M. 203

SAGE project 141
Saro-Wiwa, Ken 32

Sbarbaro, Philip 220
Securities and Exchange Commission 211
Select Committee on Culture, Media and
    Sport (House of Commons) 114
self-organizing networks 194–5, 209
self-regulation 6, 27–8, 32, 182, 186–7,
    190, 211, 230; advantages of 75; cost-
    benefit analysis of 63–4; definition of
    58–61; in different industries 67–9;
    economic or social 61; enforced or
    voluntary 65–7; forms of 58–9, 62; by
    individual firms or groups 64–5; of the
    Internet 57–62 *passim*, 65–75, 201;
    limitations of 64; by the media 312,
    315; negotiation and controls over
    60–1; taxonomy of 64–7; transparency
    in 61
self-regulatory agencies (SRAs) 75
semi-private rulemaking processes 211–13,
    226–32
'sender keeps all' (SKA) principle 165–6
Shaw, Robert 199
Singapore 75
SITA airline network 143
Sittlichkeit 50, 53–4
Sky TV 47
Smith, Adam 56
social norms 33, 53, 56, 61–2, 83, 110
social objectives 106, 108, 111, 113, 115
social obligations 112, 115
social primary goods 111
society: fragmentation of 54–5; 'locked' 81
Soete, Luc 1
Song Yongyi 265
sovereignty 14, 22, 133, 150, 166, 168, 214
Spiller, Pablo 24
standards 18, 30–2; anticipatory,
    participatory and responsive 207, 209;
    de facto 238, 247–8, 253–4; set by
    groups or organizations 235, 237, 242,
    256; *see also* open standards; technical
    standards
state, the, role of 5, 194–5
state aid 297
Strange, S. 22–3
'subcontracting' of regulation 58–9
Sudan 28
The Sun 47
Sun Microsystems 16, 30, 235, 239–42,
    244–56
SWIFT banking network 143

Tarjanne, Pekka 154, 171

Taylor, Charles 50
TCI (company) 29
technical standards 81, 126, 137–8, 152, 165
'telcos' 148, 159–63, 167
Telecom Italia 11
telecommunications: deregulation of 93, 106–7; interconnection 96–9, 102, 157–61, 166, 183–4; international regime for 124–74, 182–3; and the Internet 159–61; joint service provision 135–7, 158, 166, 183; leased circuits 134–5, 141–3, 145, 149, 151–2, 156, 160–1, 166, 168; market shares in the UK 101; network characteristics 5, 10–11, 29, 118–19; regulation of 28–30, 48, 112, 116, 184, 294; universal service provision 81–2, 95, 106, 111–15, 158; *see also* mobile telephony; Internet telephony
Telegeography Inc. 167
television 10, 12, 15, 288, 293, 313
Telewest plc 29
Texas Internet Service Providers Association 74
thinking for oneself 51–2
Tiebout model 20
Tokyo Round 185
toleration 54–5
trade barriers 178–9
trademark protection 197–202, 208, 213, 216–19, 223–4, 249–50; for famous brands 223–5, 230
tying-in of customers 85–6

Uniform Computer Information Transactions Act (UCITA), US 320–1, 323
United Nations 30; Commission on International Trade Law (UNCITRAL) 12, 189, 324; Commission on Trade and Development (UNCTAD) 10–11, 27, 189; Educational, Scientific and Cultural Organization (UNESCO) 26–7
United States: Commerce Department 9, 200–1, 208, 211, 218–19; Congress and Congressional committees 164, 230; Defense Department 141, 203; Justice Department 19, 184, 244–5, 251, 318; National Science Foundation 197, 219, 317; National Telecommunications and Information Administration 200–1;

self-regulation in 70, 73–4; Supreme Court 319; telecommunications policy 129–31, 136, 140, 149, 155, 173; trade policy 179–81; Trade Representative (USTR) 146, 181; *see also* Administrative Procedures Act; Clinton Administration; Federal Communications Commission; Federal Trade Commission; Reagan Administration; Securities and Exchange Commission
Uruguay Round 146, 150, 155, 158, 180, 185

Vail, Theodore 183
van den Beld, Jan 254
variable and fixed costs 119–20
'veil of ignorance' 111
'virtual' products 7
Vivendi (company) 9
VocalTec Inc. 162
Vodafone-Mannesman (company) 9, 11

Wang (company) 238
websites 48
Weiler, J.H.H. 23
Werbach, Kevin 109, 114
West European Telegraph Union 125, 132
Whish, Richard 2
Windows software 19, 207, 240, 244–56 *passim*
World Administrative Telegraph and Telephone Conference (WATTC) 127–9; Melbourne meeting (1988) 148–51, 153
World Bank 172, 187
world government 30
World Intellectual Property Organization (WIPO) 26, 30, 187, 189, 199, 201, 211–32, 267, 323–4; consultation process used by 220–27, 231–2; Panel of Experts 220–24
World Trade Organization (WTO) 12, 30–31, 125, 155–6, 158–9, 173, 187, 266–7, 278–9, 325; Seattle meeting (1999) 178–81, 186, 188–90
World Wide Web Consortium (W3C) 4, 207–8
Wu Jichuan 278

X.400 message handling system 161–2, 206–7
Xinhua News Agency 272